SPEAKING OF EVENTS

Speaking of Events

edited by

James Higginbotham
Fabio Pianesi
Achille C. Varzi

New York   Oxford
Oxford University Press
2000

Oxford University Press

Oxford   New York

Athens   Auckland   Bangkok   Bogotá   Buenos Aires   Calcutta
Cape Town   Chennai   Dar es Salaam   Delhi   Florence   Hong Kong   Istanbul
Karachi   Kuala Lumpur   Madrid   Melbourne   Mexico City   Mumbai
Nairobi   Paris   São Paulo   Singapore   Taipei   Tokyo   Toronto   Warsaw

and associated companies in
Berlin   Ibadan

Library of Congress Cataloging-in-Publication Data
Speaking of events / edited by James Higginbotham, Fabio Pianesi, Achille C. Varzi.
p.   cm.
Papers of an international working conference held Aug. 1995 in Trento, Italy,
which was supported by the Istituto per la ricerca scientifica e tecnologica
(IRST) of the Istituto trentino di cultura (ITC).
Includes indexes.
ISBN 0-19-512807-9; ISBN 0-19-512811-7 (pbk.)
1. Semantics Congresses.   2. Grammar, Comparative and general Congresses.
3. Events (Philosophy) Congresses.   I. Higginbotham, James.
II. Pianesi, Fabio.   III. Varzi, Achille C.
P325 .S63 1999
401'.43—dc21   99-16829

1 3 5 7 9 8 6 4 2

Printed in the United States of America
on acid-free paper

Contents

Acknowledgments

The roots of this book lie in a small working symposium on Facts and Events in the Semantics of Natural Language held in Trento, Italy, in August 1995. We gratefully acknowledge the assistance of the Istituto per la Ricerca Scientifica e Tecnologica (IRST) of the Istituto Trentino di Cultura (ITC) in organizing the conference and supporting the project that led to the preparation of this volume. We are especially grateful to Raffaella Di Iorio, Carola Dori, and Oliviero Stock for their help at various stages.

We would also like to thank Oxford University Press for their assistance in bringing the volume to fruition. Special thanks are due to Peter Ohlin, MaryBeth Branigan, and the anonymous referees for their help in preparing the final manuscript and to Barbara Conner for her expert and patient copyediting.

Contributors

Nicholas Asher
Department of Philosophy, University of Texas, Austin (USA)

Pier Marco Bertinetto
Scuola Normale Superiore, Pisa (Italy)

Johannes L. Brandl
Department of Philosophy, University of Salzburg (Austria)

Denis Delfitto
Institute for Language and Speech OTS, University of Utrecht (The Netherlands)

Regine Eckardt
Fachgruppe Sprachwissenschaft, University of Konstanz (Germany)

James Higginbotham
University of Oxford, Oxford (UK)

Alessandro Lenci
Department of Linguistics, University of Pisa (Italy)

Terence Parsons
Department of Philosophy, University of California at Irvine (USA)

Fabio Pianesi
Istituto Trentino di Cultura IRST, Trento (Italy)

Alice G. B. ter Meulen
Centre for Language and Cognition, University of Groningen (The Netherlands)

Achille C. Varzi
Department of Philosophy, Columbia University, New York (USA)

Henk J. Verkuyl
Institute for Language and Speech OTS, University of Utrecht (The Netherlands)

SPEAKING OF EVENTS

1

Events and Event Talk

An Introduction

Fabio Pianesi and Achille C. Varzi

1. Preamble

We speak of actions and other events with the same easiness with which we speak of people and other objects. We say of John that he is bright and of Bill's lecture that it is boring. We say of John's father that he is taller than Bill's and of John's life that it is better than Bill's. We say of Clark Kent that he is Superman and of Clark Kent's death that it is the death of Superman. The pervasiveness of this talk does not by itself imply that there are such things as events—that events are to be included in an inventory of the world over and above people and material objects. But one can hardly question that some theory of events is needed if one is to make sense of such talk at all. Moreover, we often speak in such a way as to suggest—implicitly—that we are talking about events. We say that Brutus stabbed Caesar with a knife. If this statement is taken to assert that a certain three-place relation obtains among Brutus, Caesar, and a knife, then it is hard to explain why our statement entails that Brutus stabbed Caesar (a statement that involves a different, two-place relation). But if we take our statement to assert that a certain event occurred (namely, a stabbing of Caesar by Brutus) *and* that it had a certain property (namely, of being done with a knife), then the entailment is straightforward. Again, these reasons do not constitute a proof that there are such entities as events. But if we are interested in an account of how it is that certain statements mean what they mean, and if the meaning of a statement is at least in part determined by its logical relations to other statements, then one can hardly ignore the relevance of facts such as these.

In the last five decades, these considerations have been the focus of considerable debate among philosophers, as well as among linguists and logicians.[1] Especially since the publication of Donald Davidson's (1967b) article 'The Logical Form of Action Sentences', it has been generally agreed that a great many natural language phenomena can be explained if (and—according to some authors—only if) we make room for logical forms in which reference to or quantification over events is genuinely admitted. Nominalization, adverbial modification, tense and aspect, factives, anaphora, plurals, naked infinitives, singular causal statements, temporal reasoning—all of these (to mention just a few) are topics that have led to the formulation of sophisticated event-based semantic theories. At the same time, a number of philosophical questions arise as soon as an ontology of events is taken into serious consideration. Are events entities of a kind? If so, how do they differ from other kinds of entities, for example, from material/objects? Are events particulars or universals? Concrete or abstract? What are their identity and individuation criteria? What is their place in the causal network? Naturally, some of these questions have puzzled philosophers for a long time. But the increasing importance of the event concept, determined by its applications in semantics and linguistic analysis, has given such questions new impetus, and since the publication of Davidson's article a number of metaphysical theories have been put forward concerning the nature of events and eventlike entities.

To some extent, these two directions of research (the development of event-based semantic theories and the development of metaphysical theories about events) are independent. It is possible to work out an event-based semantics of tense and aspect (say) without explicitly committing oneself to any specific metaphysics of events, and it is possible to work out a metaphysical theory without drawing out all its implications for, and applications to, natural language semantics. All the same, in this case as in others (for instance, talk about properties or numbers), there are deep connections between metaphysical and semantic issues. Answers to questions of one sort (Was Brutus's stabbing of Caesar the same event as Brutus's killing of Caesar?) may depend on the answers one gives to questions of the other sort (What is the logical form of the statement that they were the same event?). More concretely, it is a fact that philosophers tend to rely on their linguistic intuitions when it comes to metaphysical arguments, and linguists rely implicitly on their intuitions about the nature of events when it comes to articulating a semantic theory. There is, accordingly, a distinct need for mutual cooperation in this area. The purpose of this volume is to go some way in this direction and to offer a vivid, up-to-date indication of some fruitful lines of interaction between the philosophical and linguistic articulations of the event concept.

In the remainder of this introduction, we review the main themes and set some common background to the chapters that follow. Section 2 gives an overview of the main theories of events that have been put forward in recent philosophical and linguistic literature. Section 3 focuses on the issue of event identity and individuation, which has been largely debated in the literature and whose significance underlies a number of arguments examined in the other chapters of the book. Section 4 introduces the link between events and language by reviewing the basic features of Davidson's account of the logical form of action sentences. Finally, section 5 deals with developments and linguistic applications, with special emphasis on the themes explicitly addressed in the rest of the book.

2. The Nature of Events

It will be helpful to identify some criteria for differentiating event theories. The main criterion is whether a theory categorizes events as universals (things that can recur or be instantiated at different places and times) or as particulars (things that occur at a specific place and time). This is an absolute distinction, not a matter of degree. We may, moreover, classify a theory according to whether it treats events as "thick" (concrete) or as "thin" (abstract) entities, and this is a matter of degree. An event is thick to the extent that it prevents other events from occurring in the same place at the same time. Some theories impose maximum thickness; other theories (the majority) allow for the possibility that distinct events occur in the same place at the same time, though the degree to which this is possible is a matter of controversy. We could also differentiate event theories according to the degree of reality that they ascribe to events. Some authors, for instance, take events to be basic entities, entities to be included in the basic ontological inventory. Others deny existence to events in favour of "ontological parsimony", arguing that every seemingly event-committing statement can in principle be paraphrased in terms of event-neutral statements. And between these two extremes (the eventists and the eliminativists) there are those who avoid the language of reduction while also denying that events and objects are coordinate and equally basic. We shall not consider here the eliminativist approach. But we shall see that the other positions are variously exemplified in the theories that take events at face value.

2.1. Events as Universals

The idea that events are universals has been defended most notably by Richard Montague and by Roderick Chisholm. It is a conception that has not found many applications in recent works; but it is worth starting from because it immediately provides a good indication of the delicate interplay between metaphysical and semantic issues. (The reader will find concrete evidence of this interplay in Johannes Brandl's chapter and in the first section of James Higginbotham's chapter.)

According to Montague, events are properties, specifically properties of moments or intervals of time:

> The event of the sun's rising will be the property of being a moment at which the sun rises, and events in general will form a certain class of properties of moments [or intervals] of time. (1969: 149–150)

(Whether an event is a property of moments or of intervals depends on whether the event is *instantaneous*, such as two balls coming into contact, or *protracted*, such as the American presidential campaign.) Montague's account is thus reductionist. Events are not entities of a kind; they are, rather, a kind of property, and to say that a certain event P occurs at a moment t (in a world i) is simply to say that the property P is exemplified by t (in i).[2] Naturally, this is meant as a characterization of what Montague called *generic* events (what some authors would call event types). A generic event such as the sun's rising recurs every morning in the same sense in which the property of being a chair 'recurs' in every single chair. In fact, Montague also recognized *particular* events, such as the rising of the sun that we witnessed this morning. But for Montague the distinction between generic and particular events is not categorical. Particular events are not tokens of a type. They, too, are properties, albeit properties of a very restricted sort, 'properties of a great degree of particularity' (p. 176). Particular events are properties of such a degree of particularity as to be exemplified only once.

Chisholm, too, takes events to be recurrable entities, rejecting any categorical distinction between events that do in fact recur and events that occur only once. Chisholm's account, however, is based on an assimilation of events to states of affairs (i.e., entities that can be the objects of propositional attitudes) rather than to properties:[3]

> A proposition could be defined as any state of affairs which is necessarily such that either it or its negation does not occur. . . . An event is any contingent state of affairs which is not a proposition and which implies change. (1970: 20)

In other words, an event is a state of affairs that is not time-bound and that therefore is such that both it and its negation may occur. (If it does not imply change, Chisholm calls it a state, but we may ignore this distinction here.) The sun's rising is such an event because it occurred this morning but did not occur last night, whereas the sun's rising this morning is not an event (it is a proposition) because it is necessarily such that either it occurred or its negation did.

Now, one of the main intuitions behind the view that events are universals, whether in Chisholm's or Montague's form, is that it provides a simple account of certain familiar ways of speaking. We say that the sun rose this morning and that the same thing happened yesterday. We complain that a certain inconvenient event—missing a train connection—happened to us twice in a row. We say that John takes the same walk every evening. If events are recurrables, then these assertions can be taken literally and Montague's and Chisholm's theories give us a metaphysics supporting this account: there is something—that walk of John's—which occurs over and over every evening. On the other hand, the interesting question here is precisely whether such assertions are to be taken literally. When we say

(1)   John takes the same train every evening

we are not implying that John travels exactly on the same rail car every evening. The word 'same' in this context does not express individual identity but, rather, type identity, and we naturally understand (1) as

(1a)   There is a route along which, every evening, John travels by train.

We mean to say that every evening John takes a train of the same type, departing approximately at the same time and from the same station and for the same destination. At least, this is what we mean if our ontology includes trains, understood as physical objects. So the question is whether our talk of events give us any reason to change our attitude.

Davidson (1970), and most authors since, have answered in the negative. The sentence

(2)   John takes the same walk every evening

can be paraphrased as

(2a)   There is a route along which, every evening, John takes a walk

in perfect analogy to the paraphrase of (1) as (1a). Of course, it is by no means clear that every case of event recurrence can be understood along these lines. (See Brandl's chapter.) Moreover, paraphrasability is a necessary but not a sufficient condition for doing away with certain seeming ontological commitments. Nevertheless, if sentences that seem to imply the existence of recurrent events can be analysed in such a way as to imply only the occurrence of events of the same type, then the main linguistic motivation for endorsing a metaphysics of recurrable (universal, generic) events is undercut. As Higginbotham points out in his chapter, once particular events are admitted, the natural thing to do is to commence with these and to obtain generic events as kinds by whatever procedure is at work in similar cases (e.g., object kinds).

It is probably for this reason that a metaphysics of events as universals has not found many supporters in recent literature. But there is another point worth making, and this concerns the fact that both Montague and Chisholm treat events as *thin* entities. Properties and states of affairs alike have very fine-grained identity conditions, and many of them may therefore be instantiated in the same place at the same time. In Montague's theory, for instance, one would naturally distinguish between the generic event of the sun's rising and the generic event of the sun's rising solemnly since not every moment t that exemplifies the property of being a rising of the sun exemplifies the property of being a solemn rising of the sun. Likewise, these events would be distinct for Chisholm since one can have different propositional attitudes towards them (and, for Chisholm, states of affairs are identical just in case they are objects of the same propositional attitudes). What about particular events? Here the two theories deliver different diagnoses. Take the question of whether Brutus's stabbing of Caesar is the same event as Brutus's killing of Caesar. Montague's treatment is neutral with respect to this question. That highly particular property that was the stabbing of Caesar and that highly particular property that was the killing of Caesar may very well turn out to be the same property (under different names), in which case we would be talking of one and the same event; or they may turn out to be different properties, in which case we would be talking of distinct events. For Chisholm, by contrast, only the second answer is available, for certainly we can have different propositional attitudes towards the stabbing and towards the killing. (We might know that Brutus killed Caesar but not that he stabbed him.) By the same pattern, Chisholm's theory distinguishes Brutus's killing of Caesar from his

violent killing of Caesar, his killing Caesar with a knife, his killing Caesar intentionally, and so on. Indeed, Chisholm would insist that Brutus's killing of
Caesar must be distinguished also from Brutus's killing of the Roman emperor.
For we can say of the latter, but not of the former, that had Rome been a republic at that time, the event in question would not have occurred. The adequacy of
such an argument is not unproblematic, and we shall come back to this issue in
section 3. But insofar as it reflects Chisholm's views, it gives an idea of the extreme consequence that the theory may have and that most authors have found
unacceptable.[4] From this perspective the neutrality of Montague's theory is note-
worthy. But it leaves a deep gap between semantics and metaphysics, and most
authors would regard this, too, as a limitation rather than a virtue of the theory.

2.2. Events as Particulars

Let us, then, consider the view that events are particulars. Here it is possible to
distinguish a much wider variety of philosophical positions, which we may display ideally along the continuum determined by the thick/thin coordinate.

At one extreme we find the theory of W. V. O. Quine. A Quinean event is
constituted by the totality of what occupies (i.e., goes on at, or perhaps is exemplified at) a certain spatiotemporal region:

> Physical objects . . . are not to be distinguished from events. . . . Each
> comprises simply the content, however heterogeneous, of some portion of
> space-time, however disconnected or gerrymandered. (1960: 131).

On this view, events and objects collapse into a single category of four-
dimensional entities, and the problem of explaining our event talk extends to the
problem of explaining our talk of ordinary entities *tout court*. However, one need
not go that far. One can accept a Quinean ontology of events while at the same
time insisting on a more traditional ontology of objects as three-dimensional
entities that *endure* through time (as urged, e.g., by Davidson 1985b). What
matters is that if events are indeed construed so as to completely fill their spatiotemporal location, much of our event talk is better explained as involving different descriptions of the same events rather than descriptions of different
events. If the Earth is rotating and simultaneously heating up, then the rotation
and the heating up of the Earth are one and the same event even though, of
course, the property of rotating and the property of heating up are distinct. If
through exactly the same spatiotemporal span John swims the Hellespontus,
catches a cold, and counts his blessings (to use an example from Davidson
1967c: 125), then again these events are one and not three, in spite of the different descriptions.

Note that in this latter example the exact spatiotemporal location of the event
is no straightforward matter. More generally, there are events for which it
seeems preposterous to postulate the existence of a determinate spatiotemporal
boundary. *Where* exactly did John catch a cold? *When* exactly did the industrial
revolution begin? *What* exactly are the spatiotemporal boundaries of an event

such as Lady Di's campaign to internationaly ban the use of land mines? Some may take these questions seriously and conclude that a Quinean ontology is inherently vague or that it is an ontology of vague entities (entities with vague spatial or temporal boundaries). However, for a Quinean, those are semantic questions, not metaphysical ones. They are instances of the general question: What events are we talking about? And this question may not have a definite answer simply because our way of speaking may be vague, not because we may be speaking about vague entities. (To each region of space-time there is a corresponding unique, determinate event. But a locution such as 'Lady Di's campaign' is just too poor to uniquely and determinately pick out any such event.)

Quine's view occupies one extreme position on the thick/thin continuum, corresponding to the thickest possible theory. At the other extremity, the continuum is open-ended: there is no thinnest possible account of events as particulars. There is, however, a certain account that is radically thin (or so people have been arguing) insofar as it distinguishes an indefinitely large number of events that can occur in the same place at the same time. This is the account of those philosophers, such as Jaegwon Kim, who construe events as property exemplifications:

> We think of an event as a concrete object (or *n*-tuple of objects) exemplifying a property (or *n*-adic relation) at a time. (1973: 8)

Exactly what is meant by the locution 'exemplifying' is a delicate issue. Moreover, there is some uncertainty about what is to count as a property in the relevant sense. Presumably running and stabbing count, whereas being self-identical or greater than five do not count, but there are no obvious criteria for making a thorough demarcation (see Kim 1976). At any rate, leaving these issues aside, it is clear that this account tends to multiply the number of events far beyond the thick account of Quine. John's swimming the Hellespontus, his catching a cold, and his counting his blessings are regarded as three distinct events in Kim's account insofar as they involve exemplifications of distinct properties; and clearly enough, identical events must be exemplifications of the same properties (or relations) by the same objects (or *n*-tuples) at the same time. Likewise, when we speak of Brutus's stabbing of Caesar, we are not, in this account, speaking of his killing of Caesar: for the first event is the exemplification (by Brutus and Caesar) of the binary relation expressed by the predicate 'stabbing', whereas the second event is an exemplification (by the same Brutus and Caesar) of the relation expressed by the predicate 'killing'. Since these two relations are distinct, so are the events. In fact, by the same pattern, Brutus's stabbing of Caesar is to be distinguished also from his violent stabbing of Caesar, his knifing of Casear, his murderous knifing of Caesar, and so on. All of these are to be counted as different events (rather than different descriptions of the same event) because they are exemplifications of different properties.

At least, this is how Kim himself understands the property-exemplification account. For Kim, the constitutive property or relation of an event is the one named by the predicative part of an appropriate description of that event. So if two event names involve predicates with different intensions (as in the above examples) they denote distinct events. It is precisely this ontological proliferation that makes Kim's a radically thin theory (and which makes Kim's events much more similar to Chisholm's proposition-like entities than to Quine's concrete entities). However, one may resist this classification. As Jonathan Bennett (1988) has observed, one could subscribe to Kim's metaphysics without subscribing to his semantics: the metaphysical thesis that Brutus's stabbing of Caesar was an exemplification of a certain relation, R, does not by itself imply the semantic thesis that any name of that event must contain a predicate that fully connotes R. Accordingly, we may pick out R by the predicate 'stabbing', but that is not to say that R is the relation of stabbing. It is, more likely, a relation that is only partially described by that predicate. Should the need arise, we could describe it more fully as, say, 'stabbing with a sharp knife, violently, and in such a way as . . .' and so on. It is the same for Brutus's killing of Caesar. Surely the relation involved in this event, call it R', includes the relation of killing. But it seems perfectly plausible to suppose that R' is much more specific than that. If we wanted to be more precise, we could describe it as 'killing with the help of a sharp knife, and in such a way as . . .' and so on. When fully spelled out, this relation may even turn out to be the same relation as R. And in that case the two event names 'Brutus's stabbing of Caesar' and 'Brutus's killing of Caesar', though obviously distinct with regard to their senses, would have the same actual reference. A similar account, of course, would apply to Brutus's violent killing, his murderous knifing, and so forth. From this point of view, the property-exemplification account is not necessarily thin. It enjoys the same sort of neutrality as Montague's account—a neutrality that leaves a gap between semantics and metaphysics. (For more on this way of separating out semantic and metaphysical aspects, see the exchange between Kim 1991 and Bennett 1991, 1996.)

There are many variants of Kim's theory, from the early proposals of Richard Martin (1969) and Alvin Goldman (1970) to Barwise and Perry's (1983) theory of situations. Moreover, interesting generalizations of the theory can be obtained by relaxing the requirement that the participants of an event be concrete objects. For instance, allowing an event to consist in the exemplification of a property by another *event* (or the exemplification of a relation by an n-tuple some members of which are events rather than objects) makes room for 'higher order events' such as Brutus's stabbing of Caesar causing Caesar's death. (See Peterson 1989, 1997.) All of these theories share Kim's insight that events are very thin entities. In each case, however, the underlying metaphysics is compatible with the more neutral semantic account suggested by Bennett.

Be it as it may, between the radically thick position of Quine and the radically thin position of Kim there is a lot of middle ground. We find here those theories that allow for the possibility of two or more events occurring simultaneously in the same place (contra Quine) while resisting the tendency to multiply events on the basis of mere linguistic differentiations (contra Kim). Davidson is perhaps the chief representative of this intermediate position, at least in his early works.[5] For Davidson, events are identified by their position in the causal network, and it seems plausible to suppose, on the one hand, that events with different causal relations may occur at the same spatiotemporal region and, on the other hand, that events corresponding to different descriptions may have the same causal relations:

> Events are identical if and only if they have exactly the same causes and effects. Events have a unique position in the framework of causal relations between events in somewhat the same way objects have a unique position in the spatial framework of objects. (1969: 179)

Of course, whether or not particular events have the same causes and effects is itself a question that involves issues of sameness, for causes and effects may themselves be events. Moreover, whether an event x causes an event y is itself a question that seems to rest on identity issues: in Davidson's (1967a) own relational account, x caused y just in case x and y are identical with events described in some true causal law; in an alternative, counterfactual account (Lewis 1973; Swain 1978), x caused y just in case y would not have occurred had x not occurred, and this, too, calls for some identity criteria, namely, criteria for identity across possible worlds. So Davidson's principle should not be taken as expressing a necessary and sufficient condition to *establish* sameness of events but rather as expressing a central ingredient of the event concept. If John's catching a cold and his counting his blessings have different causes or effects, then they are distinct events (obviously), even if they occur in the same place and at the same time; otherwise they are one and the same.

Incidentally, that causation is a relation between individual events is a thesis that Davidson (see 1967a) has explicitly defended. One might suppose that the causal relata are facts and that a statement such as

(3)   Sirhan's shot *caused* Robert Kennedy's death

could be analysed as a sentential compound in which the causal predicate is replaced by a causal connective, as in

(3a)   Sirhan shot, *and as a consequence* Robert Kennedy died.

But this—Davidson argues—is impossible. For, on the one hand, causal contexts are referentially transparent: if Robert Kennedy is the Democratic candidate, then (3a) has the same truth value as

(4)   Sirhan shot, *and as a consequence* the Democratic candidate died.

On the other hand, there is a well-known argument (due essentially to Frege) to the effect that referentially transparent sentential contexts are fully truth-functional.[6] Thus, the italicized connective in (3a) would have to be truth-functional, which is absurd: even though 'Robert Kennedy died' and 'the *Titanic* sank' have the same truth value, (3a) need not (and in fact does not) have the same truth value as

(5)   Sirhan shot, *and as a consequence* the *Titanic* sank.

If accepted, this argument does not only lend support to the idea that the causal network may provide a comprehensive framework for identifying events. It also lends support to the very idea that events are objects of reference and quantification in the first place. Any eliminativist account would *have* to analyse (3) along the lines of (3a), thus facing Davidson's objection. (See Horgan 1978, 1982, for some ways of resisting this line of reasoning.[7])

As it turns out, not many authors followed Davidson's specific account of event identity in terms of causal relations. Davidson (1985b) himself eventually rejected it, opting for a Quinean account instead. Nevertheless, the idea that events are spatiotemporal particulars whose identity criteria are moderately thin—the idea, that is, that events are somewhat intermediate between Quine's and Kim's characterizations—has found many advocates both in the philosophical and in the linguistic literature. In some cases (e.g., Brand 1977, 1984) the idea comes with the claim that events are truly basic entities, ontologically on a par with material objects. In other cases (e.g., Lombard 1979, 1986) the idea comes instead with the suggestion that events are in some way dependent entities, that all truths about events supervene on truths about objects and their properties.[8] These theories are different from Davidson's. But they all share with Davidson's the hope for a "middle ground" account of the number of particular events that may simultaneously occur in the same place.

3. Identity and Indeterminacy

This being the general philosophical background, it is apparent that the links between semantic and metaphysical issues are subtle and tricky. Different conceptions of events tend to suggest different answers when it comes to assessing the referential pattern of our event names; but no metaphysical theory includes a general recipe for determining the reference of the event names used in ordinary language (hence for determining the truth or falsity of an identity statement of the form 'event x is the same as event y').

Bennett takes all this as evidence that although there are limits to what we can say about events (about specific events, as well as about events in general), no systematic theorizing about events is possible:

> The meanings of ordinary [event] nominals don't lie at any determinate point in the Quine-to-Kim continuum. The facts that give truth to predications on a nominal include much more than just the fact actually expressed by the nominal (so Kim is wrong), and they must be connected with the expressed fact by some closer link than merely being about the same zone (so the Quinean is wrong). That is as far as we can go with any general account of the matter; from there on, it depends on local context and unprincipled intuitions. (1988: 128)

This may well be too drastic a conclusion. One wonders, for instance, whether this sort of indeterminacy does not also arise in the case of ordinary material objects. Arguably, whatever indeterminacy our concept of an object may involve, we seem to be able to theorize about objects and to account for the semantics of our talk about objects. Why should the case of events be any worse? (See, e.g., Lombard 1998 for this line of reply.)

We do not aim to answer this question here. But notice that the relevant sense of indeterminacy is not just one of vagueness. We have seen, in connection with Quine's theory, that there are event names which are vaguely defined insofar as they do not specify the exact spatiotemporal boundaries of their referents. This introduces a certain degree of indeterminacy in our event talk, but in a way that calls for a general theory of vagueness—a theory that must in any case be provided to account for the semantics of a great deal of natural language expressions (including names and descriptions of material objects). The indeterminacy that threatens the semantics of our event talk, in the sense here under examination, is one that arises even in the absence of vagueness. Let us suppose that we know the exact spatiotemporal location of the events we are talking about. Let us suppose, in particular, that 'x' and 'y' pick out events that occur exactly in the same spatiotemporal zone. Is there any way of articulating an answer to the question of whether x and y are distinct events? To the extent that this challenge gets a negative response, to that extent the semantics of our event names is indeterminate.

It is instructive, here, to look at one line of argument that has often been invoked precisely to articulate answers of the desired sort. It is based on the obvious idea that events, like any other entities, must satisfy Leibniz's principle of the indiscernibility of identicals. Thus, events that can be shown to have different properties—different contingent, modal, temporal, or causal properties—must be distinct. Critics of Quine and Davidson have often relied on such arguments to provide support for a more fine-grained account of event individuation.

Consider, for instance, the stabbing and the killing of Caesar by Brutus. Quine as well as Davidson—and many other philosophers who occupy a moderate position on the thick/thin continuum of event theories—would say that these are one and the same event under different descriptions. But one could argue thus: (a) Caesar could have survived the stabbing; (b) Caesar could *not* have survived the killing; thus, (c) the stabbing and the killing have different (modal) properties and must be distinguished. (By the same pattern, one could indeed argue that Brutus's stabbing of Caesar must be distinguished also from his violent stabbing of Caesar, his knifing of Caesar, and so on. So this line of argument would seem to provide independent support to a Kimean semantics of event names, contrary to Bennett's analysis.)

Is this line of argument acceptable? The underlying intuition, of course, is that there are possible worlds in which Brutus stabbed Caesar without killing him (e.g., because the stabbing inflicted only a flesh wound) and possible worlds in which Brutus killed Caesar without stabbing him (e.g., by strangling him). This intuition can hardly be questioned, except for a determinist. But does it follow from these possibilities that two distinct events *actually* occurred? Does it follow that Brutus committed two actions?

There are two ways of cashing out the above intuition, depending on whether our event talk is understood *de dicto* or *de re*. Let us look at both of them. Compare the two premises of the argument:

(6)   Brutus's stabbing of Caesar could have been survived by Caesar.

(7)   Brutus's killing of Caesar could not have been survived by Caesar.

In a *de dicto* reading, the first one reads

(6a)   There is a possible world *w* such that Brutus's stabbing of Caesar in *w* is survived by Caesar in *w*.

This amounts to the assertion that there is a possible world *w* in which the description 'Brutus's stabbing of Caesar' picks out an event that does not result in Caesar's death (e.g., because it inflicted only a flesh wound)—which is certainly true except for a radical essentialist or a radical determinist. The second premise reads

(7a)   There is no possible world *w* such that Brutus's killing of Caesar in *w* is survived by Caesar in *w*.

And this is true too, if not analytic. No event in any world *w* can satisfy the description 'Brutus's killing of Caesar' unless it results in Caesar's death. Thus, in a *de dicto* reading, both premises of the argument are naturally accepted. However, in this reading the truth of (6) and (7) does not support the conclusion of the argument that Brutus performed two actions. For if we are interested in the temporal properties of the events that *actually* occurred—the events picked out by the descriptions 'Brutus's stabbing of Caesar' and 'Brutus's killing of Caesar' in *this* world—then we should not look at the *alternative* referents of our event names. Obviously, if those names have different senses (and in our example they surely do), they could have different referents. (Clearly, 'the morning star' and 'the evening star' could have different referents.) But that is not the issue. The issue is not whether our two event names *could* have different referents. It is whether they *do* have different referents, whether they have different referents in *this* world. So, in a *de dicto* reading the premises may well be true, but the argument is not valid. The conclusion does not follow.

It is the *de re* reading that matters, then. But in a *de re* reading, (6) and (7) are in the same boat:

(6b)   Brutus's stabbing of Caesar—that particular event—is such that there is a possible world *w* in which *it* is survived by Caesar.

(7b)   Brutus's killing of Caesar—that particular event—is such that there is no possible world *w* in which *it* is survived by Caesar.[9]

If the stabbing *is* the killing, then *that particular event* is the same in both cases, so (6b) and (7b) cannot be both true. (Which of them is false will depend on whether one takes being survived by Caesar to be an essential property of the event in question.) If, on the other hand, the stabbing is not the same as the killing, then we are certainly speaking of two different events, and perhaps we can say that (6b) and (7b) are both true. But this opposition is *prior* to our modal speculations—it cannot be inferred from them and calls for independent grounds. In short, as Neale (1990: §4.6) has pointed out, on a *de re* reading the argument is valid but question begging: one can have reasons to accept both premises only if one already has reasons to distinguish between Brutus's stabbing of Caesar and his killing of Caesar in the first place.[10] Since the *de re* reading is the only one that matters (and since in a *de dicto* reading the argument is invalid anyway), this means that the argument fails to establish the intended conclusion.

Of course, the argument still presents a problem for those who wish to identify the stabbing and the killing. For if these are one and the same event, there are only two options: either one denies (6) or one denies (7). The denial of (7) seems awkward: how could Caesar survive his killing? So one seems to be forced to reject (6), and that is a radically essentialist route to take.

This problem is only apparent, though. Surely there is some awkwardness in the denial of (7), that is,

(8)   Brutus's killing of Caesar could have been survived by Caesar.

Even in a *de re* reading, this statement sounds very implausible. But what follows from this? It follows that such a statement is not a good way of expressing the proposition that the event we are talking about could have been survived by Caesar—the proposition that being followed by Caesar's death is not an essential property of our event.If we think that that proposition is true, then we would rather express it by using a different sentence. In particular, if we think the event in question is nothing but Brutus's stabbing of Caesar, we would express our proposition by asserting (6), for that way of speaking is not at all awkward. Awkwardness is a guide to pragmatics, not to ontology.

Here is a different way of making this point. Consider a purely temporal version of the argument examined above (as in Thomson 1971). Brutus stabs Caesar at time t, but Caesar only dies at a later time, t'. (Let us not worry now about the exact coordinates of these two times.) How can the stabbing be the same as the killing in this case? How can a killing occur before the death of the victim? The answer is that if we think the stabbing *is* the killing, then only one event occurred at t, although we cannot *call it* a killing until we have a death, at t'. We have two event names, 'Brutus's stabbing of Caesar' and 'Brutus's killing of Caesar', and these two names clearly have different senses. At t, when Brutus takes his stab at Caesar, the first name can be used to refer to what happened: Brutus's stabbing of Caesar has indeed taken place. The other event name cannot be used to refer to that event at t, for obviously we cannot say that we have a killing until we have a death, and that only takes place at t'. So at t only one event name names an event. But when Caesar's death does take place, at t', we *can* refer to the stabbing by the name 'Brutus's killing of Caesar'. For then, at t', our event does fit this description. At t one of the names refers, and the other does not; at t' they both refer, and they may well refer to the same event: different senses, same reference.

Bennett (1973) and Anscombe (1979) actually pointed out that this sort of awkwardness may arise all the time: a person cannot be called a killer before the death of the victim, and a man cannot truly be referred to as the father of the president before one of his children is elected president. When Clinton was elected, no new individual was brought to life. Rather, Clinton became the forty-second president and Clinton's father became the father of the forty-second president. (Clinton's father might even have been deceased at the time of the election, but that would not prevent us from referring to him as the father of the forty-second president, now and in the future.) Likewise, then, an event may come to acquire new properties as the result of later happenings. The act performed by Brutus, the stabbing of Caesar, became a killing when Caesar became dead. Or so one could coherently argue.[11]

Of course, in the specific case at issue there is room for disagreement. One can insist that every killing must *include* the death of the victim as a part. (This was Thomson's 1971 point.) If so, then one cannot accept that the stabbing and the killing are one and the same; rather, one would say that the stabbing is a proper part of the killing—that the killing is the (temporally scattered) mereological fusion of the stabbing *and* the death. But this different attitude need not involve a different metaphysics. On the contrary, one could still agree with the above account of what happened: just one event at t (a stabbing) and one event at t' (a death). Only, in the account above, 'Brutus's killing of Caesar' is just another name for the first event; in the alternative account it would be a name for the mereological fusion. (Compare: there is one fountain pen on the table, with a nice cap. One of us uses 'the pen' to refer exclusively to the writing instrument, without the cap. The other uses 'the pen' to refer to the writing instrument *and* the cap. A minor disagreement; a difference in our idiolects—but we can easily resolve it without revising our ontologies.)

As a final example, consider a causal version of the argument (Goldman 1971, Lewis 1986). We can say of Brutus's stabbing of Caesar that it caused Caesar's death. But the statement that Brutus's killing of Caesar caused Caesar's death sounds awkward. More strikingly, we can say of Sihran's pulling of the trigger that it caused the gun's going off; but the statement that Sihran's assassination of Robert Kennedy caused the gun's going off sounds bizarre. (See Regine Eckardt's chapter in this volume for more examples of this sort.)

There is no doubt that such examples bring out a problematic feature of our event talk. But in these cases the same analysis may be offered as in the temporal examples considered above. A statement such as

(9)   The killing of Kennedy caused the gun to go off

is bizarre. But if the pulling of the trigger and the killing of Kennedy are one and the same event—if the pulling *became* the killing upon Kennedy's death—the bizarre sound can be removed by paraphrasing (9) as

(9a)   The event which (as things turned out) was the killing of Kennedy by Sirhan caused the gun to go off.

This is no different from the way the bizarre sound of a statement such as (10) is removed by paraphrasing it as (10a):

(10)   The widow stuck her husband with a knife.
(10a) The person who (as things turned out) is now the widow stuck her husband with a knife.

(See Anscombe 1979.) One could go even further in this line, defending the identification of shooting and killing by analysing every action sentence 'x φed y' as a causal statement 'x caused y to be φed' (Lombard 1978a). Davidson (1985a) himself had something similar in mind, though he would rather say that the analysis should display two events: something x did and something that happened to y, the first event qualifying as a cause of the second. Be that as it may, the main point remains:

> We cannot speak of an action as [an] action that has [a certain consequence] until the time of the consequence arrives. But the arrival of the consequence does not change the cause. It merely changes what we can, in the present tense, say of it. (Davidson 1985a: 236–237)[12]

4. Events and Logical Form

So much for issues relating to explicit event talk and the seeming indeterminacy involved in the referential pattern of the names and descriptions that we can use to pick out events explicitly. Let us now review the idea, mentioned at the beginning, that much ordinary discourse involves *implicit* reference to (or quantification over) events. It is indeed in this form that the notion of event has acquired a dominant role in recent semantic theorizing, and it is mainly with this idea that the other chapters of the book are concerned.[13]

One could, in fact, argue that our understanding of an event name x is in some way parasitic on our understanding of a sentence that reports the event referred to by x but without explicitly employing x. This is so because most event names (such as 'Caesar's death') are descriptive expressions obtained by nominalizing a sentence ('Caesar died'). Accordingly, although such sentences do not explicitly contain event-referring expressions, it seems plausible to suggest that their logical form does in some way imply an ontology of events. (Some authors would rely on the mechanics of nominalization also to explain the links and differences between event talk and fact talk, following the footsteps of Vendler 1967b.[14] See Nicholas Asher's chapter in this volume for more on this subject.)

4.1. Hidden Quantification

A first articulated formulation of this view may be traced back to Frank Ramsey:

> 'That Caesar died' is really an existential proposition, asserting the existence of an event of a certain sort, thus resembling 'Italy has a king', which asserts the existence of a man of a certain sort. The event which is

of that sort is called the death of Caesar, and should no more be confused with the fact that Caesar died than the king of Italy should be confused with the fact that Italy has a king. (1927: 37)

The same suggestion—that many ordinary sentences imply an ontology of events through the use of verbs, if not through explicit naming—is also scattered in the work of other early authors, most notably Hans Reichenbach (1947), Arthur Prior (1949), and Gilbert Ryle (1949). It is, however, Donald Davidson's (1967b) article that made the suggestion explicit, and it is this article that most authors regard as a seminal contribution toward an understanding of our event talk. According to Davidson, verbs of action such as 'stabbed', 'died', or 'swimmed' involve implicit existential quantification over events. More precisely, they are to be analysed as containing one more argument place than usually recognised, and this place is occupied by a hidden quantified variable ranging over actions (a type of event). Insofar as existential quantification is ontologically revealing, this means that such an account involves an ontology of events: events are entities to which we implicitely refer when we use action verbs.

Take, for example, a sentence such as

(11)   Brutus stabbed Caesar.

In ordinary logic textbooks, this is analysed as an "atomic" sentence, a sentence consisting of a binary predicate, 'stabbed', flanked by two singular terms, 'Brutus' and 'Caesar'. In Davidson's analysis, by contrast, (11) is not atomic. It is, rather, an existentially quantified sentence involving a three-place predicate with a bound event variable. It asserts that a stabbing of Caesar by Brutus took place—that is, overlooking tense-related complexities, that there exists some event e which was a stabbing of Caesar by Brutus. In other words, (11) is analysed as in (11b) rather than (11a):

(11a)   Stabbed(Brutus, Caesar).
(11b) $\exists e$(Stabbing(Brutus,Caesar, e)).

From the perspective of generative grammar, this amounts to the hypothesis that the thematic grid of a verbal predicate has an extra (eventive) position

(12)   stab: $\langle x, y, e \rangle$

in such a way that the verb 'stab' is true of things x, y, and e if and only if e is a stabbing of y by x. This extra position is subject to the usual repertoire of semantic and syntactic manipulations that affect ordinary variables. It is not, however, subject to the usual mechanisms of thematic discharge, such as thematic marking. Rather, the event variable is bound by default existential closure. (See Heim 1982, Higginbotham 1985.)

There are several reasons underlying this analysis. One that played a major role in Davidson's original arguments is that it allows for a simple and effective solution to the problem of the variable polyadicity of action verbs, which we mentioned at the beginning of section 1. This is the problem, pointed out by

Anthony Kenny (1963: Ch. 8), of accounting for the various apparent logical relations between a sentence such as (11) and any of the following:

(13)   Brutus stabbed Caesar violently.
(14)   Brutus stabbed Caesar with the knife.
(15)   Brutus stabbed Caesar violently with the knife.

Clearly, (15) entails (and is not entailed by) the conjunction of (13) and (14), each of which in turn entails (11). Yet there is no clear way one can do justice to such logical connections in standard predicate logic. One cannot just treat (11) and (13) through (15) as atomic sentences built up with the help of distinct, logically autonomous predicates with various numbers of argument places:

(13a)   Stabbed-violently(Brutus, Caesar).
(14a)   Stabbed-with(Brutus, Caesar, the knife).
(15a)   Stabbed-violently-with(Brutus, Caesar, the knife).

For in that case the relevant entailments could only be explained in terms of *ad hoc* meaning postulates. Nor can one just treat (11), (13), and (14) as elliptic for (15), or of some suitably detailed extension of (15), for that would presuppose the existence of a definite upper bound to the number of adverbial modifications that can affect a verb such as 'stabbed'.[15] In short, one cannot do justice to the relevant logical connections by treating action verb phrases as ordinary predicates. By contrast, Davidson's analysis enhances the internal structure of such phrases—hence their intimate relationships—by allowing the function of adverbial expressions such as 'violently' and 'with the knife' to be explained in terms of predication of events. In Davidson's construal, (13) through (15) are analysed as (13b) through (15b), and standard predicate logic becomes fitted for explaining the relevant adverb-dropping inferences:

(13b) $\exists e$(Stabbing(Brutus, Caesar, e) & Violent(e)).
(14b) $\exists e$(Stabbing(Brutus, Caesar, e) & With(the knife, e)).
(15b) $\exists e$(Stabbing(Brutus, Caesar, e) & Violent(e) & With(the knife, e)).

(This account is not dissimilar from other cases of "sub-atomic semantics", to use Parsons's 1990 expression. A Davidsonian analysis of the internal structure of 'stabbed' makes it possible to appreciate the relationships between (11) and (13) through (15) just as, say, a Russellian analysis of 'the knife' will account for the relationships between (14) and

(16)   Brutus stabbed Caesar with a knife.

In both cases, standard logic does the job as soon as the relevant sentences are associated with a suitable logical form.)

There are several other linguistic phenomena—besides adverbial modification—that can be offered as evidence for an event-based analysis of this sort. For instance, quantification over events seems necessary to account for certain relationships between implicit and explicit reference to events. Compare (13) with

(17)   Brutus's stabbing of Caesar was violent.

In a Davidsonian/Russellian analysis there is a very close link between these two sentences, namely, the same link that exists between (16) and (14). Sentence (13) asserts the existence of a violent stabbing; sentence (17) asserts the existence *and uniqueness* of a violent stabbing. Likewise, the analysis appears to do justice to the logical structure of arguments that involve explicit and implicit quantification over events (Parsons 1985: 237), as in

(18)   Whenever there is a killing, there is a death.
(19)   Brutus killed Caesar in the Senate.
(20)   Therefore, somebody died in the Senate.

This is also true for arguments in which the event quantification is lexicalised exclusively through a temporal adverbial (Rothstein 1995), as in

(18a)   Whenever somebody is killed, somebody dies.

Additional evidence along these lines (e.g., concerning the analysis of tensed statements, plurals, or perceptual reports) can be found in the chapters that follow.[16] Here it will suffice to point out that to deal with a wider spectrum of phenomena some authors have found reasons to emendate Davidson's account in various ways. For instance, building on a suggestion of Hector-Neri Castañeda (1967)—initially rejected by Davidson (1967c)—Terence Parsons (1980, 1985) and others have advocated an analysis in which the event participants are separated out, placing the subject (agent) and the object (patient) in different conjuncts along with the other thematic roles (such as the instrumental role of 'with the knife').[17] In this account, (11b) is further analysed as

(11c) $\exists e$(Stabbing(e) & Subject(Brutus, e) & Object(Caesar, e))

(and (13b) through (15b) expanded accordingly). This allows one to do justice, for instance, to the entailment by (11) of

(21)   Brutus did something to Caesar

which cannot be explained if (11) is analysed as in (11b).

How are these accounts related to the metaphysical questions concerning the nature of events and their identity criteria? It may be observed that they appear to be relatively neutral. True, insofar as events are treated as first-order variables of quantification, these accounts imply that events must be particulars rather than universals. But there seem to be no major implications concerning the nature of such particulars with respect to the thick/thin coordinate. Indeed, Kim has argued that his notion of an event is perfectly compatible with a semantic account of action sentences à la Davidson—that is, that there are no irreconcilable differences between 'Davidson's theory of event discourse as a semantical theory' and 'the property-exemplification account of events as a metaphysical theory' (1976: 42). Things are not so smooth, however. For one thing, not all accounts à la Davidson are equally neutral. Parsons (1985) has noted that the refined account exemplified by (11c) may force distinctions with respect to which Davidson's original account remains neutral. For example, suppose Amelie plays a clarinet sonata. Then the events reported by the following sentences:

(22)   Amelie played a sonata
(23)   Amelie played the clarinet

must be distinguished in Parsons's account since the object of the former is a sonata whereas the object of the latter is a clarinet. (At least, this is what one is forced to do if both 'a sonata' and 'the clarinet' are treated as instances of the same thematic role 'Object', as Parsons does.) In Davidson's account, by contrast, one may maintain that (22) and (23) report one and the same event, which was both a playing of a sonata and a playing of the clarinet.

Another, more significant example concerns the adverb-dropping account discussed above in connection with (11) and (13) through (15). If we treat 'violently' as a predicate of the event e which was a stabbing of Caesar by Brutus, then the stabbing and the violent stabbing are not to be distinguished ontologically (just as the stabber and the violent stabber need not be distinct). This is indeed compatible with a Kimean metaphysics. But it is compatible *only if* we follow Bennett in purging that metaphysics from all of its semantic connotations (as discussed in section 2.2). Otherwise we would need a different account of the logic of 'violently'—and of adverbial modification generally.

Similarly, consider the scenario discussed by Eckardt in her chapter in this volume. Pat came home late last night, because of a traffic jam, and she started cooking spaghetti at 11 p.m. The statement

(24)   The traffic jam caused Pat's cooking spaghetti late

is true (say). But the statement

(25)   The traffic jam caused Pat's cooking spaghetti

is up for grabs. Some (e.g., Eckardt) would regard it as false. Others (following Davidson) would insist that (25) is about the same event as (24) and must therefore have the same truth value as (24) in spite of the appearances.[18] Hence, the possibility of dropping the modifier 'late' in (24) depends crucially on our intuitions concerning the identity of the relevant events. This means that a Davidsonian solution to Kenny's problem is not neutral with regard to such intuitions.

Of course, if (24) were understood as a statement about facts rather than events—contra Davidson's argument in section 2.2—then the issue would not arise.[19] For, on the one hand, it is uncontroversial that facts have very fine identity criteria; on the other hand, the logical form of (24) and (25) would not be an existential but a sentential compound:

(24a)   There was a traffic jam, and as a consequence Pat cooked spaghetti late.
(25a)   There was a traffic jam, and as a consequence Pat cooked spaghetti.

It is an interesting question whether or to what extent the temptation to attribute different truth values to statements such as (24) and (25), if not to statements such as (6) and (7), depends on a tendency to read these statements as expressing fact causation. If so, then Kim's compatibility statement might be right after all, except that whereas one is concerned with event talk, the other seems more concerned with fact talk.

4.2. Problems and Alternatives

Davidson's analysis (with or without the refinements stemming from the work of Parsons and others) has been extremely influential, lending further support to the idea that events are to be included in the domain of ordinary discourse. It is not, however, the only viable account. And it has its own problems.

Let us focus on adverbial modification. Davidson's point is that adverb-dropping inferences such as those linking (13) through (15) to (11) must be explained as a matter of logical form rather than lexical semantics. And the evidence for this view is also psychological: speakers of English do make such inferences even in the absence of the relevant lexical competence. (It is not necessary to know what "stab" means in order to see that (13) implies (11).) However, the burden of the claim rests on the availability of clear criteria for separating matters of meaning and matters of form. As Bennett (1988: 166) points out, presumably the inference from (26) to (27)

(26)   John is a grandfather
(27)   John is a parent

depends on the meaning of the relevant predicates, 'grandfather' and 'parent'. Yet the inference becomes valid as a matter of logical form as soon as (26) is analysed as

(26a) $\exists x \exists y (\text{Father}(\text{John}, x) \ \& \ \text{Parent}(x, y))$.

More generally, there is the fact that the adverb-dropping inferences do not always go through. For example, a Davidsonian analysis of

(28)   Jones filled the tank halfway

would yield the wrong result, sanctioning the inference to

(29)   Jones filled the tank

(see Thomason and Stalnaker 1973: 218). So here one is *forced* to resort to matters of meaning—'halfway' is just not the sort of adverb that can be dropped (unlike, say, 'patiently' or 'in the garage'). This might well be the right thing to say, disregarding Davidson's own views on matters of form. The point of an event-based analysis of action sentences—one could insist—is to treat adverbs as predicates of events, not to claim that all adverbs can be dropped. And the fact that some adverbs cannot be dropped is the natural analogue of the fact that certain adjectives (predicates of objects) cannot be dropped. Compare

(30)   This is a metal sphere.

(31)   This is a half sphere.

The same goes for such problematic adverbs as 'allegedly' and the like: alleged events may or may not take place, so they are not, of course, a kind of events.[20] But this sort of reply is still deficient. To use an example from Verkuyl (1993: 245ff), the adverb-dropping pattern may fail in other cases—for instance, when the subject phrase involves a monotone-decreasing quantifier:

(32)   At most three students filled the thank in the garage.

Here 'in the garage' cannot be dropped. Yet this cannot be explained by reference to the semantics of the modifier; for that same modifier *can* be dropped in

(33)   Jones filled the thank in the garage

to reach the conclusion in (29).

In his chapter in this volume, Verkuyl argues that such difficulties bear witness to Davidson's bias in favour of first-order predicate logic. Even the intuitive evidence offered by Davidson at the very beginning of his 1967b article is—according to Verkuyl—biased. Take a context such as

(34)   Jones filled the thank. He did it in the garage.

Davidson wants the antecedent of 'it' to be a singular term and he takes this to be one reason for introducing events as particulars. But consider the following, similar example:

(35)   Three students filled the thank. They did it in the garage.

Here there might have been three, two, or even just one event jointly perfomed in the garage by the three students. Hence, Verkuyl concludes that the anaphoric reference of the pronoun 'it' is sloppy and should be treated accordingly. And this, for Verkuyl, calls for an analysis in terms of lambda abstraction of the sort familiar from the literature on *do so*-constructions, as in

(36)   Jones filled the thank and Piet did so too.

(See Verkuyl 1972: 142ff. For more material on the delicate issue of anaphoric reference to events, see also Alice ter Meulen's chapter in this volume.)

On the face of it, these objections appear to undermine Davidson's rationale for introducing events in the ontology. We still have reasons to take event talk seriously inasmuch as our language involves explicit reference to and quantification over events. But as far as the indirect reference of action sentences is involved, one may want to resist the event-based account.

Are there any alternatives? If we wish to stay within the bounds of ordinary first-order logic, the answer is arguably in the negative. But if we are willing to allow for higher order types, as urged by Verkuyl, then a different approach is available. It consists in treating adverbial and prepositional phrases literally as predicate modifiers. Syntactically this is straightforward: if P is an n-place predicate and M is a modifier, then $M(P)$ is an n-place predicate too. This leads to the following alternative analysis of (13) through (15):

(13c)   Violently(Stabbed)(Brutus, Caesar).
(14c)   With-the-knife(Stabbed)(Brutus, Caesar).
(15c)   With-the-knife(Violently(Stabbed))(Brutus, Caesar).

And the semantic explanation is straightforward too. An n-place predicate P is naturally interpreted as an n-place relation on the given domain D; a modifier M can be interpreted, accordingly, as a function sending each n-ary relation to a (different) n-ary relation. Of course, one must be careful and distinguish different kinds of modifiers. Some will restrict the extension of their arguments, as is the case with the standard modifiers in (13) through (15). In these cases, $M(P)x$ entails Px, so the modifier is droppable. Others cases will yield the opposite result and $M(P)x$ will entail not-Px This is what happens with the modifier 'halfway' in (28), or 'half' in (31), which therefore are not droppable. Other cases are possible too, depending on how the extension of the argument is modified. But the taxonomy is relatively simple, so a modest apparatus could be sufficient to keep the logic under control without resorting to a mass of meaning postulates.

One advantage of this account—whose main features go back to Montague (1970)[21]—is that it would allow one to stay close to the surface. In some cases, this would even result in greater perspicuity, as with the pair

(37)   Brutus cruelly stabbed Caesar violently.
(38)   Brutus stabbed Caesar cruelly and violently.

As Parsons (1970) pointed out, a Davidsonian analysis of the relevant difference would involve a complicated story involving quantification and identity. By contrast, the predicate-modifier analysis would represent the difference between (37) and (38) in the obvious way:

(37a)   Cruelly(Violently(Stabbed))(Brutus, Caesar).
(38a)   Cruelly(Stabbed)(Brutus, Caesar) & Violently(Stabbed)(Brutus, Caesar).

In some cases, however, it is the event-based account that seems to fare better. For example, Taylor (1985: 17ff) has pointed out that a Davidsonian analysis allows one to do justice to the ambiguity involved in a sentence such as

(39)   Henry gracefully ate all the crisps.

The distributive reading (Henry ate each of the crisps gracefully) corresponds to the logical form in (39a), whereas the collective reading (Henry's eating of the crisps was overall graceful) corresponds to (39b):

(39a) $\forall x(\text{Crisp}(x) \rightarrow \exists e(\text{Eating}(\text{Henry}, x, e) \ \& \ \text{Graceful}(e)))$.   (distributive)
(39b) $\exists e(\forall x(\text{Crisp}(x) \rightarrow \text{Eating}(\text{Henry}, x, e)) \ \& \ \text{Graceful}(e))$.   (collective)

The rival theory cannot account for the difference so easily. The distributive reading is straightforward, but the collective reading calls for the full apparatus of lambda abstraction:

(39c) $\forall x(\text{Crisp}(x) \rightarrow \text{Gracefully}(\text{Eat})(\text{Henry},x))$.   (distributive)

(39d) $\text{Gracefully}(\lambda y \forall x(\text{Crisp}(x) \rightarrow \text{Eat}(y,x)))(\text{Henry})$.   (collective)

4.3. Events and States

One important feature that the predicate-modifier analysis shares with the event-based account is a natural uniformity among different sorts of modification (e.g., adjectival and adverbial modification) which is lost in the standard algorithm for translating English into first-order logic. Indeed, the predicate-modifier analysis applies to all sorts of adverbial modification, whether the context is an action sentence or a stative sentence, as in

(40)   Caesar loved Brutus wholeheartedly.

(41)   John is extremely happy.

Can a similar account be given in Davidsonian fashion? If action sentences are given an analysis that exploits the event-as-particular idea, can a similar account be extended to stative sentences?

A number of authors (beginning with Montmarquet 1980) have answered in the affirmative. The suggestion is that the domain of quantification should be extended to contain individual *states*, as well as events, and that the semantics feature stative variables, as well as eventive ones. Thus, for instance, a basic stative sentence such as

(42)   Caesar loved Brutus

should not be analysed as atomic:

(42a)   Loved(Caesar, Brutus).

Rather, its logical form should be construed as (42b), or perhaps as (42c), in perfect analogy to (11b) and (11c):

(42b) $\exists s(\text{Loving}(\text{Caesar}, \text{Brutus}, s))$.

(42c) $\exists s(\text{Loving}(s) \,\&\, \text{Subject}(\text{Caesar}, s) \,\&\, \text{Object}(\text{Brutus}, s))$.

The modifier 'wholeheartedly' in (40) would, of course, be treated accordingly, as a (droppable) predicate of the state s. Thus, the analysis would be beneficial for the same reasons put forward in the case of action sentences: descriptive fittingness, explanatory adequacy, simplification in the combinatorics, and so forth.

A detailed articulation of this proposal was given by Parsons (1987/88, 1990), but with the acknowledgment that the evidence in favour of the "underlying state analysis" is much less conclusive than that in favour of the "underlying event analysis". In this volume, Parsons reconsiders the problem. He shows that the tests that lend support to the event analysis do not seem to work in the case of stative predicates. The evidence is meager in many cases and absent (if not running counter to the thesis) in others. To illustrate, consider what Parsons calls the *modifier nonconjunction* criterion. It amounts to the aforementioned fact that, with eventive predicates, the truth of (13) and (14) does not entail that of (15):

(13)   Brutus stabbed Caesar violently.
(14)   Brutus stabbed Caesar with the knife.
(15)   Brutus stabbed Caesar violently with the knife.

The point here is that even if both (13) and (14) are true, they may be made so by different events, so that the truth of (15) does not follow. Parsons takes this property as criterial for his event analysis, arguing that the facts in (13) through (15) are correctly predicted by such an analysis but remain unexplained in a theory that does not quantify over individual events. In the case of stative predicates, however, these neat results cannot be easily replicated. For there are circumstances when it actually seems possible to import the modifiers from the antecedent sentences while preserving truth. Consider:

(43)   Socrates lies in the marketplace.
(44)   Socrates lies under an awning.
(45)   Socrates lies in the market under an awning.

If this were really the case, it would constitute counterevidence to the underlying state analysis because it would show that stative sentences may violate the nonconjunction criterion.

This is not, however, Parsons's conclusion. The force of the entailment from (43) and (44) to (45) lies in the fact that people cannot be in different places at the same time. But this is an empirical fact, not a logical fact. If it were possible for people to violate this law, then the inference would be invalid. If it were possible for Socrates to be in different places (or, more generally, in different states) at the same time, then the seeming counterevidence to the underlying state analysis would be blocked. And that this is possible is shown by Parsons with reference to a simple scenario: just suppose that people can travel in time. Suppose, for instance, that Socrates is in the marketplace at a given time t, and suppose that at a later time $t' > t$ he time-travels back to t, but to a different place, under an awning. Now, under the hypothesis that there is just one Socrates, it must be concluded that at t the very same person is in two different places (states). Hence the truth of (45) does not follow any more from that of (43) and (44), and the modifier nonconjunction test is successful. Parsons's conclusion, then, is that the seeming failure of the underlying state analysis is due to interfering factors leading to a confusion between empirical and logical possibilities. As soon as these factors are detected, the tests that lend support to the underlying event analysis now also work properly in the case of stative sentences.

At this point one might be tempted to go even further. One might be tempted to go for an enlarged theory that quantifies over all sorts of property instances (tropes). Though this is not Parsons's proposal, it certainly suggests itself. But then a serious difficulty arises for we appear to be condemned to an infinite regress. If 'Caesar loved Brutus' is regimented as asserting, among other things, the existence of a state s, which was a loving and whose subject was Caesar, then why should not '*s* was a loving' be analysed as asserting, among other things, the existence of a state *s'*, which was a being-a-loving and whose subject was *s*? What prevents us from further analysing (42c) as

(42d) $\exists s \exists s'$(Being-a-love(s') & Subject(s,s') & Subject(Caesar,s) & . . .).

And if that is allowed, then what prevents us from iterating this analysis over and over?

This slippery slope was pointed out by Bennett (1988: 177, following a remark of Zemach 1978: 87). We need not be bothered by the possibility of infinite regress if what is being offered is only a "logic of language" (as Bennett calls it). But, of course, the difficulty is a real one if what is being offered is a psychology—an account of the logical principles that operate (unconsciously) in the mind of a native speaker of a language such as English. As with the problematic entailments mentioned in section 4.2, we are facing here the delicate boundary between strenght and limits of event-based semantics.

5. Linguistic Applications

We need not go any deeper into the analysis of the pros and cons of this approach to logical form. Our purpose was simply to set up the general background for the remainder of the book, and we refer to the chapters that follow for further illustrations and critical discussion. Let us simply add that, in spite of the difficulties that we have mentioned, psychological considerations play also a positive role in explaining the success of Davidson-style semantics among linguists. Especially from the perspective of generative grammar, one of the guiding principles for conceptual and empirical linguistic inquiry is adequacy with respect to language acquisition. A semantic theory—a theory of the meaning/ form connections—must be capable of explaining not only what competent speakers of a given language know about the way semantic values are attached to syntactic structures, but also how competent speakers come to have such a knowledge. Such an explanation is possible only insofar as the theory of linguistic knowledge is learnable by a child on the basis of his or her ordinary, limited experience (as Davidson himself has argued at length in 1983). And this, in turn, requires that the semantic theory be restrictive enough not to entail a search space that is too wide for a language learner. From this point of view, the hypothesis that predicates introduce an extra position for events (and states) provides for a theory of semantic combinatorics that appears to be restrictive in the desired sense, at least if compared with alternative accounts of the sort mentioned above, which rely heavily on higher-order machinery.

By way of conclusion, let us now take a look at two concrete lines of development growing out of such a general background. One of these concerns the telicity/atelicity distinction, and is discussed in some length (and from different perspectives) in Higginbotham's and Verkuyl's chapters; the other line is the treatment of adverbial quantification, and ties in with the chapters by Denis Delfitto and Alessandro Lenci with Pier Marco Bertinetto.

5.1. Aspectual Phenomena and the Telicity/Atelicity Distinction

The notion of telicity arises in connection with sentences such as those in (46) through (49), which seem to convey the idea that the relevant events reach a sort of privileged end point, or *telos*:

(46)   John ate an apple.
(47)   John ran home.
(48)   John reached the top.
(49)   John died.

In (46), not only is it the case that the event in question (the eating of the apple) is finished. It must also be true that a certain goal, the telos or *terminus ad quem*, has been attained—for example, that the whole apple has been consumed in the course of the eating. Similarly, the truth of (47) does not require only that the subject was involved in an activity of running directed towards home; it is also necessary that the telos—namely, John's being at home—is obtained by virtue of that very running. Concerning (48) and (49), it may be observed that in these cases there is no explicit mention of an activity leading to the relevant teloi. Nonetheless, the truth of these sentences require that the teloi be attained.

Teloi are "privileged" end points of events in the following sense. If we are told (47), we know not only that the event of running performed by John and directed towards his own place got to an end but also that that event could not have possibly continued any further. On the other hand, there are infinitely many ways in which an event of a similar kind could have finished: John might have stopped running halfway home, almost close to home, far away from home, and so on. In each case a continuation (until the telos 'John is at home' is reached) seems to be possible. *Atelic* sentences, by contrast, do not involve such a notion of privileged end point:

(50)   John ate apples.
(51)   John ate.
(52)   John ran.
(53)   John pushed the cart.

As in (46) through (49), these examples are about finished events. However, there is a sense in which the reported events in (50) through (53) might well have continued: John might have eaten more apples, he might have run a little longer, he might have pushed the cart some distance further. In this sense, the notion of atelicity does not simply capture the fact that, for example, in (50) no telos is specified. The point is that a telos for (50) cannot even be envisaged.

This intuitive characterisation of the telic/atelic distinction can be given firmer empirical grounds by resorting to the well-known *for-time/in-time* adverbial test. It can be observed, in fact, that sentences that have been classed as telic can be modified by in-time adverbials but not for-time ones.

(54)   John ate an apple in/*for ten minutes.
(55)   John ran home in/*for ten minutes.

(56)   John reached the top in/*for ten minutes.

(57)   John died in/*for ten minutes.

Conversely, atelic sentences admit the latter and yield unfelicitous results with the former:

(58)   John ate apples #in/for ten minutes.

(59)   John ate #in/for ten minutes.

(60)   John ran #in/for ten minutes.

(61)   John pushed the cart #in/for ten minutes.

Finally, the telic/atelic distinction is affected by the nature of the arguments the verb combines with. Thus (54), where the direct object is countable, is telic, whereas (58), with a bare plural, is atelic. Similarly, (55), with a prepositional locative phrase, is telic, whereas (60), where such a phrase is missing, is atelic.

The problems that must be addressed are therefore the following: why can't for-time adverbials felicitously combine with telic predicates, and conversely, why can't in-time adverbials combine with atelic predicates? What is the role of arguments in allowing or disallowing telicity? And, finally, what does the telic/atelic distinction amount to in an event-semantics framework? What are its ontological implications?

5.21. Event-based Accounts

An event-based approach to these questions seems promising. One possibile answer to the last questions is to follow Parsons (1990) and directly stipulate the distinction by means of two predicates, *Cul* and *Hold*, meant to apply to telic and atelic events (and states), respectively. In this way, the difference between, say, (46) and (50) can be expressed through the logical forms

(46a) $\exists e \exists t$(Eating(e) & Subject(e, John) & Object(e, an apple) & Cul(e, t)).

(50a) $\exists e \exists t$(Eating(e) & Subject(e, John) & Object(e, apples) & Hold(e, t)).

(Again, we omit here tense-related complexities.) *Cul* is a two-place relation holding between an event e and a time t if and only if e culminates (reaches the telos) at t. On the other hand, *Hold* is meant to apply to an event e and a time t if and only if the event is developing at t.[22] If an event satisfies *Cul* it also satisfies *Hold*, but the converse may fail. So (50a) might be true even when (46a) is not.

Although it captures some intuitions behind the telic/atelic distinction, such a proposal does not seem capable of providing an answer to some of the questions above. For instance, it cannot explain the role of direct objects in the determination of the telic/atelic distinction nor the observed patterns with in-time and for-time adverbials.[23] The role of direct objects suggests that the telic/atelic distinction should be better seen as a property of complex eventive predicates—that is, as a property of verb-phrase predicates—and as stemming from the interaction between the interpretive properties of the verb and those of the direct object. Using the relation *part-of* as the basic structuring device, Krifka (1989, 1992) implements such an idea within an algebraic semantics, splitting the carrier for the model into two lattice-theoretic structures, one for ordinary objects and one for events.[24] He then defines a number of higher order predicates and relations characterising different reference types. For instance, *cumulative* reference—the property holding of predicates that are closed under the join operation—can be used to model masses (e.g., *wine*; *bread*); bare plurals (*apples*); and in the eventive domain, atelic predicates (*drink wine*; *eat apples*). Indeed, given two quantities of wine, apples, bread, and so on, their join is still a quantity of wine, apples, bread, and so on. Likewise, in the eventive domain, given two runnings e_1 and e_2, it seems straightforward to conclude that their mereological sum (the lattice join $e_1 \sqcup e_2$) is still a running.

In telic cases, the corresponding predicates have *quantised* reference—that is, given two events in the extension of the predicate, it is never the case that one is part-of the other. In the eventive case, this means that no proper part of an eating-an-apple event is an eating-an-apple event. Krifka also tries to find a counterpart of the notion of telos, by exploiting the idea of *terminal point*.[25] Intuitively, the terminal point of an event is the last time in the temporal trace of the event. Then an eventive predicate P has the *set terminal point* property if and only if any given event e in the extension of P is such that all of its parts that are in P have the same terminal point as e. This characterisation of telicity straightforwardly applies to predicates with quantised reference. In these cases, in fact, the set of parts of e that are in the extension of the quantised predicate P consists only of e, so that the terminal point condition is satisfied. On the other hand, it is easy to see that cumulative predicates lack the set terminal point property, thus showing justice to their atelicity.[26]

As for the impact of argument, Krifka proposes that aspectual shifts are due to the fact that the referential properties of the argument can carry over to those of the eventive predicate. Thus, the quantised reference of *an apple* forces the corresponding property on the predicate *eat an apple*. Conversely, the cumulativity of *apples* determines the cumulativity of *eat apples*. The necessary connection between the verbal predicate and the argument is provided by the thematic relation holding between them, which acts as an homomorphism between the objectual and the eventive domain.

Krifka's proposal has been quite influential and has inspired a number of works that explore the consequences of the theory in various languages (Filip 1992; Ramchand 1997; Singh 1998). Criticisms have also been raised. For instance, Verkuyl (1993 and this volume) points out that some of Krifka's basic properties do not work the way they should. To illustrate, Verkuyl observes that every verb is cumulative and that every thematic relation is cumulative. Hence the differences between (46) and (50) should be accounted for by exploiting only the different denotations of the objects. Krifka treats bare plurals as involving existential quantification over the size of the denoted set—analysing the bare plural *apples* as

(62) $\exists y \exists n (\ldots \text{Apple}(y, n) \ldots)$.

This makes bare plurals basically akin to such expression as *some apples*, in that they both involve an unspecified number of objects. However, *some apples* induces telic readings, as in

(63)   John ate some apples in ten minutes,

whereas bare plural objects induce atelicity. In the end, it is not clear how to deal with the different status of (46) and (50) and as a consequence that the capability of satisfactorily dealing with aspectual composition is not granted.

It is worth observing that in Krifka's theory, the telic/atelic distinction applies to (complex) predicates rather than to events themselves. One consequence of this view (emphasized in Krifka 1998) is that the distinction itself is a matter of description—that is, one and the same event can be described as falling in the extension of a quantised predicate in a telic construction or in the extension of a cumulative predicate in an atelic construction. This means that (46) and (50) (and (51)) can both be made true by the same event, *just as with the stabbing/ killing case*. The alternative account—which a broadly Davidsonian event semantics makes available—consists in taking the notion of telos at face value and letting a distinguished individual event correspond to it. This is the possibility explored by Higginbotham in his chapter in this volume. Higginbotham argues that telic sentences differ from atelic ones because the logical form of the former involves a pair of eventive variables, whereas the logical form of the latter contains only one variable. The two variables of the telic case are such that the first refers to the *processual* part of the reported event and the second to the *telos*. For example, for a sentence such as

(64)   John ate an apple in ten minutes

we have a structured truth-maker consisting of two parts, e_1 and e_2, such that e_1 is the eating activity John was engaged in, e_2 is the telos of that activity (e.g., the state consisting in the apple's being in John's stomach), and the two stand to each other in the relation expressed by the relevant in-time adverbial:

(64a) $\exists e_1 \exists e_2 (\text{Eating}(\text{John, an apple}, \langle e_1, e_2 \rangle) \ \& \ \text{In-ten-minutes}(e_1, e_2))$.

In other words, in Higginbotham's view, teloi are explicitly represented in the truth conditions of telic sentences and have an encoding at the level of logical form, thus becoming available for syntactic manipulations.[27] (This is not to say that events must be multiplied to account for the relevant semantic difference. The point is that the logical form of a telic sentence such as (64) calls for a complex truth-maker consisting of two events, whereas the logical form of an ordinary atelic requires only a simple truth-maker consisting of a single event. But one can always identify the latter event with part of the complex event—namely, the processual part.)

One consequence of this view is that the relationship between (a)telicity and (in)homogeneity is reversed: whereas the common attempt was to explain telicity from inhomogeneity (and/or cumulativity; see above), now it turns out that the former entails the latter. Indeed, a telic event e is nonhomogeneous since its proper parts either lack a telos or, if they have one, it cannot be of the same type as that of *e*. Conversely, homogeneity/cumulativity entails atelicity; that is, whenever the eventive predicate applying to event *e* also applies to its proper parts, that predicate cannot be telic.

Given the conceptual priority of (a)telicity with respect to such properties as cumulativity and quantisation and the referential treatment of telicity, it would seem that aspectual shifts must be explained in a different manner than Krifka's. The absence of telic readings in a sentence such as (50), *John ate apples*, now points towards a role of direct objects in the identification of the telos—therefore in the identification of complex events. There are at least two options in this respect, depending on the underlying hypothesis concerning the way teloi are introduced in syntax. The first option is the one explored by Higginbotham in his chapter. Suppose that the complex/simplex event distinction is lexically encoded—that is, that the lexicon has two distinct lexical entries for a verb such as *eat*, one with a simplex event, yielding atelic readings, and the other with a complex event, accounting for telic readings. Then it must be the case that bare plurals and mass nouns objects fail (either syntactically or semantically) to be involved in the telos. The second option is that verbal lexical entries only encode the simplex event variant, and that the simplex/complex event distinction corresponds to structural differences. That is, the telos (event) arises only when given syntactic structural relationships hold between the verb(al projection) and the direct object, possibly with the crucial contribution of functional categories.

A question related to the origin of teloi concerns the role of verbal lexical predicates. If the distinction between simplex and complex events is lexically encoded, does the predicate *eat* of the complex variant classify both events or just the first (the processual part)? If the second alternative turns out to be better, so that the verbal predicate does the same job in the two variants, how should the telos be classified? These questions seems less important if the second, structural alternative sketched above is taken. For in this case the basic predicate classifies the same entities—namely, processual parts—both in telic and in atelic sentences. The status of the telos, on the other hand, is determined by whatever plays a role in the structural mechanisms responsible for the complex event reading (functional categories, the direct object, and the verb itself).

Let us conclude by observing that the telicity/atelicity opposition constitutes an interesting case study also for those theories that advocate a nonrealist position with regard to an ontology of events.[28] A leading account is Henk Verkuyl's (1993 and this volume). Rejecting the idea that the thematic grids of verbs (and logical forms tout court) include an event position, Verkuyl attempts to reconstruct aspectual facts by resorting to (abstract) times structures and noun phrase denotations, using the tools of generalised quantifier theory. In particular, he takes the meaning of a verb phrase as consisting of a function that relates the denotation of the subject to the denotation of the object at different times. Time, in turn, is given a discrete structure, basically akin to that of the natural numbers. Therefore, the role of a verb phrase denotation is to relate the subject denotation with pairs that consist of a time and an abstract *position* in the object denotation, where the 'position' is conceived of as a member of a given partition of the noun denotation. To use a metaphor, the verb provides a clock whose functioning specifies a *path* for the subject through the object denotation. It is from this basic structure—the path in the object denotation—that aspectual phenomena stem.

One of Verkuyl's goals is to explain the apparent role of cardinality information, concerning the direct obejct denotation, in the telic/atelic distinction. Already in his 1972 work, Verkuyl pointed out that what distinguishes telicity-inducing objects from atelicity-inducing ones is some abstract notion pertaining to cardinality, which he called SQA (specified quantity of A, where A is the noun denotation). Thus a direct object such as *an apple* differs from the bare plural *apples* in that the former has a constraint on the cardinality of its denotation (one element), which the second lacks. Generalising this property to all the determiners to which the +SQA specification applies, and given that the verb denotation (the clock) works on members of a partition of the nominal phrase denotation, if the latter does not have a specified cardinality then the partition lacks a specified cardinality as well. But this means that it is not possible to determine when the clock *stops*. This, Verkuyl argues, is the basis of the distinction between telicity and atelicity. When there is cardinality information, there is also a determinate point at which the clock stops (i.e., a point in the noun denotation from which there is no way to continue the *path* any further)—thus telicity. When cardinality information is missing, no such a determinate end point in the abstract *path* can be specified—thus atelicity.

The notion of event plays no role in this account. Verkuyl explicitly argues that the notion is not a primitive one for linguistic theory; it is, rather, a side effect of the working of the apparatus he proposes.[29]

5.2.2. The Role of Morphosyntax

While refining the basic conceptual tools, it is also possible that the chances of event-based semantics to contribute to an explanation of aspectuality depend on the acknowledgment of greater explanatory role for syntax and morphosyntax.[30] That such a flexibility is most probably needed is shown by recent comparative works (e.g., Ramchand 1997; Singh 1998) that call attention to facets of aspectuality so far ignored or overlooked. It has been noted, for instance, that there are languages—for example, Hindi or Scottish Gaelic—in which aspectual shifts are virtually absent. In these languages the aspectual value of a sentence seems to be solely determined by the nature of the aspectual morphemes and by case-theoretical considerations, and it is substantially unaffected by changes in the direct argument. Given the role aspectual shifts have played in the theoretical discussion about events and aspect, it is possible that a closer analysis of these facts will reveal the necessity to redefine the roles of syntax, morphosyntax, and semantics in accounting for aspectuality.

A similar picture concerning the architecture of the theory of aspectuality seems to emerge also from the analysis of the interplay between the telicity/atelicity dimension and the related perfective/imperfective distinction. For instance, Romance languages morphologically distinguish imperfective and perfective aspects, the former being available to express the so-called *continuous* aspect.[31] This morphological distinction is absent in English.[32] And the question arises of the place of the continuous aspect in the telic/atelic distinction. Is such a distinction applicable in this case? There is some evidence that the answer should be in the negative, given that the traditional in-time/for-time test does not seem to apply (compare Mittwoch 1980):

(65)   *John mangiava una mela in/per dieci minuti.
        John ate (IMPERFECT) an apple in/for ten minutes.

(66)   *John mangiava mele in/per dieci minuti.
        John ate (IMPERFECT) apples in/for ten minutes.

These examples are ungrammatical, in the semelfactive reading, with both kinds of adverbials—though the in-time version is acceptable with the habitual reading. That is, (65) and (66) cannot mean that John was in the process of eating an apple/apples and that that process lasted ten minutes. On the other hand, the in-time/for-time test applies to Romance perfective forms, mirroring the results obtained in English:

(67)   John mangiò/ha mangiato una mela in/*per dieci minuti.
        John ate (PERFECT)/has eaten an apple in/for ten minutes.

(68)   John mangiò/ha mangiato mele *in/per dieci minuti.
        John ate (PERFECT)/has eaten apples in/for ten minutes.

Thus, it seems that the telic/atelic distinction applies only to perfective predicates. Depending on the place of continuous imperfective predicates in the theory, these facts might therefore require a major rethinking of the role of the distinction itself. [33]

In this connection, it is interesting to observe that the events discussed by Davidson (and by most linguists afterwards) correspond to the "terminated" events: *John ate apples, Jones buttered the toast, Brutus killed Caesar*, and so on.[34] These events are on a par with regard to terminativity regardless of whether the reporting sentence is atelic (as in the first case) or telic—that is, regardless of whether the event might or might not have continued. Virtually all the theoretical setups proposed in the literature, including those rejecting event semantics, concur on this point: descriptively, the "events" they consider are all terminated. The relevance of the notion of *terminativity* might be difficult to see if attention is limited to English data. But it becomes very clear when constrasting the continuous (imperfective) and the perfective aspects of, say, Romance or Slavonic:

(69)   John mangiò/ha mangiato una mela.   (finished)
        John ate(PERFECT)/has eaten an apple.

(70)   John mangiava una mela.   (not finished)
        John ate (IMPERFECT) an apple.

There is a clear sense in which the event of (69), even in the atelic version with the mass noun object, is terminated at the utterance time. By contrast, (70) leaves open the possibility for the event to be still going on at the utterance time—that is, it need not be terminated.

The phrases that require nonfinished events are not limited to the continuous verbal forms of Romance or Slavonic. The eventive nominals of most (if not all) languages have the same property: noun phrases such as *the eating* or *the conference* do not necessarily refer to finished events, this specification being usually being provided by the context:

(71)   La conferenza fu noiosa e me ne andai.   (finished)
       The conference was (PERFECT) boring and I left.

(72)   La conferenza era noiosa e me ne sono andato.   (not finished)
       The conference was (IMPERFECT) boring and I left.

In (71) the conference must be over at the time of utterance, whereas in (72) it might still be going on.

These considerations, together with the derivational link between event nominals and verbal forms, suggest that "nonterminated" events are more basic than finished ones. At least, they provide evidence against the hypothesis that one kind of event sentence is more basic than the other.[35] More generally, these considerations pose a challange to any theory of events, however construed. For one must explain, first, how imperfective continuous sentences differ from perfective ones.[36] And, second, it must be possible to explain why continuous sentences do not participate in the telic/atelic distinction, whereas perfective sentences do.

5.2 Quantifying on Events

We conclude by looking at the material discussed in the chapters by Delfitto and Lenci with Bertinetto.

Within event semantics, it has become customary to analyse such adverbs as *often*, *always*, *rarely*, and the like as devices of quantification, elaborating on a suggestion by Lewis (1975).[37] For instance, (73) can be given the form in (73a), where *often* is analysed as a determiner in the sense of the theory of generalised quantifiers—namely, as a relation between two predicate-like denotations:

(73)   Last year, John often fainted.
(73a) (Many t) [Part(t, Last-year)] $\exists e$(At(e, t) & Fainting(e) & Subject(John, e)).

The development of this so-called *relational* analysis of generic and habitual sentences has further exploited the possibility of quantifying over eventive variables by hypothesising the existence of a hidden quantifier, *Gen*, endowed with a sort of universal force and responsible for intensional effects observed with generics and habituals.[38] For example:

(74)   When he was young, John smoked.
(74a) (Gen t)[Young(John, t)]$\exists e$(Smoking(e) & At(e, t) & Subject(John, e)).

Now, one problem for this analysis concerns the *origin* of the hidden quantifier *Gen*. It has been suggested that *Gen* is a sort of default choice, exploited whenever a quantificational format is provided by the syntax without any explicit quantifier being available. (See, e.g., Krifka et al. 1995.) This proposal, however, is open to the objection that there are languages that exploit overt morphemes to encode habituality, so that the alleged default behavior of *Gen* in, say, English would be construed as a language-specific phenomenon. Furthermore, even in languages in which no such morphemes are available, habitual/generic readings show distributional restrictions that one would not expect if *Gen* were a real default option. Thus, contrast (75) with (76):

(75)   John fumò.
        John smoked (PERFECT).

(76)   John fumava.
        John smoked (IMPERFECT).

In Italian, the use of the imperfective tense allows the habitual reading of (76), whereas the perfective past permits only the semelfactive reading of (75). However, if *Gen* were a real default option, we would expect an habitual reading with (76) also, contrary to facts. More generally, besides languages that overtly mark habitual readings, we find languages—such as the Romance ones—that morphologically distinguish between perfective and imperfective verbal forms and invariably use the latter to express habituality. These observations point towards a role of verbal morphology in ruling habitual/semelfactive readings and require the relational analysis to be more specific about the origin of *Gen*.

Another problem for the relational account concerns the quantificational analysis itself and is common in cases of overt and hidden (habitual/generic) quantification. Despite analogies with the semantics of quantification in the nominal domain, there are clear syntactic differences in the verbal domain that need to be addressed. In general, the strict structural relationships found in the nominal domain (a determiner that combines both syntactically and semantically with a nominal predicate—the restrictor—forming a generalised quantifier) are lost with adverbial quantification.

Moving from this background, Delfitto and Bertinetto's chapter in this volume is an attempt to clarify the interactions between morphosyntax and semantics by focusing on the role of aspectual morphology in habituals and semelfactive readings. Their suggestion is that aspectual morphology directly encodes quantificational information. Accordingly, they propose to unify adverbial quantification with its counterpart in the nominal domain. Following a line of analysis going back to Larson (1988) and recently revived by Giorgi and Pianesi (1997), Delfitto and Bertinetto hypothesise that the thematic grid of verbal predicates has both an eventive and a temporal position to discharge, the latter being assigned to a temporal argument. The role of aspectual morphology would then be to regulate the form and substance of generalised quantification over time, acting much in the same way as determiners in the nominal phrases. In this view, imperfective morphology gives rise to an explicit syntactic format for generalised quantification over times, which is independent of the presence or absence of overt adverbs of quantification.[39] On the other hand, perfective morphology has no quantificational import: unless an explicit quantificational adverb is present, which by itself requires a generalised quantifier format, ordinary semelfactive readings are the result of default existential closure of the event position.[40] If correct, this account would solve both the problems discussed above: *Gen* is not a default device but is introduced by the imperfective morphology. Furthermore, generalised quantification in the verbal domain becomes even structurally similar to that obtaining with nominal phrases.[41]

In a similar spirit, Lenci and Bertinetto's contribution focuses on another problem of the '*Gen* as a default' theory. We have already observed, with reference to (76), that if *Gen* were a real default, we would expect generic/habitual readings to obtain in Italian with perfect tenses also, contrary to facts. The "default" theory seems to yield the right predictions when confronted with English facts such as

(77) a. In 1956 the members of this club always wore a hat.
      b. In 1956 the members of this club wore a hat.

Both these sentences can have a "characteristic" reading (it was a characteristic of members of this club that in 1956 they wore a hat), and in both cases the underlying quantificational force seems to be universal. Thus—the argument of the default theory goes—whenever habitual readings are at stake and there is no overt quantificational adverb, a default adverb *Gen* is exploited. [Notice that such an argument rests on the (implicit) hypothesis that the quantificational format alone suffices to explain the core properties of generic/habituals. Both (77a) and (77b) have a "characteristic" reading, and this is due to the quantificational format, regardless of the quantifier.]

Lenci and Bertinetto observe that if the hypothesis were true—that is, if there were one and the same quantificational format for generic/habitual readings in which quantificational adverbs and the default *Gen* freely alternate—we would expect any given quantificational adverb to yield the same interpretive result (modulo quantificational force) regardless of other factors. But this expectation is not fullfilled, as shown by the following examples:

(78) (L'anno scorso) John è spesso andato al cinema con Maria.
      (Last year) John often went (PERFECT) to the cinema with Maria.

(79) (L'anno scorso) John andava spesso al cinema con Maria.
      (Last year) John often went (IMPERFECT) to the cinema with Maria.

Both (78) and (79) have the same quantificational adverb, *spesso* (*often*). However, only (79) has a truly habitual meaning (reporting a past habit of John). The perfective sentence (78), by contrast, is a *factual* statement to the effect that John often went to the cinema with Maria. This suggests that the "characteristic" meaning of habitual sentences is not due to the same format in which the quantificational adverb participates. Moreover, we must admit that *Gen* is present as soon as habitual/generic readings are available, regardless of the presence or absence of overt quantificational adverbs. Thus, in the end Lenci and Bertinetto's morale is germane to Delfitto and Bertinetto's: the carrier of the relevant properties of generics/habituals is the verbal morphology, and its contribution must be clearly distinguished from that of quantificational adverbs.[42]

Notes

1. See Casati and Varzi (1997) for an annotated bibliography.

2. Montague famously characterized properties as intensional entities, functions from possible worlds to sets of possible individuals. Thus, in effect, on this account an event such as the sun's rising is ultimately identified with a function—namely, a function that yields, for each world i, a set of moments t (those moments at which the sun rises).

3. We focus here on Chisholm's early views (1970, 1971). For an account of Chisholm's (1990) more recent theory, we refer to Brandl's contribution to this volume. See also Brandl (1997) and Zimmerman (1997).

4. For some discussion, see Davidson (1971), Johnson (1975), Lombard (1978b).

5. See especially Davidson (1967b, 1969, 1970). Davidson (1985b) accepted Quine's identity criterion in terms of sameness of spatiotemporal location.

6. The argument is known as the "slingshot" since Barwise and Perry (1981).

7. Even among the event realists, various authors since Vendler (1967a) have objected to Davidson's line, arguing that at least some causal statements concern facts rather than events. See Mellor (1995) for an extended account. Needless to say, the issues has been the focus of an intense debate about the nature of causation that goes far beyond the scope of this volume.

8. The issue of dependence has its roots in Strawson (1959: Ch. 1). See Moravcsik (1968) and Tiles (1981) for critical discussion.

9. We use standard possible world terminology here. One can reformulate both readings in terms of counterparts, if one will. In that case, the *de re* reading would amount to the statement that there is a possible world w in which the counterpart of the given event is survived by Caesar.

10. This way of putting the analysis is not quite neutral with respect to the issue of contingent identity. Davidson (1969: 171) said that the stabbing, though in fact identical with the killing, was not necessarily so. Kripke (1972) would say that the stabbing, if in fact identical with the killing, was necessarily so. We side with Kripke here, as most people today would. If Davidson were right, however, if it were possible for events to be identical as a matter of contingent fact, then the charge of circularity does not quite apply. In that case we could speculate on the modal properties of the killing and the stabbing and we could argue that these properties are distinct without begging the question of whether the killing and the stabbing are in fact identical. (We would only beg the question of whether they are necessarily identical.) The main point then becomes that the nonidentity argument, as formulated, is seriously incomplete, as there are no prima facie reasons to assume the premises to begin with.

11. Besides Anscombe, Bennett, and Davidson, this line of thought has been put forward in Vollrath (1975) and Grimm (1977) and discussed in Thalberg (1975) and White (1979/80). See Pfeifer (1989) for an extensive appraisal.

12. Of course, a Davidsonian is willing to admit that there is a sense in which the gun's going off was caused, not by Sihran's killing of Robert Kennedy, but by his pulling of the trigger. This is the sense in which 'was caused' is understood as 'is causally explained'. However, explanations relate statements, not events (Davidson 1967a: 161).

13. Some of the material reviewed in this section is also reviewed in other parts of the book. We include it here for the sake of completeness.

14. Vendler (1967b: Ch. 5) distinguished between perfect and imperfect nominals. The former include expressions such as *Mary's performance of the song* and *Mary's performing of the song*, in which the process of nominalization is complete and which can tolerate articles and prenominal adjectives (*Mary's beautiful performance*). Imperfect nominals, by contrast, are divided into *that* clauses and gerundives, such as *That Mary performed the song* or *Mary's performing the song*. These are nominals that still have— as Vendler neatly puts it—a verb alive and kicking inside them, so they tolerate tenses, auxiliaries, adverbs, and negation (*That Mary had performed the song; Mary's painfully performing the song; Mary's not performing the song*). The metaphysical hypothesis is that events are the referents of perfect nominals, whereas facts or states of affairs are the referents of imperfect nominals. The death of Socrates (an event) can be redescribed, in some appropriate circumstances, as the calm death of Socrates; but that Socrates died calmly is necessarily a different fact than the fact that Socrates died. For more details, see Nicholas Asher's chapter in this volume, especially section 2.1.

15. Rescher (1967) suggested that it would suffice to have a maximum number of *categories* of adverbial modifications—e.g., Manner, Time, and so on. But the problem reappears as soon as we admit (naturally) that a category can be instantiated more than once in the same sentence.

16. A comprehensive overview may be found in Parsons (1990). On perceptual reports see Higginbotham (1983) and Vlach (1983); on plurals see Schein (1993).

17. Similar accounts have been put forward inter alia by Carlson (1984), Bennett (1988), and Dowty (1989).

18. Davidson would of course agree that (25), if true, would sound awkward. But Davidson would also insist that statements such as this might be understood as causal explanations rather than singular causal statements proper. See note 11.

19. Another possibility is to construe causation as a relation between properties or "aspects" of events. See, for example, Dretske (1977), Sanford (1985), and the exchange in Stern (1993) and Peterson (1994).

20. Davidson himself considered this line of reply in his 1967b article. See also Davidson (1985a).

21. Seminal contributions in this direction have also been made, more or less independently, by Clark (1970, 1974), Parsons (1970), and Rennie (1971) and further developed inter alia by Schwartz (1975), Cresswell (1979), Fulton (1979), and Clark (1986). For a different approach, relaxing the characterisation of action predicates to accommodate variable polyadicity, see Grandy (1976) and Graves (1994).

22. Apparently, *Hold* also applies to states (Parsons 1990) in such a way that $Hold(s, t)$ is true if and only if the subject of s is in state s at t.

23. For a critical discussion of Parsons's aspectual theory, see Lascarides (1988) and Verkuyl (1993 and this volume).

24. On the algebraic approach to event-based semantics, see Bach (1981, 1986), Link (1983, 1987, 1998), and Landman (1991), and Moltmann (1997). On the limits and strengths of the relation *part-of* as a basic structuring device, see Pianesi and Varzi (1994, 1996a, 1996b).

25. See also the discussion above about privileged "end points".

26. One might notice that the set terminal point property, as defined by Krifka, works because it applies vacuously to predicates with quantised reference. Then, one might wonder whether there is any class of predicate to which such a property applies nonvacuously. They would be predicates P such that if e is in P then e has proper subparts that are in the extension of P and that share the same set terminal point as e—that is, predicates that are telics but do not have quantised reference. If no such predicates exist in natural languages, then a theory exploiting the set terminal point notion should provide an explanation for this fact. Also, in case such predicates do not exist, it is reasonable to ask whether the connection between quantisation and telicity should not go the opposite way than that explored by Krifka—namely, that it is quantisation/inhomogeneity that is determined by telicity.

27. On this point, see Higginbotham's discussion of purpose clauses.

28. There are also more traditional treatments, of course. See, for example, Taylor (1977), Mourelatos (1978), and Dowty (1979).

29. At places, Verkuyl seems to admit that event reference (construed as discourse referents in the manner of Discourse Representation Theory) has a role to play in discourse phenomena.

30. This is in a way obvious within a broad Davidsonian perspective, where the emphasis is on matters of logical form (and where logical form is a byproduct of syntax and morphosyntax).

31. For a discussion of some properties of the imperfect tense in Romance languages, see Delfitto and Bertinetto (1995 and this volume), Giorgi and Pianesi (1995, 1997), Ippolito (1997), Hoepelman and Rohrer (1980). See also the chapter by Lenci and Bertinetto in this volume.

32. It can be argued that English lacks not only a morphological means to express the continuous aspect but also such an aspect altogether. (See, e.g., Giorgi and Pianesi 1997 and Bonomi 1998.) The English form that expresses the closest meaning is the progressive construction, which nevertheless needs to be distinguished from true continuous forms because it has an intensional meaning that the former lack.

33. The continuous aspect has been discussed, under the headin of *neutral* aspect, by Smith (1991).

34. Terminativity is not a side effect of tense, as the events of such sentences remain terminated if the tense is changed to the future. It is interesting, though, that the present-tense versions of these sentence do not exist (unless such sentences are interpreted habitually). On the other hand, as pointed out in the text, nonterminative readings are available when an imperfective verbal form is used, regardless of tense. Incidentally, our use of such terms as *finished* or *terminated* is completely intuitive and pretheoretical. It should not be confused with the *terminative/durative* opposition exploited by Verkuyl (1993 and this volume). His classification is built on the basis of the in-time and for-time test and correspond to the distinction between telics and atelics.

35. For an attempt at reversing the perspective, see Giorgi and Pianesi (1997), who argued in favour of taking "continous events" as linguistically primitive, all the others (including the "terminated ones" of ordinary English sentences) being derived by means of aspectual manipulation.

36. The explanation cannot simply be that in both cases you have the same event variable and that the difference is merely a matter of perspective, with continuous sentences allowing the speaker to locate his or her viewpoint within the event and perfective sentences disallowing such a possibility. The real question is why this should be so.

37. See also de Swart (1991), Kamp and Reyle (1993), and Rothstein (1995).

38. The relational analysis of generic and habitual sentences has been developed as a response to the difficulties encountered by a previous theory (Carlson 1977a, 1977b) whereby unary, rather than binary, operators were posited. A good survey of the topic can be found in Krifka et al. (1995) At the same time, it has became increasingly clear that focus/topic considerations play a role in the choice of the material that fills the restriction or the nuclear scope of the quantified clause: see Rooth (1985, 1995), Diesing (1992), Chierchia (1995), and Delfitto and Bertinetto (this volume).

39. In their discussion of the relationships between imperfectivity and habituality, Delfitto and Bertinetto do not try to link habituality and the other interpretive possibility open to (Romance) imperfective forms—namely, the continuous/neutral aspect. Yet it seems that in languages that distinguish perfective and imperfective verbal forms (and lack dedicated habitual morphemes) habituality or genericity goes together with imperfectivity rather than with perfectivity. This is significant since it bears on the nature of verbal aspectuality and its interpretive role. A possible line of explanation, suggested by Delfitto and Bertinetto themselves and by Lenci and Bertinetto, is to hypothesise the presence of a functional category (Asp). Noting that the imperfective is no aspect—for instance, it does not affect the simplex/complex event distinction of section 5.1—one can conclude that imperfective tenses do not contribute an Asp category by themselves (see Giorgi and Pianesi 1997, 1998). Continuous readings would then be associated with such aspectual configurations. Habituals and generics, on the other hand, would arise because of the presence of a null Asp morpheme, which is interpretively spelled out as *Gen*. Finally, the incompatibility of habituals with perfective predicates could be a consequence of the fact that perfective morphology actually contributes its own aspectual projection, thereby preventing the possibility that the same category be realised as *Gen*.

40. In the case of overt adverbs of quantification with perfective predicates, the intensional component, typical of habituals/generics, is absent, thus showing the crucial role of imperfectivity for licensing the "characterising" reading of habituals.

41. Technically, Delfitto and Bertinetto adopt a feature-theoretic solution (Chomsky 1995). The imperfective morphology contributes a noninterpretable feature [+*quant*] to Asp, which must be checked or erased by the interpretable temporal feature of the temporal argument or of the verb phrase when the latter functions as a predicate of times. Checking, in turn, requires movement of the relevant phrase. As a result, a structural configuration is formed in which all the elements necessary for generalised quantification are explicitly given: the determiner *Gen*, because of the imperfective morphology, and the two phrases that contribute the temporal predicates, by virtue of the movement.

42. This is so despite the fact that both Delfitto and Bertinetto and Lenci and Bertinetto give a quantificational analysis of habituality. The idea (not explicitly addressed in either chapter) is that the quantificational format established by the imperfective verbal morphology also encodes the intensionality of habituals, whereas quantificational adverbs are neutral with respect to the intensionality/extensionality dimension.

References

Anscombe, G. E. M., 1979. Under a Description. In *Noûs* 13: 219–233.

Bach, E., 1981. On Time, Tense and Aspect: An Essay in English Metaphysics. In P. Cole (ed.), *Radical Pragmatics*, 63–81. Academic Press, New York.

Bach, E 1986. The Algebra of Events. In *Linguistics and Philosophy* 9: 5–16.

Barwise, K. J., and J. Perry, 1981. Semantic Innocence and Uncompromising Situations. In P. A. French, T. Uehling, and H. K. Wettstein (eds.), *Foundations of Analytic Philosophy* (Midwest Studies in Philosophy, vol. 6), 387–403. University of Minnesota Press, Minneapolis.

Barwise, K. J., and J. Perry, 1983. *Situations and Attitudes.* MIT Press, Cambridge (Mass.).

Bennett, J., 1973. Shooting, Killing, Dying. In *Canadian Journal of Philosophy* 2: 315–323.

Bennett, J., 1988. *Events and Their Names.* Clarendon Press, Oxford.

Bennett, J., 1991. Reply to Reviewers. In *Philosophy and Phenomenological Research* 51: 647–662.

Bennett, J., 1996. What Events Are. In R. Casati and A. C. Varzi (eds.), *Events*, 137–152. Dartmouth, Aldershot.

Bonomi, A., 1998. Semantical Considerations on the Progressive Reading of the Imperfective. Talk delived at the *Conference on the Syntax and Semantics of Tense and Mood Selection*, Bergamo (Italy).

Brand, M., 1977. Identity Conditions for Events. In *American Philosophical Quarterly* 14: 329–377.

Brand, M., 1984. *Intending and Acting. Toward a Naturalized Action Theory.* MIT Press, Cambridge (Mass.).

Brandl, J., 1997. Recurrent Problems. On Chisholm's Two Theories of Events. In L. E. Hahn (ed.), *The Philosophy of R. M. Chisholm*, 457–477. Open Court, La Salle (Ill.),

Carlson, G., 1977a. *Reference to Kinds in English.* Ph.D. dissertation, University of Massachusetts, Amherst.

Carlson, G., 1977b. A Unified Analysis of English Bare Plurals. In *Linguistics and Philosophy* 1: 413–456.

Carlson, G., 1984. On the Role of Thematic Roles in Linguistic Theory. In *Linguistics* 22: 259–279.

Casati, R., and A. C. Varzi, 1997. *Fifty Years of Events. An Annotated Bibliography 1947 to 1997.* Philosophy Documentation Center, Bowling Green (Ohio).

Castañeda, H-N., 1967. Comments on Davidson's "The Logical Form of Action Sentences". In N. Rescher (ed.), *The Logic of Decision and Action*, 104–112. Pittsburgh University Press, Pittsburgh.

Chierchia, G., 1995. Individual Level Predicates as Inherent Generics. In G. N. Carlson and F. J. Pellettier (eds.), *The Generic Book*, 176–223. University of Chicago Press, Chicago.

Chisholm, R. M., 1970. Events and Propositions. In *Noûs* 4: 15–24.

Chisholm, R. M., 1971. States of Affairs Again. In *Noûs* 5: 179–189.

Chisholm, R. M., 1990. Events Without Times. An Essay on Ontology. In *Noûs* 24: 413–428.

Chomsky, N., 1995. *The Minimalist Program.* MIT Press, Cambridge (Mass.).

Clark, R., 1970. Concerning the Logic of Predicate Modifiers. In *Noûs* 4: 311–335.

Clark, R., 1974. Adverbial Modifiers. In R. Severens (ed.), *Ontological Commitment*, 22–36. University of Georgia Press, Athens.

Clark, R., 1986. Predication and Paronymous Modifiers. In *Notre Dame Journal of Formal Logic* 27: 376–392.

Cresswell, M. J., 1979. Interval Semantics for Some Event Expressions. In R. Bäuerle, U. Egli, and A. von Stechow (eds.), *Semantics from Different Points of View*, 90–116. Springer-Verlag, Berlin and Heidelberg.

Davidson, D., 1967a. Causal Relations. In *The Journal of Philosophy* 64: 691–703. Reprinted in Davidson, D., 1980. *Essays on Actions and Events*, 149–162. Clarendon Press, Oxford.

Davidson, D., 1967b. The Logical Form of Action Sentences. In N. Rescher (ed.), *The Logic of Decision and Action*, 81–95. University of Pittsburgh Press, Pittsburgh. Reprinted in Davidson, *Essays on Actions and Events*, 105–123.

Davidson, D., 1967c. Replies. In N. Rescher (ed.), *The Logic of Decision and Action*, 115–120. University of Pittsburgh Press, Pittsburgh. Reprinted with slight revisions in Davidson, *Essays on Actions and Events*, 123–129.

Davidson, D., 1969. The Individuation of Events. In N. Rescher (ed.), *Essays in Honor of Carl G. Hempel*, 216–234. Reidel, Dordrecht. Reprinted in Davidson, *Essays on Actions and Events*, 163–180.

Davidson, D., 1970. Events as Particulars. In *Noûs* 4: 25–32. Reprinted in Davidson, *Essays on Actions and Events*, 181–187.

Davidson, D., 1971. Eternal vs. Ephemeral Events. In *Noûs* 5: 335–349. Reprinted in Davidson, *Essays on Actions and Events*, 189–203.

Davidson D., 1983. *Inquiries into Truth and Interpretation*, Oxford University Press, Oxford.

Davidson, D., 1985a. Adverbs of Action. In B. Vermazen and M. B. Hintikka (eds.), *Essays on Davidson: Actions and Events*, 230–241. Clarendon Press, Oxford.

Davidson, D., 1985b. Reply to Quine on Events. In E. LePore and B. McLaughlin (eds.), *Actions and Events: Perspectives on the Philosophy of Donald Davidson*, 172–176. Blackwell, Oxford.

Delfitto, D., and P. M. Bertinetto, 1995. A Case Study in the Interaction of Aspect and Actionality: The Imperfect in Italian. In P. M. Bertinetto, V. Bianchi, J. Higginbotham, and M. Squartini (eds.), *Temporal Reference, Aspect and Actionality. Volume 1: Semantic and Syntactic Perspectives*, 125–142. Rosenberg & Sellier, Torino.

de Swart, H., 1991. *Adverbs of Quantification: A Generalised Quantifier Approach.* Ph.D. dissertation, Rijksuniversiteit Groningen.

Diesing, M., 1992. *Indefinites*. MIT Press, Cambridge (Mass.).

Dowty, D. R., 1979. *Word Meaning and Montague Grammar. The Semantics of Verbs and Times in Generative Semantics and Montague's PTQ*. Reidel, Dordrecht.

Dowty, D. R., 1989. On the Semantic Content of the Notion of "Thematic Role". In G. Chierchia, B. H. Partee, and R. Turner (eds.), *Properties, Types and Meaning, Volume II: Semantic Issues*, 69–129. Kluwer Academic Publishers, Dordrecht.

Dretske, F., 1977. Referring to Events. In *Midwest Studies in Philosophy* 2: 90–99.

Filip, H., 1992. Aspect and Interpretation of Nominal Arguments. In *Papers from the Twenty-eight Regional Meeting of the Chicago Linguistic Society*, 139–158. Chicago.

Fulton, J. A., 1979. An Intensional Logic of Predicates. In *Notre Dame Journal of Formal Logic* 20: 811–822.

Giorgi, A., and F. Pianesi, 1995. From Semantic to Morphosyntax: The Case of the Imperfect. In P. M. Bertinetto, V. Bianchi, J. Higginbotham, and M. Squartini (eds.), *Temporal Reference, Aspect and Actionality. Volume 1: Semantic and Syntactic Perspectives*, 341–364. Rosenberg & Sellier, Torino.

Giorgi, A., and F. Pianesi, 1997. *Tense and Aspect: From Semantics to Morphosyntax.* Oxford University Press, New York.

Giorgi, A., and F. Pianesi, 1998. Present Tense, Perfectivity and the Anchoring Conditions. In A. Z. Wyner (ed.), *Proceedings of the Thirteenth Annual Conference of the Israel Association for Theoretical Linguistics (IATL-5)*, 75–95. Akademon, Jerusalem.

Goldman, A., 1970. *A Theory of Human Action.* Prentice-Hall, Upper Saddle River (N. J.).

Goldman, A., 1971. The Individuation of Actions. In *The Journal of Philosophy* 68: 761–774.

Grandy, R., 1976. Anadic Logic and English. In *Synthese* 32: 395–402.

Graves, P. R., 1994. Argument Deletion Without Events. In *Notre Dame Journal of Formal Logic* 34: 607–620.

Grimm, R., 1977. Eventual Change and Action Identity. In *American Philosophical Quarterly* 14: 221–229.

Heim, I., 1982. *The Semantcs of Definite and Indefinite Noun Phrases.* Ph.D. dissertation, University of Massachusetts, Amherst.

Higginbotham, J., 1983. The Logic of Perceptual Reports: An Extensional Alternative to Situation Semantics. In *The Journal of Philosophy* 80: 100–127.

Higginbotham, J., 1985. On Semantics. In *Linguistic Inquiry* 16: 547–593.

Hoepelman, J. P., and C. Rohrer, 1980. On the Mass-Count Distinction and the French Imparfait and Passé Simple. In C. Rohrer (ed.), *Tense, Time and Quantifiers. Proceedings of the Stutttgart Conference on the Logic of Tense and Quantification,* 85–112. Niemeyer, Tübingen.

Horgan, T., 1978. The Case Against Events. In *The Philosophical Review* 87: 28–47.

Horgan, T., 1982. Substitutivity and the Causal Connective. In *Philosophical Studies* 42: 427–452.

Ippolito, M., 1997. M.A. dissertation, Oxford University, Oxford.

Johnson, M. L., 1975. Events as Recurrables. In K. Lehrer (ed.), *Analysis and Metaphysics,* 209–226. Reidel, Dordrecht.

Kamp, H., and U. Reyle, 1993. *From Discourse to Logic.* Kluwer Academic Press, Dordrecht.

Kenny, A., 1963. *Action, Emotion and Will.* Routledge & Kegan Paul, London.

Kim, J., 1973. Causation, Nomic Subsumption, and the Concept of an Event. In *The Journal of Philosophy* 70: 217–236.

Kim, J., 1976. Events as Property Exemplifications. In M. Brand and D. Walton (eds.), *Action Theory,* 159–177. Reidel, Dordrecht.

Kim, J., 1991. Events: Their Metaphysics and Semantics. In *Philosophy and Phenomenological Research* 51: 641–646.

Krifka, M., 1989. Nominal Reference, Temporal Constitution and Quantification in Event Semantics. In J. van Benthem, R. Bartsch, and P. van Embde Boas (eds.), *Semantics and Contextual Epressions,* 75–115. Foris, Dordrecht.

Krifka, M., 1992. Thematic Relations as Links Between Nominal Reference and Temporal Constitution. In I. Sag and A. Szabolcsi (eds.), *Lexical Matters,* 29–54. CSLI Publications, Stanford (Calif.).

Krifka, M., 1998. The Origins of Telicity. In S. Rothstein (ed.), *Events and Grammar,* 197–235. Kluwer Academic Publishers, Dordrecht.

Krifka, M., F. J. Pellettier, G. N. Carlson, A. ter Meulen, G. Chierchia, and G. Link, 1995. Genericity: An Introduction. In G. N. Carlson and F. J. Pellettier (eds.), *The Generic Book,* 1–124. University of Chicago Press, Chicago.

Kripke, S., 1972. Naming and Necessity. In D. Davidson and G. Harman (eds.), *Semantics of Natural Language,* 253–355, addenda 763–769. Reidel, Dordrecht and Boston. Reprinted as Kripke, S., 1980. *Naming and Necessity.* Harvard University Press, Cambridge (Mass.).

Landman, F., 1991. *Structures for Semantics.* Kluwer Academic Publishers, Dordrecht.

Larson, R., 1988. On Double Object Constructions. In *Linguistic Inquiry* 16: 595–621.

Lascarides, A., 1988. *A Formal Semantics of the Progressive*. Ph.D. dissertation, University of Edinburgh, Edinburgh.

Lewis, D. K., 1973. Causation. In *The Journal of Philosophy* 70: 556–567.

Lewis, D. K. 1975. Adverbs of Quantification. In E. Keenan (ed.), *Formal Semantics of Natural Languages*, 3–15. Cambridge University Press, Cambridge.

Lewis, D. K., 1986. Events. In *Philosophical Papers*, vol. 2, 241–269. Oxford University Press, New York.

Link, G., 1983. The Logical Analysis of Plurals and Mass Terms: A Lattice-theoretic Approach. In R. Bäuerle, C. Schwarze, and A. von Stechow (eds.), *Meaning, Use and Interpretation of Language*, 303–323. De Gruyter, Berlin.

Link, G., 1987. Algebraic Semantics for Event Structures. In J. Groenendijk, M. Stokhof, and F. Veltman (eds.), *Proceedings of the Sixth Amsterdam Colloquium*, 243–262. Institute for Language, Logic and Computation, Amsterdam.

Link, G., 1998. *Algebraic Semantics in Language and Philosophy*. CSLI Publications, Stanford (Calif.).

Lombard, L. B., 1978a. Actions, Results, and the Time of a Killing. In *Philosophia* 8: 341–354.

Lombard, L. B., 1978b. Chisholm and Davidson on Events and Counterfactuals. In *Philosophia* 7: 515–522.

Lombard, L. B., 1979. Events. In *Canadian Journal of Philosophy* 9: 425–460.

Lombard, L. B., 1986. *Events. A Metaphysical Study*. Routledge & Kegan Paul, London.

Lombard, L. B., 1998. Ontologies of Events. In S. Laurence and C. Macdonald (eds.), *Contemporary Readings in the Foundations of Metaphysics*, 277–294. Blackwell, Oxford.

Martin, R., 1969. On Events and Event-descriptions. In J. Margolis (ed.), *Fact and Existence*, 63–73, 97–109. Basil Blackwell, Oxford.

Mellor, D. H., 1995. *The Facts of Causation*. Routledge, London and New York.

Mittwoch, A., 1980. The Grammar of Duration. In *Studies in Language* 4: 201–227.

Moltmann, F., 1997. *Parts and Wholes in Semantics*. Oxford University Press, Oxford.

Montague, R., 1969. On the Nature of Certain Philosophical Entities. In *The Monist* 53: 159–194. Reprinted in Montague, R., 1974. *Formal Philosophy*, R. H. Thomason (ed.), 149–187. Yale University Press, New Haven (Conn.).

Montague, R., 1970. English as a Formal Language. In B. Visentini et al. (eds.), *Linguaggi nella società e nella tecnica*, 189–224. Edizioni di Comunità, Milano. Reprinted in Montague, *Formal Philosophy*, 188–221.

Montmarquet, J. A., 1980. Whither States? In *Canadian Journal of Philosophy* 10: 251–256.

Moravcsik, J. M. E., 1968. Strawson and Ontological Priority. In R. J. Butler (ed.), *Analytical Philosophy*, Second Series, 106–119. Barnes & Noble, New York.

Mourelatos, A. P. D., 1978. Events, Processes, and States. In *Linguistics and Philosophy* 2: 415–434.

Neale, S., 1990. *Descriptions*. MIT Press, Cambridge (Mass.).

Parsons, T., 1970. Some Problems Concerning the Logic of Grammatical Modifiers. In *Synthese* 21: 320–233.

Parsons, T., 1980. Modifiers and Quantifiers in Natural Language. In *Canadian Journal of Philosophy*, suppl. vol. 6: 29–60.

Parsons, T., 1985. Underlying Events in the Logical Analysis of English. In E. LePore and B. McLaughlin (eds.), *Actions and Events: Perspectives on the Philosophy of Donald Davidson*, 235–267. Blackwell, Oxford.

Parsons, T., 1987/88. Underlying States in the Semantical Analysis of English. In *Proceedings of the Aristotelian Society* 88: 13–30.

Parsons, T., 1990. *Events in the Semantics of English. A Study in Subatomic Semantics.* MIT Press, Cambridge (Mass.).

Peterson, P. L., 1989. Complex Events. In *Pacific Philosophical Quarterly* 70: 19–41.

Peterson, P. L., 1994. Facts, Events, and Semantic Emphasis in Causal Statements. In *The Monist* 77: 217–238.

Peterson, P. L., 1997. *Fact Proposition Event.* Kluwer Academic Publishers, Dordrecht.

Pfeifer, K., 1989. *Actions and Other Events: The Unifier-Multiplier Controversy.* Peter Lang, New York and Bern.

Pianesi, F., and A. C. Varzi, 1994. The Mereotopology of Event Structures. In P. Dekker and M. Stokhof (eds.) *Proceedings of the Ninth Amsterdam Colloquium,* 527–546. Institute for Language, Logic and Computation, Amsterdam.

Pianesi, F., and A. C. Varzi, 1996a. Events, Topology, and Temporal Relations. In *The Monist* 78: 89–116.

Pianesi, F., and A. C. Varzi, 1996b. Refining Temporal Reference in Event Structures. In *Notre Dame Journal of Formal Logic* 37: 71–83.

Prior, A. N., 1949. Determinables, Determinates and Determinants. In *Mind* 58: 1-20.

Quine, W. V. O., 1960. *Word and Object.* MIT Press, Cambridge (Mass.).

Ramchand, G. C., 1997. *Aspect and Predication.* Oxford University Press, Oxford.

Ramsey, F. P., 1927. Facts and Propositions. In *Proceedings of the Aristotelian Society,* suppl. vol. 7: 153–170. Reprinted in Ramsey, F. P., 1990. *Philosophical Papers,* D. H. Mellor (ed.), 34–51. Cambridge University Press, Cambridge.

Reichenbach, H., 1947. *Elements of Symbolic Logic.* Macmillan, New York.

Rennie, M. K., 1971. Completeness in the Logic of Predicate Modifiers. In *Logique et Analyse* 55: 627–643.

Rescher, N., 1967. Aspects of Action. In N. Rescher (ed.), *The Logic of Decision and Action,* 215–220. Pittsburgh University Press, Pittsburgh.

Rooth, M., 1985. *Association with Focus.* Ph.D. dissertation, University of Massachusetts, Amherst.

Rooth, M., 1995. Indefinites, Adverbs of Quantification, and Focus Semantics. In G. N. Carlson and F. J. Pelletier (eds.), *The Generic Book,* 265–299. Chicago University Press, Chicago.

Rothstein, S., 1995. Adverbial Quantification over Events. In *Natural Language Semantics* 3: 1–31.

Ryle, G., 1949. *The Concept of Mind.* Hutchinson, London.

Sanford, D. H., 1985. Causal Relata. In E. LePore and B. McLaughlin (eds.), *Actions and Events: Perspectives on the Philosophy of Donald Davidson,* 282–293. Blackwell, Oxford.

Schein, B., 1993. *Plurals and Events.* MIT Press, Cambridge (Mass.).

Schwartz, T., 1975. The Logic of Modifiers. In *Journal of Philosophical Logic* 4: 361–380.

Singh, M., 1998. On the Semantics of the Perfective Aspect. In *Natural Language Semantics* 6: 171–199.

Smith, C., 1991. *The Parameter of Aspect.* Kluwer Acamedic Publishers, Dordrecht.

Stern, C. D., 1993. Semantic Emphasis in Causal Sentences. In *Synthese* 95: 379–418.

Strawson, P. F., 1959. *Individuals: An Essay in Descriptive Metaphysics.* Methuen, London.

Swain, M., 1978. A Counterfactual Analysis of Event Causation. In *Philosophical Studies* 34: 1–19.

Taylor, B., 1977. Tense and Continuity. In *Linguistics and Philosophy* 1: 199–220.

Taylor, B., 1985, *Modes of Occurrence: Verbs, Adverbs and Events*, Blackwell, Oxford.

Thalberg, I., 1975. When Do Causes Take Effect? In *Mind* 84: 583–589.

Thomason, R. H., and R. C. Stalnaker, 1973. A Semantic Theory of Adverbs. In *Linguistic Inquiry* 4: 195–220.

Thomson, J. J., 1971. The Time of a Killing. In *The Journal of Philosophy* 68: 115–132.

Tiles, J. E., 1981. *Things That Happen*. Aberdeen University Press, Aberdeen.

Vendler, Z., 1967a. Causal Relations. In *The Journal of Philosophy* 64: 704–713.

Vendler, Z., 1967b. *Linguistics in Philosophy*. Cornell University Press, Ithaca (N.Y.).

Verkuyl, H. J., 1972. *On the Compositional Nature of the Aspect*. Reidel, Dordrecht.

Verkuyl, H. J., 1989. Aspectual Classes and Aspectual Composition. In *Linguistics and Philosophy* 12: 39–94.

Verkuyl, H. J., 1993. *A Theory of Aspectuality. The Interaction Between Temporal and Atemporal Structure*. Cambridge University Press, Cambridge.

Vlach, F., 1983. On Situation Semantics for Perception. In *Synthese* 54: 129–152.

Vollrath, J. F., 1975. When Actions Are Causes. In *Philosophical Studies* 27: 329–339.

White, A. R., 1979/80. Shooting, Killing and Fatally Wounding. In *Proceedings of the Aristotelian Society* 80: 1–15.

Zemach, E. M., 1978. Events. In Y. Yovel (ed.), *Philosophy of History and Action*, 89–95. Reidel, Dordrecht.

Zimmerman, D., 1997. Chisholm and the Essences of Events. In L. E. Hahn (ed.), *The Philosophy of R. M. Chisholm* (Library of Living Philosophers), 73–100. Open Court, La Salle (Ill.).

2

On Events in Linguistic Semantics

James Higginbotham

1. General Considerations

There is no doubt that reference to events and states is a pervasive feature of human thought and language. How is such reference made available through the syntactic and lexical resources of human speech, and what is the nature of the objects referred to? In this chapter I defend and elaborate one view on these questions, derived ultimately from Davidson (1967) but subsequently developed and extended by a number of researchers. The elaboration leads to a number of interconnected points that I believe deserve further study.

The inquiry pursued here lies within *linguistic* semantics, so that the first interest of the subject is taken to be psychological, not metaphysical (although metaphysical questions inevitably arise). As I understand it, the aim of linguistic semantics is to determine what native speakers of human languages know about the relations of form to meaning, in virtue of which they are able to speak to others and understand them, and to explain how they came to know these things. If we turn from the question of the semantic competence of the native speaker to the problem of acquisition, then our conceptions of the formal information provided by syntax and the nature of semantic values and projection rules must satisfy a requirement of *learnability*: it must be possible for a first-language learner, on the basis of ordinary linguistic experience, to grasp these conceptions. In semantics, as in syntax, the learnability requirement can be satisfied only if the theory is sufficiently restrictive—that is, if it does not offer a wide space of alternatives, given the data. I argue below that a signal use of event and state reference in semantic theory is precisely to provide a restrictive semantic framework. I begin with some history and a sketch of alternatives.

1.1. Davidson and Montague on Events

In the setting outlined above, the proposal of Davidson (1967)—that there is reference to events in human language through the medium of an unapparent argument position in verbal heads—may be introduced as part of a theory of semantic competence. I take up Davidson's proposal here, following terminology I have used elsewhere (Higginbotham 1985), as the hypothesis that there is a special argument position, the *E-position*, associated with every predicative head in the $\overline{\text{X}}$ system and thus with all of V, N, A, and P.

According to the E-position hypothesis, a head H has, besides the positions $1, 2, \ldots, n$ for arguments that it will θ-mark, also a position E for events (in a wide sense, thus including states; I use the term *situation* when there is need for an expression that explicitly covers both), and therefore a θ-grid with at least the structure $\langle 1, 2, \ldots, n, E \rangle$. H is then an $n + 1$–place predicate whose interpretation is known by the native speaker to be satisfied by an appropriate sequence of objects just in case some condition Φ holds of them. For expository purposes we may represent this state of knowledge by interpreting H as

$$\lambda x_1 \lambda x_2 \ldots \lambda x_n \lambda e. \ (\Phi(x_1, x_2, \ldots, x_n, e)).$$

On the E-position hypothesis as I have stated it there need be no assumption that the things that may appropriately be assigned to it are objects of a metaphysically special sort (except insofar as they are events); on the contrary, one may follow Davidson in taking events to be objects.

Alternatives are possible. For one of the most interesting, I refer back to Richard Montague's article 'On the Nature of Certain Philosophical Entities' (the version of 1967, in Montague 1974). For Montague, events count as *philosophical* entities, at least in the sense that they are routine in language and routinely suspect in metaphysics. Montague proposed that events (together with some other types of things, which will not concern us here) be thought of as properties of moments of time, in the sense of *property* that he himself made familiar through possible-worlds semantics—that is, the intension of a predicate.

If events are properties in Montague's sense, then they are a type of universal: Montague called them *generic* events. On Montague's view there is, for instance, a generic event of the sun's rising, which is, for each possible world i, the set of moments t in i such that the sun rises at t. The predicate *rises* is understood as $rises(x, t)$, expressing a relation between individuals and times. The generic event of x's rising is

$\hat{t} \ rises(x, t)$

derived by intensional abstraction over times and possible worlds. Montague held that English definite gerunds like *the rising of the sun* typically refer to generic events.

But besides generic events, Montague recognised that there are also *particular* events, for example, the particular event of the sun's rising that occurred in Manhattan on August 13, 1967. A particular event is again a property of moments of time, but as it were, a very restricted property, typically quantified over or referred to by an indefinite gerund or mixed nominal. The nominal *rising* as it occurs in (1), for example

(1)   (They witnessed) a rising of the sun

is understood as *rising(P, x)*, for *P* the kind of property of moments of time that answers to the individual risings of *x*. Various axioms are proposed to link the two predicates *rise* and *rising*.

Montague's view of events and event reference in semantics is thus fundamentally different from the view encapsulated in the hypothesis of the E-position. The difference between these views affects all of the conceptions that form the substance of a semantic theory. On the hypothesis of the E-position, the arguments of a head must reserve a place for events; Montague's theory does not recognise such a place. Semantic values for nominals must for Montague include higher types, and the combinatorial semantic principles, projecting meaning from parts to wholes, will (even for the simple sentences discussed above) include the application of functions whose arguments are of a higher type. But higher types do not appear in connection with the E-position, and as Davidson noted in part, and as I explain more fully below, with the E-position hypothesis a certain simplification and principled restriction of semantic combination becomes possible—at the cost, of course, of positing the E-position itself.

In a footnote, Montague remarked that he believed his view to be consistent with Davidson's work on action sentences and causal relations, but he added that Davidson did not inquire into the "ontological status" of individual events (Montague 1974: 178, n.18). The remark is somewhat obscure since Davidson did in fact have a view about the ontology of events—namely, that they are individual objects, rather than universals of any sort. However, the question certainly arises of how the contexts that Montague treated should be analysed in a semantics that assumes the E-position but not the higher-order apparatus of Montague's article.[1] To this end, we would need to see how, once the E-position is admitted in ordinary predicates, both generic and particular events are accommodated, and we require a theory of the semantic relation between a root V or VP and its nominalisations, as in (1).

The semantics of nominalisation is straightforward. On the E-position hypothesis, the nominalisations that refer to or quantify over events are those that pick out the E-position as the position to be bound by the determiner. Thus *a rising of the sun* is just an indefinite description:

(2)   an *e* such that rise(the sun, *e*).

This same semantics goes for derived nominals in their event interpretation, as in (3):

(3)   a. examination (of the students)
       b. murder (of the policeman)

and the like.[2] I call it *E(vent) Nominalisation*, on a par with the agentive nominalisation expressed in English by *-er*, as in *examiner, murderer*, and *riser*, and the nominalisations that select the internal argument of the verbal root, as in *examinee, employee, belief, gift*, and so on. Thus the position that Montague recognised for individual events in gerunds and nominals derives immediately from the corresponding position in the head.

Events and states must be associated with time, and in particular must have temporal locations. In a system with the E-position, temporal adjuncts take for their subjects the position in the verb. Thus sentences like (4) express a predicational structure as in (5):

(4)   The sun rose at eight
(5)   rise(the sun, e) $\wedge$ at(eight, e)

and temporal adjuncts may relate events to other events, as in (6), whose structure is as in (7):

(6)   The sun rose before I woke.
(7)   rise(the sun, e) $\wedge$ before(e, e') $\wedge$ wake(I, e').

What now of the generic events? Well, just as we have sorts of *things* whenever we have a predicate that ranges over objects other than events, so we will have sorts of *events*—really, sorts of things, each member of which is an event—whenever we have a predicate that ranges over events. Suppose, following Montague and using the account of kind reference developed first in Carlson (1980), that a generic object or kind can be identified with the property of being an object of that kind, so that, for example, the kind *dinosaur* is

$\hat{x}$ dinosaur(x).

Then we will identify the generic event that is the rising of the sun with

$\hat{e}$ rise(the sun, e),

that is, with the property of being a sunrise. Here, then, we have properties since we are taking kinds to be properties; but they come in, not as part of the fundamental apparatus, but alongside the properties that answer to kinds of objects of all sorts.

It remains to verify that the construction of generic events just suggested will be adequate to the purposes for which Montague invoked them. In this place I consider two analogic points of comparison.

Following the original discussion in Carlson (1980), reference to kinds coming from nominals for individuals is seen in examples like (8) and (9):

(8)   Rabbits are plentiful/widespread.
(9)   The dinosaur is extinct.

The predicates *plentiful*, *widespread*, and *extinct* are truly applied only to kinds. Thus for (9) we have an interpretation as in (10):

(10)   extinct($\hat{x}$ dinosaur(x)).

There are examples for events and states, using derived nominal subjects, that are parallel to generics like (8) and (9):

(11)   Happiness is widespread.
(12)   Murder is far too commonplace.

The subject of (11), for instance, refers to a kind of state, not the state of any particular individual. The interpretation of (11) should therefore be as in (13):

(13)   widespread($\hat{e}$ happy(e)).

Besides kind predications, there are generic sentences involving events that are on a par with generics involving ordinary objects; thus compare (14) with (15):

(14)   Dogs bark.
(15)   Barking frightens me.

In Carlson's original discussion, (14) would have involved reference to the kind *dogs*, and (15) presumably to the kind *barking*, a generic event in Montague's sense. However, adopting the "relational" theory of generics sketched in Carlson (1989), we may see (14) as a conditional (perhaps with a *generic* quantifier; but see below), as in (16):

(16)   If x is a dog, x barks.

The quantification in (16) is over individual dogs, not kinds. Applying the same account to (15) we would have (17):

(17)   If e is a barking, e frightens me

(with the usual, ill-understood provisions for exceptions). The quantification now is over individual events of barking, not the kind. Generic events are therefore not required for these cases; moreover, the fact that *barking* is a predicate of events stems directly from the E-position in the root *bark*.

The philosophical literature on events, especially that defending generic events, or events as universals, has made use of the fact that we often speak of the same event occurring again, or recurring. If events are taken as individuals, following Davidson, then this talk either cannot be taken literally or, if so taken, points to a defect in the system. Suppose I have a toothache during the day, Saturday, which fades Saturday night but returns to me on Sunday morning. I can express my condition by saying, *The toothache is back again*, and in fact did express it by supposing that *it* returned on Sunday. But the Saturday toothache and the Sunday toothache are individual events, each confined to its own temporal location; and the larger event, the toothache of which the Saturday episode is one part and the Sunday episode another, is also a single event, incapable of recurrence. How, then, can I speak of the same toothache at two different times? The obvious answer is that the notion of sameness employed in these locutions is qualitative, not numerical, identity, as when we speak of *A owning the same car as B*, when all we mean is that they own cars of the same kind. Similarly, when I say that my toothache is "back again", I mean only that I have another toothache of the same kind as the toothache that I had the day before, perhaps implicating as well that the new toothache shares the etiology of the old. There is certainly more to be said about questions of qualitative identity. But it is sufficient for present purposes to note that arguments for generic events on the grounds that events can recur are fully analogous to arguments for generic objects on the grounds that we speak of different individuals as being *the same*.

In sum, Montague's approach is to commence with events as universals, specifically properties of moments of time, and then to construct individual events whose link with the generics could be guaranteed only by special axioms; however, the approach that suggests itself once Davidson's E-position is adopted is to commence with events as individuals, obtaining generic events as kinds by whatever procedures give names of kinds of objects from predicates of objects of other sorts.

1.2. Generalising the E-position

Davidson (1967) proposed the E-position only for action predicates. The extension to statives suggests itself for sentences such as (18):

(18)   John's happiness lasted ten years.

Sentence (18) is obviously virtually interchangeable with (19):

(19)   John was happy for ten years

and the semantic problem is to explain not only why it is interchangeable but also why this property is obvious. It is, in fact, an advantage of Montague's approach over Davidson's original idea that it can associate events (again, in a wide sense) with any predicate having a temporal parameter. A response to Montague therefore requires an E-position, not only in action predicates, but also in predicates of all sorts. But pairs such as (18) and (19) provide direct evidence for this position. I consider one by one the steps leading to the full analysis.

In Davidson's original formulation, and in most subsequent work, simple sentences (bearing a tense but lacking modals or aspectuals) are existentially general with respect to events—that is, a sentence such as *Caesar died* is true just in case there is some (past) death of Caesar or another, the information that Caesar died but one death being no part of the logical form. In more contemporary terms, and assuming that there is a close connection between INFL and existential quantification over the E-position, the proposal is that in a structure

$$[\ \overline{\text{INFL}}\ +\text{past VP}]$$

the interpretation of $\overline{\text{INFL}}$ is obtained by existential closure as in

$$[\exists e\colon e < e']\ \Phi(e),$$

where e' is anchored to the utterance time or some other time in a narrative, and Φ represents the interpretation of VP.[3]

Applying the account first to the simple sentence *John was happy*, we assume an LF structure:

$$[\ \overline{\text{INFL}}\ +\text{past AP}].[4]$$

The AP *John happy* expresses the condition

happy(John, e)

with free variable e. The sentence then expresses

[∃e: $e < e'$] happy(John, e).

For (19) itself, we take up the adjunct *for ten years* as a predicate of e, measuring its temporal duration. The interpretation of the LF structure for (19) is then as in (20):

(20) [∃e: $e < e'$] [happy(John, e) ∧ for ten years(e)].

For (18), we have, first, to consider the predication (21):

(21) ___ lasted (for) ten years.

This predicate expresses a temporal measure of states and activities (*the war, the drought*) but also of other objects, where it is often understood that their "lasting" is with reference to a normal or working state, as is seen in (22) and (23), for example:

(22) The Chrysler lasted for ten years (before it broke down).
(23) The apple only lasted a week (before it became rotten).

Of course, the predicate may simply measure the lifetime of an object, as in

(24) The aftershave lasted a month (then it was all used up).

In (18), the predicate is applied to the E-nominalisation of the adjective *happy*; the subject is definite and expresses (25):

(25) (the e) happy(John, e).

Taking account of the past tense, we have finally (26):

(26) For $e_1 =$ (the e) happy(John, e), $e_1 < u$ ∧ last ten years(e_1)

where u is the utterance. The predicates of situations *last (for) ten years* and *(for) ten years* have the same meaning: the word *last* is vacuous with respect to states and activities, as *happen* is vacuous with respect to events.[5] But (26) trivially implies (20); and if we assume that there is a unique state e (in the past) such that happy(John, e), then (20) implies (26). The close semantic relationship between (18) and (19) therefore follows from the theory.

We have seen that there is compelling evidence for the E-position in AP, derived from the properties of nominalisations. Evidence for the E-position in NP is similarly obtained, on the basis of examples like (27), using the derived nominal *presidency*:

(27) George Bush's presidency lasted four years.

English PP resist derived nominalisation (**the being in London of John*), but arguments from anaphora show that there must be states derivable from ordinary PP predicates. Consider (28):

(28)   John was in the kitchen, but it didn't last long.

The pronominal evidently refers to the state of John's being in the kitchen—that is, to

(the e) in the kitchen(John, e).

Finally, besides the nominalisations *happiness, presidency, examination*, and so on, licensed by derivational morphology, consider the fully productive construction, which indeed has already been used in explaining the import of these nominalisations, exemplified by DPs such as (29)and (30):

(29)   the state of being happy/in the kitchen/a philosopher.
(30)   the event of the sun's rising/my going to London.

The examples in (30) are evidently definite descriptions, purporting to refer to particular events. The expressions in (29) become somewhat awkward with lexical subjects rather than PRO:

(31)   ??the state of John's being happy/my being in the kitchen/Mary's being a philosopher
(32)   ?John's state of being happy

but this syntactic feature should not obscure the fact that they, too, can be understood as definite descriptions, purporting to refer to particular states if the subject is realised circumlocutorily, as in, for example, (33):

(33)   the state of being happy that John is in.

We thus conclude that the syntax of the construction in (34) must always be capable of yielding an event description and that in (35) of yielding a state description:

(34)   [D event [of PRO/DP's [$_{\overline{V}}$ -ing]]].
(35)   [D state [of PRO$_i$ [being AP/PP/NP (that DP$_i$ is in)]]].[6]

If we assume the E-position, these nominals, where the type of state or event in question is given through the gerund, receive an analysis in the terms shown in (36) for the second example in (30):

(36)   (the e) (event(e) $\wedge$ go to London(I, e)).

But statives too, as well as *I-level* predicates in the sense of Kratzer (1995), will be so analysed, so that (33) will have the semantics shown in (37):

(37)   (the e) (state(e) $\wedge$ happy(John, e)).[7]

I conclude that if we agree with Montague that there are events, states, or situations corresponding to all ordinary predicates, or at least all of those involving time, then having adopted the E-position hypothesis for action predicates, there is no choice but to adopt it for all. But the evidence leads in that direction independently anyway.

2. The Visibility of E

We now take up the E-position hypothesis together with the attendant theory of event nominalisations, including gerunds and derived nominals, and generic events as described. In simple sentences the E-position is very nearly invisible, being realised only through existential closure. In nominalisation and in the construction of generic events, on the other hand, it performs actual semantic work, or, is as I shall say, *visible*.

A good bit of the evidence in favour of the E-position hypothesis comes from tracking the environments where it can be supposed to be visible, as, for example, in mediating the causative-inchoative alternation, following Parsons (1990). There are many other applications. As Davidson remarked at length, recognition of a position for events also permits a simplification of the combinatorics of adverbial modification; and as a number of people have observed, the quantificational adverbs can bind positions for events, as well as other indefinites. Thus the hypothesis of the E-position serves to capture the roles of adverbial modifications by manner adverbs, as in (38), or adverbs of quantification, as in (39):

(38)   John walked slowly.
(39)   John usually walks to work.

In (38) the adverb *slowly*, whose interpretation is just the same as that of the adjective *slow*, when predicated of events, is semantically conjoined with *walk*, so that the interpretation of the predicate in (38) (ignoring tense) is as in (40):

(40) $\text{walk}(e) \wedge \text{Actor}(\text{John}, e) \wedge \text{slow}(e)$.

In (39) there is quantification over events as contextually determined (e.g., John's travels to work), the assertion (39) being to the effect that usually they are walks. We have

(41)   [Usually e: $C(e)$] walk to work(John, e)

where C is the contextually supplied background condition. Besides these well-known applications, I will consider some others, involving adverbials. These will constitute further evidence for the E-position.

2.1. Adverbial Interpretation

Consider the ambiguity of (42):

(42)   Mary quickly objected.

On the interpretation in which *quickly* is taken as a manner adverb, (42) has it that Mary's objection was quickly delivered. On the other interpretation, which I call *thematic*, the objection could have been delivered at any speed but came quickly after the proposal to which it was an objection. This second interpretation is evidently paraphraseable by (43):

(43)   Mary was quick [PRO to object].

Any explanation of the ambiguity of (42) must explain the adequacy of the paraphrase (43) as well. I will show that with the E-position it is straightforward to distinguish these interpretations.

We take the V *objected* to be as in (44):

(44) $\lambda x \lambda e.$ objected(x, e)

where the θ-position marked by x will be assigned to the surface subject. The manner interpretation is derived by taking *quickly*, like *slowly* above, as a predicate of events and derives for the modified V the interpretation shown in (45):

(45) $\lambda x \lambda e.$ objected$(x, e) \wedge$ quick(e).

For the thematic interpretation, we take a cue from the paraphrase (43). In that example, *quick* is a transitive adjective whose complement is an argument. The example tells us that the θ-grid of the transitive *quick* has two argument positions. The nonfinite complement is an indefinite description of an event, so that the interpretation is as in (46):

(46) $\exists e \exists e'$(quick(Mary, e', e) $\wedge$ object(Mary, e')).

But now the very same semantic combination that we see in (43) may be applied to (42) itself, as follows.

We assume that the syntactic structure for (42) shows a VP-internal subject trace, as in (47):

(47)   [Mary [quickly [t objected]]].

The adverb *quickly* takes the VP as complement, within which the trace t is a free variable, whose value will be assigned as the value of its antecedent when that is encountered. We compute the interpretation of the predicate as shown in (48):

(48)   *quickly*: $\lambda x \lambda e \lambda e'.$ quick(x, e', e)
          t objected: $\lambda e''.$ object(y, e'')
          quickly [t objected]: $\lambda x \lambda e \lambda e'.$ (quick$(x, e', e) \wedge$ object(x, e'))

The combination represents a kind of unification of θ-positions (E-positions in this case) or θ-identification in the sense of Higginbotham (1985). Notice that on this account the subject *Mary* is the subject both of *quick* and of *object*. Hence the subject trace behaves semantically as if it were PRO occupying a position of control, a point to which I return in the discussion of subject-oriented adverbs.

Further support for the above interpretation of the ambiguity of adverbial modification comes from examples such as (49), which like (42) has no clausal complement, and from nominals like (50):

(49)   Mary was quick with her objection.
(50)   Mary's quick objection (was appreciated by everyone).

Both examples are ambiguous, in just the way (42) is. Thus the adjective is the fundamental ambiguous form, with the adverb retaining the same semantics.

Davidson (1967) considered adverbs that, in the present terminology, are thematic only, such as *intentionally*. As he ultimately agreed in response to a comment from H.-N. Castañeda, the adjectival form *intentional* not only takes two arguments, one for the subject and one for the action of which the subject is the agent, but also shows the semantic equivalent of control of the agent by the subject. Thus the context in (51) is referentially opaque with respect to the position of *Jocasta* but transparent with respect to *Oedipus*:

(51)   Oedipus's marrying Jocasta was intentional (of him).

The same is true, of course, for (52):

(52)   Oedipus intentionally married Jocasta.

If we pursue the path suggested by these applications of the E-position hypothesis, then two lines of thought present themselves.

The first is that the semantics of human languages contains, insofar as these constructions are concerned anyway, no modifications of higher types. In giving the semantics of any construction, the question arises of what is the nature of the projection rule that binds the pieces together: the semantic glue, so to speak. In the case of heads and their arguments, it is simply the filling of an argument slot. For overt nominal quantification it is what may be called θ-binding by D of the open position in the head by the determiner: thus *every* binds the open position in *dog* in the DP *every dog*. Simple modifications, including relative clauses, can be understood as conjunctions, and hence as glued together by truth functions. But there are modifications that the simple picture does not seem to fit, and for these, higher types have often been invoked. Thus one could regard *leave slowly* as denoting the value of the result of applying the denotation of *slowly* to the denotation of *leave*, so that the denotation of the adverb is a function whose argument is itself a function. The adverb then has a denotation of higher type than that of predicates. As just noted, however, no such view of the adverb need be taken if we have the E-position, for then *slowly* falls into place with other modifiers as forming, with its head, a conjunctive predicate (40). Similarly, we do not understand *leave intentionally* as representing the action of the adverb on a verbal denotation; rather, we understand *intentional* as a relation between an actor and an event (and having its own E-position), so that *leave intentionally* is interpreted as shown in (53):

(53)   *intentionally*: $\lambda p \lambda x \lambda e.\,\text{intentional}(x, p, e)$
       t leave: $\lambda e'.\,\text{leave}(y, e')$
       t leave intentionally: $\lambda x \lambda e.\,(\text{intentional}(x, {}^\wedge\text{leave}(x, e)) \wedge \text{leave}(x, e)).$

The θ-grid assigned to *intentional* in this analysis is supported directly by sentences like (54):

(54)   John's leaving was intentional (of him).

The semantics for (54), or the simpler 'John left intentionally', is ultimately as in (55):

(55)   For x = John, $\exists e$(intentional(x, $^\wedge$leave(x, e)) $\wedge$ leave(x, e)).[8]

The second line of thought has already been illustrated in the semantics of (42) and other examples. It is that one should always seek to understand modifiers as they occur in *simple* sentences, of which they themselves are the main predicates. If, for instance, we want to know the θ-structure of an adverb such as *quickly* or *intentionally*, we should look at cases in which the adjective from which it is derived is the main predicate of AP, as in the examples above. Ideally, the θ-structure that is discernible in the simple cases should carry over to the complex.

When the strategy of carrying modifiers back to main predicates is successful, it frequently happens that what is from a syntactic point of view an adjunct functions semantically as the head of the expression that it modifies, and conversely that the syntactic head is semantically part of an argument. Comparing the syntactic structure of (42) to the interpretation shown in (46), we see that the main predicate in (42) is *quickly*, not *objected*. Let us say that the *semantic head* of an expression $Z = X - Y$ is whichever of X and Y θ-marks the other. Then we might sum up the situation by saying that the syntactic head of an expression may, but need not, be its semantic head. I argue for further instances of the divergence of syntactic and semantic headedness below.

2.2. Syntactic Constraints

In a right-branching language such as English the licensing positions of adverbs are correlated with their linear position.[9] Following Bowers (1993), I assume that C licenses the sentential or speech-act adverbs such as *clearly*, *frankly*, and *apparently*; that INFL licenses the subject-oriented adverbs such as *reluctantly* and *intentionally* and adverbs of appraisal such as *probably*; and that V licenses manner adverbs. Within the account proposed here, this diversity of positions, with associated correlation in types of meaning, is to be expected.

Consider the hypothesis that, stylistic rearrangement aside, adverbs may θ-mark only their sisters and may modify, by θ-identification, only as they occur adjoined to nodes where the positionswith which they are to be identified remain open. We expect, then, that sentential adverbs must be sisters to whole clauses. Thus (56) has only the (somewhat strange) meaning that John's learning was clear, whereas (57) and (58) both express that it is clear thatJohn learned French:

(56)   John learned French clearly.
(57)   Clearly, John learned French.
(58)   John clearly learned French.

The sisters IP to C and VP to INFL are both clausal structures. Assuming that the subject moves to Spec(IP) or a higher position, we have in both (57) and (58) a structure

[clearly [. . . [Subject-Predicate] . . .]]

suitable for θ-marking. If the predicate in (56) is constrained to be generated as

$[_{\bar{V}} [_{\bar{V}}$ learn French] clearly]

then the relevant structure is not present and the sentential-adverb interpretation impossible.

Subject-oriented adverbs can be licensed by INFL and will θ-mark the subject in the position Spec(IP) to which it raises. Suppose that *reluctantly*, for example, has the θ-grid of the adjective *reluctant*, which is transparent from examples like (59):

(59)   Mary was reluctant [PRO to leave].

The adjective takes two arguments, referring to Mary and the proposition about her that she leave, respectively, and has its own E-position. It is therefore

$$\lambda p \lambda x \lambda e.\ \text{reluctant}(x, p, e).$$

Suppose then that the (relevant part of the) structure of (60) is as in (61), with t the trace of *Mary*:

(60)   Mary reluctantly left.

(61)

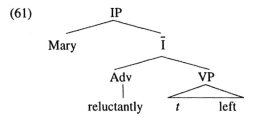

The trace of the subject is interpreted as a free variable, say the i-th one, so that the interpretation of the clausal sister of the adverb is the proposition $\hat{x}_i$ *left* that x_i left. The adverb takes the clause as an argument. The subject *Mary* is θ-marked once through the V *left* but again by INFL' through the adverb, an independent θ-marker. The interpretation of the whole is then (62):

(62)   For Mary $= x_i$, reluctant($x_i, \hat{x}_i$ left, e).

Semantically, then, the trace behaves exactly as if it were PRO, coindexed with the subject.

We have seen that (59) and (60), despite their syntactic difference, behave similarly from the point of view of semantic projection. They differ, however, in presupposition. The adjective *reluctant* is not factive, so that (59) is neutral on the question of whether Mary left. The adverbial construction, however, does presuppose that Mary left. Negation will normally be understood as applying only to the modifier, so that the speaker of (63) will implicate that Mary left:

(63)   Mary didn't leave reluctantly.

The presuppositional difference between (59) and (60) is no accident but characteristic of the constructions themselves. To express it, we must allow that the IP is a conjunction, as in (64):

(64)   For Mary $= x_i$, reluctant$(x_i, \hat{x}_i$ left, $e) \wedge x_i$ left.

Consider now the passive (65):

(65)   Mary was reluctantly instructed t (by Joan).

The adverb is by hypothesis free to θ-mark the subject *Mary*, just as it did in (42). It is not free to θ-mark *Mary* in the corresponding active since it is never a sister of that expression:

(66)   Joan reluctantly instructed Mary.

From this point of view, the semantics of subject-oriented or passive-sensitive adverbs is trivial: they may θ-mark whatever element emerges in the subject position. What is problematic is that the adverb retains its ability to select the agent as its subject, whether the agent is overtly present or not. The latter interpretation may involve θ-identification between the open positions or implicit arguments represented by the agent of the V *instruct* and the experiencer of *reluctant*. This interpretation is available even when no *by* phrase can be appended, as in (67):

(67)   the reluctantly instructed student (*by Joan)

From a semantic point of view, the verbal passive unsupported by a *by* phrase shows a default existential closure, whose scope is below that of the external argument. Assuming a phrase structure as in (68), with the adverb higher than passive *-en*, we may allow closure to apply freely at the subordinate point Y or superordinate point X:

(68)

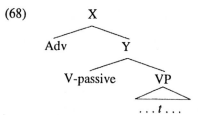

with t the trace of V. If closure applies "too soon"—that is, at Y—then the adverb in (67) will lack a subject, violating the θ-criterion; otherwise, its subject may be identified with the subject of V-passive, and closure will apply at X.

Finally, for adverbs that are ambiguous between manner and subject-oriented interpretations—for example, *clumsily* as in J. L. Austin's (1956) pair (69) and (70)—positioning disambiguates:

(69)   Clumsily, he trod on the snail.
(70)   He trod on the snail clumsily.

The manner adverb, a predicate of the E-position in *tread*, must appear at a low adjunction site, before that position is bound, and hence below INFL, if INFL binds that position. But the sentence-initial adverb must adjoin at INFL or above. So (69) is unambiguous and cannot mean that the treading was clumsy.

Conversely, the subject-oriented adverb must be able to θ-mark a clause and so cannot appear in an adjunction site lower than INFL.

The semantic analysis I have suggested for subject-oriented adverbs, in fact for all thematic adverbs, including *intentionally* and the thematic interpretation of *quickly* (discussed above), raises a question for application of the θ-criterion. In the syntactic structure (66) we must allow the subject *Joan* to be simultaneously (a) the head of the chain (*Joan, t*), θ-marked by *instructed*, and (b) the head of the trivial chain (*Joan*), θ-marked by the complex *reluctantly instructed*, through the adverb. In this sense we must allow the subject position in Spec(IP) to be a θ-position, at least in the sense that it can receive from the adverb a *secondary θ-role* in the sense of Zubizarreta (1982).

How should the θ-criterion be revised so as to allow the analysis given above, while retaining the usual consequences of its application to syntactic structures? Turning from adverbs to other elements with similar effect, we consider the pair (71) and (72), cited in Higginbotham (1989):

(71)   John seems to be a nice fellow.
(72)   John is seeming to be a nice fellow.

As noted there, the assertion of (72) carries the implication, not shared by (71), that John is actively engaged in giving off the appearance of being a nice fellow. Suppose (now extending the discussion in the article cited) that the Progressive, a functional head Prog, is acting in (72) as a secondary θ-marker of the subject *John*, also θ-marked through the chain (*John, t*) by the NP *nice fellow*. We then have the syntax shown in (73), with the semantics computed as for the adverbial cases:

(73)   [John [Prog [seem [*t* to be a nice fellow]]]].

Examples of this type may iterate, so that in (74), for example, the subject will be θ-marked in three distinct ways—namely, the thematic adverb, the progressive, and the lower predicate:

(74)   John quickly appeared [*t* to be seeming [*t* to be a nice fellow]].

The examples suggest that where $C = (A_1, \ldots, A_n)$ is a maximal A-chain, the sister Σ of an element A_i may θ-mark the initial segment $(A_1, \ldots, A_i)$ of C, provided only that the head $H(\Sigma)$ of Σ does not θ-mark any element immediately containing a θ-marker of a larger segment $(A_1, \ldots, A_i, \ldots, A_m)$ of C.

The proviso, or some conditions implying it, is necessary to rule out the existence of heads that have the syntactic properties of raising but the semantic properties of control. For discussion of interactions with semantic theory, see Higginbotham (1996).

3. Telicity

In the last section we saw the E-position as visible for adverbial modification, including syntactic and semantic aspects. In this section I argue for a greater complexity within the E-position itself, whose visibility explains some puzzling aspects of the telic/atelic distinction in English (see also Higginbotham 1995).

The temporal adverbials *for NP* and *in NP* distinguish telic from atelic predicates, inasmuch as *for NP*, uncontroversial with atelics, forces telics into the *activity* mode (as explained more fully below), and *in NP*, uncontroversial with telics, forces atelics to be interpreted as incomplete expressions. The reason is that an expression like *for NP* (*for an hour*, for instance) merely has the function of measuring duration, whereas *in NP* requires two arguments, given either as times *simpliciter* or as the times of events, and measures the temporal distance between them. Thus in

(75)   John will run in an hour

the meaning is this: John will run in an hour from now. That is, an hour will transpire between now and the onset of John's running; and in a sentence such as

(76)   The patient walked in an hour,

we have the interpretation that the onset of the patient's walking took place in an hour from some unspecified earlier point. In the case of an achievement predicate, as in

(77)   The patient died in an hour,

the earlier point can and typically will be taken as the onset of the process that led to the patient's death, so that the first temporal point is given in terms of an event. For accomplishment predicates, it is natural to suppose that both process and telos are supplied, so that

(78)   John solved the problem in an hour,

contains both elements, the work on the problem and the arrival at the solution, within the θ-grid of the head *solve*.

Simple durational adverbs like *for an hour* combine with verbal complexes through conjunction (θ-identification). For the case of *in an hour* we may suppose either (a) that the thematic structure of the V *solve* shows two E-positions or (b) that it shows only one, but from this it is possible to extract both process and telos. Adopting the first hypothesis, if the distinction between adverbials such as *in an hour* and *for an hour* is as stated, the E-position may itself be satisfied by events represented as complex—that is, as made up of two parts, of which the second is the *terminus ad quem* or telos of the first. For (78), then, we take *solve* as having an E-position that is in turn broken down into two positions forming an ordered pair $\langle e_1, e_2 \rangle$. The semantics for (78) is then as follows:

(79) $\exists \langle e_1, e_2 \rangle$ (solve(John, the problem, $\langle e_1, e_2 \rangle$)$\wedge$ in an hour(e_1, e_2)).

3.1. Argument Parameters

Consider now the problem of explaining why quantificational or singular-term internal arguments make for telic predications, whereas bare plural internal arguments and incorporated nouns do not. The contrast is exemplified in (80) and (81):

(80)   Mary drew a circle in/for an hour.
(81)   Mary drew circles in/for an hour.

Sentence (80) with *in* has the expected meaning that an hour elapsed between Mary's commencing to draw and her completion of a circle; with *for* the sentence is false since a circle once drawn cannot be drawn again. Compare (82):

(82)   Mary drew John's face for an hour.

Here we have the "over and over" reading, in which Mary drew for an hour, producing some number of representations of John's face. In (82) with *for* we have also an "over and over" reading, with the difference that the individual acts of drawing are said merely to have various representations as their objects, and nothing is said about what they represent.[10] In (81) with *in* there is a natural interpretation, discussed in Higginbotham (1995), where Mary's circle drawing is regarded as the telos or final state coming to be following some unspecified process, so that the meaning is, roughly, "It took an hour for Mary to get to drawing circles". If we pass over this phenomenon, the problem is to explain why (81) with *in* cannot be an ordinary telic, and inversely, taking *for*, why it can be an atelic.

Telic interpretations are derived under rather specific circumstances—namely, when the arguments are singular terms or certain other quantificational expressions, and the predicate headed by V, which involves a telos, is also taken as singular (I justify the talk of singularity below). Singular terms include not only names of objects and definite descriptions with count-noun heads but also individual variables. Thus Verkuyl (1993: 20) is right to say that a sentence such as

(83)   Judith ate no sandwich

is (in his terminology) *nonterminative*, despite the fact that in

(84)   Judith ate no sandwich in an hour

we have an ordinary telic. The point is that (84) is taken as

(85)   For no sandwich x did (Judith eat x in an hour)

where the parenthetical clause is telic, so that the interpretation (in relevant respects) is

(86)   [No x: sandwich(x)] $\exists \langle e_1, e_2 \rangle$ [eat(Judith, x, $\langle e_1, e_2 \rangle$)$\wedge$ in an hour(e_1, e_2)].

What is excluded is the (somewhat strained) reading: there is a situation of Judith's eating no sandwich that lasted an hour (but see the discussion of "negative events" below).

By speaking of the singularity of the predicate, I mean to exclude the case in which the existential closure over the E-position is a plural quantification, seen in the salient interpretation of

(87)   John shot ducks for an hour,

which we give as

(88)   (for some Γ) (for all $\langle e_1, e_2 \rangle$ in Γ) ($\exists x$: duck(x)) (shoot(John, x, $\langle e_1, e_2 \rangle$))).

Even though each $\langle e_1, e_2 \rangle$ in Γ has a process and a telos, the family Γ itself does not; hence (87) is atelic, like (82). In general, the "over and over" readings represent a pluralisation of the E-position of the predicate, independent of the nature of the arguments of the head.

Tenny (1994) argues that telic interpretation is restricted to what I am calling singular-term internal arguments because only in this way can the verbal head *measure out* the change in objects that it indicates. Thus when one draws a circle, there is a measuring out of the process of creating the circle up to the point of its completion. Similarly, in an example like (89), the internal argument *the apple* supplies the object relative to which the measuring out is taken:

(89)   John ate the apple in an hour.

I redirect this proposal so that what Tenny calls *measuring out* is a consequence of telicity and not a basis for it. If the event e satisfying the $\overline{X}$ *eat the apple* is separable into a process $\pi(e)$ and telos $\tau(e)$, then the sense of measuring out that Tenny rightly discerns derives from the fact that, at least normally, attainment of the telos (the apple's being consumed) through the process (taking one bite after another from the apple) is an affair that involves a systematic change in the apple, such that the attainment of the telos is brought closer and closer.

Returning now to our earlier question, we ask what prevents a telic interpretation in cases in which the internal argument is a mass noun or bare plural, as in (90) and (91)?

(90)   John ate apples/chicken in an hour.
(91)   Mary drew circles/clothing in an hour.[11]

Bach (1986), among others, has called attention to the fact that (in the terms we are employing here) the events that would make it true that John ate apples for an hour, or Mary drew circles or clothing for an hour, are in a sense *homogeneous*. Roughly, an event of apple eating is made up of subevents of the same type; an event of repeated circle drawing is made up of subevents that are also circle drawings. Moreover, sums of events of the type are again events of the type. The analogy, as Bach especially points out, is to the homogeneity (as far as it goes) of mass terms, the intuition that parts of gold—down to molecules anyway—are gold and that a substance whose parts are gold is again gold.[12]

However, the notion of a *subevent* is a technical one, requiring interpretation. To fix ideas, let us suppose that where an event e has for its time $T(e)$ some interval $I = (t_1, t_2)$ of real numbers, possibly closed at either extremity and possibly trivial (when $t_1 = t_2$), a subevent of e is determined by confining e within any proper subinterval (t'_1, t'_2) of I (again, possibly closed at either or both extremities and possibly trivial).[13] Then we may say that the subevents of an apple eating, or at least all of those that are describable as eating at all, are events of apple eating.

Let x be an apple. Why is an event of eating x *not* homogeneous? We cannot say that it is not homogeneous because its proper subevents cannot be described as *eating an apple*; for our question was why this is so. The answer suggested by the analysis of the verb in terms of process and telos is that eating x is not homogeneous because (none of) its proper subevents—the event of eating half of it, say—are such that the telos of eating x is attained. If so, then it is telicity that is responsible for inhomogeneity, and not conversely.

But now we have the result that homogeneity implies atelicity. If a verbal projection has the property that the subevents of an event e that it classifies are of the same type as e, then the E-position in that projection cannot be $\langle e_1, e_2 \rangle$: the subevents in question, for instance, the initial segments of e_1, are not both (a) telic and (b) of the same type as that classified by the verbal projection. Where the projection, for instance, is that of *eat x*, the telos is, say, the onset of the state of x's being in the agent's stomach (by ingesting x through the mouth).[14] Subevents of the process can well be telic (e.g., an event of taking a bite of the apple) but will not in general have a telos that satisfies the condition on e_2.[15]

This argument, if correct, shows why homogeneity should be a sufficient condition for atelicity but does not make it also a necessary condition. This result is perhaps fortunate since it is unclear, for example, how homogeneous an event of apple eating really is when it consists of taking only one bite. To avoid the distraction of implicatures with plurals, consider a case with a mass-noun object and the reduced determiner written as *sm*, as in (92):

(92)   John ate sm apple.

If we regard an event as (purportedly) described in (92) as homogeneous, then we must take the V *ate* as having a simplex E-position, not an ordered pair. But what if it need not be regarded as homogeneous, and we insert the complex *ate*, whose E-position is broken down as $\langle e_1, e_2 \rangle$? We have to say that the (denotation of the) bare mass noun is incapable of being involved in the telos.

The telos of (92), by parity of reasoning, would be the onset of the state of having some (sm) apple in one's stomach, ingested through the mouth. But this state must exist if the process comes off at all. Hence the bare mass noun cannot give a telos: attainment of that telos is *inseparable* from the occurrence of the process itself—that is, the telos comes about if the process does.[16]

Thus far I have considered object quantifications in construction with telic heads only inasmuch as these quantifications are taken as binding variables in the object position and appear outside the scope of the quantification over events. We can now extend the analysis to inner quantifications, in which the quantification over events is primary. Consider, for example, (93):

(93)   I examined three pictures in an hour (each).

With the distributive *each*, the interpretation is given by

(94) $[3x: \text{picture}(x)]\ [\exists\langle e_1, e_2\rangle]\ \text{examine}(I, x, \langle e_1, e_2\rangle) \wedge \text{in an hour}(e_1, e_2)$.

But without *each*, the most natural, and perhaps the only, interpretation is that there was an examination of pictures that took an hour, in the course of which three pictures were examined. Under this inner quantification, in part following Schein (1993), (93) is as in (95):

(95) $\exists\langle e_1, e_2\rangle[\text{examine}(\langle e_1, e_2\rangle) \wedge \text{Agent}(I, \langle e_1, e_2\rangle) \wedge \exists X[3(X) \wedge \forall y(X(y) \rightarrow \text{picture}(y)) \wedge \forall z.\theta(z, \langle e_1, e_2\rangle) \leftrightarrow X(z)) \wedge \text{in an hour}(e_1, e_2)]$,

where θ expresses the thematic relation between the event, or ordered pair of events, and its internal argument. The sense may be paraphrased as:

> There is a process and telos $\langle e_1, e_2\rangle$ constituting an examination, of which I was the agent, and to which there were in the relation θ three objects, all of which were pictures, and the temporal distance between the onset of the process and the onset of the telos is one hour.

It remains to discuss the nature of the telos for this case. Analogous to (92) are examples with measure phrases in construction with mass nouns, which give telic predicates as in (96):

(96)   John ate a box of chocolates/a pint of ice cream.

Atelicity reappears when the measure is a bare plural, as in

(97)   John ate boxes of chocolates/pints of ice cream,

so that these examples fall under the general point of view given above—that is, they involve plural quantification, like (86). Phrases such as *a box of chocolates* are ambiguous, denoting in one interpretation the chocolates in some box or other and, in the other, a *measure* of an amount of chocolates; this holds similarly for *a glass of wine*, for example. It is the measure interpretation that calls for further analysis. Following the conception and the notation in Higginbotham (1994a), the predicate *a pint of ice cream* is interpreted as

$$\text{ice cream}(X) \wedge \mu_{\text{pint}}(X) = 1.$$

That is, X is ice cream, and its pint measure is the number 1 (corresponding to the indefinite article, which in this case functions as a numeral).

To bring out the peculiarity of the situation, consider that *eat*, taken as a telic, is understood as $eat(\langle e_1, e_2\rangle)$, where

(98)   For some α:
     e_1 is a process of eating directed toward α;
     e_2 is the state of α's being properly inside the agent.

(The terms *directed toward* and *beeing inside the agent* should be understood as conveying primitive notions, the former being the thematic relation e_1 bears toward the reference of the internal argument of V, and the latter indicating the final state of α.) Now, in the typical event of eating a pint of ice cream X, e_1 is directed toward X; but the telos is not X's being properly inside the agent but rather that the measure of eaten X should be a pint. Nor is it true in general that X should be a pint: when one eats a pint of ice cream from a quart container, intending to and succeeding in eating a pint, there is no particular pint measure of stuff X that one intended to eat; one may have just intended to eat from the container until a pint had been consumed.

It follows that the characterisation (98) of *eat* as a telic is somewhat different for measure-phrase objects.[17] We may propose (99):

(99)   For some X:
   e_1 is a process of eating directed toward X;
   e_2 is the state of measure $\mu_K(X)$ being properly inside the agent,

where the object must supply both the value of K and the identity of the measure.

In closing this section, I compare briefly the suggestions in the text to the construction in Krifka (1992). Whereas I have supposed that a V like *eat* is systematically ambiguous between the atelic *eat(e)*, with a single E-position, and the telic *eat($\langle e_1, e_2 \rangle$)*, with two, Krifka takes V to be univocal, with a single E-position. Predicates then become telic through the nature of the arguments with which V is in construction. Krifka gives a metaphysical argument for this view—namely, that conditions in event identity suggest that telicity is a matter of event descriptions rather than events themselves. Suppose I eat a pint of ice cream, and thereby eat ice cream. Then, the suggestion is, my eating of a pint of ice cream is identical with a certain event of my eating ice cream; but then the event of eating cannot be telic or atelic in itself but only as described.

In the construction I have suggested, however, Krifka's argument does not go through. My eating of a pint of ice cream is an event $e = \langle e_1, e_2 \rangle$ with the properties stated. But the events of my eating ice cream (of which there will be many when I eat a pint of ice cream) are none of them identical to e; in particular, e_1 is only the first coordinate of $e = \langle e_1, e_2 \rangle$, and not e itself.

In a similar case, involving individual objects rather than measures of amount, suppose that I walk around the Trevi fountain, making one complete revolution, and suppose that this project takes ten minutes. Then both (100) and (101) are true:

(100)   I walked around the fountain in ten minutes.
(101)   I walked around the fountain for ten minutes.

There is an implication of (100) that (101) lacks—namely, that I made one complete revolution of the fountain; (101) can be true if I made no revolutions at all or many. In the case I have described, however, there is just one 10-minute walk, whose trajectory makes (100) and (101) both true, or so it would seem. So it appears that the same event makes both (100) and (101) true. But if an event considered in itself either has or does not have a telos, and what we have assumed about temporal adverbials is correct, then one or the other of (100) and (101) should not be satisfied by the event in question, contrary to fact. In this case, I think, we have an ambiguity in the preposition. In one meaning, *around* means *go all the way around*, and *walk around* means *circumambulate*—that is, go all the way around by walking. In the other meaning, *around* is simply a predicate of the path of the walking itself. Notice that it is only in the second, atelic, interpretation that the PP *around the fountain* is a true adjunct, or modifier, of V. In the telic interpretation, this PP is itself the main predicate, semantically speaking, and the V serves as the modifier, giving the means of locomotion.[18]

The puzzles of event identity known to me admit solution in the above or other ways; if they are generally soluble as suggested, then we need not say with Krifka that it is only event descriptions, and not events themselves, that may be classified as telic or atelic.

There are predicates that can be understood as telic or atelic without appeal to "over and over" interpretations, as in (102):

(102) I ran upstairs in/for 10 minutes.

The predicate *run upstairs* must therefore be ambiguous, evidently between (a) an atelic predicate true of running events *e* that go in the upstairs direction and (b) a telic predicate whose use with *in* in (102) implicates that the top of the stairs was reached. Krifka's construction would require elaboration to deal with these cases, especially since the expression *upstairs* is not a singular-term argument of *run*. The proposal above would take the atelic interpretation, as in (103), and the telic, as in (104):

(103) $\text{run}(e) \wedge \text{upstairs}(e) \wedge \text{for an hour}(e)$.
(104) $\text{run}(\langle e_1, e_2 \rangle) \wedge \text{upstairs}(e_2) \wedge \text{in an hour}(e_1, e_2)$.

The ambiguity is then located in the ambiguity of the word *upstairs*, between a predicate true of motions, giving their direction, and a predicate true of states, giving the location of an object involved in them. The latter predicate is independently found in statives, as in *your bedroom is upstairs*.

3.2. Purpose Clauses: The Visibility of the Telos

Above I have discussed several cases in which the E-position is visible to syntactic and semantic processes, and I have proposed that accomplishment predicates should be thought of as containing two positions within E, one each for process and telos. This proposal, if correct, establishes that the telos in particular is syntactically represented and not merely supplied by the semantics of the verbal projection. I argue in this section that to capture the distribution of purpose clauses in English we must also suppose that teli are syntactically represented; it is not sufficient that they be supplied through entailments or commonsense understanding.

The English purpose clause is exemplified by the bracketed constituent in (105) and similar examples:

(105) I bought bones [to give to the dog].

I assume the syntactic account of Chomsky (1977), in which the purpose clause 'gap' is taken to reflect *Wh*-movement of an empty operator *O* (notwithstanding the analysis in Jones 1991). We then have:

(106) I bought bones [*O* [PRO to give *t* to the dog]]

where *O*, or the chain *O-t*, is linked to the antecedent *bones*.

As observed in Bach (1982), acceptability of a purpose clause requires not only that the gap be linked to some matrix argument, usually the theme, but also that the fulfilment of the purpose in question be consequent on some state that is in turn consequent on the truth of the main clause. In (105), the state is that of the bones' coming to be in my possession; it is because they are in my possession that I am in a position to give them to the dog. The consequent state is therefore the state whose onset is the telos of the main clause *I bought bones*. I argue first that this identity is no accident.

We can make Bach's proposal more explicit by filling in a semantics for the purpose clause along the lines suggested in Whelpton (1995). Whelpton proposes that the operator in a purpose clause expresses λ-abstraction and that its argument structure is as in (107):

(107) $\lambda P\lambda e\lambda x.\ C(x, e, P)$,

where *x* is an individual, *P* is a property (in the sense of Montague, noted above), and *e* is the consequent state. The meaning of *C* is to a first approximation as in (108):

(108) *e* is a state that is (or is intended to be) causally efficacious in bringing it about that *P(x)*.

The predicate (108) applies in turn to the property, expressed by the purpose clause—the consequent state—and the argument to which the operator is linked.

Atelic matrix clauses can host purpose clauses, as in (109) and (110):

(109) The sign hung in the window [for people/PRO to read].
(110) John pushed the cart along the road [for the crowd to see]/[PRO to show to the crowd].

But some pure activities disallow purpose clauses:

(111) *I wiped the table [for Mary/PRO to impress the guests with].

Compare (112), where the consequent state is manifest:

(112) I wiped the table clean/free of dirt [PRO to impress the guests with].

What is the distinction between (109) and (110) on the one hand, and (111) on the other? Following Whelpton's semantic analysis, we would conclude that whereas the event in the main clause (109) and (110) is causally efficacious in bringing about the accomplishment of the purpose—the sign's hanging in the window is what brings it about that people read it; the pushing of the cart along the road is what gets the crowd to see it or gets me to show it to the crowd—the event of wiping the table (i.e., going through the movements of wiping) is not of itself efficacious in getting the guests impressed with it. In (112), on the other hand, the consequent state following on the wiping—namely, the cleanliness of the table—is causally efficacious in impressing the guests with it. The efficacy of the wiping derives from the fact that it brought about the consequent state, whose onset was the telos of the wiping.

We can now ask more generally whether purpose clauses are licensed whenever it is a matter of common knowledge that there is a consequent state of a particular kind that will inevitably follow upon the successful completion of a given activity, or whether specifically linguistic information is required. The answer suggested by the contrast between (110) and (111) is that common knowledge of a consequent state is not sufficient. Thus we do not have examples like (113) or (114):

(113) *They deprived the prisoner of food [to starve].
(114) *The pitcher threw at the batter [to knock down].

We know that starvation is the consequence of food deprivation and that the pitcher's purpose in throwing at the batter is to knock him down. Nevertheless, the examples are unacceptable.

From these examples, we may tentatively conclude that the formulation (108) of the interpretation of the nexus in the purpose clause should be supplemented by the condition that e not merely be causally efficacious but also be the *immediate* cause of the object x's having the property P—that is, that it not cause x to have P only because it caused some intermediate event e' that in turn caused x to have P. The events described in the atelics (109) and (110) have this property with respect to their purpose clauses. In (111), however, the state (of cleanliness) into which the table is to be put by the wiping action, which is something that the action causes and in turn causes or is intended to cause the guests to be impressed, is left implicit. In (113) and (114), similarly, the consequent states (the prisoner lacks food; the ball strikes the batter), although matters of common knowledge, are not linguistically present. We thus conclude that in the formulation of the nexus of the purpose clause in (107) the position marked by e must be in the linguistic material, with C now being understood to involve immediacy of causation.

If this is correct, we have strong evidence that the telos of a telic predicate, which is not realised by any overt secondary predicate such as the resultative *clean* of (112), is available to be the second argument of the purpose-clause nexus only because it is syntactically present. Our first example, *I bought bones*, already illustrates the general theme since the telos, the bones' being in my possession, can only be made available through thematic information in the predicate *buy*.

The capacity of a verbal projection to license a purpose clause may depend on the specifically lexical information that is a part of what is understood when its meaning is fully grasped. Compare, for example, (115) to (116):

(115) *I pounded the meat [to improve the taste of].

(116) I pounded the meat [to fit into the pan].

Example (115) is unacceptable, though it is known that tenderisation of the meat is a state that is a causal consequence of pounding it, that putting the meat into that state is salient among the reasons for doing so, and that its being in the tender state improves its taste. The intermediate state, the meat's being tenderised, is not explicit in the sentence. If it is explicit, then the purpose clause is acceptable, or at any rate more acceptable:

(117) (?)I pounded the meat tender [to improve the taste of].

On the other hand, (116) is acceptable as it stands, so that the state that consists in the meat's having a certain shape mediates between the activity, pounding, and the purpose for which it is intended. These and similar examples invite the conclusion that the V *pound* is in fact ambiguous, having, on the one hand, a pure activity meaning and, on the other, a meaning that incorporates the telos of putting the patient, the object pounded on, into some shape.

4. Can Events Be Negative?

If there can be events such as John's playing golf last Saturday, can there also be events such as John's not playing golf last Saturday? If there are events such as my turning off the light, can there also be events such as my not turning off the light? If there are contexts for negative events, then this question looms large for any account of events and states in which they are taken to be individuals, and larger still if events lack a structure of complementation; but conversely if these contexts are restricted, then the liberality that complementation would give is itself suspect. In this section, I defend a limited account of negative events within the Davidsonian framework and contrast it with what would be available for Montague and for any account of events that endows them with an intrinsic Boolean structure.

We are concerned here with contexts in which negation is understood *in propria persona* and therefore put aside the contexts in which it is otherwise interpreted. I have argued (Higginbotham 1983) that naked infinitive complements to verbs of perception express existential quantification over events, as given by the E-position of the verbal head. If events could be negative, we would expect reference to them, or quantification over them, in such complements with overt negation *not*. But I have argued also that in fact the word *not* within these complements does not express negation but a kind of contrariness. Consider the perception-verb context (118):

(118) Mary saw John not play golf last Saturday.

The acceptability of (118) depends on conceiving the complement as expressing something stronger than negation and contributing to the complement as a whole a meaning such as this: John pointedly refrained from playing golf; or John didn't play golf when he might have been expected to; or, more figuratively,

John played golf so poorly that he could hardly be said to have been playing the game; or something similar. What Mary saw, if her assertion in (118) is true, is an event *suspending* the prospect of John's playing golf or interfering with his playing it properly: what sort of event Mary intends must be gleaned from the context. If this is right, then cases like (118) should not be analysed in terms of negative events.

Negative events also, and more obviously, do not come into the picture in connection with propositional or factive complements, no matter how these may be syntactically realised. However, there are arguments for negative events stemming from causal contexts and from the behaviour of temporal adverbials. Thus in contexts like (119), we seem to make reference to a negative event with causal consequences:

(119) I kept the child awake by not turning out the light

and the ambiguity of sentences like (120) suggests that negation can receive internal as well as external scope:

(120) John didn't play golf until noon.

In the external reading, the speaker of (120) denies that John's golf playing went on until noon; in the internal reading, the speaker asserts that until noon there was no golf playing by John. I take these cases in turn.

The case for negative events in (119) cannot be dismissed by saying that if my not turning out the light kept the child awake, then there is some event non-negatively described, that is, the light's continuing to burn, that was actually responsible for the child's being awake; for there are many cases in which we do not know what events of that kind there are, or even whether there are any. Notice furthermore that my not turning out the light may not have been a refrainment on my part but simply an omission; hence negation in cases like (119) cannot be assimilated to the antonymic negation of naked infinitive complements.

A system that, as in Montague's work, took events as universals, and could in principle construct them from any predicate with a free temporal variable, will admit negative events of all sorts (although the issue is not discussed in Montague 1974). Thus there is a property of moments of time that holds (in a given possible world) of those moments t such that the light is not turned off at t; and the set of moments instantiating this property in the actual world might be said to be causally responsible for the child's being awake. Similarly, if the property of being a moment t such that John does not play golf at t is one that each moment before noon has in the actual world, then, identifying the event of John's not playing golf with this property, we can say that as things are it lasted until noon. In this way, locutions such as (119) and (120) are admitted, describing negative events.

To accommodate negative events within the Davidsonian setting adopted in section 1.1, we must think of some situations as given to us merely through the family of moments of time that belong to them. Situations of all sorts are in time, and we postulate that for each situation e there is a unique set of moments of time $T(e)$ that constitute the *time* of e. Where H is an ordinary predicate classifying situations and (t_1, t_2) is a temporal interval (open, closed, or neither, where we allow the possibility that $t_1 = t_2$), if there is no event e of kind H whose time overlaps (t_1, t_2), then we may posit the existence of a unique H-*complement* event e' whose time $T(e')$ is (t_1, t_2). Relative to the given interval, e' is an event of non-H-ing. Thus the situation of my not turning off the light—between 7 and 10 P.M., say—exists and has the interval in question as its time provided that there is no situation of my turning off the light within the interval. More formally, given H, we introduce a predicate $\bar{H}$ and the axiom (121):

(121) $\quad \forall I(\neg \exists e(O(T(e), I) \wedge H(e)) \rightarrow \exists e'(\bar{\bar{H}}(e') \wedge T(e') = I)$,

where O is the relation of overlapping between temporal intervals. Our assumption is that overt negation may express the operation, yielding $\bar{H}$ from H, thus giving rise to what are intuitively negative events.

The construction just given posits negative events e' of kind $\bar{H}$ only for antecedently given event classifiers H and only relative to temporal intervals I; it goes, therefore, only partway toward a full complementarity that would be realised, for instance, in a Boolean structure. Nevertheless, it is adequate for examples like (119), and also for negation within derived nominals, as in (122) and (123):

(122) the nonexplosion of the gases

(123) Bill's nondeparture

Moreover, the generosity toward negative events that would follow in Montague's theory (and in any theory that endowed events with an intrinsic structure of complementarity) seems not only unnecessary but even profligate. Recall that in Montague's view nominals such as (124) refer to generic events:

(124) the rising of the sun

The adjective admits negation, so that we have

(125) the nonrising of the sun,

which would presumably denote the generic event that is the property of moments of time t such that the sun does not rise at t. There will also be existential quantifiers ranging over particular events, nonrisings of the sun. In allowing complementarity at all, we have pulled closer to Montague's point of view; but we do not have full complementarity from the beginning.

Consider now the second type of example, (120). A state of John's not playing golf is any state s whose time $T(s)$ does not overlap with any $T(e)$ such that e is an event of John's playing golf. On the internal reading of the negation in (120), there is said to be such a state throughout the period ending at noon. Invoking complementarity to allow this reading, we are not far from Montague's construal of events as properties of moments of time. The construals nevertheless differ in what they take to be given and what must be constructed from the basic apparatus.

5. Concluding Remarks

In this discussion I have endeavoured to explain part of the scientific background that seems to me operative in linguistic semantics, guiding the psychological inquiry, and to give some examples of applications of the hypothesis of the E-position within that theory. The arguments in favour of the hypothesis point toward a restricted theory of linguistic organisation: events enter semantic computation only as they are linguistically represented through thematic grids, and discharge of open positions takes place only under structurally controlled conditions. The theory pays in ontology for what it buys semantically—that is, the cost, if it is a cost, of the combinatorial simplification is the positing of objects, reference to which is not immediately manifest in linguistic structures. The formalisation of the theory, and its application to a greater variety of human languages, is a matter for the future; in the meantime, the theory receives some support from the fact that it makes many of what we take to be obvious implications really obvious and from the degree to which it fits a reasonable conception of what is learned in mastering a language.[19]

Notes

1. Obviously, the higher-order apparatus can be invoked for the purposes that explicitly require it, such as Montague's own interpretation of the phrase 'the property of being a moment of time t such that the sun rises at t' in his theory of properties.

2. See Grimshaw (1991) for a discussion of the types of derived-nominal interpretations.

3. For a defence of the thesis that +*past* expresses a relation between events, see Higginbotham (1995) and references cited there.

4. I am assuming here that the overt subject is, first, AP-internal and moves to the pre-copular position without semantic effect. In section 2.2 I give an application that depends on the internality of subjects of XPs.

5. The latter point is observed in Montague (1967).

6. Choice of determiner D in these schemata is not limited to the definite article. Furthermore, although PRO in state descriptions with bare PRO subjects has the usual property of uncontrolled PRO that it is confined to humans, PRO may be controlled by a non-human DP, as in

the state of [PRO being in the frying pan that the steak is in].

7. The proposed semantics, therefore, has the consequence that the hypothesis of Kratzer (1995) that I-level predicates lack an event argument should be rejected, and the data that show that this argument is in a number of contexts not available to the semantics should be reanalysed so that the argument, although present, is in some way (perhaps differently for different contexts) unavailable. For one hypothesis along these lines, see Chierchia (1995), and for discussion of the diversity among the cases, see Higginbotham and Ramchand (1997).

8. Notice that, on this view, "John left intentionally" is stronger than the conjunction "John intended to leave, and he left". To intend to leave is merely to intend that there be such as thing as one's leaving; and one leaves if there is such a thing. But, according to

(55), to leave intentionally involves passing from the state of intending to leave to a state in which one intends, of a particular thing that one is doing, that it constitute leaving and for it in fact to be so. I believe this view to be correct and its correctness even to be manifested in ordinary experience. For example, I can intend to express my displeasure at someone's remark and be surprised to discover myself already frowning. If such cases are accepted, then I can intend to express my displeasure and express it, without expressing it intentionally. (For discussion on this point I am indebted to Hans Kamp.)

9. In recent work following especially the suggestions of Kayne (1994), it may be suggested that these correlations are universal.

10. In the most natural interpretation—that is, a circle can also be what is represented in a drawing of a circle, and in this case one can draw what is represented (the sacred circle, say) for an hour.

11. These examples are, of course, fully acceptable when another coordinate for the adjunct *in an hour* is given, say by adding the phrase *from when he/she finished work.* In that case, as remarked above, the onset of the event classified by the V acts as the final state, the difference between which and the supplied coordinate the temporal adjunct measures.

12. This point of view is heavily exploited in Krifka (1992).

13. The subevents of *e* need not be *parts* of *e* in any interesting sense since they may cross the boundaries that we regard as delimiting the parts.

14. Of course, the open texture of language makes the telos (and for that matter the process) somewhat elastic; but stereotypical cases are sufficient to illustrate the point.

15. Again, open texture plays a role here. Suppose there is an organism that can only (finish) eating something by ingesting it three times. Such an organism might be said to have to eat an apple three times in order to eat it. Even so, when this organism eats an apple, there will be atelic subevents, properly describable as apple eating but not as eating an apple.

16. This suggestion is perhaps related to, but the inverse of, one that I have heard presented by David Dowty, that in cases like (91) no unique final state can be specified.

17. As noted in Higginbotham (1994a: 478), these objects are not quantificational since they observe a definiteness effect.

18. For elaboration on this theme, see Higginbotham (1994b).

19. A version of this article, itself descended from versions given in various venues since 1993, was read at the Trento Conference on Facts and Events in the Semantics of Natural Language, 1995. I have profited from comments and questions both there and at subsequent presentations at the University of California, Los Angeles, and at the founding meeting of the Society for Semantics, Tübingen, Germany. Even though for want of space I have not been able to take account of all of these, I should like particularly to thank Kit Fine, Hans Kamp, David Kaplan, Anna Szabolcsi, and Ede Zimmermann for their remarks and discussion.

References

Austin, J. L., 1956. A Plea for Excuses. In *Proceedings of the Aristotelian Society* 57: 1–30. Reprinted in Austin, J. L., 1961. *Philosophical Papers*, 123–152. Clarendon Press, Oxford.

Bach, E., 1982. Purpose Clauses and Control. In P. Jacobson and G. K. Pullum (eds.), *The Nature of Syntactic Representation*, 35–57. Reidel, Dordrecht.

Bach, E., 1986. The Algebra of Events. In *Linguistics and Philosophy* 9: 5–16.

Bowers, J., 1993. The Syntax of Predication. In *Linguistic Inquiry* 24: 591–656.

Carlson, G., 1980. *Reference to Kinds in English*. Garland, New York.

Carlson, G., 1989. On the Semantic Composition of English Generic Sentences. In G. Chierchia, B. H. Partee, and R. Turner (eds.), *Properties, Types, and Meaning II*, 167–192. Kluwer, Dordrecht.

Chierchia, G., 1995. Individual-level Predicates as Inherent Generics. In G. Carlson and F. J. Pelletier (eds.), *The Generic Book*, 176–223. University of Chicago Press, Chicago.

Chomsky, N., 1977. On WH-movement. In P. W. Culicover, T. Wasow, and A. Akmajian (eds.), *Formal Syntax*, 71–132. Academic Press, New York.

Chomsky, N., 1981. *Lectures on Government and Binding*. Foris, Dordrecht.

Davidson, D., 1967. The Logical Form of Action Sentences. In N. Rescher (ed.), *The Logic of Decision and Action*, 81–95. University of Pittsburgh Press, Pittsburgh. Reprinted in Davidson, D., 1980. *Essays on Actions and Events*, 105–123. Clarendon Press, Oxford.

Grimshaw, J., 1991. *Argument Structure*. MIT Press, Cambridge (Mass.).

Higginbotham, J., 1983. The Logic of Perceptual Reports: An Extensional Alternative to Situation Semantics. In *The Journal of Philosophy* 80: 100–127.

Higginbotham, J., 1985. On Semantics. In *Linguistic Inquiry* 16: 547–593.

Higginbotham, J., 1989. Elucidations of Meaning. In *Linguistics and Philosophy* 12: 465–517.

Higginbotham, J., 1994a. Mass and Count Quantifiers. In *Linguistics and Philosophy* 17: 447–480. Reprinted in E. Bach, E. Jelinek, A. Kratzer, and B. H. Partee (eds.), 1995. *Quantification in Natural Language*, 383–419. Kluwer Academic Publishers, Dordrecht.

Higginbotham, J., 1994b. *Sense and Syntax*, 1–27. Inaugural Lecture, Oxford University. Clarendon Press, Oxford.

Higginbotham, J., 1995. The Semantics of Tense. Unpublished ms., Oxford University.

Higginbotham, J., 1996. Semantic Computation. Unpublished ms., Oxford University.

Higginbotham, J., and G. Ramchand, 1997. The Stage-level/Individual-level Distinction and the Mapping Hypothesis. In *Oxford Working Papers in Linguistics, Philology, and Phonetics* 2, 53–83.

Jones, C., 1991. *Purpose Clauses: Syntax, Thematics, and Semantics of English Purpose Constructions*. Kluwer, Dordrecht.

Kamp, J. A. W., 1981. A Theory of Truth and Semantic Representation. In J. Groenedijk, T. Janssen, and M. J. Stokhof (eds.), *Formal Methods in the Study of Language*, 277–322. Mathematical Centre, Amsterdam.

Kayne, R., 1994. *The Antisymmetry of Syntax*. MIT Press, Cambridge (Mass.).

Kratzer, A., 1995. Stage-level and Individual-level Predicates. In G. Carlson and F. J. Pelletier (eds.), *The Generic Book*, 125–175. University of Chicago Press, Chicago.

Krifka, M., 1992. Thematic Relations as Links Between Nominal Reference and Temporal Constitution. In I. Sag and A. Szabolcsi (eds.), *Lexical Matters*, 29–53. CSLI Publications, Stanford (Calif.).

Montague, R., 1969. On the Nature of Certain Philosophical Entities. In *The Monist* 53: 159–194. Reprinted in Montague, R., 1974. *Formal Philosophy*, R. H. Thomason (ed.), 149–187. Yale University Press, New Haven (Conn.).

Parsons, T., 1990. *Events in the Semantics of English*. MIT Press, Cambridge (Mass.).

Schein, B., 1993. *Plurals and Events*. MIT Press, Cambridge (Mass.).

Tenny, C., 1994. Aspectual Roles and the Syntax-Semantics Interface. Kluwer, Dordrecht.

Verkuyl, H., 1993. *A Theory of Aspectuality: The Interaction Between Temporal and Atemporal Structure*. Cambridge University Press, Cambridge.

Whelpton, M. J., 1995. *Syntactic and Semantic Functions in Control Theory*. D.Phil. dissertation, Oxford University.

Zubizarreta, M.-L., 1982. *On the Relationship of the Lexicon to Syntax*. Ph.D. dissertation, MIT, Cambridge (Mass.).

3

Underlying States and Time Travel

Terence Parsons

1. The Theory of Underlying Events for Event Sentences

The theory to be discussed is at least as old as Plato's *Sophist*. It is that verbs stand for kinds of events and that several other parts of sentences contribute additional information about those events, sometimes standing for things that are related to the event in common ways. For example, in

(1)   Brutus stabbed Caesar violently with a knife

the whole sentence asserts that an event of a certain kind occurred, the verb tells what kind of event it was (a stabbing), the tense on the verb tells when it occurred (sometime in the past), the subject indicates the agent of that stabbing, the direct object says who the object of the stabbing was, and the modifying phrases supply additional information about the event: that it was violent and that it was with a knife. All told, this information can be summed up in this logical form for (1):

(1')   For some event *e*:
      e is a stabbing   \<verb\>
      e culminated in the past   \<tense\>
      the agent of *e* is Brutus   \<subject\>
      the object of *e* is Caesar   \<direct object\>
      e was violent   \<adverb modifier\>
      e was with a knife   \<prepositional phrase\>

In predicate calculus notation (which is optional), this is

(2) $\exists e(\text{Stabbing}(e) \wedge \text{Cul}(e, \text{past}) \wedge \text{Agent}(e, \text{Brutus}) \wedge \text{Object}(e, \text{Caesar}) \wedge \text{Violent}(e) \wedge \text{With}(e, \text{knife}))$.

The question naturally arises of why anyone should attribute such a complex form to the sentence. It has an intuitive appeal, but does it yield any particular theoretical fruits or is it merely an engaging way to view things? In Parsons (1990) I argue that such logical forms yield several important consequences. The main ones are summed up in the next two sections. The remainder of this chapter concerns extending the theory to state sentences.[1]

1.1. The Logic of Verb Modifiers in Event Sentences

The first piece of evidence for underlying quantification over events in event sentences stems from the logic of verb modifiers. It is a striking fact that of these sentences,

(3)   Brutus stabbed Caesar violently with a knife
(4)   Brutus stabbed Caesar violently
(5)   Brutus stabbed Caesar with a knife
(6)   Brutus stabbed Caesar

(3) entails both (4) and (5), and each of these entails (6). Thus any *modifier drop-off* is valid, in any order. But equally important is the fact that the conjunction of (4) and (5) does not entail (3). If Brutus stabbed Caesar gently with a knife and violently with an icepick, both (4) and (5) are true but (3) is not; there are two stabbings, each of which satisfies one of (4) and (5) but neither of which satisfies (3). I call the first entailment the *modifier drop-off* and the second nonentailment the *modifier nonconjunction.* The logical forms proposed above satisfy both. Those forms are

(3')   For some e:
        e is a stabbing,
        the agent of e is Brutus,
        the object of e is Caesar,
        e is violent,
        e is with a knife.

(4')   For some e:
        e is a stabbing,
        the agent of e is Brutus,
        the object of e is Caesar,
        e is violent.

(5')   For some e:
        e is a stabbing,
        the agent of e is Brutus,
        the object of e is Caesar,
        e is with a knife.

(6')   For some e:
        e is a stabbing,
        the agent of e is Brutus,
        the object of e is Caesar.

Ordinary predicate logic then accounts for both the *modifier drop-off* and the *modifier nonconjunction*. That is, these logical forms are such that (3') entails both (4') and (5') in the predicate calculus, and these both entail (6'). But there is no predicate calculus entailment of (3') by the conjunction of (4') and (5'). Thus these forms validate the distinctive logic of verb modifiers, which is the first sort of evidence for the quantification over events.

1.2. Perception Statements for Event Sentences

The second sort of evidence has to do with the semantics of perception statements whose perception verbs take *small clauses*. Examples are

(7)   Mary saw Brutus stab Caesar.
(8)   Sam heard Mary shoot Bill.
(9)   Agatha felt the boat rock.

These are logically independent of similar constructions with the same verbs that take *that* clauses:

(10)   Mary saw that Brutus stabbed Caesar.
(11)   Sam heard that Mary shot Bill.
(12)   Agatha felt that the boat rocked.

Thus, a different semantic treatment is necessary. If simple sentences routinely contain underlying quantifications over events, it is possible to attribute to the former constructions forms like these:

(13)   Mary saw Brutus stab Caesar = there is an event of seeing whose subject is Mary, and whose object is a stabbing of Caesar by Brutus.

The advantage of these forms is that they validate equivalencies such as the following:

(14)   Mary saw Brutus stab Caesar if and only if Mary saw a stabbing of Caesar by Brutus.

This provides a foundation for a robust set of other equivalencies, such as

(15)   Mary saw Brutus stab Caesar violently if and only if Mary saw a violent stabbing of Caesar by Brutus.

There must be some connection, for example, between the use of 'violent' as an adjective of events and the use of 'violently' as an adverb of event verbs; on the account in question these both contribute the same ingredient to logical form: a predicate true of events.

   The point of this chapter is not to engage in detailed assessment of the evidence just outlined. Instead, I take for granted that it is promising, and I ask whether there is similar evidence for attribution of underlying states in simple stative sentences. In section 2, I assess the evidence known to date, and in section 3, I argue that discourse about time travel provides better evidence.

2. Are There Underlying States for State Sentences?

In this section, I review evidence for underlying states in stative constructions: state verbs, adjectives, locative modifiers, and common nouns. For simplicity, I confine myself throughout to an examination of the logic of modifiers and of perception sentences.

2.1. Underlying States for State Verbs

State verbs include verbs like the following:

(16)   John *has* a dog.
(17)   It *resembles* a small horse.
(18)   Mary *believes* it is friendly.

The question is whether these simple sentences have the simple forms attributed to them in logic texts, or whether they have more complicated forms analogous to those associated with simple sentences with event verbs. Consider example (16). At issue is the contrast between the two kinds of forms in (19a) and (19b):

(19a) $\exists x(\text{Dog}(x) \ \& \ \text{Has}(j, x))$ (no underlying states)
(19b) $\exists x(\text{Dog}(x) \wedge \exists s(\text{Having}(s) \wedge \text{Object}(s, x) \wedge \text{In}(j, s)))$ (underlying states)

2.1.1. The Logic of Modifiers with State Verbs

At first glance there is no evidence to be assessed for modifiers, since the kinds of modifiers that appear with event sentences (primarily adverbials of manner, instrument, and so forth) do not occur with state verbs. The following are not even grammatical:

(20)   *Brutus has a dog quietly.
(21)   *Brutus resembles a cat violently with a knife.

There is a small number of cases in which the constructions occur with locatives and in which there is some tendency to see a positive case for underlying states. Consider the following sentence with the stative reading of *sit*:

(22)   The TV sits on the desk by the lamp.

This allows us to infer either of (23) and (24):

(23)   The TV sits on the desk
(24)   The TV sits by the lamp,

and either of these allows the inference to

(25)   The TV sits.

This *modifier drop-off* is not relevant to the issue before us since it is accounted for by either kind of form—namely, the one based on underlying states and the form not resorting to them. For example, we have

(26a) Sits(TV) $\wedge$ On(TV, desk)
$\therefore$ Sits(TV)

(26b) $\exists s$(Sitting(s) $\wedge$ Theme(s, TV) $\wedge$ On(s, desk)).
$\therefore$ $\exists s$(Sitting(s) $\wedge$ Theme(s, TV)).

But what about *modifier nonconjunction*? The symbolisation without underlying states falsifies this, whereas the one with underlying states satisfies it. The question is which is right. For example, is this a valid inference?

(27) The TV sits on the desk.
The TV sits by the lamp.
$\therefore$ The TV sits on the desk by the lamp.

Normally we would make such an inference without hesitation. But things are not completely clear. Imagine a TV set perched partly on a desk and partly on a table with a lamp on the table next to it. Is this situation a counterexample to this inference? If so, it is evidence for the underlying state form. If not, the general absence of such inferences would seem to favour the simpler form without underlying states. The data here are inconclusive.

2.1.2. Perceptual Idioms with State Verbs

With perception sentences, the situation is clear: the evidence does not occur. The following sentences are not grammatical:

(28) *We watched her believe that snow is white.
(29) *We saw her resemble a unicorn.

This is strange. Suppose that my pony resembles a unicorn and that we find this out by looking and seeing. Why can't we then say that we saw it resemble a unicorn? If the underlying event form for perception sentences with event clauses were correct, the absence of such constructions for state sentences might have a simple explanation: there are no underlying states for state sentences.

2.2. Underlying States for Adjectives

When we turn to adjectives, the issue is between the two sorts of forms in (31a) and (31b):

(30) Mary is clever.

(31a) Clever(m)   (no underlying states)
(31b) $\exists s$(Cleverness(s) $\wedge$ In(m, s)).   (underlying states)

2.2.1. The Logic of Modifiers with Adjectives

Again, the relevant constructions mostly do not occur. We do not have sentences such as:

(32) *Mary is clever in Prague with a knife.

However, examples can be given that seem to favour the underlying state view:

(33)   The board is coarsely grooved.

These constructions favour the underlying state view because they obey the *modifier nonconjunction* phenomenon; the following is not valid:

(34)   The board is coarsely grooved.
        The board is grooved along its edge.
        ∴ The board is coarsely grooved along its edge.

Suppose the board is coarsely grooved across one end and finely grooved along its edge; the premises then can be true without the conclusion. The problem about these constructions is that they seem to occur only when the adjective is spelled like the past participle of a verb: *grooved* is an example. The construction is thus quite restricted and special and cries out for some special explanation;[2] as a result it does not clearly provide strong support for the underlying states option.

2.2.2. Perceptual Idioms with Adjectival Phrases

Adjectives *do* occur in the relevant perception sentences, and the pattern from the event case seems to work fine:

(35)   She saw him naked = There is an event of seeing, whose agent is her, and whose object is a state of his being naked.

If there is to be a good parallel, we also need to have an equivalence between these sentences and ones with explicit reference to states. These do occur, in examples such as

(36)   She saw him naked if and only if she saw his nakedness.

The second clause here has an archaic ring, and not everyone accepts the equivalence. So this is provocative but inconclusive as evidence.

2.3. Underlying States for Locative Prepositional Phrases

With locatives the competing forms are

(37)   Socrates is at the marketplace.

(38a)   At(Soc, m).   (no underlying states)
(38b) $\exists s$(Being-at(s) $\wedge$ Object(s, m) $\wedge$ In(Soc, s)).   (underlying states)

2.3.1. The Logic of Modifiers: Locatives

As usual, both proposed forms satisfy the *modifier drop-off* condition but differ concerning the *modifier nonconjunction* condition. Which is right? In most cases it appears that the *modifier nonconjunction* condition does *not* apply to these cases. The following kind of inference seems generally unproblematic:

(39)   Socrates is in the market.
        Socrates is under an awning.
        ∴ Socrates is in the market under an awning.

There are a few counterexamples to this pattern; consider

(40)   IBM is in Paris.
        IBM is in a hilly region.
        ∴ IBM is in a hilly region in Paris.[3]

But people generally have trouble with cases of this sort, feeling that there is something fishy going on. (In section 4, I speculate about what this is.) Since the counterexamples are few in number and problematic in interpretation, they do not provide compelling evidence for the underlying state account.

2.3.2. Perceptual Idioms with Locatives

These perceptual idioms occur; we have, for example,

(41)   Mary saw Socrates under an awning.

They provide moderate evidence for the underlying state account for copulative sentences with locatives.

2.4. Underlying States for Nouns

The competing analyses here are

(42)   Socrates is a boy.

(43a)   Boy(Soc).   (no underlying states)
(43b) $\exists s(\text{Boy}(s) \wedge \text{In}(s, Soc))$.   (underlying states)

A key part of the assessment of these cases is what happens when the nouns are modified in some way. I assume here a parallel with verbs, so that the competing analyses are those such as

(44)   Socrates is a boy under 1.5 metres tall.

(45a)   Boy(Soc) ∧ Under-1.5(Soc).   (no underlying states)
(45b) $\exists s(\text{Boy}(s) \wedge \text{Under-1.5}(s) \wedge \text{In}(Soc, s))$.   (underlying states)

2.4.1. The Logic of Modifiers with Nouns

Again, both analyses obey the *modifier drop-off* condition, and this seems to be borne out by the data (ignoring special cases such as 'former'). They differ with respect to the *modifier nonconjunction* condition, and here the underlying state approach seems to be wrong because arguments of this sort appear to be valid:

(46)   Socrates is a boy.
        Socrates is under 1.5 metres tall.
        ∴ Socrates is a boy under 1.5 metres tall.

If such inferences are valid, this provides strong evidence against the underlying state approach, which entails that they are invalid. (Below, I suggest that in spite of appearances to the contrary, they are indeed invalid.)

2.4.2. Perceptual Idioms with Nouns

The relevant perceptual constructions do not occur with nouns:

(47)   *I saw her (be) a doctor.

This is consistent with the view that the underlying state view is wrong for nouns.

2.5. Summary

Based on the considerations reviewed above, it would appear that the underlying state analysis is not compelling for any kind of the constructions reviewed here and is not even plausible for some (e.g., for nouns). There are a few outstanding problems that the underlying state analysis might solve, such as how to give a semantics for perception sentences with adjectival clauses, but for the most part the weight of evidence seems to go the other way. In the next section we look at some new evidence.

3. Considerations from Time Travel

Time travel raises a number of fascinating issues for philosophers. Is it possible? If not, why not? If so, what are its consequences? For want of a convincing proof that time travel is impossible, we are free to explore some conceptual puzzles that arise as soon as we contemplate its being carried out. These problems provide nice tests for our concepts of how the world operates. David Lewis has written about some of the problems that arise in cases of time travel, and I agree with his assessment that a world in which time travel takes place is, to us, very strange—strange, but not impossible to conceive. And contemplation of cases of time travel can force us to clarify our theories about ordinary situations.

Consider a story in which time travel takes place, either by means of some marvellous application of scientific principles or by magic or supernatural means; the issues to be discussed don't depend on how it happens. Socrates, let us suppose, at age eighteen, engages in a discussion with Parmenides, the discussion that is portrayed in Plato's dialogue *Parmenides.* So we find Socrates, at high noon on the Ides of March, 452 B.C., sitting outside the city walls and talking to Parmenides. A month later, driven to distraction by the metaphysical conundrums of that conversation, he stumbles into a time warp and travels back in time one year. He emerges from the time warp a year before he stumbled into it. He ponders his discussion with Parmenides for several months, and here he is again on the Ides of March, lying down in the marketplace, cursing the gods.

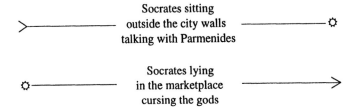

How are we to describe what takes place at noon on the Ides of March, 452 B.C.? Here are some of the things we want to say:

(48)   Socrates is sitting outside the city walls.
       He is sitting outside the city walls talking to Parmenides.
       Socrates is lying in the marketplace.
       He is not lying in the marketplace talking to Parmenides.
       Socrates is not sitting in the marketplace.
       Socrates is Socrates.
       There is only one Socrates.
       Socrates is in two places at the same time.

Let me focus for a moment on the penultimate claim: there is only one Socrates. Obviously, people aware of Socrates in the marketplace and of Socrates outside the city walls, and unaware of the fact of time travel, would assume that these are two distinct but similar people, both named Socrates. But they would be wrong. There is only one person, Socrates. Recall that we are exploring the consequences of a hypothesis, and the hypothesis is that Socrates time-travelled— that is, Socrates entered a time warp and *he* emerged from it a year earlier. The hypothesis is not that some person very like Socrates emerged from the time warp a year earlier; the hypothesis is that *he* did. The hypothesis of time travel entails that the very same person who entered the warp emerged from it at a time at which he already existed. And so, for a year, he overlapped himself in time.

So there is only one Socrates. But this claim seems easy to disprove. Since Socrates is sitting outside the city walls at noon on the Ides of March, he is sitting. Since he is lying in the marketplace, he is in the marketplace. Hence, at noon on that day he is sitting and he is in the marketplace; so he is sitting in the marketplace:

(49)   Socrates is sitting.
       Socrates is in the marketplace.
       ∴ Socrates is sitting in the marketplace.

But that's absurd; for all we know, *nobody* is sitting in the marketplace at noon on the Ides of March. If time travel commits us to conclusions like this, it can't occur.

If this is a good argument, then the scenario we are discussing is impossible, and by parity of reasoning, other cases are as well, and so time travel is impossible. Perhaps some person very like Socrates could emerge from a time machine, but *he* couldn't.

The other option, of course, is that the story under consideration is coherent, and we need a semantics that will avoid the appearance of incoherence. The underlying state semantics discussed in the previous section is just that. If the story is coherent, then it provides most of the missing evidence in favour of underlying states. I review the points at issue in the order in which they are introduced above.

3.1. Underlying States for State Verbs

3.1.1. The Logic of Modifiers with State Verbs

Consider again an argument of this sort:

(50)   Socrates is sitting outside the city walls.
       Socrates is lying in the marketplace.
       ∴ Socrates is sitting in the marketplace.

We can now see that this is invalid. And this invalidity is explained by the underlying state analysis. On this view, the first sentence entails that there is a sitting state that Socrates is in, and the second entails that there is an in-the-marketplace state that he is in. But the conclusion says that these are the *same* state; it says that there is a state that is both a sitting state and an in-the-marketplace state that he is in. So the conclusion says something beyond what is said in the premises.

(51)   For some state s: s is a state of sitting $\land$ Socrates is in s $\land$ s is a state of being outside the city walls.

       For some state s: s is a state of lying $\land$ s is a state of being in the marketplace $\land$ Socrates is in s.

       ∴ For some state s: s is a state of sitting $\land$ s is a state of being in the marketplace $\land$ Socrates is in s.

This inference is just like the inference involving Brutus's stabbing of Caesar; there may have been two stabbings in that case, and in this case there may be two different unrelated states that Socrates is in. Socrates is, in fact, simultaneously in these two different states:

(52)   State 1: sitting, outside the city walls, talking with Parmenides.
       State 2: lying, in the marketplace.

We can't infer that he is sitting in the marketplace because there is no state having both of the properties: being a sitting state and being an in-the-marketplace state. This form of analysis solves the apparent paradox we thought we were led into above. (Here is where it is essential that there is only one Socrates. If there were two Socrates, then one premise in the above argument would refer to one of them and the other premise to the other, and the argument would commit a fallacy of equivocation.)

For the remainder of the cases I merely give the relevant example; the import of the example is clear from the discussion above.

3.1.2. Perceptual Idioms with State Verbs

(53)   She saw him sitting in the marketplace.

This example is grammatical and needs a semantical account. The underlying state theory provides one.

3.2. Underlying States for Adjectives

3.2.1. The Logic of Modifiers with Adjectives

The relevant constructions are still not grammatical; but there are closely related ones that are grammatical and that are explained by the underlying state analysis:

(54)   He is tall over here.
(55)   He is not tall over there.

(These could be handled instead by supposing that *over here* and *over there* create nonextensional contexts. I think that other hypotheses are more plausible, and these also work best with the underlying state approach.[4])

3.2.2. Perceptual Idioms with Adjectival Phrases

These constructions do occur with modals, and they seem to require something like the underlying state analysis:

(56)   Here you can see him tall, and there you can see him short.

3.3. Underlying States for Locative Prepositional Phrases

3.3.1. The Logic of Modifiers: Locatives

The *modifier nonconjunction* phenomenon occurs and is evidence for the underlying state analysis. It explains why this argument is invalid:

(57)   Socrates is under an awning.
       Socrates is in the marketplace.
       ∴ Socrates is in the marketplace under an awning.

3.3.2. Perceptual Idioms with Locatives

The *modifier nonconjunction* phenomenon affects these cases as well. The following is invalid:

(58)   She saw him under an awning.
       She saw him in the marketplace.
       ∴ She saw him under an awning in the marketplace.

3.4. Underlying States for Nouns

3.4.1. The Logic of Modifiers with Nouns

Suppose that Socrates was a boy under 1.5 metres tall talking to Parmenides but that he was a man over 1.5 metres tall lying in the marketplace. Then this is clearly invalid:

(59)   Socrates is a boy under 1.5 metres tall.
       Socrates is a man over 1.5 metres tall.
       ∴ Socrates is a boy over 1.5 metres tall.

Likewise, our test inference for the modified nouns is invalid:

(60)   Socrates is a boy.
       Socrates is over 1.5 metres tall.
       ∴ Socrates is a boy over 1.5 metres tall.

3.4.2. Perceptual Idioms with Nouns

Again, the constructions occur awkwardly with modals and seem to favour the underlying state analysis:

(61)   Here you can see him a boy, and there you can see him a man.

3.5. Summary

Considerations of how we describe what takes place in time-travel stories suggest that there are underlying states in stative sentences involving state verbs and copulative sentences with adjectives, locatives, and nouns.

4. A Problem of Default Information

If there are underlying states in simple state sentences, that leaves us with a problem. Inferences of the following sort are normally made and are normally unproblematic:

(62)   Mary is at the desk.
       Mary is in the living room.
       ∴ Mary is at the desk in the living room.

(63)   She is a doctor.
       She is female.
       ∴ She is a female doctor.

Yet according to the proposed theory they are fallacious. This needs some explanation. I suggest that such inferences are valid enthymemes. There is some background information that we normally presuppose and that renders the inferences valid when conjoined with the premises. The problem is to identify what it is.

The information must include the fact that we are not dealing with a case of time travel. But this is much too special to provide a general solution. Perhaps the key lies in the idea that Socrates can be sitting and be in the marketplace without being sitting in the marketplace *because* he is in two places at once. *We* can't do that because we are not in two places at once. So perhaps the piece of background information is that the entities under discussion are not in two places at once:

(64)   *Typical default assumption*: The entities in question are not in two places at once.

This also meshes with part of the previous evidence discussed in section 2: the reasons that IBM can be in Paris and also in a hilly region without being in a hilly region in Paris is that IBM *is* the sort of entity that can be in two places at once—indeed, in many places at once.

But what is the connection between not being in two places at once and the inferences in question? The following would do the trick:[5]

(65)   If x is not in two places at once, then if x is in state s_1 and x is in state s_2, then $s_1 = s_2$.

Whether this is plausible as an overall account is difficult to assess without additional evaluation.

Notes

1. I discussed the question of extending the theory to state sentences in Parsons (1990) and, earlier, in Parsons (1987/88). I have not been satisfied with the conclusions drawn in either of these earlier works.

2. As in Parsons (1990: §12.7), we can imagine that the adjectives derive from the verbs by a somewhat regular process, and that the adverbs come along for the ride without there being any underlying states.

3. This example is from Barry Schein.

4. See Parsons (1990: §11.2) on frame adverbials.

5. Perhaps this is too strong when we turn our attention to the discussion of mental phenomena. We may need a limitation on the states in question to physical states.

References

Parsons, T., 1987/88. Underlying States in the Semantical Analysis of English. In *Proceedings of the Aristotelian Society* 88: 13–30.

Parsons, T., 1990. *Events in the Semantics of English. A Study in Subatomic Semantics.* MIT Press, Cambridge (Mass.).

4

Do Events Recur?

Johannes L. Brandl

1. Introduction

The idea that events can happen more than once is a familiar one. We often re-
gret that something happened again (e.g., an accident at Kennedy airport) or we
are surprised to see things happen again (e.g., the Jazz beating the Lakers four
times in a row). But can we take this way of speaking literally? Do events *recur*
in the strict sense of this term? This is the question I want to discuss.

There is a widely accepted view in ontology, called *particularism*, according
to which statements about recurring events should be paraphrased as statements
about particular events resembling each other in some way. I critically examine
this position by comparing it with two proposals concerning how a literal understanding of recurrence might be achieved. Although these alternatives are not
convincing in themselves, they suggest a way of restricting the particularist position: there may be a special category of basic events that actually recur in a
literal sense. Admitting this exception to the particularist point of view means
driving a wedge between ontological questions concerning the nature of events,
on the one hand, and linguistic questions concerning our way of talking about
events, on the other.

2. Events as Particulars: The Standard Approach

That events are unrepeatable particulars is the accepted view in the field. It is
common ground both for those who favour a fine-grained principle of individuation, like Kim and Goldman, and those who individuate events in a more
coarse-grained way, like Davidson (for a survey of these issues see Pfeifer 1989
or Stoecker 1992). Since all parties in this dispute agree that events cannot literally recur, it will do no harm if I concentrate on Davidson's theory as representative of the standard approach.

Davidson suggests that many of our ordinary language statements should be
analysed as statements about events. Take, for instance, the sentence

(1)   John kissed Mary.

According to Davidson, this sentence expresses a statement not only about John and Mary but also about the kissing that is going on between them.[1] We can bring this out by introducing a quantifier for each entity involved. (The notation is taken from Parsons 1990):

(2) $\exists e(e$ is a kissing $\wedge$ subject(John, $e)\wedge$ object(Mary, e)).

The advantage of this analysis becomes apparent when we consider adverbial modifications. John may kiss Mary timidly or passionately, he may kiss her in the morning or in the evening, and so on. In Davidson's analysis these adverbial modifiers become predicates, which are ascribed to the event in question. Thus the sentence

(3)   John kissed Mary passionately in the morning

is translated into our semiformal language as

(4) $\exists e(e$ is a kissing $\wedge$ subject(John, $e)\wedge$ object(Mary, e) $\wedge$ e is passionate $\wedge$ e occurs in the morning).

It is worth noting that this analysis by itself does not prove the existence of events. It only links their existence to the truth conditions of sentences. Given that sentence (3) is true and given that (1) is a logical consequence of (3), the proposed analysis provides strong reasons for accepting events in our ontology. If the logical data can be explained otherwise, events may still turn out to be superfluous entities (see Horgan 1978; see also Thalberg 1985 for a response to this kind of attack on events).

It is not these worries that I want to pursue here, however, but a specific problem that arises with sentences like the following:

(5)   John kissed Mary three times.

Is the adverbial modification in (5) also to be represented by adding a conjunctive clause to (2)?

(6) $\exists e(e$ is a kissing $\wedge$ subject(John, $e)\wedge$ object(Mary, e) $\wedge$ e occurs three times).

In Davidson's view (6) would be necessarily false because no event can satisfy the predicate *occurring three times*. If sentence (5) should come out to be true, Davidson needs a different kind of analysis. He suggests that "recurrence may be no more than similar, but distinct, events following one after another" (1970: 184). The same view about recurrence is proposed by Lombard (1986: 63ff, 200f) and in the following remark by Myles Brand: "for the particularist, locutions concerning event recurrence are best understood as locutions about events of the same type occurring" (1976: 143). Applied to our example, this means that we should distinguish as many different token events as there have been cases of kissing:

(7) $\exists e_1 \exists e_2 \exists e_3 (e_1$ is a kissing $\wedge$ subject(John e_1) $\wedge$ object(Mary, e_1) $\wedge$ e_2 is a kissing $\wedge$ subject(John, e_2) $\wedge$ object(Mary, e_2) $\wedge$ e_3 is a kissing $\wedge$ subject(John, e_3) $\wedge$ object(Mary, e_3) $\wedge$ $e_1 \neq e_2 \wedge e_1 \neq e_3 \wedge e_2 \neq e_3$).

This analysis is again supported by the fact that John may kiss Mary three times in three different ways. Whereas his first kiss may be on the cheek, his second may be on the shoulder, and his third one on the lips. Ascribing the corresponding predicates to the three different events distinguished in (7), we get

(8) $\exists e_1 \exists e_2 \exists e_3 (e_1$ is a kissing $\wedge$ subject(John, e_1) $\wedge$ object(Mary, e_1) $\wedge$ e_1 is on the cheek $\wedge$ e_2 is a kissing $\wedge$ subject(John, e_2) $\wedge$ object(Mary, e_2) $\wedge$ e_2 is on the shoulder $\wedge$ e_3 is a kissing $\wedge$ subject(John, e_3) $\wedge$ object(Mary, e_3) $\wedge$ e_3 is on the lips $\wedge$ $e_1 \neq e_2 \wedge e_1 \neq e_3 \wedge e_2 \neq e_3$).

The question now is whether this kind of analysis will work in all cases. Davidson himself considers several hard cases for his theory (see 1970: 184f.). Take, for instance, the sentence

(9)   Jones bought a leopard, and Smith did the same thing.

This sentence is ambiguous because of two possible readings of 'the same thing': Jones and Smith may have bought two different animals or they may have bought the very same animal twice.[2] The following analysis might be suggested to make this ambiguity explicit:

(10)   a. $\exists z(z$ is the buying of a leopard $\wedge$ subject(Jones, z) $\wedge$ subject(Smith, z)).
        b. $\exists x \exists z(x$ is a leopard $\wedge$ z is a buying of x $\wedge$ subject(Jones, z) $\wedge$ subject(Smith, z)).

But for Davidson, (10a) and (10b) are not correct readings of (9). These sentences suggest that Smith and Jones cooperated in performing one individual action, which is not what is meant by (9). To get at the real ambiguity in (9), we must first paraphrase it in the following way:

(11)   Jones and Smith did similar things: they bought something and what they bought was a leopard.

The interpretation of (11) depends on how we explain the similarity of their actions. Two cases of buying may be similar either because their objects are similar, or because their objects are identical. Thus the appropriate readings of (11), and hence of (9), are as follows:

(12)   a. $\exists x \exists y \exists z_1 \exists z_2 (x$ is a leopard $\wedge$ y is a leopard $\wedge$ $x \neq y$ $\wedge$ z_1 is a buying of x $\wedge$ z_2 is a buying of y $\wedge$ subject(Jones, z_1) $\wedge$ subject(Smith, z_2)).
        b. $\exists x \exists y \exists z_1 \exists z_2 (x$ is a leopard $\wedge$ y is a leopard $\wedge$ $x = y$ $\wedge$ z_1 is a buying of x $\wedge$ z_2 is a buying of y $\wedge$ subject(Jones, z_1) $\wedge$ subject(Smith, z_2)).

As this example shows, the trick is to distinguish the relevant respects in which events may be similar. This is not always so easy. Consider the sentence

(13)   He danced the waltz eight times.

This sentence is paraphrased by Davidson (1971: 192) as

(14)   The number of waltzes such that he danced them was eight.

This will not quite do. If our dancer danced eight different waltzes, (13) would be false and (14) would still be true. What we have to count is the number of *similar* waltzes that he danced. But when are two particular dances similar enough so that we can count them as dances of the same waltz? The similarity here might consist in nothing else but the intention of the dancer to do the same thing again. The particularist owes us an explanation of what *intending to do the same thing* means here.

Another problem for Davidson's analysis arises with such sentences as

(15)   A certain event happened exactly twice.

Sentences like this fit the particularist scheme only if the context of utterance provides additional information that could be added in a 'namely' phrase—for example,

(16)   A certain event happened exactly twice, namely, that John kissed Mary.

Davidson classifies sentences like (15) as exceptional cases, which are "less than clear or less than literal" (1971: 193). But in fact such cases are quite common. *John did it three times, Mary enjoyed it every time,* and so on. Do we understand these sentences only after tacitly completing them with information provided by the context of utterance? It seems that they tell us something about John and Mary even if we do not know from the context what exactly the pronoun *it* refers to.

Let me summarise these considerations. We have seen how natural language sentences can be analysed as sentences about events, whereby adverbial modifications provide the main reason for taking this approach. The standard analysis proceeds by adding events to the domain of quantification, where events are taken to be unrepeatable particulars. Sentences that apparently talk about repeatable events are paraphrased as sentences about event reduplications—that is, as statements about a number of different event particulars resembling each other in some respect (though without quantifying over respects). This strategy proves difficult in two sorts of cases: those in which it is hard to specify the similarity relation on which the paraphrase depends, and those in which context information is needed for getting the paraphrase started in the first place. Keeping these difficulties in mind, let us turn to some alternatives to the standard approach.

3. Events as Properties: Montague's Approach

What is the alternative to treating events as particulars? If they are not particulars, they are some sort of universal. The most common sort of universal are properties. So why not treat events as properties? This idea was first put forward by Richard Montague (1969).

Montague starts by distinguishing several kinds of events. First he considers what he calls *instantaneous generic events*. As the term 'instantaneous' indicates, he thereby means events that occur at a certain moment of time (or a short stretch of time), like a sunrise. The term 'generic', on the other hand, indicates that these events are repeatable. Events of this kind, Montague suggests, may be conceived as *properties of moments of time*: "Thus the event of the sun's rising will be the property of being a moment at which the sun rises, and [instantaneous, generic] events in general will form a certain class of properties of moments of time" (1969: 150).

According to this proposal, the occurrence of an event amounts to the exemplification of a certain property by a moment of time. Consequently, for an event to recur means that the same property is exemplified at (or by) different moments of time. Take, for instance, the property *being a moment of time at which the sun rises*. This property is exemplified again and again every day by some moment of time at each place on the Earth. That makes it a daily recurring event.

Apart from these generic events, Montague also introduces *instantaneous individual* events. One way of individuating events is to fix their date. Montague resists this move, however, because he does not want to rule out that, for instance, the individual sunrise of this morning may have occurred a minute earlier or later. This would be impossible if the moment at which an event occurs were part of the property that is exemplified at this moment.[3] But what else could an individual event be? Here is Montague's proposal:

> I propose that the individual risings of x be identified, like other instantaneous events, with properties of moments of time, but in this case with the properties of a great degree of particularity, what we might regard as the various particular occurrences that constitute risings of x. (1969: 176)

Thus individual events are also properties, but properties of such a specificity that every single sunrise is to be identified with a different property. Does this imply that individual events are not repeatable? Not necessarily. The more specific a property is, the less likely that it is exemplified more than once. In the end, Montague suggests, it may be a matter of convenience whether we say that, at two different times, *two risings of x have occurred* or *that a single rising of x has occurred twice* (1969: 177).

What should we think of this theory? I have omitted here the formal apparatus that Montague uses for analysing our event talk in accordance with his theory. His intensional approach requires a much richer language than the simple language of first-order predicate logic used by Davidson. This may count as a disadvantage of his theory, but the use of intensional languages may be justified on independent grounds. The real difficulty with Montague's theory, I think, lies elsewhere: it threatens to conflict with our intuition that events are located in space and time. Properties are usually taken to be abstract entities that exist outside space and time. So how could a concrete event be identical with an abstract property?

In reply to this objection, Montague might deny one of its assumptions—namely, that events are located in space-time or that properties are not so located. But a better reply would be, I think, to make the theory consistent with these assumptions. This is the route taken by Roderick Chisholm.

4. Events as States: Chisholm's Approach

Chisholm originally defended the view that events are a species of (abstract) states of affairs (1970, 1971). In the mid-1980s, however, he changed his theory in accordance with the intuition that events are located in space, and especially in time. I have discussed the development of Chisholm's views on events elsewhere (Brandl 1997); here I concentrate on his position as it is expounded in Chisholm (1985/86, 1989: ch.16, 1990, and forthcoming).

The basic idea behind Chisholm's current theory can be put thus: let events be like properties, but properties that exist *in* space and time. These temporally (and perhaps also spatially) bounded properties Chisholm calls *states*. States are dependent on contingent things: they necessarily exist *at a* contingent substance and they vanish with their bearers. This makes them part of the concrete world. They have temporal and spatial location and they enter into causal relations. (See Chisholm 1985/86: 103; 1989: 152; 1990: 419; and forthcoming).

Still there is a very close relationship between properties and states, as can be seen from the following principle (Chisholm 1985/86: 99; 1989: 150):

(17)   For every x, there is the state x-being-F if and only if x *exemplifies* being-F.

This principle tells us that if, for instance, *redness* (the property of being red) is exemplified by a tomato, the tomato is in a state of which the tomato itself is a constituent. This state ceases to exist when the tomato changes its colour or when the tomato disappears. The colour itself, on the other hand, remains unaffected by any changes in the contingent world.

Now if states are distinguished from properties in this way and if events are identified with states, what happens with the idea of recurrence? In his earlier writings Chisholm made it a constraint on any acceptable theory of events that it should be "adequate to the fact of recurrence, to the fact that there are some things that . . . happen more than once" (1970: 15). Does Chisholm's present theory satisfy this constraint?

Chisholm tries to satisfy it by distinguishing, like Montague, between individual and generic events. He defines a generic event as the *content* of an individual event, that is, of a passing state of an individual thing. If a tomato is in the state of being red, the property of being red would be the content of this state. And this content, Chisholm assures us, is a repeatable generic event.

But isn't this just a terminological manoeuvre? As Chisholm notes himself, his theory is very close to Kim's property-exemplification view of events, which takes events to be particulars (Chisholm 1989: 155 n. 2; 1990: 426, n. 3). The only difference lies in the fact that Chisholm prefers tensed properties whereas

Kim makes use of moments of time. Of course, Chisholm can *call* certain properties generic events, but the real events in his theory, one would like to say, are the contingent states of things. And these do not recur.

Thus far our efforts to find a theory that allows us to take statements about recurrent events literally has not been successful. Either the proposed theory turned out to violate our intuitions about the spatiotemporal location of events or it threatened to collapse into a version of the particularist view. Before we retreat to this view, however, we should consider one final alternative.

5. Events as Concrete Universals

If events are not particulars, they must be universals. But they need not be properties, as in Montague's or in Chisholm's theory. What other universals could they be?

Consider once more the category of states. Chisholm assumes that every state is a *one-time thing*. He justifies this by the metaphysical principle that *nothing is capable of two beginnings of existence* (1970: 17; 1989: 153; forthcoming). But why should we accept this principle? It has no better foundation than, for instance, the principle that no entity can exist at the same time at different places. This latter principle is thrown into doubt by the existence of masses. It is possible to conceive of masses, like water or gold, as a nonindividual stuff that exists wherever there is water or gold around. Similarly, generic events could exist in time and yet have more than one beginning, thus violating the principle Chisholm takes for granted. They would then belong, together with masses, to the category of *concrete universals*.

The concept of a concrete universal is a controversial one. In the case of masses it must be defended against a position that identifies masses with spatially discontinuous individuals, what Quine calls *scattered objects* (1960: §§19–20). I will not try such a general defence here. All I need, for the sake of argument, is the idea that masses may be a special kind of stuff, irreducible to the category of individuals. This idea is based on two mereological principles. On the one hand, individual things are divided into parts, where each part is a *different* individual. For instance, if you cut an apple in half, you get two new individuals. Masses, on the other hand, are divided into quantities, where each quantity is the very *same* mass. If you divide a pool of water, what you get is just water again. (The two pools are new individuals but not new masses.) This still leaves a lot of questions open, but it suffices for our present purposes. (For a deeper inquiry into the ontology of masses see Zimmerman 1995.)

Granted that masses could be concrete universals, could events be, too? In a remarkable passage Davidson attempts to show that "even if one allows only particular, unrepeatable events, then, it is possible to give a literal meaning to the claim that the same event occurs on two or more occasions." This is how it is supposed to go:

> One way is this: events have parts that are events, and the parts may be discontinuous temporally or spatially (think of a chess tournament, an ar-

gument, a war). Thus the *sum* of all my droppings of saucers of mud is a particular event, one of whose parts (which was a dropping of a saucer of mud by me) occurred last night; another such part occurred tonight. We need three events to carry this off, but they have the same ontological status. (1970: 184)

Davidson does not pursue this proposal any further, considering it as too obscure. "Is this strange event-sum", he asks, "really what we refer to when we say, 'The same thing happened again'?" (1970: 184). However, the obscurity of the proposal may result only from the particular examples Davidson uses. We simply do not know what it means to add one dropping of a saucer to another dropping of a saucer. And in the case of chess games, where such an addition makes sense, we do not get a larger event of the same kind but a completely new kind of event—namely, a tournament.

What one needs to make the parallel between generic events and masses plausible are *homogeneous* events, that is, events picked out by terms that satisfy the following two conditions: (1) if P applies to an entity e, then it also applies to the parts of e, and (2) if P applies to entities e_1 and e_2, then it also applies to the mereological sum of e_1 and e_2. Mass terms like 'water' and 'gold' satisfy these conditions (or conditions very similar to these; see Higginbotham 1994: 455 ff.). The question is this: Are there any event predicates that pass this test?

The only candidates that come to my mind are predicates like *growing, increasing, moving*, and so on. If something grows, that is an event each part of which is itself a case of growing. And if the temperature increases at different times or at different places, we can imagine the sum of these events as a more extensive increasing of temperature. This seems the closest we can get to homogeneous events.

What should we say about this concrete universal approach? I think it has several interesting consequences, partly vindicating and partly undermining the particularist viewpoint. First, in this approach recurrence turns out to be a quite rare phenomenon. Most of the events that we commonly talk about are not homogeneous and therefore cannot recur. Only a rather small number of events may be said to happen all the time at various places and times. Just as a great number of individuals are made up of few kinds of stuff, so a large number of individual events would be made up of a few generic events.

This implies, second, that no theory of events can be correct that treats recurrence as an all-or-nothing affair—that is, that holds that either all kinds of events are repeatable or none. This assumption is shared both by the particularist theory and by the alternative theories proposed by Montague and Chisholm.

Third, it is not to be expected that the two kinds of events—those that can recur and those that cannot—can be distinguished on linguistic grounds. In this respect the situation may be different from the case of masses. Terms that designate masses might be picked out by syntactic and/or semantic criteria (cf. Pelletier and Schubert 1989). No similar procedure is in sight for distinguishing terms for generic events like *growth* and *movement* from terms for individual events like *accident* or *game*. The distinction would have to be made on purely ontological grounds without a linguistic foundation.

Finally, a defender of the concrete universal approach can agree with the particularist that our talk about recurrent events is a loose way of speaking, not to be taken seriously from an ontological point of view. The reason for this, however, is different from that which a particularist thinks. It is not that events, by their very nature, are unrepeatable. The explanation is that there are only very few events for which recurrence is possible. What is misleading in our common way of talking about recurring events is not the notion of recurrence itself but the liberal way in which we apply this notion.

Notes

1. I follow here the common practice of treating actions as a kind of event. I also ignore the distinction between sentences and statements. Both distinctions are irrelevant for my present concerns.

2. Davidson draws attention to a further ambiguity in the sentence *Jones bought a leopard for his wife and Smith did the same thing*. This could mean that Smith bought the same (or a different) leopard either for Jones's wife or for his own wife. I am not concerned with these further complications here.

3. Montague (1969: 175) does not reject dated properties of moments of time in general; he only thinks that not all instantaneous individual events are of that type.

References

Brand, M., 1976. Particulars, Events, and Action. In M. Brand and D. Walton (eds.), *Action Theory*, 133–157. Reidel, Dordrecht.

Brandl, J. L., 1997. Recurrent Problems—On Chisholm's Two Theories of Events. In E. L. Hahn (ed.), *The Philosophy of Roderick Chisholm*, 457–477. Open Court, Chicago.

Chisholm, R. M., 1970. Events and Propositions. In *Noûs* 4: 15–24.

Chisholm, R. M., 1971. States of Affairs Again. In *Noûs* 5: 179–189.

Chisholm, R. M., 1985/86. On the Positive and Negative States of Things. In *Grazer Philosophische Studien* 25/26: 97–106.

Chisholm, R. M., 1989. *On Metaphysics*. University of Minnesota Press, Minneapolis.

Chisholm, R. M., 1990. Events Without Times. An Essay on Ontology. In *Noûs* 24: 413–428.

Chisholm, R. M., forthcoming. Substances, States, Processes and Events. To appear in G. Haefliger and P. Simons (eds.), *Analytical Phenomenology*. Kluwer, Dordrecht.

Davidson, D., 1970. Events as Particulars. In *Noûs* 4: 25–32. Cited from the reprint in Davidson, D., 1980. *Essays on Actions and Events*, 181–187. Clarendon Press, Oxford.

Davidson, D., 1971. Eternal vs. Ephemeral Events. In *Noûs* 5: 335–349. Cited from the reprint in Davidson, *Essays on Actions and Events*, 189–203.

Horgan, T., 1978. The Case Against Events. In *Philosophical Review* 87: 28–47.

Higginbotham, J., 1994. Mass and Count Quantifiers. In *Linguistics and Philosophy* 5: 448–480.

Lombard, L. B., 1986. *Events. A Metaphysical Study*. Routledge & Kegan Paul, London.

Montague, R., 1969. On the Nature of Certain Philosophical Entities. Reprinted in R. H. Thomason (ed.), *Formal Philosophy. Selected Papers of Richard Montague*, 148–187. Yale University Press, New Haven (Conn.).

Parsons, T., 1990. *Events in the Semantics of English. A Study in Subatomic Semantics*. MIT Press, Cambridge (Mass.).

Pelletier, F. J., and L. K. Schubert, 1989. Mass Expressions. In D. Gabbay and F. Guenther (eds.) *Handbook of Philosophical Logic*, vol. 4, 327–407. Reidel, Dordrecht.

Pfeifer, K., 1989. *Actions and Other Events: The Unifier-Multiplier Controversy*. Peter Lang, Frankfurt.

Quine, W., 1960. *Word and Object*. MIT Press, Cambridge (Mass.).

Stoecker, R., 1992. *Was sind Ereignisse?* De Gruyter, Berlin.

Thalberg, I., 1985. A World Without Events. In B. Vermazen and M. Hintikka (eds.), *Essays on Davidson. Actions and Events*, 137–155. Basil Blackwell, Oxford

Zimmerman, D., 1995. Theories of Masses and Problems of Constitution. In *Philosophical Review* 104: 53–110.

5

Causation, Contexts, and Event Individuation

Regine Eckardt

1. Introduction

The kind of events used in linguistic theories are rather coarse-grained. For the purpose of tense semantics, it is sufficient to identify events with intervals of time. Although this view will not be tenable for more subtle phenomena, people still agree that events can have several properties and be described in various ways. Parsons (1990), for instance, suggests a rule that "every stabbing is a killing". Or, we would like to be allowed to assume that if Sue repaired something in e, and this something was indeed her car, then Sue repaired her car in e. There is a philosophical tradition, however, that perceives events as very fine-grained objects. This tradition was originated by a suggestion by Davidson (1969) to individuate events: two events e and f are identical iff they have the same causes and effects. If this criterion is adopted, the linguist's simple objects are no longer sophisticated enough. Tension arises as soon as the linguist starts using event causation. Using a *CAUSE* relation between events is appealing in certain cases. Should the linguist, then, reshape his ontology to make sure that the *CAUSE* relation does the right things? This question has never been answered thoroughly.

The structure of this chapter is the following: I start by presenting two examples that demonstrate why causation seems to require fine-grained events. Next, I discuss Lewis's definition of *CAUSE* as a relation between events. I show that he misuses the fine-grainedness of events to hide shortcomings in his theory. A repair of Lewis is then developed, based on a suggestion by Dowty for a *CAUSE* relation between propositions. This new *CAUSE* is still a relation between events. The new theory does not make any claims about the nature of events in and of itself. I show that the philosophical notion of events leads to wrong predictions in certain, up to now unnoticed cases. I thus suggest using the Dowty-style *CAUSE* with linguistic events and reanalysing the prominent counterexamples as counterfactual statements involving a focus. I show that this perspective leads to interesting predictions in a wide range of examples, including the problematic cases above.

2. Event Individuation by Causal Relations

Davidson (1969) suggests the following criterion to individuate events: two events are identical if and only if they have the same causes and effects. At least one direction of this equivalence is a necessity, once we assume that events stand in causal relations. Let me give two examples that illustrate why this assumption leads to events that differ only in very subtle ways.

(1)   a. Pat came home late last night because of a traffic jam. She started cooking spaghetti at 11 P.M. which caused the neighbour to call the police.

     b. The traffic jam caused Pat's cooking spaghetti.   (false)

     c. The traffic jam caused Pat's cooking spaghetti late.   (true)

    ∴ The event of Pat's cooking spaghetti is not the same event as the event of Pat's cooking spaghetti late.

(2)   a. Bob was tied to the railway line where the train would pass in a few minutes. However, the departure of the train from the preceding station was delayed. Therefore Bob was still alive when Pat accidentally came by and could rescue him. Just when she had pulled him off the railway, the train thundered past.

     b. The delayed departure caused Bob's rescue.   (true)

     c. The departure caused Bob's rescue.   (false)

    ∴ The train's departure is not the same event as the train's delayed departure.

Whereas the linguist would be happy to have only *one* event of cooking or only *one* event of departure, the philosopher will have to accept at least two. These events admittedly look very similar, and it was claimed (see, e.g., Lewis 1973) that the difference between such events was due to the choice of properties that are essential for the respective event. Thus, the event e_1 of the train's departure can occur at earlier times in other worlds. The event e_2 of the train's delayed departure, on the other hand, necessarily occurs too late. We will see where this leads us.

3. Lewis: A Formal Theory of Causation

David Lewis (1973) has set up a formal theory of event causation, building on Davidson's intuitive notion of event causation. Starting out from his theory of counterfactual implication, Lewis gives the following definition:

(D.1) The relation O is a unary relation on the domain of events. $O(e)$ is true in
        a world w iff e occurs in w.
        An event c causes an event e, $c\ CAUSE\ e$, iff
        a. $O(c) \Box\!\!\rightarrow O(e)$ and
        b. $\neg O(c) \Box\!\!\rightarrow \neg O(e)$.

If the events e and c both occur in w, then condition (a) is trivially true and (b)
roughly says: "If c had not occurred, e would not have either." This seems to be
a correct way to formalise the kind of reasoning we actually do to establish c as
a cause of e. However (D.1) turns out to have the tendency of mistaking necessary preconditions as causes. Let us look at an example:

(3)   Imagine that Joe had a bad accident, e_1, in 1989. Luckily, Dr. Spock came
        by and give first aid (e_2). He managed to get Joe's heart beating again (e_3)
        and thus saved his live. One year later, Pat (who is a member of the
        mafia) shot at Joe (e_4). Joe died as a consequence of the shot (e_5).[1]

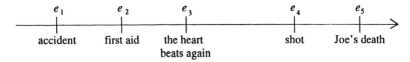

Intuitively one would like to find two causal relations in this diagram: $e_2\ CAUSE$
e_3 and $e_4\ CAUSE\ e_5$. Lewis's definition however, if innocently applied, makes the
prediction that, for instance, $e_2\ CAUSE\ e_5$ because, if Dr. Spock had not saved
Joe's life in 1989, the actual death would not have occurred in 1990.

    Lewis tries to come up with a solution for this problem by discussing the cir-
cumstances in which an event e occurs in some possible world and those in
which it doesn't. The notion of occurrence is a central ingredient of Lewis's
theory and interacts with the notion of essential property: if an event e occurs in
a world w, then it has to have all its essential properties in w. On the other hand,
if something occurs in w that has all essential properties of e, then e does occur
in w. (It is easy to check that (D.1) relies on these assumptions.) However, a
fine-grained distinction of events does not help to avoid $e_2\ CAUSE\ e_5$. Let me
show why.

    If we take Lewis's writings seriously, we must assume that his reaction to ex-
ample (3) would be as follows: when uttering a sentence such as

(4)   Dr. Spock's first aid caused Joe's death

we never know which one of a multitude of events of *Dr. Spock's first aid* we
are referring to. Context will make clear how *stable* or *fragile* the event referred
to must be.[2] If we argue, for example, that

(5)   Dr. Spock's first aid caused Joe's heart to start beating again

is a true sentence, we assume that we talk about an event $e_2{}'$ of first aid and an
event $e_3{}'$ of heartbeat with the following properties: $e_2{}'$ is comparatively stable—
that is, we have to go to remote possible worlds in order for $e_2{}'$ not to occur.

Event e_3' on the other hand is comparatively fragile—that is, it ceases to occur easily enough as we move away from the actual world. Thus, in worlds where e_2' does not occur (= far away), e_3' does not either; therefore sentence (4) is true.

Can we make use of this kind of reasoning to prevent the causation relation between Dr. Spock's first aid and Joe's actual death? We want to argue that (4) is false. Thus, we have to show that there are worlds where Dr. Spock's first aid does not occur but Joe's death still does. We can either claim that the event e_2'' we refer to in (4) is so fragile that it easily ceases to occur. In particular, we have to find worlds where this actual first aid does not occur yet Dr. Spock does something to save Joe's life. In such worlds $\neg O(e_2'') \wedge O(e_5)$ holds true. Therefore e_2'' does not cause Joe's death. Alternatively, we can claim that the event e_5'' denoted by 'Joe's death' in (4) is very stable. It even occurs in worlds where Dr. Spock's help, e_2'', does not occur, and therefore there are again worlds where $\neg O(e_2'') \wedge O(e_5'')$ holds true. This kind of event of Joe's death can probably be described as *Joe's death no matter when*.

Lewis claims that our choice of events is contextually driven. Context tells us what is essential for the event in question: "Don't say: here we have the events—how fragile are they? . . . Our standards of fragility might be both vague and shifty. . . . [The] resolution of vagueness is influenced by context" (1986: 196ff.). However, there is no independent notion of context in the examples above. The term "context" is used to hide our pretheoretic intuitions. In short, "context" can tell us which standards of fragility to use iff this "context" knows whether we want to prove or reject a causation relation.

I conclude that the distinction of causes and necessary preconditions cannot be made by relying on the fact that each event-denoting expression can refer to many events of varying stability. It may be useful in other respects to have many events at hand, but it is not with respect to this problem.

I also refuse the following kind of answer: "Maybe Dr. Spock's first aid does cause Joe's death one year later, in an abstract sense". This kind of extension of a theory to the borderline cases may be an elegant simplification in some cases, but it is not here. It would, for example, not be able to explain why we have an intuitive notion of *occurrence of an event* and of *causation*. If we stick to the good intuitions about event occurrence, we get the bad causations and vice versa. In a good theory, however, the good intuitions about the objects and concepts involved should converge in the core cases, and the shaky intuitions should correlate to the borderline cases.

4. Dowty's Repair

The definition of causal dependence in (D.1) was made in such a way that one of the two defining clauses would always be trivially true or false. We now develop a modified version of (D.1) by getting both clauses to work.

What really happened in the above example was that necessary preconditions c of later events e had a strong tendency to be analysed as causes of e. We can fruitfully construct hard cases for Lewis by telling stories in which some necessary precondition c of e took place but without literally causing e. The kind of examples that will contradict our intuitions most clearly is of the following shape. Assume that some event c takes place at some time and that it prevents another event e, which would otherwise have taken place, from happening. For instance, Carol might find and switch off a ticking bomb, which would have otherwise exploded and destroyed the White House. Assume, moreover, that this makes it possible for some other event of the same kind as e to occur later. In our example, the bomb might be reused years later to blow up the Kremlin. One would clearly hesitate to say that Carol's finding the bomb caused the Kremlin to explode. Yet, this is what our theory predicts. Sentence (4) is an example of this kind.

Why are we so sure that Pat's shooting at Joe was cause for him to die but not Dr. Spock's first aid? In some sense, we seem to think that Joe might have lived on for many years after the first aid he was given by Dr. Spock. Nothing at the time of Joe's accident in 1989 points in a direction that inevitably leads to Pat's shot one year later.[3] There are possible worlds close to the actual one where Dr. Spock's first aid occurs but *not* the alleged effect, Joe's death from a shot in 1990. Causes, however, should in the simplest case always lead to the effects, as long as no mystery occurs in between.

Can we flesh out condition (D.1.a) so as to capture this observation? Lewis himself made a similar suggestion in order to handle a different problematic case: some course of events may be transferred into other worlds where "it keeps its intrinsic features" and exhibits the same sort of behaviour, but matters differ in other respects (1986: 206f.). Lewis added that such an operation was not in the spirit of his whole enterprise. The problem is that standing in any other world, we will always find a world in which both c and e occur and which is very similar to the actual world—namely, the actual world itself. We can't say something like (6):

(6)   An event c causes an event e iff
        a. For all worlds where $\neg(O(c) \wedge O(e))$, there is a world w' that is closer
           to the actual world and where $(O(c) \wedge O(e))$ holds true.
        b. $\neg O(c) \: \square\!\!\rightarrow \neg O(e)$.

In Lewis's framework we always decide relative to a (counterfactual) proposition Φ how close a possible world w is to the actual one. (In fact, Lewis only *compares* possible worlds where Φ is true in their relative closeness to the actual world, where Φ is false.) So, there is nothing like a set of worlds being *close* to ours in any absolute term.

Dowty (1979) discusses Lewis's notion of causation and notes the theory's tendency to mix up necessary preconditions with causes. He develops a modification that mimics our desired definition (6). His definition does not provide an absolute criterion to distinguish causes from preconditions. The perspective is the following: Lewis's theory gives us an enormous number of causes for every event. We want to find the "strongest" causes—those that can be already omitted by making minimal changes in the actual world. To find the strongest causes, we compare the possible causes pairwise. This is Dowty's definition, adapted for the event case:

(D.2) a. *e depends causally on c* iff $O(e)$, $O(c)$, and $\neg O(c) \,\Box\!\!\rightarrow\, \neg O(e)$.

    b. c is a *causal factor* for e iff there is a series of events $c, c_1, \ldots, c_n, e$ ($n \geq 0$) such that each member of the series depends causally on the previous member.

    c. 'c *CAUSE e*' is true iff c is a causal factor for e and, for all other c' such that c' is a causal factor for e and all $\neg(O(c) \wedge O(c'))$-worlds w in which $\neg O(c')$ is true, there is some $\neg O(c)$-world w' which is equally or more similar to the actual world w_0 than the other $\neg(O(c) \wedge O(c'))$-worlds. As a formula:

$$\forall w(w \vDash \neg O(c') \rightarrow \exists w'(w' \vDash O(c') \wedge \neg O(c) \wedge d(w_0, w') \leq d(w_0, w)))$$

where d measures the distance of w_0 from counterfactual worlds induced by the counterfactual formula $\neg(O(c) \wedge O(c'))$.

Apart from adapting Dowty's definition for the event case, I have included some refinements while keeping the idea that we compare weightier causes and lighter causes. The differences are of a rather technical nature. The definitions will have to be refined even more if we want them to work in cases in which more than two potential causes for an event are to be compared. They should result in a partial order among a finite set of potential causes. I omit such details here.

Let us look at our examples again to see how (D.2) works. What about the first aid e_2 of Dr. Spock in 1989, in comparison to Pat's shooting e_4 in 1990? Now we are allowed to rely on an intuitive notion of occurrence: $\neg O(e_2)$ holds true in worlds where, basically, Dr. Spock does nothing for Joe. In these worlds Joe dies in 1989. In the same way, Pat's shooting does not occur if Pat does nothing, and Joe's death e_5 does not occur if Joe dies at another occasion, under different circumstances. Thus we find that both, e_2 and e_4 stand in the crucial counterfactual relation to Joe's death e_5. But what will worlds look like where either e_2, e_4, or both do not occur? Worlds where e_4 (= Pat's shooting) but not e_2 (= the first aid) occurs are rather outlandish. These are the worlds with Joe's spontaneous self-healing or other miracles. So we can ignore these as candidates for *most similar worlds*. If e_2 does not occur, e_4 does not happen either in the more similar worlds. A lot more things do not happen also—for example, everything Joe did between 1989 and 1990. Thus, we can claim that the worlds in which $\neg O(e_4)$ and $O(e_2)$ hold are closer to the actual world than those in which $\neg O(e_2) \wedge \neg O(e_4)$. The following holds true:

(7) $\forall w(w \vDash \neg O(e_2) \rightarrow \exists w'(w' \vDash O(e_2) \wedge \neg O(e_4) \wedge d(w_0, w') \leq d(w_0, w)))$.

On the other hand, the same does not hold true for e_2 as a cause for Joe's death. The following is *false*.

(8) $\forall w(w \vDash \neg O(e_4) \rightarrow \exists w'(w' \vDash O(e_4) \wedge \neg O(e_2) \wedge d(w_0, w') \leq d(w_0, w)))$.

The closest worlds are those in which e_4 does not occur but e_2 still does. Thus, in comparison to the more stable e_4 (Pat's shooting), e_2 (Dr. Spock's first aid) is ruled out as a possible cause. We can derive this without any additional assumptions about the essential properties of the event of Dr. Spock giving first aid to Joe.

5. A Problematic Case

Note that the Dowty-style analysis (D.2) does not solve the linguist's problem of having too many events. It avoids certain misuses of the lavish richness of the domain of events. However, examples like (1) and (2) above still motivate a rich event ontology. It is interesting that (D.2) in and of itself does not provide an independent identity criterion either. The framework will be flexible enough to host any kind of event. It is our raw intuition about sentences such as (1b) and (1c) and (2b) and (2c) that calls for a fine-grained individuation.

Let me reconsider (1) in the new framework. If we ask ourselves which of the two cooking events, the cooking of spaghetti, *cs*, or the late cooking of spaghetti, *csl*, is the one that causes the neighbour to call the police, (D.2) will give a clear answer: although both events qualify as potential causes, it is only the more fragile *csl* that actually stands in the *CAUSE* relation to the neighbour's call (*d*):

$$(csl \; CAUSE \; d) \land \neg(cs \; CAUSE \; d).$$

This does not run against our intuition. However, it leads to serious problems in the analysis of sentences of the following kind:

(9)   If Pat's cooking had occurred earlier, it would not have caused the neighbour to call the police.

The first sentence refers to an event of Pat's cooking spaghetti which can occur at earlier times in other possible worlds. It might, for instance, refer to *cs*. It may, however, not refer to *csl* because wherever *csl* occurs, it occurs late. The second sentence takes up the event with the anaphoric pronoun *it*. The sentence counterfactually states that *it* would not have stood in a certain causal relation. This presupposes that *it* actually *does* stand in that causal relation in the *actual* world. (Otherwise we would be allowed to say: ". . . it would not have caused the neighbour to call the police *either*", which is certainly odd in the above scenario.) However, the event that causes the call in the actual world is *csl*, the essentially late event of Pat's cooking spaghetti. But exactly this event was not a possible denotation for *it*. Therefore, we cannot represent a sentence like (8) in our theory of causation.

Definitions in the tradition of (D.1) and (D.2) have the effect that an event can hardly occur in other worlds without its causes and effects. An event that causes something else to happen will keep all the properties that are necessary for the causal relation in all worlds where it occurs. Therefore an event can only occur without causing if certain external parameters have changed that are also necessary for the causation to take place. The event *csl* of essentially cooking spaghetti late can then only occur without causing the call if the neighbour is deaf, for example.

However, sentence (9) demonstrates that we quite naturally talk about events that occur *without* causing what they actually *do* cause in the real world. And we do not have in mind any external changes like a change in the neighbour's perceptive abilities. This observation can't be explained in the framework discussed so far.

6. Two Kinds of Causal Statements

The conclusion to draw from examples like (9) is one that is not breathtakingly new at all:

(10)   There are sentences of the form *the A caused the B,* where *the A* and *the B* refer to events *a* and *b,* which are *not* equivalent to *a CAUSE b.*

Let us call these sentences *pseudocausal sentences* in contrast to *true causal sentences.* The existence of pseudocausal sentences was already noted by Davidson (1969). A more recent discussion to the same end can be found in Bennett (1988). Dowty (1979) doesn't have to face these questions because he defines causation as a relation between propositions, not events. He can leave the linguistic notion of *event* untouched but has to pay the prize: events no longer cause.

Remember that our final definition of *CAUSE* in (D.2) was such that it could be used with both linguistic events and philosophical events. In the rest of the chapter I elaborate (10) in such a way that

> *CAUSE* is understood as a relation between linguistic (= coarse-grained) events.

All alleged counterexamples are understood as pseudocausal sentences—that is, not referring to a causal statement *a CAUSE b.* I interpret pseudocausal sentences as counterfactual statements that involve a focus. This motivates my distinction between true causal sentences and pseudocausal sentences on independent grounds and at the same time gives a comparatively precise answer to the question "what do pseudocausal sentences say?"

I claim that there is an essential difference between true causal statements and pseudocausal statements. Let me repeat two examples:

(11)   The delayed departure caused Bob's rescue.
(12)   Dr. Spock's first aid caused Joe's heart to start beating again.

Sentence (12) will qualify as a true causal statement. We refer to the event e_1 of Dr. Spock's first aid, and to the event e_2 of Joe's heart starting to beat, and the world is such that nonoccurrence of the first would have resulted in the nonoccurrence of the second. In (11), however, matters are different. We refer to the event d of the delayed departure and the event r of Bob's rescue. But if the departure had not occurred, the rescue would have taken place all the more. I assume that (11) rather expresses that "if the departure had occurred *in a different manner* (e.g., at an earlier time), then the rescue would not have occurred". The difference between true causal statements and pseudocausal statements is this:

(13)   True causal statements talk about the nonoccurrence of certain events. Pseudocausal statements talk about the occurrence of events in a different manner.
There is no event so fragile that it could not occur in a different manner.[4]

I assume that pseudocausal statements are formally distinguished from true causal statements in that the former are understood with a focus on the crucial property. I now demonstrate that recent theories about focus can be used to straightforwardly derive the meaning of pseudocausal statements. I do not go into a formal definition of the *focus semantic value of a sentence*. However, my informal discussion is based on the interpretation of focus developed by Rooth (1985, 1992), and my terminology is coherent with his theory. If we manage to elaborate (13) in a satisfying manner, then events will prove to be solid causes and effects without becoming useless for linguistic purposes.

7. Some True Causal Statements

We distinguish true causal statements from pseudocausal statements in that the former do not contain a focus and are interpreted along definition (D.2), whereas the latter are distinguished by having a focus feature on some property in the description of the events involved, and consequently are interpreted in a different manner. In this section, we interpret some sentences as true causal statements and see what the result is. I sometimes call them *causal statements* for short, to avoid the puzzling question of "whether a true causal statement is true".
Let us begin with

(14)   Pat's cooking spaghetti, *cs*, caused the neighbour's calling the police, *d*.

This sentence, if interpreted as a causal statement, is true iff the relation

$$(cs\ CAUSE\ d)$$

holds true because of definition (D.2). We have noted in section 5 that *cs*, the event of cooking spaghetti, will in any case be a potential cause for *d*, the call. However, in section 5 we have still maintained the picture that there was another potential cause, *csl*, the cooking-spaghetti-late event. We have given up this assumption in the meantime. We assume, in best linguistic tradition, that there is only one event of cooking, which is a cooking of spaghetti, which occurs late, which is performed by Pat, and so on. Therefore *cs* has no longer to compete with other potential causes, apart from very weak ones such as the invention of the telephone, Pat's birth, and so on. We thus find that (*cs CAUSE d*) holds true, because of definition (D.2). Sentence (14) is true in our world.
The sentence

(15)   Pat's cooking spaghetti late caused the neighbour's calling the police

is true for the same reasons because (15) expresses the same causal statement as (14). The expressions 'Pat's cooking spaghetti' and 'Pat's cooking spaghetti late' denote the same event.

Now consider the sentence

(16)　The (late) departure, e, caused the rescue, r.

If we interpret (16) as a causal statement, we predict that it will be true if and only if the relation

$$(e \ CAUSE \ r)$$

holds true, because of definition (D.2). However, we have noted already that the nonoccurrence of e means that the train does not leave the station at all. In worlds where the train does not leave the station, Bob will be rescued in any case: Pat will come by, will find him lying on the railway, and free him. Therefore, e does not even qualify as a potential cause for r. Sentence (16) will be predicted to be false. (This prediction is elegantly confirmed in section 8.)

The following sentence will also be false if interpreted as a causal statement:

(17)　The traffic jam, t, caused Pat's cooking spaghetti late, cs.

As in (14) and (15), there is only one event, cs, of Pat's cooking spaghetti. If the traffic jam had not occurred, then Pat would still have cooked spaghetti, just somewhat earlier. Therefore, the relation ($t \ CAUSE \ cs$) does not hold. (Note that matters would be different had we assumed that Pat originally had intended to go to a restaurant and only cooked spaghetti because the restaurants had already closed when she came home.)

Sentence (12) is another example that becomes true if interpreted as a causal statement. I do not go through the computations.

We have seen whether some sentences are true or false if interpreted as a (true) causal statement. The results are acceptable for sentences (12), (14), and (15). However, for (16) and (17) we are left with a problem. After all, we had the feeling that they should be true in *some* sense, if they are uttered in the scenarios I gave in (1) and (2). In the next section I show that they are true if they are interpreted as pseudocausal statements (with a certain focus structure).

8. Pseudocausal Statements

Let me start from the by now well-known sentence (16) in order to give an outline of the interpretation of pseudocausal statements. I propose that we take (16) to mean something like this: "If the departure had not occurred in a *delayed* manner, then Bob would not have been rescued". To evaluate this sentence, we have to check in *nearby worlds*, where the departure was not delayed, and see whether the rescue takes place therein. However, when looking for these nearby worlds, we take into account that the departure must have a property contrasting with the delay. The departure should not be omitted altogether but should occur *early* or *in time*.

It has been shown that focusing an expression in a sentence always results in evoking a set of logically and contextually appropriate *alternatives* to the focused expression (see, among others, Krifka 1991 and Rooth 1992). Focus associates with operators that compute the value of the sentence by taking these alternatives into account. For a thorough discussion of these mechanisms, the reader is referred to Rooth (1992). Let us for now denote the set of focus alternatives for an expression α by $[\![\alpha]\!]_f$. Focus alternatives for *delayed* in (16) will be, for example, $[\![delayed]\!]_f = \{earlier, in\ time\}$.[5] As the alternatives may depend on the context in which a sentence is uttered, the set of alternatives is not determined uniquely. However, this notion of "context" is not circular, in contrast to the one in section 1. We know this use of "context" from examples that have nothing to do with causation, and we rely on the same kind of "context" in the present examples. The set of alternatives is further restricted on logical and linguistic grounds. There is no danger of misusing it as a waste bin for unresolved cases of causation.

I assume that (16) is uttered with a focus on 'delayed'. The set of focus alternatives is used to compute the set of possible worlds over which we quantify in a counterfactual statement. In short, sentence (18) is interpreted as in (19). I have spelled out Lewis's symbol '□→' of counterfactual implication as quantification over "nearby" possible worlds. Consequently, the world parameter has to turn up at all places where a world-dependent property is ascribed. To this end, an index w is exploited.[6]

(18)   The [delayed]$_{focus}$ departure caused Bob's rescue.

(19) $\forall w([\neg\exists e(\text{departure}_w(e) \wedge \text{delayed}_w(e) \wedge \exists Q \exists e_1 (Q \in [\![\text{delayed}_f\ \text{departure}]\!]_f$
        $\wedge\ Q_w(e_1))] \rightarrow \neg\exists e_2(\text{rescue}_w(e_2) \wedge \text{theme}_w(e_2, \text{BOB})))$.

Note that (19) involves existential formulas instead of making reference to events e and r in other worlds. I am open to any reformulation of the meaning of (18) in this respect. What is important is that the set of relevant alternative worlds is restricted by the focus alternatives of the property in focus. Let me comment on this point.

It was already pointed out by Dretske (1972) that focus may restrict the choice of possible alternative worlds. He discussed the following examples, giving a scenario where, because of the focus, (20) is false whereas (21) is true:

(20)   If Clyde hadn't married BERTHA, he would not have qualified for the inheritance.

(21)   If Clyde hadn't MARRIED Bertha, he would not have qualified for the inheritance.

The effect that focus has in these cases is similar to the effect outlined in (19). Thus we do not stipulate a completely new mechanism. On the other hand, it is well known that focus helps to determine the domain of quantification, both for nominal and adverbial quantifiers (see Rooth 1992; Eckardt 1995). This is again in line with the use of focus postulated in examples (18) and (19).

One might object that the foci that I diagnose in pseudocausal statements differ in one crucial point from other cases of focusing: they are rarely indicated by a pitch accent. This is indeed a severe objection because traditionally we assume that focus is made visible by an accent, at least in the normal case. I think that pseudocausal statements differ from normal sentences in that they convey very complex information in an extremely condensed way. Probably the hearer understands a pseudocausal statement only after some tacit reasoning and by making use of world knowledge. Any theory that accepts (10) will have to make some assumption of this kind. The advantage of the perspective developed in this chapter is that we get a straightforward semantic representation of pseudocausal statements with a minimum of guessing. By representing the pseudocausal statement (18) as in (19), sentence (18) becomes true in our world. We have to look at counterfactual worlds where the departure occurs with different properties and where Bob consequently will not be rescued. When (18) was evaluated as a causal statement, it was false. I think that this analysis reflects the data appropriately.

Let us look at some more examples.

(22)   The traffic jam caused Pat's cooking [late]$_{focus}$.

In (22) we face a focused property in the description of the second event. Nevertheless, the effect of focus will be again to restrict the set of possible worlds referred to in the example. The focus alternatives of 'late' might be something like {*at a normal time, early*}. We can use such a set of alternatives associated with a single item to compute the resulting alternatives for the more complex parts of the sentence, following the leads developed in Rooth (1985). This will result in a set of alternative properties of events:

$\llbracket$Pat's cooking spaghetti late$_f\rrbracket_f$ = {Pat's cooking spaghetti early, Pat's cooking spaghetti at a normal time}.

I assume that sentence (22) states something like this: "In all nearby worlds where no traffic jam occurred, there would not have been a cooking by Pat that was *late*, but instead a cooking by Pat that was *at a normal time* or *early*". This is formalised in (23):

(23) $\forall w(\neg\exists e(\text{traffic-jam}_w(e) \rightarrow \neg\exists e_1(\text{cook}_w(e_1) \wedge \text{theme}_w(e_1, \text{spaghetti}) \wedge$
       $\text{agent}_w(e_1, \text{PAT}) \wedge \text{late}_w(e_1)) \wedge \exists Q\exists e_2(Q\in \llbracket\text{Pat's cooking spaghetti late}_f\rrbracket_f$
       $\wedge Q_w(e_2)))$.

We have now seen example (18), a pseudocausal statement with a focus in the description of the subject event, and example (19), a pseudocausal statement with a focus in the description of the object event. Are there any examples in which both subject and object event description involve a focused property? Yes, I think we can find such examples. The following sentence is of that kind:

(24)   Assume that the coal prices are always low in summer and somewhat higher in late autumn because everybody has to buy coal then. Assume

further that this year the winter came surprisingly early, and people were more eager than normally to get coal in time. Then we can say:

The [early]$_{focus}$ beginning of the winter caused the [quick]$_{focus}$ rising of coal prices.

If we interpret (24) as a sentence involving two foci, as indicated in the example, then we predict the following meaning:

(25) $\forall w([\neg \exists e(begin_w(e, winter) \wedge early_w(e) \wedge \exists Q \exists e_1(Q \in [\![early_f \text{ beginning}$
of the winter$]\!]_f \wedge Q_w(e_1))] \to \neg \exists e_2(rise_w(e_2) \wedge theme_w(e_2, \text{coal-price})$
$\wedge quick_w(e_2)) \wedge \exists R \exists e_3(R \in [\![quick_f \text{ rising of coal prices}]\!]_f \wedge R_w(e_3))).$

Thus, sentence (24) says something like this: "In all worlds where there isn't an *early* beginning of the winter, but a *normal* or even a *late* beginning of the winter, in all these worlds (nearby) there isn't a *quick* but only a *normal* or even maybe *slow* rising of coal prices". This reflects our intuitive understanding of (24) in the given scenario. Sentence (24), if understood as a pseudocausal statement involving only one focus, would not match these intuitions, as (25) makes clear.

Assume, for example, that there was only a focus on 'early'. I give the corresponding structure in (26):

(26)   The [early]$_f$ beginning of the winter caused the quick rising of coal prices.

Sentence (26) would be treated like sentence (22) and would result in the following formula:

(27) $\forall w([\neg \exists e(begin_w(e, winter) \wedge early_w(e) \wedge \exists Q \exists e_1(Q \in [\![early_f \text{ beginning}$
of the winter$]\!]_f \wedge Q_w(e_1))] \to \neg \exists e_2(rise_w(e_2) \wedge theme_w(e_2, \text{coal-price})$
$\wedge quick_w(e_2))).$

However, (27) only states that without an early beginning of the winter, there would not have been a quick-rising-of-the-coal-prices. It leaves the possibility open that the coal prices remain constant in those worlds. That is, either the winter starts early, and the coal prices rise quickly, or the winter starts normally, and the coal prices remain constant. This is not what (24) was originally meant to express.

Can we give a systematic interpretation scheme for pseudocausal statements? The examples discussed in (18)through (27) have shown that we have a certain pattern to follow. All pseudocausal statements are of the following kind:

(28)   *A* caused *B*

where *A* and *B* are event descriptions, and at least one of them contains a focused property. These statements are interpreted as universal quantifications over worlds:

(29)   a. $\forall w(\neg \exists e(A_w(e)) \wedge \exists Q \exists e_1(Q \in [\![A]\!]_f \wedge Q_w(e_1)) \to \neg \exists e_2(B_w(e_2))).$

      b. $\forall w(\neg \exists e(A_w(e)) \to \neg \exists e_1(B_w(e_1)) \wedge \exists Q \exists e_2(Q \in [\![B]\!]_f \wedge Q_w(e_2))).$

   c. $\forall w(\neg\exists e(A_w(e)) \wedge \exists Q \exists e_1(Q \in [\![A]\!]_f \wedge Q_w(e_1)) \to \neg\exists e_2(B_w(e_2)) \wedge$
      $\exists R \exists e_3(R \in [\![B]\!]_f \wedge R_w(e_3)))$.

Interpretation (29a) corresponds to the statement with only a focus in the subject, (29b) to the statement with only a focus in the object, and (29c) to a double-focused statement. The interpretation in (29) show that the effect of focus is the same in all three cases—namely, that of restricting the set of worlds in question by means of the focus alternatives of the original noun phrase. The verb 'cause' must then be understood as a doubly focus-sensitive operator whose meaning is as described in (30). I do not go any further into the consequences such a definition will have for the syntax-semantics interface.

(30) $\text{cause}(A, B) =$

   a. $\forall w(\neg\exists e(A_w(e)) \wedge \exists Q \exists e_1(Q \in [\![A]\!]_f \wedge Q_w(e_1)) \to \neg\exists e_2(B_w(e_2)))$
      if $[\![A]\!]_f \neq \varnothing$ and $[\![B]\!]_f = \varnothing$[7]

   b. $\forall w(\neg\exists e(A_w(e)) \to \neg\exists e_1(B_w(e_1)) \wedge \exists Q \exists e_2(Q \in [\![B]\!]_f \wedge Q_w(e_2)))$
      if $[\![A]\!]_f = \varnothing$ and $[\![B]\!]_f \neq \varnothing$

   c. $\forall w(\neg\exists e(A_w(e)) \wedge \exists Q \exists e_1(Q \in [\![A]\!]_f \wedge Q_w(e_1)) \to \neg\exists e_2(B_w(e_2)) \wedge$
      $\exists R \exists e_3(R \in [\![B]\!]_f \wedge R_w(e_3)))$ otherwise, i.e., if $[\![A]\!]_f \neq \varnothing$ and $[\![B]\!]_f \neq \varnothing$.

9. More Examples

In the previous sections I have given a perspective in which two kinds of sentences of the form *A caused B* are distinguished. There are true causal statements, which refer to a causation relation *CAUSE*. *CAUSE* is defined as in (D.2) and relies on the linguistic notion of event. There are, on the other hand, pseudocausal statements, which involve the focusing of at least one property in the event descriptions involved and are interpreted as focus-sensitive counterfactual statements. We were motivated to make a distinction between true causal statements and pseudocausal statements because examples like (9) had shown that without this distinction, definition (D.2) (and similar ones) would fail under any notion of event. Let us now come back to the problematic example (9) and see whether we can analyse it under the present perspective.

    There is only one event of cooking by Pat, which actually did occur late but might have occurred earlier in other worlds (see section 7). It also actually did cause the neighbour's call, where 'cause' means *CAUSE* in the sense of (D.2). Therefore we can analyse (9) as follows:

(31)   In all worlds where the cooking, *cs*, occurs earlier, there is no event, *d*, that is the neighbour's calling the police and that is caused by *cs*.

Sentence (9), moreover, meets the presupposition that *cs* actually does cause *d* in the real world.

    We can make an interesting comparison between (9) and a parallel example where such a presupposition is not met, according to the theory it stands by now. Consider the sentence

(32)   If the train's departure had occurred in time, it wouldn't have caused Bob's rescue.

This sentence cannot be truly uttered in the scenario given for (2). It seems that in spite of (2) we do not think that the departure literally causes the rescue in the sense of (D.2). It is interesting that, as noted in section 7, the departure of the train, according to our present view, indeed does *not* cause (= *CAUSE*) the rescue, although the cooking of spaghetti still does cause (= *CAUSE*) the call. Therefore we are able to predict the difference between (9) and (32). Sentence (32) is bad because the second clause presupposes that the departure *CAUSE*d the rescue in the strong sense of (D.2). This presupposition is not met in the scenario in (2). The difference between (9) and (32) is one that no theory that uniformly treats all causal sentences alike can predict. It is certainly a difference that cannot be predicted if we use (D.2) together with fine-grained events.

10. Conclusion

We started from the question of whether the linguist can safely use causation as a relation between events. Event causation in the tradition of Lewis cannot be integrated into linguistic theory in a simple way. I have argued that event causation in the tradition of Lewis has another unwelcome feature—namely, that the causal relations events stand in have a strong tendency to become essential properties of the event.

I have outlined a new perspective on sentences of the kind *A caused B*. We distinguish true causal statements from pseudocausal statements. The former involve causation in the strong sense of definition (D.2). The latter are counterfactual statements that involve the focusing of a certain property. Sentences of the form *A caused B* can be interpreted in both ways (at least in many cases). They might be true in one sense but false in the other. Whereas the interpretation of causal statements is more or less unproblematic, pseudocausal statements are more vague. I have outlined a theory for the interpretation of pseudocausal statements that is safely based on current theories of focus interpretation and allows us to compute the meaning of a pseudocausal statement in a deterministic way. Thus, the concept of *pseudocausal statement* does not stand for a black box where all cases of unexplainable causation sentences are collected.

The predictions of the present theory are confirmed by exactly the kind of data that were problematic for the original account. Moreover, the linguist is free to use the relation *CAUSE* for linguistic events.[8]

Notes

1. Note that I avoid talking about a *killing*. I do not want to take a stand about whether the killing event is the same as the shooting event, or more.

2. According to Lewis, an event is *"fragile* if, or to the extent that, it could not have occurred at a different time, or in a different manner. A fragile event has a rich essence; it

has stringent conditions of occurrence" (1973: 196). According to such a definition, a fragile event is one of the first to be dropped when we are looking for worlds most similar to ours. On the contrary, a *stable* event, because of its less stringent conditions of occurrence, is likely to be found also in worlds that are far away from the actual one.

3. We ignore the possibility of a totally deterministic world. I think that if we really believed in determinism, our intuitions about causation would also be radically different from those we actually have.

4. I do not mean to claim that any event can have any property, in some possible world. I don't think that the departure might have been Peter's birthday. However, I do not think that there is a delayed departure that could not have occurred earlier. This is what the slogan is meant to express.

5. Note that in the notation of Rooth, the focus value would be $[delayed]_f = \{delayed,$ *earlier, in time*}. We could stay coherent with his theory. However, this would make the semantic representation of pseudocausal statements more complex. I avoid these difficulties for now.

6. In this section I ignore all complications having to do with the fact that there are no "nearby worlds", in absolute terms. A more carefully formulated variant of (19) that comes up for this point might be paraphrased like this: "For all worlds w_1 where there is no *delayed* departure, but a *normal* or *early* one, and where Bob does get rescued anyway, there is a world w_2 where there is no *delayed* departure, but a *normal* or *early* one, and where Bob does not get rescued, and such a world is closer to the actual world than w_1".

7. In the framework of Rooth (see note 5), these conditions have to be replaced by $[A]_f = [A]_0$ and $[A]_f \neq [A]_0$, respectively.

8. I want to thank the participants of the 1995 Trento Conference on Events for valuable comments and discussions. My original view of things has been seriously reshaped by a remark made by James Higginbotham, which I understood to its full extent only recently.

References

Bennett, J., 1988. *Events and Their Names.* Clarendon Press, Oxford.

Davidson, D., 1967. The Logical Form of Action Sentences. In N. Rescher (ed.), *The Logic of Decision and Action*, 81–95. University of Pittsburgh Press, Pittsburgh. Reprinted in Davidson, D., 1980. *Essays on Actions and Events*, 105–123. Clarendon Press, Oxford.

Davidson, D., 1969. The Individuation of Events. In N. Rescher (ed.), *Essays in Honor of Carl G. Hempel*, 216–234. Reidel, Dordrecht. Reprinted in Davidson, *Essays on Actions and Events*, 163–180.

Dowty, D., 1979. *Word Meaning and Montague Grammar.* Reidel, Dordrecht.

Dretske, F., 1972. Contrastive Statements. In *Philosophical Review*, 8: 411–437.

Eckardt, R., 1995. Focus and Nominal Quantification. In P. Bosch and R. van der Sandt (eds.), *Focus and Natural Language Processing. Proceedings of the Focus Conference 1994*, vol. 2 (Working Papers of the ILL). Heidelberg.

Krifka, M., 1991. A Theory for Multiple Focus Constructions. In *Proceedings of the SALT-I Conference*. Department of Modern Languages and Literatures, Cornell University, Ithaca (N.Y.).

Lewis, D. K., 1973. Causation. In *The Journal of Philosophy* 70: 556–567. Reprinted in Lewis, D., 1986, *Philosophical Papers*, vol. 2, 159–172. Oxford University Press, New York.

Lewis, D. K., 1986. Postscripts to "Causation." In Lewis, D., *Philosophical Papers*, vol. 2, 172–213. Oxford University Press, New York.

Parsons, T., 1990. *Events in the Semantics of English. A Study in Subatomic Semantics.* MIT Press, Cambridge (Mass.).

Rooth, M., 1985. *Association with Focus.* Ph.D. dissertation, University of Massachusetts, Amherst.

Rooth, M., 1992. A Theory of Focus Interpretation. In *Natural Language Semantics* 1: 75–116.

6

Events, Facts, Propositions, and Evolutive Anaphora

Nicholas Asher

1. Introduction

Events have peculiar effects on anaphoric processes. When a discourse introduces an event of creation, a new object becomes available for anaphoric reference in the subsequent narrative. When an event of destruction is introduced, an
object that was available for anaphoric reference is no longer available. Or at
least that is what intuitively one would think. This interaction between events
and anaphora in discourse is part of what is known as the problem of *evolutive
anaphora*, and an analysis of this phenomenon, or at least the beginnings of one,
is the object of this chapter.

To understand evolutive anaphora, we need a clear conception of what events
are in the metaphysical framework suggested by our talk—a framework that I
have called, following Bach, *natural language metaphysics*. To this end, in the
first part of the section I reexamine and defend some distinctions among facts,
events, and propositions that I argued for in Asher (1993). I review differences
based both on linguistic tests and on certain metaphysical principles that I laid
out there. I also introduce a new source of difference between the abstract entities and semiconcrete entities (eventualities)—their dynamic aspects. I argue
that events can change the world, whereas facts do not. Facts are rather part of
the world. I then work out the consequences of this dynamic difference, in particular for anaphora (so-called evolutive anaphora). Evolutive anaphora, in particular those cases involving anaphoric reference to objects that are either created or destroyed by the events being described, pose problems for a purely semantic analysis like that in DRT. Briefly, the problem is that we cannot say
when anaphora in those cases is licensed by purely compositional and lexical
semantic means. Rather, the licensing conditions have to do with the discourse
structure and in particular the rhetorical relation with which the constituents in
the discourse structure are connected.

2. Natural Language Metaphysics

2.1. Vendler's Discussion of Facts vs. Events

Vendler (1967: Ch. 5) was one of the first to make a systematic study of sentential nominals in response to a dispute between Strawson and Austin on the existence and nature of facts.[1] His study of the distributional properties of sentential nominals in English supports a distinction between events and states, on the one hand, and abstract entities like propositions, on the other.

Vendler first distinguishes two types of nominals: *perfect* and *imperfect*. Examples of perfect nominals are *of -ing* gerund phrases like *kissing of Mary* or derived nominals like *invention*. Here are some traits common to all perfect nominals: they require determiners to constitute full noun phrases; they admit prenominal adjectival modification, possessives, prepositional phrases, and pluralisation; they do not admit adverbial modification or negation. Their behaviour makes them very similar to common noun phrases. But they do still retain something of their verbal heritage, that is, the argument structure of the verb, as syntacticians call it. When combined with *of -ing* gerund phrases, possessives and certain prepositional phrases play special roles when we think of the sentence corresponding to this nominalisation. The NP in the possessive attached to the *of -ing* gerund phrase, as (1) below corresponds to the subject of the sentence, whereas the NP in the prepositional phrase headed by *of* corresponds to the object. The subject can also be an NP in a *by* prepositional phrase, as in (2):[2]

(1)   Shem's kicking of Shawn
(2)   The kicking of Shawn by Shem

Imperfect nominals, like *kissing Mary*, in contrast to perfect nominals, are more verblike than nounlike. They do not take determiners to make noun phrases; instead they combine either with a possessive NP to form POSS-*ing* gerunds as in (3) or a simple NP to form an ACC-*ing* gerund as in (4).

(3)   Shem's kicking Shawn
(4)   Shem kicking Shawn

Other traits common to imperfect nominals are that they admit adverbial modification and negation and certain forms of tense; they do not admit prepositional phrases or pluralisation.[3] POSS-*ing* and ACC-*ing* gerunds in fact have many of the same properties as *that* clauses, another form of imperfect nominal (that functions like an NP). In Asher (1993) I classified *that* clauses as imperfect nominals also.

Given the distinction between perfect and imperfect nominals, Vendler observes that these different types systematically serve as arguments to different sorts of predicates or, as he calls them, *containers*. The Vendlerian explanation for these distributional differences is a semantic one. He argues that the two types of nominals when turned into complete NPs denote different types of objects.

Vendler also notes that some containers accept both imperfect and perfect nominals, whereas others accept only perfect nominals. Here are some contexts that admit perfect nominals felicitously but sound bad with imperfect nominals (# denotes awkwardness or infelicity):

(5) a. #Mary hitting Fred occurred at noon (took place in the park; was bloody; made him angry; is an event).

     b. #Mary's mowing the lawn took an hour (lasted for three days; began an hour ago).

Other contexts admit both perfect and imperfect nominals with varying degrees of success:

(6) That Mary mowed the lawn (Mary's mowing the lawn; Mary's mowing of the lawn; for Mary to mow the lawn) bothered Fred (was a possibility).

The denotations of *that* clauses, infinitivals, POSS-*ing* and ACC-*ing* gerund phrases cannot occur felicitously within some Vendlerian containers, in particular spatiotemporal or concrete adjectival modifiers.

Vendler's explanation for why this is so seems to be this: if a predicate cannot felicitously combine with a nominal of a certain type but the nominal does combine with predicates of the *same syntactic category*, then the incompatibility evident between the predicate and its argument does not lie with the content of the particular nominal or in some syntactic restriction but rather points to an incompatibility between the type of object denoted by the nominal and the semantics of the predicate type. The fact that no imperfect nominals accept spatiotemporal predicates is quite different from the incompatibility between particular predicates and particular arguments—as in the incompatibility, for instance, between *this square* and the predicate *is round*. The incompatibility Vendler noticed indicates that the *type* of object denoted by such nominals cannot have spatiotemporal properties, though they can have properties denoted by expressions of the same syntactic category as those expressing spatiotemporal properties.

If eventualities are taken to be those objects that can take spatiotemporal and concrete adjectival modifiers, then Vendler's argument implies that perfect nominals denote eventualities, whereas imperfect nominals denote some other sorts of objects that do not take spatiotemporal modifiers or concrete adjectives. These are the more abstract objects in the spectrum of world immanence, the facts and propositions. In Asher (1993: ch. 4–5), I develop a DRS construction procedure that compositionally builds up the appropriate values for perfect nominals along with an analysis of their argument structures. All the Vendlerian data about proper and improper nominals are accounted for there.

2.2. Facts vs. Propositions in NLM

To understand events and their influences on anaphoric properties better, we need to understand better what facts are. One way to do this is to examine the distinction between facts and propositions. In Asher (1993) I extended

Vendler's argument to distinguish between the denotations of various sorts of imperfect nominals that Vendler lumps together. In (7), for instance, a large number of propositional attitude verbs take NPs and *that* clauses as objects, but no gerunds:

(7)   a. Fred knew the fact that an earthquake had destroyed the city in 1300 B.C.
      b. ??Fred knew (*doubted) the earthquake's destroying the city in 1300 B.C.
      c. Sam believed that Fred hit Mary.
      d. Sam believed the claim that Fred hit Mary.
      e. *Sam believed Fred's hitting Mary.
      f. ??Sam believed Fred's hitting of Mary.

The containers in (7) are all verbs of propositional attitude; many such verbs take *that* clauses but don't take derived nominals or *of-ing* gerund phrases that intuitively denote events, thus indicating that the denotations of imperfect nominals are not a subset of the set of eventlike objects. Here are some other containers that admit *that* clauses but aren't open to perfect nominal arguments or gerunds of any kind:

(8)   a. *Mary's hitting of Sue is true.[4]
      b. *Mary's hitting Sam is true.
      c. That Mary hit Sue is true.
      d. *Fred's hitting of Sam is a thought that hadn't occurred to me.
      e. ??Fred hitting Sam is a thought that hadn't occurred to me.
      f. That Fred hit Sam is a thought that hadn't occurred to me.

A Vendlerian argument distinguishes between the denotations of ACC-*ing* and POSS-*ing* gerund phrases, on the one hand, and certain uses of *that clauses*, on the other. The examples in (8) show that paradigm proposition containers do not readily accept ACC-*ing* and POSS-*ing* gerund phrases. But they do accept NPs; so the reason for excluding ACC-*ing* and POSS-*ing* gerunds is not a syntactic one since these also are NPs. So unless we wish to beg the question by postulating gerund phrases as a distinct syntactic category, by Vendler's argument, there appears to be a semantic distinction between the type of objects denoted by POSS-*ing* and ACC-*ing* gerund phrases and the denotation of *that* clauses in certain contexts. On the other hand, the gerund phrases, as well as *that* clauses, occur as arguments to supposedly factive contexts such as *indicate*; *show*; causative verbs; and predicates like *is a fact*, which is a container that denotes a category of facts in natural language metaphysics. So if we take factive contexts and propositional contexts to be satisfied by different types of entities, it would seem that *that* clauses may denote either facts or propositions.

The distinction between events, facts and propositions receives support from other data, such as those involving quantification and anaphora.[5] For example, with respect to the differences between propositions and facts, these tests show that it is difficult to admit a quantificational structure like

$$Q(x)(R(x), P(x))$$

where P is a spatiotemporal property and R a property proper to facts or propositions or where P is a fact distinguishing property and R a property that is satisfied by a proposition. Such tests confirm a natural language metaphysical difference between facts and propositions, on the one hand, and a distinction between facts and events, on the other.

These arguments imply an ontological distinction, but they do not tell us anything about these types. To do so, we must examine the different contexts. By looking at the logic of these contexts, we can again construct arguments to distinguish their arguments ontologically.

Factive contexts suggest that fact-type objects have different identity conditions from those that satisfy proposition contexts. The arguments assume that *indicate* and *show* denote, like propositional attitude verbs, two place relations with a subject and an object argument place. For both types of verbs, the object argument place may be filled by a *that* clause. As with naked infinitival perception contexts, it appears that the objects denoted by *that* clauses within *indicate* and *show* contexts obey the following identity principle:

> **Identity principle.** Suppose that φ is an expression denoting an abstract entity, that φ contains an occurrence of a name α, and that the denotation of α is the same as the denotation of β, then $denotation(\varphi) = denotation(\varphi[\beta/\alpha])$.

To see this, consider the valid argument in (9), in which we have two sets of documents, A and B.

(9)   Documents A indicate that Cicero was the most highly regarded philosopher of his time.
        Cicero = Tully.
        Documents B indicate that Tully was the most highly regarded philosopher of his time.
        Therefore, documents A and B indicate the same thing.

Factual contexts also validate arguments in which we have substitution of expressions denoting the same property, whereas propositional contexts do not. Consider the argument in (10), from Cresswell (1985):

(10)   The map indicates that it is 7 + 5 kilometres to Upper Moutere.
        Therefore, the map indicates that it is 12 kilometres to Upper Moutere.

Again (10) is valid, whereas the corresponding argument with a propositional attitude context substituted for the factual context is not. Similar distinctions in the logic of factive and propositional contexts show up with complex noun phrases of the form *the fact that p*, *the claim that p*, and *the indication that p*. These nominals, I will assume, have an analysis in which the objects they denote are arguments of a context introduced by the noun that heads the noun phrase.

(11)   a. The fact that Cicero was the most highly regarded philosopher of his time is identical to the fact that Tully was the most highly regarded philosopher of his time.

   b. The belief that Cicero was the most highly regarded philosopher of his time is identical to the belief that Tully was the most highly regarded philosopher of his time.

   c. The fact that it is 12 kilometres to Upper Moutere is identical to the fact that it is 7 + 5 kilometres to Upper Moutere.

   d. The belief that it is 12 kilometres to Upper Moutere is identical to the belief that it is 7 + 5 kilometres to Upper Moutere.

Statements (11a) and (11c) strike many speakers as true, whereas many who work on propositional attitudes would suppose that (11b) and (11d) are false. The discrepancy in truth value suggests that there is an ontological difference between the arguments of factual contexts and the arguments of attitude contexts, or to put it ontologically, between propositions and facts.[6] Facts don't have such fine-grained identity criteria; propositions have contextually sensitive identity criteria, as I have argued in Asher (1986, 1987; see also Kamp 1990).

Another, metaphysical difference between facts and propositions is that, as Moore argued, facts and propositions have different existence criteria. Propositions exist "eternally," or at least they exist independently of whether they are true or not. The proposition *that* φ exists in any possible world w whether or not φ is true at w, for an agent may bear some attitude to the proposition even when φ is not true. But the fact that φ cannot exist at w if φ is not true at w.[7] This distinction captures an important aspect of natural language metaphysics and provides more evidence that facts and propositions are distinct.[8] Like facts, eventualities and situations are contingent entities; the events that actually happened typically might have happened otherwise. Facts, events, and situations all share this property with concrete individuals. The facts of one world are another world's possibilities. Thus, possibilities and facts are closely related. Both are distinct from propositions; possibilities must only be actual in at least one world, whereas propositions must be actual in all. It is also this tie to a real world and to a particular realisation that gives facts their causal efficacy.

A final, distinguishing feature of facts as opposed to propositions is that facts appear to have causal efficacy, whereas propositions do not. Consider for instance (12):

(12)   a. The fact that John had a headache made him crabby.
   b. John's crabbiness resulted in the fact that everyone avoided him.
   c. John's crabbiness resulted in everyone avoiding him.

These statements seem to show that facts may either cause or be caused by states or other facts. Propositions, on the other hand, do not have causal efficacy. How could they, given that these propositions do not depend for their existence on any realisation?

How might we account for these observations about facts and propositions in a formal system? In Asher (1993), ACC-*ing* and POSS-*ing* gerund phrases denote facts or possibilities (unrealised facts) but not propositions, whereas *that* clauses may denote any sort of abstract object. The way this works out technically in the DRS construction procedure is not worth bothering about here in detail. Roughly, what happens is that *that* clauses introduce sub-DRSs, whereas full NPs such as the gerund phrases always introduce discourse referents. These discourse referents must be of a particular type, for example, fact type, proposition type, or event type; the gerunds that are imperfect nominals, I hypothesise, always introduce fact-type discourse referents into a DRS. When *that* clauses are part of a noun phrase such as *the fact that Susan is pregnant*, then the sub-DRS serves to characterise the fact discourse referent introduced by *the fact*. (For details see Asher 1993.) Thus DRSs are conceptual structures designed to reflect the ontological type structure of natural language metaphysics, which is to be distinguished from the type structure of *real* metaphysics, the way the world *really* is (or the way we model the way it really is). The latter is represented in my scheme by the models into which one embeds DRSs to give them a truth definition. At the level of the models, I suppose there is one type of abstract conceptual structure that can characterise discourse referents of different types. These are equivalence classes of DRSs.

2.3. Facts vs. Events Again

The distinction between facts and propositions is relatively straightforward. One may not want to make such a distinction to handle the semantics of various nominal constructions. But one can make such a distinction, and I show how this distinction can handle the various distributional data noted above (Asher 1993). But it seems to me that the distinction between facts and events is perhaps more delicate to make out. In this section I offer some more reasons for distinguishing between these two kinds of entities at the level of natural language metaphysics.

2.3.1. Closure Principles

Another way of examining types of abstract objects in natural language metaphysics concentrates on their logical closure principles. The investigation of closure principles answers questions like this: if δ denotes an object of type T, does $\neg \delta$ also denote an object of type T? If so, then objects of type T are closed under some sort of operation of complementation, corresponding to the meaning of negation. The closure principles for an entity of type T define an algebraic structure for the domain of objects of type T. Different closure principles differentiate between various sorts of abstract objects and provide a more systematic treatment of natural language metaphysics.

An answer to the question of what is the structure of the domain of facts or events, however, depends on what we are postulating a structured domain *for*. I can think of two possible reasons. The first concerns the possibilities for propositionhood, eventhood, facthood, and so on. That is, what sort of abstract entities does natural language allow us to talk about? This is, I believe, the sort of question that has motivated those interested in the *algebra of events*. Such theories of the structure of an ontological domain should ensure that the entities to which one can refer anaphorically exist. They should also provide denotations for combinations of expressions that each denotes an entity of a particular kind. A second concern is to characterise the domain of propositions put forward by a bit of natural language discourse. That is, the task is to discover just what propositions, events, or other types of objects are introduced by a particular bit of natural language discourse. This is a concern of theories sensitive to discourse structure like Segmented Discourse Representation Theory, or SDRT. But I shall not go into this here.

Let's look first at closure principles for the domain of events. One interesting aspect of the domain of events, as Link, Krifka, and others have observed, is that events can be summed together to yield new events. Of course, the same is true of the domain of individuals, though when individuals are summed together they form groups to which we anaphorically refer with plural pronouns. One cannot use a plural anaphoric pronoun alone to pick up a group of events, in the way that one can use a plural pronoun to pick up a group of individuals.

(13) a. Three men raised$_i$ the flag of the republic. They$_i$ took the ruling junta by surprise.

   b. Three men raised$_i$ the flag of the republic. It$_i$ took the ruling junta by surprise.

Statement (13a) cannot be used to mean that there were three events of raising the flag, the group of which took the junta by surprise. One can use the plural definite description *these events* to pick up the group, a fact familiar from plural anaphora generally. On the other hand, in using the singular pronoun to refer to this group of events, as in (13b), an acceptable sentence with the same intended anaphoric interpretation results. These anaphoric data provide some support for the notion developed by Bach (1981), Link (1983), and Krifka (1987, 1989) that events in natural language metaphysics are a structured domain, closed under a summation operation. In such a conception, events sum together to form a new event. More precisely, the space of events is closed under a *join* or *sum* operation, as in (E1):[9]

(E1) $\exists e_2 (e_2 = e \oplus e_1)$

The linguist's algebraic view of events refines an older philosophical theme that events are subject to mereological principles.[10] This principle of summation appears to work generally with all kinds of events—even achievements and accomplishments, which behave similarly, as Krifka (1987) has argued, in counting noun denotations. If this is right, then it appears that we have two ways of forming collections for events: a principle that takes individual events and fuses them into a larger individual event (the masslike summation principle) and a principle that takes individual events and forms a plural group from them (the *count* summation principle).

The domain of events is not closed with respect to complementation, however. To use Cresswell's (1985) example, the train's arrival may be an event, but whatever *the train's nonarrival* denotes, it does not denote an event. Why?, one might ask. Well, first, intuitively the phrase tells us that something did not happen, not that a non-something happened. Second, *the nonarrival of the train* does not accept the standard perfect nominal containers—as witnessed by (14):

(14)   *The nonarrival of the train occurred at 10 A.M. (lasted many hours; took place at the station in Victoria).

So in virtue of Vendler's criteria, the denotation of *the nonarrival of the train* should not be classified as an event. Further, *the nonarrival of the train* can be paraphrased by a *that* clause; the positive derived nominal phrase *the arrival of the train* cannot be—*that the train arrived* is not synonymous with *the arrival of the train*. At best we might think that certain types of temporally extended events, that is, processes, activities, and accomplishments, are closed under a principle of relative complementation (E2):[11]

(E2) $\forall e \forall e_1((\text{Temporally-extended}(e) \wedge \text{part-of}(e_1, e)) \rightarrow \exists e_2 \, (e_2 = e\backslash e_1))$.

It is also very unclear whether the disjunction of two event descriptions yields another event. A sentence such as

(15)   John's kissing Mary or his pinching her led her to knock him unconscious with her handbag

appears to indicate not that some sort of disjunctive event led her to knock him unconscious but that one or the other event (perhaps the speaker doesn't know which) did. What could a disjunctive event even be? Conditional events seem to be even more peculiar. We seem to have no such conceptual categories. So the domain of events has only two closure principles, (E1), concerning summation, and (E2), concerning complementation.

Contrast now the domain of events with the domain of facts. The syntax of *that* clauses allows us to speak happily of *conditional, negative,* or *disjunctive* facts:

(16)   a.   The fact that if Mary came home late, John would be in a bad mood forced her to leave work earlier than the others.

Similarly, our language allows us to construct expressions that denote facts that are the complements (or the contradictories) of other facts, just as it does for propositions.

(16)   b.   That no one bothers any more about doing a good job is not a legitimate excuse for distributing goods of poor quality.

Natural language metaphysics also countenances some facts as *generalisations* of other facts. Reference to disjunctive facts in natural language also seems fine; see, for instance, (17):

(17)   The fact that the children were either asleep or playing quietly in their room allowed Mary to get some work done.

Thus, facts and events seem to have quite different closure principles. One might argue that certain types of eventualities—that is, states—have closure principles that resemble those for facts much more closely. But the case is problematic. States, like events of various kinds, rely on existence of their actors or participants; it is these actors and participants that help determine the spatiotemporal extent of eventualities. A state is always a state *of* some object.[12] Can there be the state of nothing existing? What spatiotemporal extent would it have? Presumably none since there isn't anything that exists, including, one can assume, a spatiotemporal manifold. If the object a exists, it is not in the state φ if and only if it is in the state of $\neg\varphi$. But obviously if a does not exist, then there may be no state in which a φ's but yet not be a state in which a has the state $\neg\varphi$. So states cannot be closed unrestrictedly with respect to complementation, as are facts.[13]

2.3.2. Identity Criteria

Facts also differ from events in natural language metaphysics in their identity criteria. In fact, we might take these principles of logical inference to be a part of closure principles (though I didn't represent them as such in Asher 1993). Suppose that δ denotes a fact and that it contains a definite description α. Suppose further that $\alpha = \beta$. There appear to be readings of $\delta[\beta/\alpha]$ such that it does not denote the same fact as δ. To see this, let's examine the *indicates* construction, which I have taken to be a fact context (taking as it does both gerunds and *that* clauses as arguments):

(18)   The thirty-three rings indicate that this tree was thirty-three years old when it was cut down.
        This tree = the first tree that Jack Webber, extraordinary woodsman, felled on December 7, 1987.
        Therefore, the thirty-three rings indicate that the first tree that Jack Webber, extraordinary woodsman, felled on December 7, 1987, was thirty-three years old when it was cut down.

There is a reading in which the argument in (18) is not valid, whereas there is no similar ambiguity for the similar inference in which coreferential proper names are substituted for each other; compare (9).

Consider the same argument concerning event descriptions. Suppose that a sentential nominal δ denotes an event and suppose it contains an occurrence of a singular term α. Now suppose $\alpha = \beta$. But obviously, the death of Caesar happens at t just in case the death of the Roman conqueror of Gaul happens at t; the death of Caesar is the same event as the death of the Roman conqueror of Gaul. The substitution of coreferential definite descriptions does not affect the denotations of event nominals. Fact descriptions then appear to differ from eventuality descriptions in such identity of reference principles. One simple explanation for this difference is that the identity criteria for the two types of objects are different. We could suppose that events are individuated by their actors and some event-describing property, regardless of how the actors are described, whereas the identity criteria of facts may depend on the descriptions of the individuals that may be part of their realisation.

There are those, like Jagewon Kim, who would argue that the identity criteria just presented for events are also those for facts. Kim would say that both events and facts are individuated by their constituent properties and individuals. Kim's proposal would still have to explain the difference we noted earlier between facts and eventualities; but perhaps this is possible, and so Kim's proposal merits a closer look. Even in a Kimian view of events, however, there seems to be a difference between facts and events. Not all properties define eventualities, whereas it seems any property may constitute a fact. Consider for example mathematical properties. It is clearly a fact that $2 + 2 = 4$, but is there a state of the number 2 that is defined by this property? At least we don't speak this way; such states are not part of natural language metaphysics. Further, what would the spatiotemporal extents of such states be? It seems that there would be none or it would be everything. So it seems that events and states have to do with contingent beings and their contingent properties, whereas facts do not.

This line of thought suggests a much more striking difference between facts and eventualities: facts are atemporal or eternal; events and states are transitory. First, consider the thesis that facts are eternal. The facts denoted by natural language noun phrases of the form

the fact that p

where p expresses a dated proposition, are eternal, for if the sentence holds, it holds at all times t. What about fact descriptions that do not contain dates? Given the evidence below, it appears that natural language metaphysics does not countenance time-dependent facts:

(19) a. #It was a fact that Susan got the highest grade in the class, but it is a fact no longer.
      b. #It was a fact that Susan gets (will get) the highest grade in the class, but it is no longer a fact.
      c. #It will be a fact that Susan gets (will get) the highest grade in the class, though it is not one now.

Sentence (19a) strikes many speakers as nonsense; it certainly does me. Such sentences do not get any better if the verb in the subordinate clause is in the present, as in (19b). Sentences about future events, as in (19c), don't sound perhaps as bad as (19a) and (19b), but they don't sound very good either. The thesis that facts are eternal or atemporal predicts that (19a–c) are nonsense; eternal or atemporal objects can't come into existence at some time or cease to exist at another. Further evidence is forthcoming from the behaviour of fact-denoting nominals. As we saw with example (5), fact nominals do not take temporal properties at all. They don't last for any definite length of time, and they aren't

punctual either. This would suggest that facts lie outside the realm of time altogether. Such atemporal objects would clearly not be transitory, and if they exist
at all must exist eternally.

One can of course use temporal adverbials, as in

(20)   The fact of John's singing the Marseillaise at 6 o'clock in the morning

to situate the event described by the singing, but this is not the same as assigning
the fact a temporal location. The fact itself *is* that a certain event has a certain
temporal location.

The events in fact-denoting expressions get temporally constrained by the
semantics of the predicates to which the fact-denoting expressions occur as arguments. For instance, the semantics of *bother* in (21) would coerce the temporal localisation of the eventuality described by the fact to overlap the main
eventuality of bothering Mary, as shown in the DRS below ('O' represents temporal overlap).

(21)   John's singing the Marseillaise bothered Mary.

$$
\boxed{
\begin{array}{l}
\quad x,\ e,\ n,\ f,\ u,\ v \\[4pt]
\hline \\[-6pt]
\text{Mary}(x) \\
\text{John}(u) \\
\text{Marsellaise}(v) \\
e\text{-bother}(f, x) \\
e < \text{now} \\[6pt]
f \approx \boxed{
\begin{array}{l}
e' \\
e'\text{-sing}(u, v) \\
O(e', e)
\end{array}}
\end{array}}
$$

But this is still not the same as locating the fact within some temporal span.

We have now to argue for the transitoriness of states and events. That an
event is temporary is crucial to our understanding it as a transition between two
states: a *pre-state* in which the conditions for the event's occurrence are met and
a *post-state*, in which the effects of the event obtain. We think of an event as
having a pre- and a post-state. If events weren't temporary, such pre-states and
post-states wouldn't make sense. Such pre-states and post-states are essential
parts of the way we look at many if not all events, and they reveal a close connection between states and events. The paradigm events that are changes of
states are things like accomplishments and achievements. What about activities
and processes? Most activities (e.g., swimming) and processes (e.g., melting)
certainly have pre-states and post-states. Perhaps there are some such events,
however, that don't have so clearly defined pre-and post-states. States do not

seem to have pre- and post-states, though they have instead pre- and post-events that mark their temporal boundaries. Are there states that are in fact eternal? This seems difficult to determine; at any rate unlike the difficulties of talking about future facts that are not facts now, we have no difficulty in speaking of future and past states that don't exist now.

(22)   Ten minutes ago, Jim was very angry, though he isn't angry now.

The transitoriness of (many) states and all events offers another reason why states and events do not have to do with noncontingent objects (like mathematical ones), whereas facts and propositions do. Noncontingent objects and necessary properties would by definition define an event or state that is eternal and not transitory. When events happen, objects can be modified, created, or destroyed at different times and in different places.

Dynamicity is also linked to temporariness. Events are transitions between states and so are the bringers of change. Certain events bring about the existence of new objects, as it happens with verbs of creation—for example, *make, create, build*, and *construct*. Others bring about the destruction of objects, as with verbs of destruction—for example, *destroy, deconstruct*, and *undo*. Other events modify or transform objects and make them take on different properties. Facts, being eternal or timeless objects, don't have pre- and post-states and cannot be coherently pictured as changing the world in any of these respects, though of course a fact can describe any one of these transforming events.

But whereas facts are eternal or even atemporal and events are temporal and transitory objects, there is a relation between facts and events. Facts may describe events, and in turn these events realise those facts. This relation is key to defining a fact (and differentiating it from a possibility). I say that f is a fact at w if and only if there is an event in w that realises f. Notice, however, that this relation is not time-dependent. The event may occur at any moment within w. Thus, the indexing of facts, and hence their eternality, comes not from their being situated at some spatiotemporal location but rather through the quantifying out of spatiotemporal locations associated with the events that realise them.

3. Evolutive Anaphora

In this section, I take up the consequence of this distinction between facts and events—that events have a dynamic potential. I go into some detail concerning how this dynamic potential affects our talk about events, in particular talk in which we refer anaphorically to the participants of events.

3.1. The Problem of Evolutive Anaphora

We have a good idea of how to model events in which the properties of their participants are modified but the objects themselves persist, as well as our talk about such events and their participants. We take such events to be individuals à la Davidson (1967). A Davidsonian model of events is then easily incorporated within DRT or some other equivalent dynamic semantic framework, and it suffices for an analysis of anaphoric reference to the participants of such events. For although such events modify properties of objects that exist in the prestate of the event, these objects continue to exist in the post-state of the event.

What has not been explored in these or other frameworks is the problem of more fundamental change—namely, the creation and destruction of objects. Simply adopting a Davidsonian framework and placing events in a domain along with other objects will not account for our talk about such objects; in particular, the problematic anaphoric reference to objects that have been destroyed or not yet brought into existence cannot be explained within such a theory. Anaphoric reference in such contexts is what I call *evolutive anaphora*. To understand evolutive anaphora, we must make sense of a dependence between events and the existence of individuals.

The problem of evolutive anaphora is that if we have events in which objects are destroyed, then we shouldn't be able to refer to them subsequent to their destruction. But in DRT there is no mechanism to forestall this, at least if we stick to the standard DRT account of accessibility and discourse interpretation.

At the purely semantic level, it is to me unclear how to proceed. First, we must in some cases limit accessibility of discourse referents. It does not make sense, for example, to be able to continue to refer to an object that has been destroyed. Examples that might on purely conceptual grounds make sense are ruled out:

(23) a. #The bomb vaporised the/a VW_i. The police then inspected it$_i$ closely.
b. #The fire in the museum consumed a beautiful painting$_i$. The curator then tried to restore it$_i$.

On the other hand, the availability of the destroyed object does not depend completely on the semantics of the DRS and of the constituent words. It also depends on the way the information conveyed by the clauses in which the anaphor and its target occur are linked together. To see this, consider the examples in (24):

(24) a. The bomb vaporised the/a VW_i. It$_i$ disappeared in a flash.
b. The bomb vaporised the VW_i. But it$_i$ didn't run anyway.

These examples are very similar to those in (23) except that, intuitively, the propositions expressed by the sentences are linked together in a different way. In (23) we understand what happened in terms of a narrative sequence. The examples in (24) don't exemplify a narrative sequence. But the reason for this is not because the tense forms of the constituent verbs or anything about the compositional semantics of the propositions are different. Rather, we are forced to interpret (23) as narrative sequences because of the presence of the particle *then*, which is conspicuously absent in the examples in (24).

Standard dynamic semantic theories like DRT or Dynamic Montague Grammar (DMG) do not have any way of distinguishing narrative connections between propositions from other connections in virtue of the role of discourse particles like *then*. The fact that the examples in (24) seem acceptable, whereas the others are not indicates that the anaphoric links in evolutive anaphora cannot simply be a consequence of the semantics of the discourses as this is understood, even within a dynamic semantic theory like DRT or DMG.

3.2. From Dynamic Semantics to Discourse Semantics

The theory SDRT, an extension of DRT, is specifically designed to examine the various ways propositions in a discourse can be linked together and the semantic effects of these linkings. Thus SDRT represents a discourse as a *segmented discourse representation structure*, or SDRS, a structure recursively defined and consisting of DRSs and binary relations on DRSs. These binary relations are discourse relations and represent the links between propositions in a discourse. An SDRS for one of the simple discourses in (23) or (24), for example, consists of a DRS for each sentence related by one or more discourse relations. The word *then* indicates that a particular discourse relation, *Narration*, holds between the propositions introduced by the two sentences in the examples in (23). Other relations can hold between propositions, for example, *Elaboration. Elaboration* holds between the constituents derived from the two sentences in (24a). In (24b) two other relations hold, *Contrast* and *Background.*

The properties of *Narration, Elaboration,* and other discourse relations, and the conditions under which they hold, have been studied extensively in SDRT. I will not go into detail concerning this matter.[14] What is important for our purposes, however, are the semantic effects of these relations on discourse interpretation. According to SDRT's analysis, *Narration*(α, β) implies that the post-state of the event in α must overlap temporally, and so be consistent with, the pre-state of the event in β:[15]

$$Narration(\alpha, \beta) \rightarrow O(\text{post}(e_\alpha), \text{pre}(e_\beta))$$

Using certain natural assumptions about pre-states and post-states—namely, that a pre-state of e antedates the start of e and that a post-state of e comes temporally after e—we derive the following formula as a theorem:

$$Narration(\alpha, \beta) \rightarrow e_\alpha < e_\beta$$

Elaboration(α, β) implies rather the opposite—namely, that

$$Elaboration(\alpha, \beta) \rightarrow e_\beta \subset e_\alpha$$

But this in and of itself does not solve our problem.

What would it take to predict the examples in (23) to be bad without predicting (24) to be equally bad? The difference between these sets of examples lies not in the lexical or compositional semantics but rather in the way the propositions or constituents of the discourse structure are related together by discourse relations. According to SDRT, we are forced to conclude that *Narration* holds between the two constituents, α and β, derived from the two sentences. But if there is an incompatibility between the pre-state of the second eventuality and the post-state of the first, then *Narration*(α, β) cannot hold. So such an incompatibility would lead us to conclude that the discourse is inconsistent.

Now there is an incompatibility when we attempt to put two constituents as in (23) together with *Narration*. But what precisely is it? Intuitively, the incompatibility is obvious. The first sentences of (23) state that a certain object is destroyed and so no longer exists in the post-state of the event, whereas in the second sentence an anaphoric reference to this object presupposes that it exists. But if we attach with *Narration*, then the post-state and pre-state of these two events must be consistent, which here is not the case. To formalise this incompatibility, I assume that there is a function from eventualities into the domain of the model at w. I call such a function $\mathcal{D}$. Further, I assume not only that events have pre- and post-states (thus incorporating into the formalism that events are changes of state) but also that states have pre- and post-eventualities. Thus, I incorporate into the formalism the idea that states also are temporary and have both initiating events and events that terminate them. This might appear at odds with the contention by linguists that states have vague or indefinite boundaries, but I think that this talk of vague or indefinite boundaries can be put as follows: there are boundaries for a state, but these boundaries are not determined by temporal adverbials or tense markers; hence they can be taken to be vague or indefinite as far as semantics is concerned.

Now we can make a first pass at formalising the lexical entry of a verb of destruction φ as follows. I assume a bottom-up construction procedure for DRSs such as that in Asher (1993), where verbs introduce relations that will combine with noun phrase denotations to yield DRSs for clauses:

$$\lambda x \lambda y \lambda e \quad \boxed{\begin{array}{l} x, y \in \mathcal{D}(\text{pre}(e)) \\ e\text{-}\varphi(x, y) \\ y \notin \mathcal{D}(\text{post}(e)) \end{array}}$$

Note that the lexical entry of the destruction verb lambda abstracts over the main eventuality, as well as over the subject and object argument places. This lambda abstract will combine with the translation of the object noun phrase to form a verb phrase denotation. Then the translations of the inflection node and of the subject noun phrase will introduce an eventuality discourse referent and an objectual discourse referent, respectively, so that the output of the semantic translation of the first sentence of (23a), for example, is a completed DRS like the following:

$$\boxed{\begin{array}{l} x, y, e \\ \\ \text{bomb}(x) \\ \text{VW}(y) \\ x, y \in \mathcal{D}(\text{pre}(e)) \\ e\text{-vaporise}(x, y) \\ y \notin \mathcal{D}(\text{post}(e)) \\ e < \text{now} \end{array}}$$

One further assumption that we need concerns the treatment of the presuppositions of a sentence. Following Kamp and Rossdeutscher (1994), I assume that the presuppositions of a sentence that describes an event must already hold in the pre-state of that eventuality. This assumption, together with the representation of destruction eventualities, yields the incompatibility between $post(e_\alpha)$ and $pre(e_\beta)$ that would preclude *Narration*. For example in (23a), when we link the propositions expressed by the first and second sentences by *Narration*, which is forced by the presence of the particle *then*, we must infer that where $e_{23a.1}$ is the eventuality in the first sentence of (23a), $O(post(e_{23a.1}), pre(e_{23a.2}))$. By the semantics of *vaporise*, which is a destruction verb, we deduce $y \notin \mathcal{D}(post(e_{23a.1}))$. But we also identify the discourse referent introduced by the pronoun in (23a) with the car; so we infer by our assumption about presuppositions that $y \in \mathcal{D}(pre(e_{23a.2}))$. But this ensures that $\neg O(post(e_{23a.1}), pre(e_{23a.2}))$; inconsistent states cannot overlap temporally. So we deduce an inconsistency from the axiom concerning *Narration* and the lexical entries for the verbs. The finished SDRS is inconsistent because we deduce both *Narration*(α, β) and $\neg$*Narration*(α, β) because of the incompatibility of $post(e_\alpha)$ and $pre(e_\beta)$.

On the other hand, when the two constituents in the discourse structure are linked by *Elaboration*, no such inconsistency ensues and we can construct a coherent discourse structure for an example such as (24a):

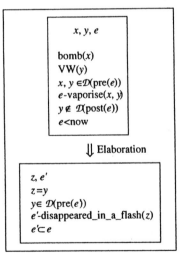

In this particular case, the first constituent is as before, and once we construct a DRS for the second sentence and attach it by means of *Elaboration*, we infer $e_\beta \subset e_\alpha$ from the axiom about the consequences of *Elaboration*. The resulting SDRS is evidently consistent. The condition imposed by the presupposition of the anaphoric pronoun in the second sentence is that y, the car, must exist in $pre(e_\beta)$. But we only know that the car ceases to exist in $post(e_\alpha)$, and since e_β is a part of e_α, we are not forced to conclude that $pre(e_\beta)$ overlaps with $post(e_\alpha)$—rather the opposite. We don't know that $pre(e_\beta)$ overlaps with $pre(e_\alpha)$, although this is possible; what *Elaboration*(α, β) tells us about the car is that the car's existence continues at least through the $pre(e_\beta)$, which could overlap part, though not all, of e_α (since e_β must also be a part of e_α).

Sentence (24b) offers yet another example of how discourse relations can affect anaphoric reference in SDRT. The particle *but* in the second sentence is an indicator of *Contrast*, and so the constituents α and β must be related by *Contrast*. We must appeal to lexical semantics to support this notion of *Contrast*, and this is a matter to which I return later. Contrast in and of itself imposes no temporal relation on the eventualities in α and β. But it appears to be the function of the particle *anyway* that entails that the car didn't run prior to the eventuality in α. Thus, the SDRS for (24b), which is also evidently coherent, is the following:

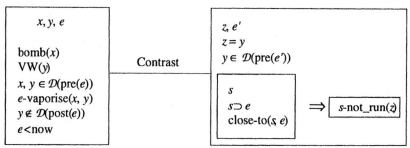

This discussion has shown how SDRT exploitation of discourse relations can account for anaphoric phenomena that elude other dynamic and more purely semantic frameworks like DRT, DPL, and so on. The theory SDRT takes into account the temporal anaphoric relations between eventualities and discourse structure, which those theories do not. To this I have added a certain lexical analysis of verbs of destruction, which requires that with each eventuality is associated a domain of objects. Together with the principles of SDRT, I can now show why examples like (23) are bad whereas an example like (24) is not. The discourse relation, *Narration*, which must bind together the two constituents in the discourse structures for (23), has semantic consequences that are inconsistent with the semantics of the destruction verb.

Once we have tackled destruction verbs in this way, we can also go on to examine creation verbs. A first pass at their formalisation is more or less the mirror image of the destruction verbs. Such verbs are typically three-place verbs with an agent, a; a described event, e; and an object, o, that gets created in e. The presupposition of such a verb is that o does not exist in the prestate of e or any time prior to e but comes to exist in e and is part of the domain of *post-state(e)*. This is reflected in the DRS conditions for the verb:

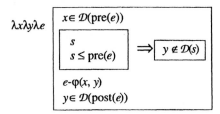

Now this lexical analysis of creation verbs, together with an analysis of tenses such as that in DRT (Kamp and Rohrer, 1983) or the much simpler tense semantics of SDRT (Lascarides and Asher 1993; Asher 1995), produces an explanation of why an example like (25a) sounds at the very least odd or contradictory.

(25) a. #John built a house last year. It had stood on the cliff high above the valley.
  b. #John baked a cake yesterday, because Susan liked it.
  c. John baked a cake yesterday. Susan wanted to eat it.
  d. John baked a cake yesterday. Susan wanted to eat one.

Let's look for illustrative purposes in the analysis of (25a). According to the SDRT analysis of the tenses, the interpretation of the pluperfect tense in the second sentence requires an anaphoric link, which can only be supplied by a time or event discourse referent. The only available discourse referent that can perform this linking role is the event discourse referent e_α introduced by *built* or the temporal discourse referent introduced by the adverbial *last year*, which contains e_α. Now the second sentence also contains another anaphoric element, the pronoun *it*, which must be linked to *a house* in the first sentence. Furthermore, this pronoun has a presupposition—namely, that its referent exists in the pre-eventuality of the state s of *standing* or rather at $end(pre(s))$. But $pre(s) < s$ by definition, so that the house must exist at the end of the eventuality that initiate s. Now, there are two possibilities to fill in the anaphoric equation concerning s. If e_α is chosen to fill the anaphoric equation introduced by the pluperfect, then we derive $s < e_\alpha$. If we choose the other possible solution, then $s < t_{\text{last-year}}$. But then we again obtain $s < e_\alpha$, given that α already specifies that $e_\alpha \subset t_{\text{last-year}}$. In the end, attempting to satisfy the presupposition of the pronoun forces us to postulate that the house exists prior to the completion of e_α, the building event. This contradicts the semantics of *build* as a creation verb since it requires that the house not exist prior to the end of e_α.

Similarly, (25b) leads to a contradiction between the semantic effects of the discourse relation introduced by the particle *because* and the presuppositions of the anaphoric pronoun. Assuming the appropriate axioms for this example, we would deduce in SDRT that the discourse relation in this case is *Explanation*. *Explanation* involves a causal relation and since effects do not precede their causes, this implies temporally:

$$Explanation(\alpha, \beta) \rightarrow \neg \exists e (e \subset e_\alpha \wedge \neg \bigcirc(e, e_\beta) \wedge \neg \bigcirc(e_\beta, e_\alpha))$$

So the pre-state of e_β in which the cake must exist, given the requirements of the anaphoric pronoun, must precede e_α, which contradicts the information conveyed by the verb of creation, *bake*.

Like (25b), (25d) is naturally interpreted so that the constituent derived from the second sentence furnishes an explanation for what happened in the first.[16] In this case, however, the anaphoric presuppositions of *one* do not clash with the presuppositions of the creation verb. In (25c), however, where the anaphoric presuppositions clash with those of the creation verb, the defeasible interpretation that the second constituent explains the first is not available. Instead, SDRT predicts that *Narration* (or perhaps *Result*, which we could infer with the requisite triggering axioms), relates the two constituents derived from the sentences of (25c).

3.3. Further Issues Concerning Verbs of Creation and Destruction

A first pass at an analysis of verbs of creation and destruction and evolutive anaphora opens up many other issues. I now discuss some of these.

3.3.1. Half-baked Cakes and Bare Ruined Choirs

The lexical semantics for creation and destruction verbs invites us to give a temporally sensitive interpretation of the NP that fills in the object position of the verb. When we say *John built a house*, is it not the case that the created object is only really a house in the post-state of the event of building? Intuitions are perhaps clearer for sentences in the progressive, such as *John was building a house but he never finished it*. There it seems that during the process of building the house, the house was not yet a house but it is called a house only because of the foreseen completion of the process. If so, then there is reason to suppose that the object NP must be interpreted as being a house only in the post-state of the eventuality. To make this interpretation plain, we adopt a proposal of Higginbotham (personal communication) according to which common nouns like *house* have a separate eventuality argument, that is, $house(s, x)$. The interpretation of *John was building a house*, then, would be that John was engaged in an activity that had as a *natural* or *typical* culmination that a house is created by John. That is, $house(s, x)$ would hold of the result state of the process in which John was engaged.

3.3.2. Remnants of Destruction and Antecedents of Creation

Our analysis of creation and destruction verbs and anaphora is not complicated enough. Consider the following examples:

(26)   a. Figaro our cat ate a huge mouse. He then digested it for a whole day.
       b. The compactor crushed a VW. A huge crane then moved it to a railcar.
       c. Core, peel, and slice the apples, and then cook them together with sugar and spices for 20 minutes. Then put them in the piecrust and bake them for forty minutes (recipe for apple pie).

These examples seem fine, yet they are structurally similar to (25a). The verbs in (25a) and (26a–c) all involve substantial change to the affected object, and so our analysis above would analyse them along the lines of the examples in (23). But the anaphoric reference does appear to work even in discourses where *Narration* holds between the constituents introduced by the two sentences, as indicated by the presence of *then* in the examples above.

This challenge to our analysis can be overcome by a more sophisticated analysis of substantial change, creation, and destruction verbs and of the lexical information contained in objects. If we follow Aristotle's intuitive understanding of substantial change, a substantial change of an object involves a change in its essential form, which is also linked to the object's function. In this case both (26a) and (26b) involve substantial change to the mouse and the VW, respectively; the form and the function of the mouse no longer exist after the destruction. But what is a substantial change to the mouse and the VW is an accidental change here to the matter of those objects. And it appears that we are referring to the matter of the VW and the matter of the mouse in examples (26a) and (26b). In (26c) we refer to the apple-sugar-spice stuff that is the result of the blending.

The behaviour of the pronouns in (26) appears to be some form of discourse coercion; it is the type requirements of the predicates as an argument to which the pronoun appears, as well as the presence of a destruction in the discourse context that coerces the anaphoric pronoun to pick up the matter of the destroyed object.[17] Pustejovksy (1991, 1995) argues that a lexical entry for each type of object has a qualia structure that reflects that type of object's Aristotelian *aitia*—namely, its fourfold causal roles of form. Pustejovksy has proposed that qualia structures are a principle of organisation in lexical semantics, and he has used them to provide an account of coercion that explains why *enjoy the book* has as a default interpretation *enjoy reading the book*.

The coercion going on in (26) is more complex than that with *enjoy* since the anaphor's reference depends on the discourse context, the eventuality in which the antecedent is a participant, and the eventuality to which the anaphor supplies a participant. My idea is that in a discourse context where the object has been destroyed and is thus no longer available as an antecedent to a pronoun that denotes a participant in some subsequent event, the matter of the object, perhaps as it has been transformed by the previous event, is at least by default available. As long as the matter associated with *X* via the qualia structure (for example, the mouse's body in the examples above) remains after the substantial change or is transformed in some determinate way as in (26c), one can refer to *X*'s matter by using an anaphoric pronoun. In effect this is a bridging type of reference that exploits the qualia structure. One uses at least a part of the qualia structure as a function to get at the original object even though it no longer exists. It is also similar to metonymy, using a part to refer to a now no longer existent whole.

Whether the matter is available or not depends on the type of destruction the object has undergone. Vaporisation of the car does not preserve the matter, though crushing it does. This hypothesis allows us to distinguish between the complete destruction of the object and the total transformation of the qualia structure in (23) from the partial transformation of the qualia structure in (26a) and (26b). To be sure the mouse has lost its mousy function after being eaten; it can no longer lead a mousy life. The mouse's matter has even been transformed during the eating process; presumably Figaro did not swallow the mouse whole. Yet at least the matter of various mouse parts lying in Figaro's stomach remains understood as a transformation of mouse matter (i.e., as an accidental change of shape of the mouse matter). Similarly, the form and the function of the VW are destroyed by the car compactor; so the VW has ceased to be. Its matter of auto parts, though transformed in shape, still remains recognisable as VW matter.

It is important to note that the matter of the object is not easily available for anaphoric reference in those cases in which the object has not been destroyed. We have a strong preference to predicate properties of the whole object where possible.

(27)   a.   The children found a mouse in the bathroom. It was 2 ounces of fur, bone, and little mouse organs.
       b.   A VW rolled down the highway. It was a 1000 pounds of metal and 200 pounds of plastic and rubber.

The pronouns in (27) in either case could refer to the matter of the mouse or the VW, but they seem to refer back only to the mouse and the car itself. This suggests that it is only when the discourse context implies that the object has been destroyed or not yet created that the matter becomes available for anaphoric reference. As we have seen, that the discourse context contains such information is a matter not only of computing the contents of the individual constituents but also of how these constituents are related in the discourse structure.

I term the hypothesis that the underlying matter of an object is anaphorically available as the *underlying matter (UM) hypothesis*. Formally, the UM hypothesis extends the set of accessible discourse referents. I assume that a qualia structure contains functions from one type of object into another type—functions such as *Matter, Form, Function*—that discourse referents have types that are associated with such qualia structures, and that $Matter(w, e)$ returns a discourse referent of a particular type.

> **The UM hypothesis.** Suppose that x is a discourse referent accessible to $z \in \mathcal{D}(e)$ for some e and constituent α in an SDRS K such that $e \in U_\alpha$. Suppose also that for some e_β, it holds that $K \vDash x \notin \mathcal{D}(post(e_\beta)) \wedge O(post(e_\beta), pre(e))$. Then $Matter(x)$ is a discourse referent accessible to z.

Let us see how the UM hypothesis accounts for examples like (26a). Figaro's eating a huge mouse destroys the mouse, and this triggers, according to the UM hypothesis, the accessibility of the discourse referent, $Matter(x)$, representing the mousy matter. The discourse relation between the constituents in the SDRS introduced by the first and second sentences is *Narration* (because of the presence of *then*), and so the prestate of the digesting must overlap with the post-state of the eating of the mouse. Nevertheless, we can identify the discourse referent $Matter(x)$ with the discourse referent introduced by the pronoun since the destruction event e does not preclude the existence of $Matter(x)$ in $post(e)$. Now $post(e)$ may in fact transform $Matter(x)$ and change its properties. In (26c), $Matter(y)$, where y is the apples, is transformed to a cooked mixture containing sugar and spices.

There are limits to the type of transformations the matter of a certain object may undergo before it is no longer recognised as being the matter of that object.

When such transformations *e* occur, we say that not only the object but also its matter no longer exist in *post(e)*. I take this to be part of the lexical entry of the verb. We may classify destruction verbs according to how they affect the matter *quale* of the destroyed object. So in (23a), for example, *Matter(x)*, where *x* is the VW, is also denied to exist in the post-state of the vaporisation. When the discourse context implies a change such that nothing remains of the qualia structure, and hence nothing recognisable of the object, then anaphoric reference to the object is not possible, at least when the anaphoric reference presupposes the existence of the anaphoric antecedent in the post-state of the change. Similarly in (23b), where the painting is consumed, anaphoric reference to the painting appears no longer possible in a subsequent eventuality. In both cases neither the VW matter (metal) nor the canvas and paints of the painting remain.

In the UM hypothesis, I have limited the exploitation of the qualia structure to the material role because only the anaphoric exploitation of this role seems warranted philosophically and only in the context where there has been an antecedent event of destruction. The reason for this depends on this understanding of substantial change as being in at least many cases an accidental change of the underlying matter. The philosophical justification for restricting the use of qualia structures in this discourse context also receives linguistic support. It appears difficult to refer to the object's form, function, or causal role with a simple anaphoric pronoun in which the object has disappeared and its function or form appears as a participant in a subsequent event. That is, it doesn't seem possible to coerce the referent of the simple pronoun to refer to the form, function, or causal role of the no-longer-existing object.

(28)   a.   ?A powerful thermonuclear device vaporised a VW. We saw it thermally etched on a wall upon our visit to the site of the explosion.

b.   A powerful thermonuclear device vaporised a VW. We saw its shape thermally etched on a wall upon our visit to the site of the explosion.

The form and function don't persist in substantial change. Natural language reflects a nominalistic, Aristotelian approach to change.[18]

The creation of an object seems not to presuppose the existence of its matter, and the matter is not accessible with a pronoun prior to the object's creation. Consider the data in (29). The attempts to refer anaphorically to the matter of a not yet created object with pronouns are terrible. With the use of bridging definite descriptions, however, these anaphoric links improve dramatically.

(29)   a.   *John baked a cake. He mixed it together and put it in the oven.

b.   John built a house last year. He started buying the materials (it*, them*) in March and finished in November.

c.   John baked a cake. He mixed the materials together and put the mixture in the oven.

In all these cases, it can be seen that the matter of the created object is not available for anaphoric reference with a pronoun contributing a participant to some event that precedes the creation. Thus, these cases seem to differ from the cases in which objects are destroyed, and the UM hypothesis would appear not to extend to them, at least as far as the material component of the qualia structure.

A possible counterexample to this claim might be (30a):

(30)   a.   John baked a cake. He put it in the oven and let it cook thirty minutes.

But this discourse, according to my intuitions, involves an *Elaboration*; John's baking a cake is elaborated on in the second sentence. In any case, it appears that the anaphoric pronoun there is not referring necessarily to the mixture but simply to the cake itself. I find (30a) no different from (30b), apart from some stylistic heaviness in the latter:

(30)   b.   John baked a cake. He put the cake in the oven and let the cake cook in thirty minutes.

I have presented evidence that matter isn't available even when it should be. But what about form? Examples such as (31) might provide evidence that the form is anaphorically available:

(31)   a.   The council drew up plans to build a bridge. The mayor liked its design.
         b.   Bob had been dreaming about a super philosophy department. When he became chairman he got the chance to realise it.

Such examples are suggestive, but I don't think they are conclusive. The mayor likes the design of the bridge as it will someday exist or as the council conceives of it existing. He doesn't like the bridge's form's design. This seems to be a category mistake. Similarly Bob has a super department in mind, an intentional object that he then has a chance to realise. But it doesn't seem that we should identify this intentional object with *the form* of the department (whatever that would be). On the other hand, we should recognise that there are all sorts of verbs that can take intentional verbs; *realise* is one, but so is *miss*:

(32)   The bomb destroyed my VW_i. I'll miss it_i.

Clearly what I miss is my VW, not its form. Thus, it would appear that creation verbs don't license the sort of type coercions that destruction verbs license.

This suggests that creation events have a quite different metaphysics from destruction events. Though natural language metaphysics does not countenance creation ex nihilo, the matter or form of an object like a cake isn't something that one can pick up anaphorically with a pronoun. It may exist but not in the requisite salient and recognisable way that the user of the anaphor can rely on, in contrast to the situation in which an object is destroyed but the matter persists. This difference is explicable if we follow the form of the UM hypothesis. The qualia structure, restricted by our conception of change, guides availability; if the object is not yet created, then neither is its qualia structure nor associated matter, form, and so on. So this train of thought predicts, apparently correctly, that prior to the creation of an object, one can neither refer to the object nor to its matter since the matter is dependent on the not yet created object for its identification.

The analysis of destruction and creation verbs proposed in this section suggests a classification of destruction verbs in terms of how they treat the matter of the objects they destroy, as I mentioned earlier. But this treatment should extend naturally to an analysis of the aspectual verbs like *stop*, *start*, *cease*, and so on. In effect these are destruction and creation verbs concerning events and processes. But I leave this analysis to another time.

4. Conclusions

In section 3 I have shown how the dynamicity of events affects the structure of natural language discourse and also reflects a broadly Aristotelian view of change. In particular, I have argued that this conception of change helps us understand the behaviour of anaphoric pronouns in contexts where objects are being created or destroyed—the so-called contexts of *evolutive anaphora*. But discourse structure and compositional semantics (especially tense) also affect evolutive anaphora; my analysis has had to take many factors into account and so is quite complex. The reason for these complications are, I hope, by and large clear. One can, of course, refer to individuals who no longer exist, as in (33):

(33)   The bomb vaporised a VW. It had been parked near the Federal Building.

But we must use the tense system and discourse structure to do it properly. The use of the pluperfect here provides a clue in SDRT that the second sentence functions to give the background of what went on in the first.[19] The car's being parked must, by the anaphoric theory of the pluperfect in SDRT, be prior to the explosion, and so the anaphoric link between *it* and *a VW* does not conflict with the consequences of a destruction verb like *vaporise*. My analysis of evolutive anaphora would treat such a discourse as consistent and coherent. But to do this we need a theory not only of lexical semantics but also of discourse structure and compositional semantics to make such predictions. A formal theory like SDRT supplies the requisite tools for this analysis.

The dynamicity of events, exemplified in the analysis of evolutive anaphora, is a key feature of events, distinguishing them from facts. Dynamicity follows directly from the temporal locatedness and transitoriness of events. Facts do not exhibit dynamicity because they are atemporal. Along with the other distinguishing features of facts and events that I reviewed in section 2, dynamicity strongly suggests that in natural language metaphysics facts and events constitute distinct kinds.

Notes

1. See "Unfair to Facts" in Austin (1961).

2. There are many interesting observations about the way PPs and possessive NPs fill in the argument structure of the nominal. See Grimshaw (1992) and also chapters 4 and 5 of Asher (1993).

3. For examples and a detailed discussion, see Asher (1993).

4. I differ here from Vendler in my judgments about the acceptability of the container *true* with gerunds and derived nominals.

5. See Asher (1993: ch. 1).

6. The description of the differences between facts and events is made more complex by the need to treat highly intensional contexts that appear to take facts as arguments like those below. There is a reading, for instance, on which (a) is true but (b) is false:

(a)   The fact that Superman was vulnerable interested Lex Luthor.
(b)   The fact that Clark Kent was vulnerable interested Lex Luthor.

For a discussion see Asher (1993).

7. This reconstruction of Moore's argument is given in Fine (1981).

8. Many philosophers who adopt a correspondence theory of truth take this argument to support the view that facts ground the truth of propositions. For a discussion, see Hochberg (1978).

9. One can with Krifka (1987) and Link (1987) go on to assume ⊕ to be commutative, idempotent, and associative.

10. Davidson (1967) states that events are subject to mereological principles.

11. As Krifka (1987) has noted, there is a problem with events and negation if events are not closed under complementation. It affects a theory of events on which events are not closed under restricted complementation. Suppose that we adopt the general account of a large class of adverbial modifiers in the way proposed by Davidson, and suppose we analyse *for two hours* as a predicate of events. But if that is the case and events are not closed under negation, how can we make sense of (a) in the reading in which the adverb is understood to have wide scope over the negative quantifier *no one*?

(a)   No one talked for over two hours.

If we try to carry out the standard event-based approach to such adverbial modifiers, we cannot write down a coherent logical form for (a) that captures the intended reading. For the logical form for *No one talked* would be $\neg\exists x\exists e(\text{talk}(x, e))$, and if we make *for two hours* a predicate of e, we must end up with the logical form $\neg\exists x\exists e(\text{talk}(x, e) \wedge \text{for-two-hours}(e))$, which assigns (a) incorrect truth conditions. This difficulty can be dealt with, however: we give up the idea that these adverbial modifiers are predicates of the events in question; rather they are predicates of times that are always introduced outside the scope of any possible negation operator. These times are introduced within the processing of the inflection node of the syntactic structure as is negation. See Asher (1993) and Amsili and Le Draoulec (1995).

12. There are perhaps difficulties with states such as those described by *it's raining*. But one can always defend the dependence of states upon objects by saying that this describes a state of the local atmosphere or of the weather.

13. For more discussion of states and the problem of event negation, see Asher (1993) and Amsili and Le Draoulec (1995).

14. The axioms for deriving discourse relations in SDRT divide into three parts. First there are general axioms, expressed by means of weak defeasible conditionals, that allow us to infer particular discourse relations:

$\langle \tau, \alpha, \beta \rangle > Narration(\alpha, \beta)$
$(\langle \tau, \alpha, \beta \rangle \wedge \text{D-permissible-subtype}(\alpha, \beta)) > Elaboration(\alpha, \beta)$
$(\langle \tau, \alpha, \beta \rangle \wedge \text{D-permissible-cause}(\alpha, \beta)) > Explanation(\alpha, \beta)$

Here '>' is a rather special conditional, and the nonmonotonic logic underlying SDRT allows us to infer *Elaboration*(α, β) even though both the antecedents of the *Narration*

axiom and the *Elaboration* axiom are satisfied. Other axioms define the semantic consequences of the relations, and examples of those are given in the text. All these axioms are
part of a speaker's general linguistic competence for the *Narrative* genre.

There are other axioms, which exploit lexical knowledge and even world knowledge.
These give conditions under which we can infer conditions like *D-permissible-subtype*
and *D-permissible-cause*. I have elsewhere referred, and will again refer below, to these
as *triggering axioms*. To infer the appropriate discourse relation in many cases, we need
to write appropriate triggering axioms. At present SDRT does not have a general theory
of these triggering axioms. For details see Asher (1995), and for an early application of
these axioms see Lascarides and Asher (1993).

15. The definition here is a simplification of what is needed when temporal and spatial
adverbials in β are taken into account. For details, see Asher et al. (1995). Concerning
consistency between states, the necessary and sufficient condition is that their theories—
namely, the set of sentences true in those states, or at the times at which they occur—
must be consistent.

16. Again in SDRT we would have to supply specific axioms that would trigger the
relevant licensing condition for *Explanation*.

17. This behaviour also applies to definite descriptions. For example, in (26c) we could
have continued to refer to the mixture by means of the term *the apples*, even though the
distinct apples have ceased to exist. It is unclear to me, however, how far one can analyse
the bridging use of definite descriptions in terms of the sort of coercion discussed here.

18. There still remains the question of how to handle (28b). The discourse relation
linking the two sentences is *Result*, a causal relation between facts. We can refer to the
VW here because it is the cause of the shape now etched on the wall. But this in no way
entails a commitment to the existence of the VW in the prestate of the second eventuality.
We are rather referring back to the VW in the prestate of the first clause. We could make
this clear with Higginbotham's idea that VW has an eventuality argument. We would
have to fix the eventuality argument as being the prestate of the vaporising event.

19. For more details see Lascarides and Asher (1992).

References

Amsili, P., and A. Le Draoulec, 1995. Contribution to the Event Negation Problem. In P.
    Amsili, M. Borillo, and L. Vieu (eds.), *Time, Space and Movement: Meaning and
    Knowledge in the Sensible World. Proceedings of the 5th International Workshop*,
    17–29. COREP, Toulouse.
Asher, N., 1986. Belief in Discourse Representation Theory. In *Journal of Philosophical
    Logic* 16: 127–189.
Asher, N., 1987. A Typology for Attitude Verbs and their Anaphoric Properties. In *Lin-
    guistics and Philosophy* 10: 125–198.
Asher, N., 1993. *Reference to Abstract Objects in Discourse*. Kluwer Academic Publish-
    ers, Dordrecht.
Asher, N., 1995. From Discourse Micro-structure to Macro-structure and Back Again:
    The Interpretation of Focus. In H. Kamp and B. Partee (eds.), *Semantics and Context*
    (SFB 340 Publication). Universität Stuttgart, Stuttgart.
Asher, N., M. Aurnague, M. Bras, and L. Vieu, 1995. Spatial and Temporal Adverbials in
    Discourse. *Time, Space and Movement: Meaning and Knowledge in the Sensible
    World. Proceedings of the 5th International Workshop*, 107–119. COREP, Toulouse.

Austin, J. L., 1961. *Philosophical Papers*. Oxford University Press, Oxford.

Bach, E., 1981. On Time, Tense, and Aspect: An Essay in English Metaphysics. In P. Cole (ed.), *Radical Pragmatics*, 62–81. Academic Press, New York.

Cresswell, M. J., 1985. *Adverbial Modification. Interval Semantics and Its Rivals*. Reidel, Dordrecht.

Davidson, D., 1967. The Logical Form of Action Sentences. In N. Rescher (ed.), *The Logic of Decision and Action*, 87–95. University of Pittsburgh Press, Pittsburgh. Reprinted in D. Davidson, 1982. *Essays on Actions and Events*, 105–122. Oxford University Press, Oxford.

Fine, K., 1981. First Order Modal Theories. In *Studia Logica* 39: 159–200.

Grimshaw, J., 1990. *Argument Structure*. MIT Press, Cambridge (Mass).

Hochberg, H., 1978. *Thought, Fact and Reference: The Origins and Ontology of Logical Atomism* . University of Minnesota Press, Minneapolis.

Kamp, H., 1990. Prolegomena to a Structural Theory of Belief and Other Attitudes. In C. A. Anderson and J. Owens (eds.), *The Role of Content in Logic, Language and Mind*, 27–90 (CSLI Lecture Notes 20). University of Chicago Press, Chicago.

Kamp, H., and Rohrer, C., 1983. Tense in Texts. In R. Bäuerle, C. Schwarze, and A. von Stechow (eds.), *Meaning, Use, and Interpretation of Language*, 250–269. De Gruyter, Berlin.

Kamp, H., and A. Rossdeutscher, 1994. Remarks on Lexical Structure and DRS Construction. In *Theoretical Linguistics* 20: 98–164.

Krifka, M., 1987. *Nominal Reference and Temporal Constitution: Towards a Semantics of Quantity* (FNS Bericht 17), Forschungstelle für Natürliche Sprachliche Systeme, Universität Tübingen, Tübingen.

Krifka, M., 1989. Nominal Reference, Temporal Constitution and Quantification in Event Semantics. In J. van Benthem, R. Bartsch, and P. van Embde Boas (eds.), *Semantics and Cntextual Epressions*, 75-115. Foris, Dordrecht.

Lascarides, A., and N. Asher, 1992. A Semantics and Pragmatics for the Pluperfect. In *Proceedings of the 6th Conference of the European Chapter of the Association for Computational Linguistics*, 250–259. Research Institute for Language and Speech, Utrecht.

Lascarides, A., and N. Asher, 1993. Temporal Interpretation, Discourse Relations, and Common-sense Entailment. In *Linguistics and Philosophy* 16: 437–493.

Link, G., 1983. The Logical Analysis of Plurals and Mass Terms: A Lattice Theoretic Approach. In R. Bäuerle, C. Schwarze, and A. von Stechow (eds.), *Meaning, Use and Interpretation of Language*, 303-323. De Gruyter, Berlin.

Link, G., 1987. Algebraic Semantics for Event Structures. In J. Groenendijk, M. Stokhof, and F. Veltman (eds.), *Proceedings of the 6th Amsterdam Colloquium*, 243–262. Institute for Language, Logic and Information, Amsterdam.

Pustejovksy, J., 1991. The Generative Lexicon. In *Computational Linguistics* 17: 409–441.

Pustejovksy, J., 1995. *The Generative Lexicon*. MIT Press, Cambridge (Mass.).

Vendler, Z., 1967. *Linguistics in Philosophy*. Comell University Press, Ithaca (N.Y.).

7

Chronoscopes

The Dynamic Representation
of Facts and Events

Alice G. B. ter Meulen

1. Introduction

Some essential semantic properties of our use of tense and aspect in ordinary
English discourse have been accounted for in Discourse Representation Theory
(DRT; Kamp and Reyle 1993), formalising how aspectual properties control the
reference to events and states with a classical notion of logical entailment. Further properties of our ordinary reasoning about temporal dependencies may arise
in the interpretation of discourse. The richer representational tools of Dynamic
Aspect Trees (DAT; ter Meulen 1995) captures other aspects of temporal reasoning in natural language with a situated, nonmonotonic notion of inference in
chronoscopes.

This chapter takes a closer look at three issues concerning the representation
of facts and events in DATs: (1) the use of aspectual verbs to describe the relations among the internal structure of events described in discourse; (2) differences between three kinds of stative information, and activities, treated on a par
in DRT; and (3) the application of situated inference in our reasoning in temporal domains, as opposed to the classical logical entailment.

2. General Considerations

In dynamic natural language semantics, the objective is to analyse how a given
context is affected by incorporating new information, associating with linguistic
expressions different context-change potentials (*ccp*). Reasoning about time, the
order in which information is presented to the interpreter is a particularly relevant dimension, for it constrains the inferences we draw about what happened
when. Competent English speakers share fundamental linguistic intuitions about
the ways in which the morphological inflections may be used to indicate in what
order the described events took place. Consider (1) and (2):

(1)   Jane was patrolling the neighbourhood. She noticed a car parked in an alley.

(2)   Jane noticed a car parked in an alley. She was patrolling the neighbourhood.

Either (1) or (2) makes us answer the question of whether Jane was patrolling the neighbourhood already before she noticed the car positively. The order of presentation thus does not seem to affect our judgment. This is not merely due to the background information that Jane is a member of the feared parking police in Amsterdam, who hover around a district to punish any infraction of parking regulations instantly with steep fines. Nor should our answer depend on the meaning of the particular predicates involved. Our judgment is based solely on the logical interaction of the past tense, the aspectual properties of progressive verbal morphology, and the order of presentation.

But contrast this observation to the fact that the order of presentation in (3) and (4) does affect what we answer to the question of whether Jane had turned the corner before she noticed the car:

(3)   Jane turned the corner. She noticed a car parked in an alley.

(4)   Jane noticed a car parked in an alley. She turned the corner.

We judge on the basis of (3) that she did turn the corner first, but given (4), her noticing the car must have preceded her turning the corner. These core data have set the agenda for the dynamic semantics of tense and aspect since the early 1980s, when Hans Kamp and his colleagues first proposed DRT as a new toolkit, integrating tense logical results with Reichenbachian reference times as a third semantic parameter (see van Eijck and Kamp 1997 for an updated presentation of DRT).

One may be tempted to a quick hypothesis (// denotes order of presentation irrelevant).

(H.1)   a.   PAST PROG (e_1) // PAST $(e_2) = e_1$ includes e_2, part of e_1 precedes e_2.
        b.   PAST (e_1) + PAST $(e_2) = e_1$ precedes e_2, all of e_1 precedes e_2.

But it is easy to find evidence against b; consider (1a), where the past progressive of (1) is turned into a simple past.

(1a)   Jane patrolled the neighbourhood. She noticed a car parked in an alley.

If b were valid, we should conclude that Jane patrolled the neighbourhood before she noticed the car. But our intuition does not support that conclusion, for from (1a) we still conclude to the same temporal relations as those based on (1). So what explains this difference between the two simple past-tense discourses?

The fundamental difference is one of aspectual class. If we describe what Jane does with predicates that apply homogeneously to any part of her action, the description is called an activity (ACT). If our description does not apply to a part of her action, it is called an accomplishment (ACC). Traditional semantic terminology calls the first an atelic event description, the second a telic event description; the first mode does not contain any information about the resulting state, the telos, but the second does. Our first hypothesis needs refining to make b depend on aspectual class, as below.

(H.2) a. Correct
       b. PAST $(e_1$ ACC) + PAST $(e_2) = e_1$ precedes e_2, all of e_1 precedes e_2.
       c. PAST $(e_1$ ACT) + PAST $(e_2) = e_1$ includes e_2, part of e_1 precedes e_2.

This leads to the prediction that aspectual class effects are still overruled by progressive inflections, as it cancels the dynamic force the past-tense accomplishments have. Indeed, applying this prediction to (3) and (4), we see it is borne out in our intuitive judgments concerning the temporal relations described in (3a) and (4a).

(3a)   Jane was turning the corner. She noticed a car parked in an alley.
(4a)   Jane noticed a car parked in an alley. She was turning the corner.

Was Jane turning the corner before she noticed the car? Both (3a) and (4a) make us answer positively to this question, as if her turning the corner is portrayed in slow motion.

Now one may wonder whether there is any relevant semantic difference between activities and progressive descriptions, as both seem to lead to the same conclusions about the temporal relations. Contrary to the account of these data in DRT, I would like to argue that indeed there is a significant difference. Consider the three sentence discourses in (5), a sequence of ACC, ACT, and PROG, and (6), a sequence of ACC and two PROG.

(5)   Jane noticed a car parked in an alley. She patrolled the neighbourhood. She was driving along the Rokin.   ACC + ACT + PROG
(6)   Jane noticed a car parked in an alley. She was patrolling the neighbourhood. She was driving along the Rokin.   ACC + PROG + PROG

Now was Jane driving along the Rokin when she noticed the car in the alley? If our answer is based on (5), it is not all that clear what we should say. She may have been driving along the Rokin when she noticed the car, or she may have been elsewhere. Perhaps she started her patrolling of the Rokin after she had noticed the car elsewhere. But if (6) is the information we use in answering, it is perfectly clear that both her patrolling and her driving along the Rokin must have started before she noticed the car. Hence the car she noticed must have been in an alley off the Rokin. So (6) gives us enough information to infer, as a matter of temporal logic, that she must have been driving along the Rokin when she noticed the car. Hence there is a clear inferential difference between (5) and (6) caused by the ACT versus PROG in the second sentence of these discourses.

A second example, showing another, related difference between ACT and PROG, is given in (7), starting with an ACT, and (8), starting with a PROG.

(7)   Jane drove along the Rokin. When she noticed a speeding car, she turned on the alarm.

(8)   Jane was driving along the Rokin. When she noticed a speeding car, she
        turned on the alarm.

So what do we answer to the question of whether Jane was still on the Rokin
when she turned on the alarm? Perhaps this appeals to a finer tuned intuition, but
it still seems common linguistic competence to judge that (7) makes us answer
positively, whereas (8) leaves room for doubt about the location of Jane when
she turned on the alarm. She may have pursued the speeding car, leading her
from the Rokin into the Vijzelstraat, before she got a chance to turn on the
alarm.

Systems of temporal reasoning in natural language must address the issue of
which contexts give us reason to conclude that what is described first also
happened first. The view I advocate is that we use simple past-tense clauses
either to present dynamic information, directly referring to change in the world
(i.e., events), or to present static information, descriptive of a state the world is
in (i.e., facts). The way we give information about the world is only in part
determined by what the world is like, or rather by what we collectively consider
the world to be.

3. The Toolkit: Dynamic Aspect Trees and Chronoscopes

The dynamic representation of tense and aspect in natural language must make a
fundamental distinction between ways of referring to events (i.e., giving dynamic information about change) and ways of describing states (giving static
information about what is the case). In DATs, dynamic information affects the
architecture of the representation by adding new nodes, whereas stative information merely adds descriptive labels to existing nodes and ordinarily does not
introduce new nodes.

A text provides three kinds of information:

(a)   the descriptive content,
(b)   the aspectual content,
(c)   the perspectival content.

The descriptive content determines the truth-conditional meaning; it classifies a
situation as being of a certain type or supporting that type. This descriptive content is represented in DATs by labels on nodes, where a label always consists of
a relation, an appropriate number of arguments, and a positive or negative polarity. The aspectual content of a clause or an entire text tells us how its descriptive content is integrated with the given context. In DATs this is encoded in the
open or closed nodes to represent ACT and ACC events, respectively called
holes and *plugs*, and in the stickers for stative information that are appended to
nodes without introducing new ones.[1] The perspectival content of a clause or
text determines which point in the representation is considered the point of view
of the evaluation representing the location of the interpreter drawing inferences
from the given information. It determines, for instance, the reference of indexicals and demonstratives, but it also affects the form with which available infor-

mation is reported. For example, the text may present information in the simple past tense, but later on that information should be reported as a stative *sticker* representing past-perfect clauses. The spatiotemporal location of the act of issuing the information is also included in the perspectival content. In DATs this is represented as the *source node*, unique and fixed as the rightmost terminal node. A chronoscope is a connected, acyclic path from root to terminal node, representing a cone of simultaneously satisfiable descriptive content, carried in the labels on its nodes. The current chronoscope contains the unique *current node*.

Before the data discussed in section 2 are represented in DATs, the construction rules are stated.

3.1. DAT Construction Rules

Every DAT has a unique *source node*, representing the act of issuing information, and a unique *current node*, which is shifted when the DAT is updated with a new node. At the outset, the current node is identified with the source node. When the initial past-tense clause is processed, the past-tense rule sets the current node to a newly created left sister open node, labelled PAST, to dominate all of the past-tense discourse. Subsequent past tense clauses must be represented at nodes dependent on this PAST node.

A DAT is stepwise constructed during the process of interpretation. There may be choice points at which the interpreter may decide to accept or reject certain inferences or interpretations, based on information that is not contained in the text itself. The DAT system is designed only to determine the consequences of such an interpretive choice but not to present any heuristic or normative guidelines in making the choice. This means that the DAT construction rules do not constitute a deterministic algorithm—that is, there is not always a unique next step in the construction. This is an important advantage of the DAT system, as it reflects an opening towards input interactively obtained from the interpreter when a choice point is reached. In an implementation, the DAT system may query the user for his or her preferences—for example, by asking situated temporal questions such as "Is John still asleep?" to which a positive answer provides the system with a warranty to import the sticker representing John's sleeping state into a new chronoscope.

The construction rules are presented here rather informally, for expository ease. A reader who wishes to see a formal presentation of the DAT construction should consult Seligman and ter Meulen (1995). Each DAT has a unique current node, designated with c.

(9)   *Sticker rule* for progressive and perfect clauses, simple lexical states (*be*, *have*): stack sticker label on c, if c is a plug; stack sticker label on next new node otherwise.

(10)   *Hole rule* for ACT: affix label on new hole; reset c to new hole—that is, next node to be dependent.

(11) *Plug rule* for ACC: affix label on new plug; reset c to new plug—that is, next node to be sister.

3.2. Illustrations

The construction rules are now applied to the data discussed in section 2. The first observation, based on (1) and (2), is that the order of presentation of a progressive and a simple past is irrelevant in determining the temporal relation between what they describe. So (1) and (2) should produce the same DAT, as in figure 1.

(1) Jane was patrolling the neighbourhood (*Prog* sticker). She noticed a car parked in an alley (plug).

(2) Jane noticed a car parked in an alley (plug). She was patrolling the neighbourhood (*Prog* sticker).

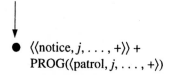

● $\langle\langle$notice, j, . . . , $+\rangle\rangle$ +
PROG($\langle$patrol, j, . . . , $+\rangle$)

Figure 1. DAT for (1) and (2).

The PROG-sticker awaits the introduction of the notice plug for (1), and for (2) it is appended to the notice plug after its introduction. For transparency, the labels are not always fully specified in these illustrations, and the source node is not displayed when it is obvious where its location is. From figure 1 we infer that Jane was patrolling the neighbourhood when she noticed the car, as a matter of DAT logic, and that she must have started her patrolling before she noticed the car, by an inference rule relating the start of an event as presupposition of its progressive. We cannot infer anything about her ending her patrolling other than that it cannot be consistent with the current node, that is, occur now.[2]

A text consisting of two ACC, both represented as plugs, is given in (3), where the introduction of the PAST node is illustrated in figure 2.

(3) Jane turned the corner (plug). She noticed a car parked in an alley (plug).

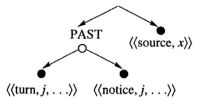

Figure 2. DAT for (3).

Since the order of presentation was here considered relevant for temporal reasoning, reversing the order, as in

(4)   Jane noticed a car parked in an alley (plug). She turned the corner (plug)

would produce an isomorphic DAT, but its labels would be reversed. The left-to-right order on nodes is used in precedence inferences—that is, from figure 2 we would conclude she first turned the corner before she noticed the car.

To represent the differences between ACT and PROG stickers in DATs, we discuss (1a). It starts with a simple past ACT, which creates a hole for Jane's patrolling with a dependent plug for her noticing the car.

(1a)   Jane patrolled the neighbourhood (hole). She noticed a car parked in an alley (plug).

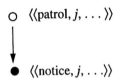

$$\circ \quad \langle\langle patrol, j, \ldots \rangle\rangle$$

$$\bullet \quad \langle\langle notice, j, \ldots \rangle\rangle$$

Figure 3. DAT for (1a).

The intended meaning of the dependency is that the noticing event took place within the time her patrolling took—that is, the down arrow represents temporal inclusion. This relation is not reversible, as it would be if there was a sticker on the plug, as in figure 1. We can also infer from figure 3 that she was patrolling the neighbourhood when she noticed the car, introducing a PROG sticker on any node dependent on a node carrying the corresponding label. In other words, figure 1 is entailed by figure 3, but not vice versa.

The same point is illustrated in texts (3a) and (4a), both creating figure 4:

(3a)   Jane was turning the corner (*Prog* sticker). She noticed a car parked in an alley (plug).

(4a)   Jane noticed a car parked in an alley (plug). She was turning the corner (*Prog* sticker).

$$\bullet \quad \langle\langle notice, j, \ldots, + \rangle\rangle +$$
$$\quad PROG(\langle turn, j, \ldots, + \rangle)$$

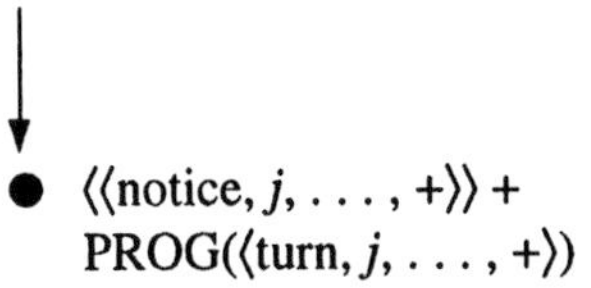

Figure 4. DAT for (3a) or (4a).

To appreciate the different behaviour of holes and stickers in a slightly more complex content, consider (5) and (6), which differ only in the second clause:

(5)   Jane noticed a car parked in an alley (plug). She patrolled the neighbourhood (hole). She was driving along the Rokin (*Prog* sticker).

(6)   Jane noticed a car parked in an alley (plug). She was patrolling the neighbourhood (*Prog* sticker). She was driving along the Rokin (*Prog* sticker).

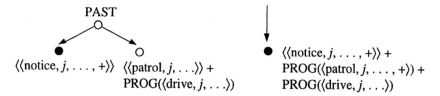

Figure 5. DATs for (5) and (6), respectively.

A difference was observed in the degree of reliability of the judgement of whether Jane was already driving along the Rokin when she noticed the car in the alley. Given (6), it would be definitely clearer that she was than given (5). This is accounted for in a DAT representation as follows. From the right DAT for (6) in figure 5 we infer, as the *drive* sticker is on the *notice* plug, that Jane must have been driving along the Rokin at the time she noticed the car. But from the left DAT in figure 5 we seem to need additional supporting information to draw that conclusion. The left DAT in figure 5 for (5) created a sticker on the *patrolling* hole, which is preceded by her noticing the car. There is no DAT inference rule that copies PROG stickers to left sisters, but there may be rules in other sources, serving as oracles to the temporal-reasoning component, based on lexical relations or explanatory modes to support a meaningful relation between her noticing that car and the duties of parking police on the Rokin.

A third illustration of the difference between progressive clauses and activities as initial clauses in discourse was presented in (7) and (8). In DAT representation, the difference is clearly visible in figure 6:

(7)   Jane drove along the Rokin (hole). When she noticed a speeding car (plug), she turned on the alarm (plug).

(8)   Jane was driving along the Rokin (*Prog* sticker). When she noticed a speeding car (plug), she turned on the alarm (plug).

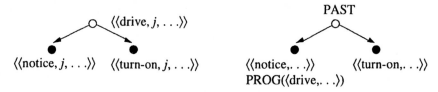

Figure 6. DATs for (7) and (8), respectively.

Importing a PROG sticker for Jane's driving in the left DAT in figure 6 is a solid DAT-inference rule, allowing any dependent node to carry the PROG sticker corresponding to a label of its dominating nodes. But in the right DAT of figure 6 we need to copy the given PROG sticker to a right sister, which is not a matter of DAT logic and should preferably be supported by additional, independent information. The DAT for (5) entails the DAT for (6), as the latter is obtained with DAT inference rules from the former, but not vice versa. Activities provide stronger information than progressives, although both preserve the perspective and the current chronoscope.

4. Three Degrees of Dynamic Involvement

Current theories in natural language semantics commonly accept the conception of meaning as a ccp, a function or relation operating on the given context to incorporate the information contained in the interpreted sentence. The DAT representations propose a structured updating operation, relating the input DAT, as a highly structured state, to one or more output DATs. Of course, it is always possible to reformalise DATs as purely set-theoretic objects, where labelled nodes are (sequences of) propositions and arrows relate them. Although this set-theoretic reformalisation may prove to be a useful exercise, offering an opportunity to sharpen the structural insights about situated inferences, it remains to be seen whether it would result in tools that are sufficiently user-friendly and heuristically fruitful to promote new explanatory insight and a broader empirical basis of linguistic theory. The advantages of the visually, directly accessible level of DAT representation reside primarily in supporting inferential judgments and structural understanding of the information a text procures. The dynamics of interpretation in DATs are located in the DAT construction, where their model-theoretic semantics, defined by embedding into event structures, remains hidden, for it is entirely determined by the DAT.

It may prove useful to indicate some important differences between DAT, DRT, and Dynamic Montague Grammar (DMG; Groenendijk and Stokhof 1991). The three semantic theories each rightfully claims to be dynamic, but it does so in different senses. Thus DMG is dynamic in adhering to the ccp view of meaning, while compositionally accounting for NP pronominal dependencies in discourse. Its dynamics resides in the update functions on information states, model-theoretic objects consisting of an assignment function and a state, which gradually delimits their possible continuations. I call this the first degree of dynamic involvement, with a tongue-in-cheek reference to Quine's (1953) notorious article 'Three degrees of modal involvement'. In DMG the dynamic interpretation of an expression encodes its constraints on discourse anaphora, but its static interpretation, computed by the update, only determines its truth conditions. In contrast, DRT exhibits the second degree of dynamic interpretation, as it explains how the reference of indexicals and other context-dependent expressions may change during the interpretation of the discourse, interpreting tense inflections as indexicals with context change potential. Both the first and the second degree of dynamics assume that the given information, resulting from updates, is always preserved in any later update—information is never lost. But in DMG and DRT, reference markers may not remain accessible to any future update, as they may be hidden in the structure of the information represented. In DRT when a reference marker is introduced into a subordinate DRS, it is inaccessible to later updates taking place at the main DRS. In DMG the discourse variable of bound pronouns dissolves in the static meaning resulting from the update, effectively hiding it in the dynamic computation of the binding. This accounts in both theories for the unacceptability of discourse anaphora with quantificational antecedents:

(12)   Every man loves his mother. *She is nice.

DAT representation constitutes a third degree of dynamic involvement, allowing the input DAT to be adjusted structurally to the requirements of the interpretation process in specific contexts to maintain consistency or accommodate presuppositions. Part of this adjustment may consist in closing off a section of the current chronoscope while preserving the section containing the dominating nodes and the root, to create a new, later chronoscope. In reporting inferences about the closed section of the old chronoscope, we must use static perfect tenses, even though the information may initially have been given with past progressives or simple past clauses describing events. Two rules regulate such adjustments: (a) a rule to plug up holes when update information is inconsistent (i.e., not simultaneously satisfiable with the current chronoscope) and (b) a rule to unplug a current plug to accommodate presuppositions, specified procedurally in (13) and (14).

(13)   *Plugging rule.* If extending the current chronoscope introduces a node with labels incompatible (i.e., not simultaneously satisfiable) with the labels of its ancestors:
   (a)   Back up to lowest node n in the current chronoscope with incompatible labels.
   (b)   If n is a hole, plug it up (i.e., make it a plug).
   (c)   Reset current node $c = n$.
   (d)   Apply plug rule.

(14)   *Unplugging rule.* If a new label with the update information simultaneously presupposes a label on the current plug c, then
   (a)   Unplug c (i.e., make it a hole),
   (b)   Introduce a dependent plug, label it with START(T), where T is the label of c which is presupposed.
   (c)   Reset current node c to this new plug and proceed with the update.

Plugging holes and unplugging plugs are the only dynamic DAT inferential operations that adjust the input DAT both in the nature of its nodes and in its structure. The DAT structure is dynamically adjusted to incoming information by checking whether the labels are simultaneously satisfiable within the current chronoscope or accommodating presuppositions. Admitting dynamic effects of inferences is characteristic of the third degree of dynamic involvement.

   To illustrate this third degree of dynamic involvement, consider the discourse in (15) and the DAT in figure 7:

(15)   After dinner (plug), Jane did her homework (hole). She was sitting on the sofa (PROG sticker). The cat slept on her lap (hole). Suddenly the doorbell rang (plug). She got up to open the door (plug). It was John (sticker). He wanted her to come with him (sticker). He did not realise she was doing her homework (negative polarity sticker). She started explaining he better leave (plug). First she said her homework was not done yet (plug).

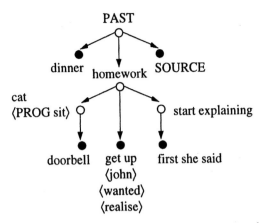

Figure 7. DAT for (15) with dynamic inference nodes.

The DAT constructed for (15) is presented in figure 7 with abbreviated labels for legibility and simplicity. The hole representing the cat sleeping on Jane's lap also carries the PROG sticker for her sitting on the sofa, according to the DAT construction rules. The plug for the doorbell is dependent on it, and so would be the plug for her getting up were it not that one cannot simultaneously be sitting on a sofa and getting up from it. The dynamic inferences cannot be displayed in the static picture other than by a hole with a plug inside. The plugging rule now plugs up the hole for the sleeping cat with the conflicting sticker for Jane's sitting on the sofa and applies the plug rule to it. It creates a new sister plug for her getting up, still dependent on the hole for Jane doing her homework. This dependency is reinforced later by the presupposition that Jane is still doing her homework, induced by the negative polarity sticker for John's failing to realise that. Had the interpreter instead chosen to interpret doing one's homework as an continuous activity that cannot be interrupted by answering the doorbell, hence plugging the higher homework hole, this presupposition would unplug that hole-turned-plug for her doing homework and repair the DAT to accommodate her getting up as the dependent plug. The plug for Jane's starting to explain, sister to the getting-up plug, requires opening when the clause is interpreted, giving information about what she said first, accommodating the presupposition that it is a temporal part of her explanation of why John better leave. This illustrates how dynamic inferences to maintain local consistency within a chronoscope and to accommodate presuppositions have structural effects in DATs. This notion of dynamic inference is contrasted with the static situated inferences that are characterised by portability conditions on stickers.

5. Dynamic Inference and Situated Inference

In classical static Montague grammar meaning postulates are formulas considered true in all models that provide "proper" interpretations of the language. They serve to constrain the set of logically possible models to those that are also plausible, incorporating word meanings or other lexically induced meaningful relations as if they were necessary, logical truths in every model. Logically valid statements and analytically true ones are no longer clearly distinguished, once meaning postulates are also exploited to implement logical operations, such as the PTQ analysis of the copula *be* with logical identity. In DATs, lexical relations may have dynamic effects in changing the current chronoscope by the plugging rule or accommodating presuppositions by unplugging, as was discussed in the previous section. Since such relations are encoded in conditional stickers labelling the DAT root, they have a local ccp, as internal consistency within a chronoscope must be maintained. Now the distinction between nonlogical, but meaningful, lexical relations and necessary logical truths may be sharpened, as only the latter have no ccp in DATs. The genuinely logically valid inferences are represented in DATs by the portability conditions of stickers. Any sticker may be copied to its dependent nodes, as the described states are continuous in the underlying interval structure. Perfect stickers represent enduring states, for once you have V-ed you will have V-ed forever. So PERF stickers may be copied onto the right sister of the node they are appended to and spread to dependent nodes from there. Simple stative stickers—for example, for *John is ill*—are very sensitive to lexically induced relations between the descriptive labels, whereas generic stickers are freely portable as long as their background conditions are not violated or inconsistencies arise between the restrictor information and the information in a chronoscope into which the generic stickers are transmitted (which may or may not give rise to an exception).

It remains for future research to employ modal operators on stickers encoding possible DAT continuations in which stickers are imported to other nodes by portability conditions. The idea is simple: necessity means the sticker is portable to all dependent nodes; right-directed necessity encodes unrestricted rightward portability. The possibility operator may then be used to encode information that the DAT is expandable with a new node, possibly constrained to a subdomain but not yet located. Such possible nodes may be useful for inferences, for instance, in inferring from the PROG sticker that its start preceded it, without being able to pinpoint when it started. Possible nodes do not constitute current nodes from which the update of a DAT proceeds. They do not create antecedents for temporal anaphora, as that requires the direct reference to events reserved to simple past clauses. Possible nodes are to be realised somewhere within a restricted domain; we just don't yet know exactly how to localise them and position them temporally with respect to events we did make direct reference to.

Listing stickers representing progressive or perfect information allows us to reason about the temporal relations between the events supporting their types. The three examples in (16) through (18) serve to illustrate the interaction of stickers and activities in discourse:

(16) Jane strolled through the dark alleys. She wore her leather bomber and her hair was all tangled. She had bought what she needed. She arrived at the coffee shop.

(17)   Jane wore her leather bomber and her hair was all tangled. She strolled through the dark alleys. She had bought what she needed. She arrived at the coffee shop.

(18)   Jane wore her leather bomber and her hair was all tangled. She was strolling through the dark alleys. She had bought what she needed. She arrived at the coffee shop.

The DAT for (16) has a past chronoscope consisting of a hole (*stroll*), a dependent hole (*wear*), and a dependent plug (*arrive*) with the list of the two stickers ⟨(*tangle*) , (PERF *buy*)⟩. But for (17), the chronoscope consists of a hole (*wear*), a dependent hole (*stroll*) with a sticker (*tangle*), and a dependent plug (*arrive*) with a sticker (PERF *buy*). The DAT for (18) consists of a hole (*wear*) and a dependent plug (*arrive*) with a list of three stickers ⟨(*tangle*), (PROG *stroll*), (PERF *buy*)⟩. The relevant sections of the three DATs are shown in figure 8 with abbreviated labels and the list of stickers in angled brackets.

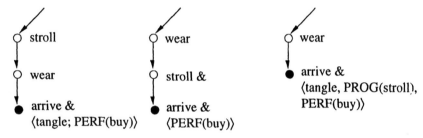

Figure 8. Partial DATs for (16), (17) and(18).

These three DATs show that the textual order in which stative information is given matters considerably to the way in which a single chronoscope in the DAT is constructed.[3]

Given the DATs in figure 8, can we make any situated inferences about the time Jane bought what she needed and her strolling around? From all three DATs we infer that she *must* have bought it before she arrived at the coffee shop and that she *may* or *may not* have bought it during her stroll. From (16) and (18) we infer that if she bought it on her stroll, her hair may, but need not, have been tangled. But only from (17) follows the conditional information that if she bought it on her stroll, her hair *must* have been tangled. Note that in both cases the inference about the condition of her hair is conditional on her having bought what she needed on her stroll. The information given in any of the three texts does not tell us whether this is in fact the case. This illustrates how situated inferences are used to reason conditionally with partial information, when the information given leaves open what is in fact the case. The first rule at work here is a constraint for the perfect sticker *PERF(T)* labelling node *c* implies that there must be an event of type *T* preceding the current node. Her buying must have preceded the state of her having bought it for all three DATs in figure 8. But only in the DAT for (14) do we import the tangle node, representing the tangled condition of her hair, to a dependent node. So if the node representing her buying is dependent on the stroll-node, then the tangle sticker is imported on that node by DAT logic.

When the list of stickers labelling c contains both a PROG(T') sticker and PERF(T), or when T' labels a node dominating c, we cannot infer anything about the temporal relation between events described by the two embedded types T and T'. This is illustrated in the following examples:

(19)   She was dialling. Her wallet had dropped on the ground.

Can we conclude from (19) anything at all about the temporal relation between her wallet dropping and her dialling? Must the wallet have dropped before she started to dial or after it? We cannot tell what the case was from the information expressed in (16)—either way is possible. But her wallet must have dropped before now, at the time she is dialling. If we change the order of these PROG and PERF stickers, the same inferential effects are observed.

(20)   Her wallet had dropped on the ground. She was dialling.

Did the wallet drop before she started to dial? Again we cannot say anything about the temporal relation between her starting to dial and the time her wallet dropped. Both have happened in the past for sure, but we don't know in what order they or their constituent temporal parts did occur. Using a progressive and a perfect cancels the dynamic effect of the embedded type, and hence (19) and (20) allow for the same inferences despite the differences in the order in which the information was given, all represented within the same chronoscope.[4.]

These illustrations demonstrate an important aspect of the interaction between holes introduced by simple past clauses, simple stickers, PROG stickers and PERF stickers. There are important restrictions on how we reason with lists of stickers, which illustrate again the significance of chronoscopes as structured temporal objects. If facts are objects described by stickers, the DAT representations characterise the context-dependent nature of facts in the associated portability conditions. Facts are still dependent on the causal connections established between the representation and the world by direct reference to events, even though facts transcend the context in which they were introduced and remain stable within more global contexts. Events, however, are objects we must directly refer to—they fix the web of referential connections that delimits the contexts within which facts are preserved. There is no such thing as a context-independent fact in this conception of the relation between facts and events.

6. Situated Inference, Default Reasoning, and Logical Entailment

Even if there is no defensible hard and fast boundary between our knowledge of meaning and our knowledge of the world, aspectual information controls what descriptive information is about. The aspectual information determines the architecture of the representation in DATs; the descriptive information determines truth-functional content, represented in the labels. What the semantic theory is to account for are the inferences based on the temporal relations between the events and states in the episode described by the text. Of course, other sources of information may provide interpretive constraints that may even overrule the DAT construction rules in specific cases. The semantic role of the portability conditions associated with the different kinds of stickers in DATs may be spelled out in a default logic, as in Lascarides and Asher (1993). But the semantic role of the aspectual classes is to determine temporal relations between events. Other stylistic registers may lead to different DAT rules, but explanatory relations between clauses need not be accounted for in semantic theory, for what counts as an explanation to someone depends holistically on all kinds of nonsemantic factors.

A key logical point of difference between DRT and DAT representations lies in their characterisation of valid inferences. For DRT the notion is classical logical consequence, quoted here from Kamp and Reyle (1996: 305).

(D.I) Let K, K' be pure (. . .) DRSs. Thus K' is a logical consequence of K (in symbols $K \vDash K'$) iff the following condition holds:

Suppose M is a model and f is a function from $U_K \cup Fr(K) \cup Fr(K')$ into U_M, such that $M \vDash_f K$. Then there is a function $g \supseteq_{U_K} f$ such that $M \vDash_g K'$.

(A DRS is *pure* if each reference marker is only declared at exactly one level; U_K is the set of declared reference markers in K; $Fr(K)$ is the set of free, i.e., non-declared, reference markers in K; and U_M is the set of all referents, i.e., the domain of the model.) This definition requires every verifying embedding of a DRS representing the premises of an argument to have an extension (this is what $\supseteq$ symbolises), preserving the verification of the premises and in addition verifying the conclusion. In other words, logical consequences do not add any new descriptive information to the DRS representing the content of just the premises.

The primary goal of DAT representation is to display in a user-friendly, visually perspicuous way what information can be validly inferred *at the current node*—that is, which inferences are situated entailments in a DAT, which by definition contains a single, designated current node at which inferences are situated. A subsidiary goal of DAT reasoning is to allow for dynamic inferences to adjust the input DAT prior to updating it. Since the free parameters or variables occurring in the labels of the current chronoscope must be assigned a value by the currently given embedding into the event structure, they are not subject to existential closure, as in DRT. This situated notion of entailment makes it possible to introduce information in the DAT by interpreting a simple past sentence and to report this information by using a different syntactic form later, when the current node is in a new chronoscope. In reasoning with DATs, the conclusion describes an event via the embedding into the event structure of the current node in a DAT that represents the information obtained by processing its premises. The premises together describe the entire episode, ending with the event described by the conclusion. This context-dependence of temporal reasoning is formalised in the notion of situated entailment in DATs:

(D.2) *Situated entailment.* Let D be a DAT for the premises $T_1, \ldots, T_n$ and let c be its current node; then $T_1, \ldots, T_n \vdash T$ iff, for all event structures S and all embeddings f of D into S, if $T_1, \ldots, T_n$ describes $f(D)$, then $f(c)$ is of type T.

The situated entailments are preserved for all perfect sticker types of conclusions in DAT extensions, so for information about such perfect states the inference relation is monotonic, corresponding to their portability. No matter what information is added to the premises, if one can infer a perfect-tense conclusion at some point, one can always infer the same conclusion at any later point in the interpretation. But, of course, the situated entailments of other information, represented by the other labels on the current node, is not monotonic, as a change of the current chronoscope in perspectival shift loses some of the situated entailments valid in the previous chronoscope. Ordinarily one can add any number of compatible stickers to a given DAT for the premises without affecting the valid situated entailments. But adding new nodes to the DAT, incorporating additional dynamic information, is bound to affect the set of situated entailments derivable from it.

Another important difference with DRT resides in the way DATs treat activities (ACT), representing them as holes and referring to events via the verifying embeddings, as discussed in section 4. The three DATs in figure 8 were intended to illustrate this point as well, as they show that the textual order in which information is given, even when it is all represented on one node, affects the DAT construction within a single chronoscope. DRT requires all the different ways of expressing stative information—which according to DRT includes at least one possible use of ACT—called *processes* to be represented by state markers including their time marker. This does not represent the textual order in which they are given, as the conditions in the same (sub)DRS are not ordered. Although there are deep and important philosophical issues to discuss regarding the nature of (direct) temporal reference, the ontological status of culmination points, and the interaction of presupposed, asserted, and entailed information in semantic representations, one important difference between DATs and DRT is that holes, representing past activities, do have end points, if only because they must precede the source node. Hence DATs predict the situated entailments (22) and (23) from the information given in the text (21):

(21) Jane patrolled the neighbourhood. She saw a car parked in an alley. She gave it a ticket.
(22) Jane must have ended patrolling the neighbourhood after she ticketed the car in the alley.
(23) Jane was patrolling the neighbourhood when she ticketed the car in the alley.

Only if the current node is labelled with information that cannot be simultaneously satisfied with the portable stickers does the DAT block the situated inferences. Hence if it is asserted that Jane went back to the police station, the DAT contains a node that provides a right boundary for the portability domain of the sticker representing the progressive clause in (23). Such information would trigger the creation of a new chronoscope by a right sister node of the hole representing her patrolling of the neighbourhood. This provides the natural end point to her patrolling, which then precedes her going back to the police station. Such inferential information is visually directly displayed in DATs and thus avoids representational clutter in which objects are introduced to which no direct reference was made.

7. Conclusions

The insights gained from this study show that (a) the shifting of reference time in DRT is better modelled directly in the structured chronoscopes of events in DATs; (b) there are important temporal logical differences between various ways in which stative information gets expressed, and the order in which stative information is given may sometimes give us information about the temporal structure of the described episode; and (c) how temporal information is preserved and reported in context change depends on how—that is, with what form and when the information was initially given, as well as in the current context. A proper account of reasoning in time about time should model dynamic and situated inferences as a context-dependent operation between representations of events described by natural language text.[5]

Notes

1. The terminology here is reminiscent of the plugs and holes in Karttunen's (1973) account of the projection of presuppositions in compound sentences, but it is applied here to the way aspectual information about events affects the context in the setting of a theory of dynamic interpretation and flow of information characteristic of the 1990s. The exact relation between the projection of presuppositions and the context-change potential of aspectual information remains an important issue for future research.

2. It would take too much space to present these inference rules in any detail. See ter Meulen (1995) and Seligman and ter Meulen (1995) for further details.

3. In DRT no semantic difference is made between activities and states, for they are all represented by requiring their DR marker to include the given reference time. It is nevertheless important for a semantic representation to retain the information in which order this information is received, if it is to account properly for situated inferences with stative information.

4. These examples may provide a good testing ground for the different predictions one can make with DAT representations and DRT representations. In DRT the current reference time would be included in all four states, but no other relation would obtain among the states, so (13), (14), and (15) would have the same content and would presumably validate the same inferences.

5. Research on this project has been supported by the Netherlands Organisation of Scientific Research (NWO) on a visitor grant for the author to the Utrecht Institute of Linguistics OTS, Rijksuniversiteit Utrecht. The author is grateful to Indiana University, Bloomington, for a leave of absence during 1997–1998.

References

van Eijck, J., and H. Kamp, 1997. Representing Discourse in Context. In J. van Benthem and A. G. B. ter Meulen (eds.), *Handbook of Logic and Language*, 179–237. MIT Press and Elsevier Science Publishers, Boston and Amsterdam.

Groenendijk, J., and, M. Stokhof, 1991. Dynamic Predicate Logic. In *Linguistics and Philosophy* 14: 39–100.

Kamp, H., and U. Reyle, 1993. *From Discourse to Logic*. Kluwer Academic Publishers, Dordrecht.

Kamp, H., and U. Reyle, 1996. A Calculus for First-order Discourse Representation Structures. In *Journal of Logic, Language and Information* 5: 297–348.

Karttunen, L., 1973. Presuppositions of Compound Sentences. In *Linguistic Inquiry* 4: 169–193.

Lascarides, A., and N. Asher, 1993. Temporal Interpretation, Discourse Relations and Commonsense Entailment. In *Linguistics and Philosophy* 16: 437–594.

ter Meulen, A. G. B., 1995. *Representing Time in Natural Language. The Dynamic Interpretation of Tense and Aspect*. MIT Press, Cambridge (Mass.). (Paperback edition with new appendix published in 1997.)

Quine, W. V. O., 1953, Three Grades of Modal Involvement. In *Proceedings of the XIth International Congress of Philosophy*, Volume 14. Amsterdam: North-Holland. Reprinted in Quine, W. V. O., 1966. *The Ways of Paradox*, 158–176. New York: Random House.

Seligman, J., and A. G. B. ter Meulen, 1995. Dynamic Aspect Trees. In L. Pólos and M. Masuch (eds.), *Applied Logic: How, What and Why*, 287–320. Kluwer Academic Publishers, Dordrecht.

8

Events as Dividuals
Aspectual Composition and Event Semantics

Henk J. Verkuyl

1. Introductory Remarks

Someone criticising event semantics is not bound to reject or evade the notion of event. The question is whether or not representations containing expressions like $\exists e(\dots e \dots)$ have explanatory value for the linguistic analysis at hand. In Verkuyl (1993) I have argued that the use of event variables may have this value, for example, in the study of discourse structure, as in Hinrichs (1981, 1986a, 1986b). However, for the study of what I call *inner aspectuality*—roughly, the domain of the verb and its arguments—there turn out to be severe problems with Davidson's (1967) claim that the notion of event is primitive.

The aim of this chapter is to show that the idea of aspectual composition is incompatible with the introduction of a primitive event variable at the level of inner aspectuality. I do this by focusing on the role of the verb phrase (VP) in the construal of aspectuality. It is interesting enough that the VP as a semantic unit may be argued to denote the value of Davidson's famous *it* in

(1)   Jones did it deliberately in the bathroom.

I argue that the VP may be taken as a factor in a multiplication. In its distributive interpretation, a sentence such as

(2)   Jones and Jackson crossed the street

may be seen as a 2×1 expression—that is, as a 1 (= Jones) $\times$ 1 (= VP) + 1 (= Jackson) $\times$ 1 (= VP), with as many copies of the VP as there are members of the external argument denotation. Davidson's *it* pertains to this VP. With Reichenbach (1947), I see no reason why one should not be able to refer to a factor, even if this turns out to be a function. I argue that as a function, the VP is a complex "dividual" built up by information conveyed by the constituent mem-

bers of the VP, the verb and its internal argument. It is only after the construal of
the VP information that one may begin to speak about events.

1.1. Some Preliminary Empirical Notions

Let me first restrict the empirical domain of this chapter to the aspectuality of
the a-sentences in (3) through (6). It helps me to clarify the terminology and to
take away possible misunderstandings:

(3)   a. Judith ate a sandwich.   terminative
          b. #Judith ate a sandwich for an hour.
          c. Judith ate a sandwich in an hour.

(4)   a. Judith ate sandwiches.   durative
          b. Judith ate sandwiches for an hour.
          c. ?Judith ate sandwiches in an hour.

(5)   a. Nobody ate a sandwich.   durative
          b. For an hour nobody ate a sandwich.
          c. ?In an hour nobody ate a sandwich.

(6)   a. Judith disliked a sandwich.   durative
          b. Judith disliked a sandwich for an hour.
          c. ?Judith disliked a sandwich in an hour.

The a-sentences illustrate the compositional nature of aspectuality: the aspectual
distinction between (3a) and (6a) can be attributed only to a difference between
the verbs. One could call *eat* a terminative and *dislike* a durative verb, but this
becomes problematic in view of the difference between (3a) and (4a): here the
verb is kept constant; yet (3a) is terminative (some say *telic*) and (4a) is durative (some say *atelic*). This proves that the internal argument plays a role in the
determination of aspectuality. The same applies to the external argument: the
only relevant difference between (3a) and (5a) is a difference between the NP
Judith and the NP *nobody*. The conclusion of this brief inspection of the data
(reached in Verkuyl 1972) is that both the verb and its arguments contribute to
the aspectuality of sentences. Although people in general seem to adhere to the
idea of a compositional approach, many of them do not take the consequences
that in my view should be drawn: to find out which basic semantic material underlies aspectual composition and how the composition proceeds at higher
phrasal levels. In this chapter, I discuss the mathematical principles underlying
aspectual composition in the a-sentences from the point of view of analysing the
notion of event as it plays a role in event semantics—that is, as a primitive notion. I will argue that this notion is as complex as aspectual composition requires
it to be.

    The adverbials in the b- and c-sentences serve the purpose of identifying
the a-sentences as being terminative or durative. I call (3a) *terminative*. The
other three a-sentences are *durative*. An adverbial such as *for an hour* applied to
(3a) excludes the single-event interpretation of (3a), the result being some other

form of aspectuality (a queer sort of repetition), but it is compatible with the durative aspectuality of the other a-sentences. The reverse holds for the *in* adverbials.

It would not be appropriate to say that the b- or c-sentences or sentences such as *Judith ate a sandwich yesterday* or *Judith ate sandwiches twice* are terminative, at least not in the same sense as (3a). The b- and c-sentences in (3) through (6) consist of their a-sentence plus an adverbial. In a way, (3a) can be seen as the aspectual "kernel" on which adverbials and other adjuncts may operate. If we extend (3a) to, for instance, *Yesterday Judith ate a sandwich in the bathroom at midnight*, this kernel remains intact and it should be the point of departure, so to say, for the determination of higher forms of aspectuality. This analysis of aspectuality differs considerably from that which follows from event semantic approaches. In this chapter, I characterise the aspectual kernel consisting of the verb and its internal argument (*a sandwich* in (3a)) and its external argument (*Judith* in (3a)). I use the term *inner aspectuality* for the aspectual information expressed by this kernel structure. The term *outer aspectuality* is used for the result of applying modifying adverbials to inner aspectual information.

The idea behind this position is that if one takes (Fregean) interpretation seriously, the proper way to go is from the bottom of phrase structure up to its top. The syntactic structure suitable for a bottom-to-top interpretation construing the aspectuality of sentences like (3) through (6) is figure 1.

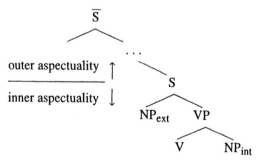

Figure 1. Basic structure of aspectual construal.

I do not go into the question of how fine-grained the phrasal structure of (3a) through (6a) should be from the syntactic point of view. It is easy to extend figure 1 with all sorts of functional projections of the generative kind, but this would not substantially alter the syntax involved in the composition of aspectuality as presented below. Therefore, figure 1 reduces a number of equivalent alternative syntactic representations to their bare minimum. In current generative theory, the lower S would correspond with the top of a V-projection (= IP), S̄ would correspond with CP, NP would be read as DP, and so on.[1] But for the purpose of this chapter, the relabeling of syntactic nodes is not important.

There is no separate AspectPhrase at this stage of the analysis. This is a matter of strategy and reasoning. Such a phrase is often assumed by those who take events as primitive individuals. I argue that if one needs such a projection, it should be allowed only to mark the transition from inner to outer aspectuality. Only in this way can certain aspectual phenomena be explained that cannot be explained otherwise.

1.2. First Order vs. Higher Order

In the belief that there are good linguistic reasons for assuming that the NP VP partition of figure 1 in sentences like (3) through (6) is motivated, the question arises of whether or not this structure may be the input of an interpretation function that yields values from the domain of discourse.

There are two positions. The first one is the standard first-order position developed on the Russell/Quine line in mathematical and philosophical logic: figure 1 is translated into the logical form of sentences like (3) through (6). This is what Russell, Quine, Chomsky, and Davidson have in common: they translate sentences into the format given in (7), with P an n-place predicate and $a_1, \ldots, a_n$ as its arguments.[2]

(7) $P^n(a_1, \ldots, a_n)$ $(n \geq 1)$

At this point there are again two options: to stop at (7) or to interpret (7) as a subset of the Cartesian product over the domain of discourse, as in (8).

(8) $[\![P^n]\!] \subseteq D_1 \times \ldots \times D_n$ $(n \geq 1)$

Although (8) represents the standard semantics of (7), neither Quine nor Chomsky nor Davidson seems to be very happy about really employing it.[3] Chomsky places the interpretation of (3) through (6) outside his grammar at LF', which makes it hard to expect any theory about aspectuality from his side if this turns out to be a semantic phenomenon. Davidson also restricts himself to (7), extending it to make it possible for him to yield the right inferences. For him it is important to show that D may contain events as individuals because of valid inferences drawn from the extended (7) and not because he is really interested in the relation between the structure of (3)-(6) and the structure of the domain D.

Turning now to the second position with respect to figure 1, we find it in Montague's work. For example, Montague (1970) explicitly defends the view that a natural language may be seen as a formal language. This means that structures like figure 1 may be interpreted in the Fregean way. The notion of Fregean interpretation based on type logic in the sense explained by Halvorsen and Ladusaw (1979) comes to mind here. The general idea is not unknown in generative circles because Katz, Fodor, and Postal used it informally in the 1960s (without paying debt to Frege). The slogan roughly is that the meaning of a sentence is made up of the meanings of its parts. For figure 1, a Fregean interpretation means that (3) through (6) are interpreted bottom-up, starting with the lexical items and yielding phrasal meanings.

Montague's model-theoretic work respects (8), even though the scheme is extended to account for intensionality, but it is primarily his use of type logic that makes it possible to do away with the format of (7) as a fixed syntactic pattern of interpretation and to leave the predicate and its arguments in situ, as in figure 1. That is, the V can be seen as a predicate of a certain functional type asking for an internal argument NP_{int} and forming a VP that combines with the NP_{ext} to form an S. I restrict myself here to this aspect of the Montagovian outlook on interpretation of syntactic structure, but I would like to add that his semantics may be put on "stable" trees, as HPSG and related grammars have shown—that is, trees as we know them from generative syntax. In other words, it is possible to consider the tree in figure 1 as a generative tree, which rather than being converted into an LF receives its interpretation either directly, as in Montague (1970), or more indirectly, as in Montague (1973), in both cases by translating the tree into an equivalent type-logical structure. For the purpose of this chapter it is not necessary to execute this translation because, for convenience and for the benefit of the exposition of the machinery involved, the semantics of the sentences in (3) through (6) is mainly given in terms of the corresponding domain structure—that is, in terms of the mathematical functions underlying sentences like (3) through (6) rather than their representations.

The distinction between two sorts of representations of sentences may contribute to a better understanding of the opposition between certain branches of event semantics and theories based on the compositionality of aspectuality, such as Verkuyl (1972, 1993). It is the purpose of this chapter to analyse some of the differences between the two approaches. Let me therefore identify the problems to be discussed.

1.3. Two Problems

First of all, the differences among (3) through (6) cannot be satisfactorily dealt with in the philosophical branch of event semantics—that is, along the lines of Davidson and Parsons. This can be shown quite easily. Before the Davidsonian extension of the standard format (7), (3a) would be represented as (9):

(9) $\exists x(\text{Sandwich}(x) \wedge \text{Eat}(j, x))$.

This is to be interpreted as being true when there is a sandwich x and the pair $\langle j, x \rangle \in [\![Eat]\!]$. The verb is a set of pairs. This makes it impossible to explain the aspectual differences among the a-sentences of (4), (5), and (6). For example, the standard logical form of (6a) is (10):

(10) $\exists x(\text{Sandwich}(x) \wedge \text{Dislike}(j, x))$.

This means that the aspectual difference between (3a) and (6a) must be found somewhere in the difference between $\langle j, x \rangle \in [\![Eat]\!]$ and $\langle j, x \rangle \in [\![Dislike]\!]$. This does not help very much, so an extension of (7) is called for anyhow.

Not in Davidson (1967) but, for example, in Parsons (1990), an appeal is made to representations like (11):

(11)   a. $\exists e(\ldots \text{Cul}(e))$.
        b. $\exists e(\ldots \text{Hold}(e))$.

That is, new predicates are postulated, which may express that an event holds or culminates. This seems to improve on (9) and (10):

(12) $\exists e \exists x (\text{Sandwich}(x) \wedge \text{Eat}(j, x) \wedge \text{Cul}(e))$.
(13) $\exists e \exists x (\text{Sandwich}(x) \wedge \text{Dislike}(j, x) \wedge \text{Hold}(e))$.

One could then point out that *Cul* is incompatible with *for an hour* and compatible with *in an hour* and that the reverse holds for *Hold*. It seems then that aspectuality comes within the reach of the extended first-order logic.

Apart from the problem that the introduction of predicates like these hardly exceeds the level of observational adequacy by just making the representation look like the semantic difference between (3a) and (6a), without giving any hope for an explanation, Parsons's version of (11) turns out to be inadequate and unilluminating, given what is known about aspectuality in the compositional tradition, as I point out in section 3.3. The general question is whether or not event semantics may be considered explanatorily adequate by treating aspectual phenomena in terms of *Cul* and *Hold*. Thus I look at event semantics from the point of view of its treatment of aspectuality.

There is a second problematic area that I want to explore. In figure 1 the VP plays a very crucial role. It carries the information of what I call the *Path* of the external argument denotation. So, aspectually the VP is taken as a unit, as is the (lower) S, but with quite different semantic properties, as I will show.

Now, recall that Davidson's (1967) famous article started with consideration of the anaphoric reference of *it* in sentences such as (14) as applied to (3a).

(14)   Judith did it slowly deliberately in the bathroom at midnight.

What does *it* refer to in (14)? This question led to the Davidsonian event semantics because Davidson could not live with the idea that *it* in (14) would pick out the VP of sentences like (3a). Why not? Because for him under the standard format in (7) a VP is not a semantic unit that can be referred to. But as I shall point out, if a phrase may refer to a function, there is no need to postulate an event as a primitive inside the area of inner aspectuality. The event is there because there is a VP that denotes it, but this VP is there only if there is more elementary information contributed by the verb and its internal argument. The presence of the VP for eventhood is only a necessary condition: there must be an appropriate mapping between the external argument and the VP, which is absent in (5a).

From this problem of anaphoric reference, which turns out to be connected with a particular choice between two sorts of logical languages, it is a small step to get into another problem that may be solved if correctly stated. Vendler's (1957) well-known aspectual classes have been defined on the verb. Dowty (1979) clearly took the notion of verb linguistically and, in particular, lexically, and many followed him on this route.[4]

In my critical analysis of his article (Verkuyl 1989), I also assumed that Vendler's notion of verb is linguistic. However, it occurs to me that Vendler may also be interpreted as taking the notion of verb much in the way Montague did—namely, as corresponding to the VP and expressing a sometimes complex, unanalysed, one-place predicate. This still does not solve the problems for Vendler, but this rather benevolent new interpretation turns out to make more sense than trying to pin Vendler down on four different lexical verb classes. In this line of interpretation, the VP gets its own place. More strongly, I will show that it is possible to bring Vendler's notion of verb as VP and Davidson's *it* into the compositional tradition by making clear that they intuitively must have referred to what can be made explicit as the Path in the localistic tradition that gave rise to the scheme in figure 1.

So, this is the theme of the chapter: to focus on the role of the VP in the making of terminative aspectuality and to show that only because of the presence of certain information in the sentence itself may one conclude that the sentence pertains to an event, a process, or a state. In this way, the notion of event is saved but it will be understood quite differently from what today seems to be the case in the (neo-)Davidsonian tradition. The remainder of the chapter is structured as follows. In section 2, a brief sketch is given of the compositional machinery of Verkuyl (1993), called PLUG$^+$. In section 3, I go into four proposals concerning the issues discussed above—proposals by Davidson, Vendler, Parsons, and Krifka—and I compare the PLUG$^+$ solutions with these proposals.

2. The PLUG$^+$ Framework

It is very informative to see that, Krifka (1989a) excepted, there is no systematic event semantic analysis available for sentences like the following:

(15) a. Judith ate three sandwiches.
      b. Two girls ate three sandwiches.
      c. Several girls ate at least three sandwiches.
      d. Many girls ate three sandwiches.
      e. Some girls ate all sandwiches.

Some of the quantifying NPs cannot be treated in first-order logic, as pointed out by Barwise and Cooper (1981). Their article, together with an interest in the behaviour of plural NPs generated by, for example, Scha (1981) resulted in serious attention for important issues in generalised quantification. All sentences in (15) are terminative, so from the point of view of temporal structure these sentences have also been under investigation. Joint work of Jaap van der Does and myself led to studies in which we set out (a) to reduce the number of readings of the sentences in (15)—Scha (1981) assigned (at least) ten readings to, for example, (15b), Link (1991) about eight—and (b) to clean up the notions of distributivity and collectivity as they were used in the literature.[5] This work resulted in a grammar called PLUG, extended in Verkuyl (1993) to PLUG$^+$ to form the basis for the analysis of aspectuality.

I give this information here just to point out how deep the connection between an aspectual theory and a theory of quantification should be. In my view, this bears directly on the criteria by which event semantics should be evaluated:

it can be taken as a serious enterprise only in the study of aspectuality of sentences if it deals with quantification.[6] However, it is also important to see that by developing a framework in which the account of plurality receives a central place, certain problems arise in the treatment of singularity, as discussed in section 3.4.

In this section, I account for the compositionally formed terminative aspectuality of the sentences in (16):[7]

(16)   a. Mary lifted four tables.
        b. Mary lifted a table.
        c. Three girls lifted four tables.
        d. Three girls lifted a table.

I intend to show that their terminative aspectuality is systematically predicted.[8] Moreover, the framework in which the sentences in (15) and (16) are treated contains a complete theory about distributivity and collectivity and subsumes Scha's cumulativity.

In brief, there are three functions involved in the composition of the aspectuality of the sentences in (15) and (16):

1. The function s contributed by the verb *lift* and providing for the sense of progress in verbs expressing change;

2. The function l amalgamating the V and its internal argument into the VP denotation $[\![VP]\!]$;

3. The function relating the members of the external argument denotation to $[\![VP]\!]$.

These functions are defined and explained in some detail in the following three subsections.

2.1. The Successor Function s

There is an aspectually important lexical distinction between verbs expressing change and verbs expressing a state. This well-known distinction is often referred to as an opposition between nonstatives and statives. To distinguish them, one may also use the feature opposition [±STATIVE]. By employing features, one follows a long linguistic tradition, the idea being that features should have a proper interpretation. In my work on aspectuality, I have been using the opposition pair [±ADD-TO] rather than [±STATIVE], to underscore that verbs of change are responsible for the property of additivity in nonstative verbs: they yield temporal structure construed from some point of origin. This treatment of verbs belongs to the localistic tradition in which change is given a dynamic treatment.

The localism involved in the account of change can be tied up very naturally with the number systems: each [+ADD-TO] verb is interpreted as introducing a well-ordered set I of indices i. Let $I := \mathbb{N}$. That is, I is taken as the set of natural numbers, which by definition (D.1) are the endpoints of intervals in $\mathbb{R}$, the set of real numbers.

(D.1) $I_V := \{(0, k) \subseteq \mathbb{R}: k \in \mathbb{N}\}.$

The successor function $s:I \to I$ is defined over I in such a way that $\forall k \in I:(s(k) = k + 1)$.[9] The connection between I and I_V is provided by a function $succ: I_V \to I_V$ defined in such a way that $\forall k \in \mathbb{N}: succ((0, k)) = (0, s(k))$. In this way [+ADD-TO] verbs meet the Peano axioms characterising natural numbers (cf. Partee, ter Meulen, and Wall 1990: 75–78 for details). Indices are introduced as part of the information expressed by a [+ADD-TO] verb. Ignoring at this stage the information about the external argument X, we see that the verb *lift* in (17) introduces indices of which the information about the argument Y is made dependent:

(17)   ... $\lambda i \lambda Y.[\![lift]\!](i)(Y)(X).$

Here, *lift* is of type $\langle i, \langle \langle e, t \rangle, t \rangle \rangle$, the type of functions taking an index and yielding a collection of sets. This is the type of the function l discussed in detail in section 2.2.[10]

The indices i contributed by the verb constitute a well-ordered set, and so there is a point of origin that is the starting point of an enumerative device. We are quite familiar with this sort of use of natural numbers when we in fact operate in the reals. We apply it when we put the daily odometre of a car on zero and start to drive. Its natural numbers give us a means to experience the sense of progress. If we take the train we make progress in the reals but we speak about the progress in terms of the stations, discrete entities in the natural numbers. Also the picture in figure 2 shows that whenever we can, we use natural numbers as representatives of stretches in the reals.

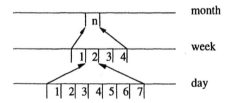

Figure 2. Days, weeks, and months as numbers and stretches.

In natural language, shrinking and expansion play a prominent role: we are used to treating days, weeks, and months both in $\mathbb{N}$ and in $\mathbb{R}$, as in figure 2. It is important to see that there is no absolute hierarchy: a month is a set of weeks, and a week is a set of days. A month is both a collection of sets of days, but it is also simply a set of days. I consider this shifting from one number system to the other as crucial for our use of language, especially when we see that the effect of these shifts is to use natural numbers as the most simple way of counting.[11]

2.2. The Path Function l

The general picture for VPs containing a [+ADD-TO] verb, as in (3a) through (5a) and in (15) and (16), is given in figure 3. The VP is $[+T_{VP}]$ (terminative) if the internal NP is [+SQA], and $[-T_{VP}]$ (durative) otherwise.

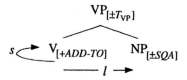

Figure 3. The Path function l.

In (16a), *Mary lifted four tables*, the internal argument NP is labelled [+SQA]. The NP pertains to what I call a *specified quantity of A*, where A is the denotation of the head noun. The label is made more precise shortly.[12] At this point it is sufficient to observe that because of the presence of the subscript [+SQA], the codomain of l is finite. The subscript [−SQA] in (4a), *Judith ate sandwiches*, indicates that the codomain of l is not finite.[13] Dependent on the plus or minus values of the NP, the VP will become VP-terminative or VP-durative.

The domain of l is the set I; its codomain $\mathbf{D}_L$ is the set of *positions p* making up the internal argument denotation:

(D.2) $l_x : I \rightarrow \mathbf{D}_L$ with $l_x = \{\langle i, p\rangle: [\![AT(p)(x)]\!]_{M,i} = 1\}$.

As the definition of the Path function contains a place for information concerning the external argument, l will be subscripted with x when necessary for the exposition. Definition (D.2) characterises the injective function l as a set of pairs $\langle i, p\rangle$ such that x is in the position p at i, given a model $\mathbf{M}$. The term "position" is used to indicate that l defines a Path in the sense of the so-called localistic tradition in the linguistic analysis of verbs expressing change.[14] The localistic element in (D.2) is the AT-predicate, which localises the external argument x in a certain position with respect to the predication involved. Thus, l_x constitutes a 'Path of x', keeping track of how x relates to the members of the internal argument denotation as far as satisfaction of the predicate is concerned. This is important for the analysis of plurality because in (16c), *Three girls lifted four tables*, there are three x's involved, each resulting in a Path—that is, a way in which they are involved in the predication.

Still stated in terms of positions, for each actualisation of a Path l, the picture in figure 4 holds.

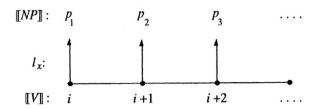

Figure 4. l forming a set of pairs—that is, a Path.

Such a figure illustrates the way in which the localistic heritage is integrated in the model-theoretic machinery. It shows how the relationship between an external argument x (Mary, in our lifting examples) and the members of the internal argument NP denotation (a set of tables) may be structured.

The information expressed by the VP is built up cumulatively. Let me demonstrate this with the help of (16a), *Mary lifted four tables*. Let the set of tables be $T = \{t_1, t_2, t_3, t_4\}$. The situation in figure 5 would make (16a) true, with three liftings involved.

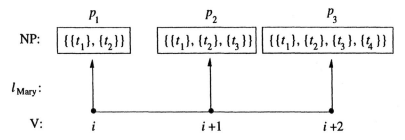

Figure 5. The information of a cell is carried over to its successors.

Each box is a collection of subsets Y of T made dependent on an index, as discussed in the type-logical explanation of the verb *lift* in (17). The last box is formed by successive steps. In this particular situation, the Path of Mary, l_{Mary}, would be $\{\langle 1, p_1 \rangle, \langle 2, p_2 \rangle, \langle 3, p_3 \rangle\}$.

(18) $\langle Mary, \langle 1, p_1 \rangle \rangle$ $\langle Mary, \langle 1, \{\{t_1, t_2\}\} \rangle \rangle$

$\langle Mary, \langle 2, p_2 \rangle \rangle$ $\langle Mary, \langle 2, \{\{t_1, t_2\}, \{t_3\}\} \rangle \rangle$

$\langle Mary, \langle 3, p_3 \rangle \rangle$ $\langle Mary, \langle 3, \{\{t_1, t_2\}, \{t_3\}, \{t_4\}\} \rangle \rangle$

$\langle Mary, \langle 3, \{p_1, p_2, p_3\} \rangle \rangle$ $\langle Mary, \langle 3, T \rangle \rangle$

The left-hand side of (18) says that l_{Mary} distinguishes three positions, at each of which the model satisfies the lift predication applied to Mary and subsets of T. Given a model **M** in which (16a) is true, Mary reached the position at which $AT(\{\{t_1, t_2\}\})(Mary) = 1$ at index 1. At index 2 a new collection was added, and so $AT(\{\{t_1, t_2\}, \{t_3\}\})(Mary) = 1$, and so on.[15] In this way, l keeps track of the way in which the individual members of the external argument of the predicate are involved in the predication. Why the function s comes to a stop is also explained: after p_3 there is no table from T available for being lifted. This accounts for the terminativity of (16a) through (16d) as well as for the sentences in (15) and for (3a).[16]

In general, one may say that (16a) is made true by a set of possible configurations, given cardinality 4, and three positions, among which is (18). The situation in (18) and figure 5 is just one of the possible combinatorial configurations that may arise because of the presence of the cardinality information in the NP. In the PLUG representation of the internal argument NP, this is provided for by the presence of an existential quantifier introducing a partition of the set that is the denotation of the head noun of the internal argument. By leaving out some details, the NP *four tables* is represented as (19):

(19) $\lambda P \exists W (W \subseteq \llbracket table \rrbracket \wedge |W| = 4 \wedge \exists Q ps W (Q = P))$.

This says that there is a set W of four tables having a cardinality of 4 structured as a partition Q, such that Q is the collection of sets of things being lifted that is denoted by the predicate P.[17] The existential quantifier over Q purports to express the degree of uncertainty about which of the possible actualisations has been the case, but it warrants that there is one. This concurs with the empirical fact that none of the sentences in (15) and (16) gives away how the sandwiches were eaten or how the tables were lifted: one by one, as a group, or in intermediate configurations.

By taking *walk* as a [+ADD-TO] verb and defining it as in (20), one explains why Zeus in *Zeus walked* may have walked indefinitely:

(20) $\lambda X \lambda i \llbracket walk \rrbracket (i)(X)$.

The difference between *lift* in (17) and the unergative verb *walk* is that there are no internal argument sets Y to bring s to a stop. We assume that in this case the codomain of l yields the empty set for every application of s.[18] The presence of cardinality information in (19) can be seen as the [+SQA] property of the NP *four tables* in (16a). For NPs such as *many tables*, *few tables*, and *at least three tables*, the [+SQA] information adopts the form $|W| = k$ where a precise value of k is not conveyed. In the case of the bare plural *sandwiches*, the representation does not contain cardinality information of the form $|W| = k$. Therefore, the codomain of l cannot be bounded, so the partitioning is unbounded and s does not come to a stop. This explains the durativity of (4a), *Judith ate sandwiches*.[19]

2.3. The Participancy Function π

A third function relating the external argument NP and the VP is required to complete the basic internal aspect construal. This *participancy* function takes as its domain the external NP denotation, assigning to each element x in it a unique l. To relate an x to its own Path, we write $\pi(x) = l_x$.

(D.3) π: $\llbracket NP_{ext} \rrbracket \rightarrow (I \rightarrow D_L)$ is the function such that, for all singletons
         $x \in \llbracket NP_{ext} \rrbracket$, $\pi(x) = l_x$, with l_x as in (D.2).

What π does in (16a) is to assign the VP denotation to the individual Mary—that is, $\pi(Mary) = l_{Mary}$. The same applies to Judith in (3a): $\pi(j) = l_j$.[20]

In Verkuyl (1988) a distinction is made between two constraints on π: such a function is either injective or constant. This turns out to be a natural division, based on the intuition that in many languages some sort of plural (all different)/singular (all one) distinction is called for. Two familiar types of function are taken into account. Given f: $A \rightarrow B$,

1. f is injective iff $\forall a,a' \in A \ (a \neq a' \rightarrow f(a) \neq f(a'))$
2. f is constant: $\forall a,a' \in A \ (f(a) = f(a'))$

Applied to (16c), *Three girls lifted four tables*, this means that the external domain $[\![NP_{ext}]\!]$ contains three elements to which π will be applied and that there are two different "modes":

(21)   a. π is injective: $l_1 \neq l_2 \neq l_3$.
       b. π is constant: $l_1 = l_2 = l_3$.

In the injective mode, each of the girls is given a unique value in the codomain of π. So there are three different images of π. In terms of predication, this means that the predicate *lift four tables* applies fully to each of the girls. It is called the *distributive* mode because it closely resembles the situation we find with simple arithmetical functions:

(22) $3 \times 4 = (2 \times 4) + (1 \times 4) = (1 \times 4) + (1 \times 4) + (1 \times 4)$.

The distributive mode lets π distribute (with respect to set membership) in the same way as the law of distributivity permits arithmetical multiplication to distribute with respect to arithmetical addition in (22). In the latter case, the number 3 is split up into 2 plus 1 and 1 plus 1 plus 1, and 4 is repeated in all splits. This is what happens in (22), where the VP is repeated according to the number of elements in the external argument domain.[21]

(23)   3 girls lifted 4 tables = . . . = girl$_1$ lifted 4 tables + girl$_2$ lifted 4 tables + girl$_3$ lifted 4 tables.

This makes it possible to recast the notion of distributivity in terms of figure 6. Possible actualisations of (16c) along the lines of figure 6 are (24) through (26), among many other configurations:

(24) $\{girl_1\} \rightarrow \{\langle 1, \{t_1, t_2, t_3, t_4\}\rangle\}$
       $\{girl_2\} \rightarrow \{\langle 2, \{t_3, t_4, t_5, t_6\}\rangle\}$
       $\{girl_3\} \rightarrow \{\langle 3, \{t_3, t_4, t_6, t_7\}\rangle\}$

(25) $\{girl_1\} \rightarrow \{\langle 1, \{t_1\}\rangle, \langle 2, \{t_2, t_3\}\rangle, \langle 3, \{t_4\}\rangle\}$
       $\{girl_2\} \rightarrow \{\langle 2, \{t_3, t_4, t_5, t_6\}\rangle\}$
       $\{girl_3\} \rightarrow \{\langle 4, \{t_3, t_4, t_6, t_7\}\rangle\}$

(26) $\{girl_1\} \rightarrow \{\langle 1, \{t_1\}\rangle, \langle 5, \{t_2, t_3\}\rangle, \langle 6, \{t_4\}\rangle\}$
       $\{girl_2\} \rightarrow \{\langle 2, \{t_1, t_2, t_3, t_4\}\rangle\}$
       $\{girl_3\} \rightarrow \{\langle 4, \{t_1, t_2, t_3, t_4\}\rangle\}$

An important advantage of the index dependency of the tables in (23) is that the indices create the room for varying over all combinatorial possibilities. Thus, there are two ways of distinguishing between two tables:[22]

$\langle i, \{t_1\}\rangle \neq \langle j, \{t_1\}\rangle$
$\langle i, \{t_1\}\rangle \neq \langle i, \{t_2\}\rangle$

Definition (D.4) captures the range of combinatorial possibilities of NP denotations illustrated in figure 6.[23]

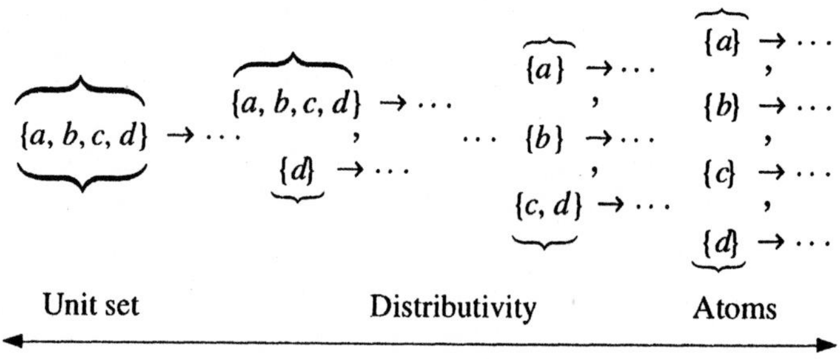

Figure 6. Distributivity in the new sense.

(D.4) **X** is *distributive* iff for all $X, Y \subseteq D$:
(a) If $X \in$ **X** $\wedge$ $Y \subseteq X$, then $Y \in$ **X**.
(b) If $X \in$ **X** $\wedge$ $Y \in$ **X**, then $(X \cup Y) \in$ **X**.

When π is a constant function we obtain for (16c) the situation in (27):

(27) $\pi(g_1) = l_{g_1} = \pi(g_2) = l_{g_2} = \pi(g_3) = l_{g_3}$.

The most natural (terminative) sentences for obtaining this interpretation are given in (28), although they have a distributive interpretation in the sense explained above.

(28) a. The twelve passengers killed that horrible villain.
      b. Hans and Uwe wrote that introductory book about DRT.

In both cases none of the individuals involved may claim the VP predicate itself. So, the passenger Sean may not say, *I have killed that horrible villain*. Likewise, Uwe may not say that he wrote that introductory book about DRT. It is exactly this reading, which I call the *kolchoz-collective* or *totalising* sense of the predicate, that is accounted for by making use of the constant.[24] In the PLUG framework, for any collection of sets **X**, given a domain D, *kolchoz-collectivity* is defined as follows:

(D.5) **X** is *totalising* with respect to the collections A, B iff:
      (a) $(A \cap B) \subseteq$ **X**.
      (b) There is no $X \subseteq D$ such that $(X \subseteq \bigcup(A \cap B) \wedge X \in$ **X**$)$.

This says that the unit set $\bigcup(A \cap B)$ satisfies the predicate denoting **X**, and it precludes the predicate from being applied to any proper subset of $\bigcup(A \cap B)$. Note that the distinction between the notions of distributivity and kolchoz-collectivity concurs with the old distinction between count nouns like *child, passenger, book*, and so forth, and group nouns like *herd* and *committee*. Although the set denoted by *herd* contains individuals, the use of the noun *herd* prevents any member of a herd from being called a herd. The lowest level at which we may quantify is the group level, whereas regular count nouns allow us to "enter" the set of children and get at its subsets. Similar considerations apply to the difference between (D.4) and (D.5).[25]

2.4. The Three Functions Working Together

The three functions s, l, and π do not account only for terminativity; they also account properly for distributive and collective facts. The result of the interaction among s, l, and π is given in figure 7. It comprises all the different sorts of terminativity discussed so far:

1. $n = 1$ as in (3a), (15a), (16a), and (16b). Here the difference between the distributive mode and the totalising mode is irrelevant: they collapse.

2. $n \geq 1$ in $dom(\pi)$ as in (15b) through (15e), (16c), and (16d). Here there are two possibilities:

   (a) $n = 1$ in $ran(\pi)$: totalisation, as defined in (D.5).
   (b) $n \geq 1$ in $ran(\pi)$: distributivity, as defined in (D.4).

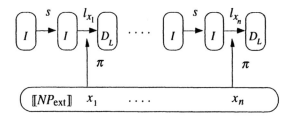

Figure 7. The relation among s, l, and π.

If figure 7 is the right picture of the involved compositional process, it follows rather straightforwardly that events are not individuals. Which part of the system making up the information should be called an event seems to be a matter of convention. In (16c), *Three girls lifted four tables*, one might call each $s + l + \pi$ combination an event, even though the indices provided by s are the same from the temporal point of view. Note also that parts of a Path may be called an event. But one might also call the VP an event. If so, then one conclusion should be that mereological approaches to event structure tend to blur the differences between the levels at which we speak about events.

2.5. Tense and Progressive Form

Tense is syntactically defined as taking a tenseless S of type $\langle\langle\langle i, t\rangle, t\rangle, t\rangle$ to form a tensed $\overline{S}$: $\overline{S} = INFL(S)$.[26] Its semantics is given in (29), where α varies over the different tenses:

(29) $[\![INFL]\!] = \lambda S \exists I \exists I_V (S(I) \wedge I = Ent^+(I_V) \wedge Tense_\alpha(I_V)(i^*))$.

In (16a), *Mary lifted four tables*, $\alpha = '<'$ because of its past tense. When (29) applies to it, it yields

(30) $\exists I \exists I_V(\text{Mary-lift-four-tables}(I) \wedge I = \text{Ent}^+(I_V) \wedge \text{Tense}_<(I_V)(i^*))$.

This says that there is a set of indices I (in the natural numbers) and an interval I_V (in the real numbers) such that I is associated with Mary's lifting of four tables, I represents the stretch I_V, and this stretch is before the point of speech i^*.[27]

The progressive form PROG applies before INFL and is syntactically defined as taking a tenseless S to form a tenseless S: $\overline{S}$ = PROG(S):[28]

(31) $[\![\text{PROG}]\!] = \lambda S \lambda J' \exists J(S(J) \wedge J' \subset J)$.

For (32a), the application of PROG to the tenseless [*Mary lift four tables*] yields (32b), after which INFL is applied, yielding (32c):

(32)   a.   Mary was lifting four tables.
       b. $\lambda S \lambda J' \exists J(S(J) \wedge J' \subset J) \, (\text{M-lift-FT}) = \lambda J' \exists J(\text{M-lift-FT}(J) \wedge J' \subset J)$.
       c. $\exists I \exists I_V \exists J(\text{M-lift-FT}(J) \wedge I \subset J \wedge I = \text{Ent}^+(I_V) \wedge \text{Tense}_<(I_V)(i^*))$.

This says that the Mary-lift-four-tables predication—*M-lift-FT*—associated with J can only be warranted as to its truth as far as its proper subset I is concerned. That is, only the I-part of J is given as actualised in the real numbers and Tense commits itself only for I and not for its complement in J.

This is a nonmodal treatment of the progressive form as far as the application of a rounding-off function is nonmodal. It assumes that a tenseless S contains the information that supplies a full Path. Tense takes only part of it, as the progressive demands.

2.6. Some Ontological and Representational Conclusions

From the point of view in which the terminative aspectuality of sentences like (3a), (15), and (16) is formed on the basis of Frege's principle of compositionality, there is hardly room for the notion of event as an individual—that is, as an explanatory notion. As pointed out above, the term *event* can be tied up with different phrasal levels such as VP or S. This is actually what corresponds with normal intuitions about the notion of event: it is as flexible as we want to have it. One might say that in distributive sentences like (16c), *Three girls lifted four tables*, and (16d), *Three girls lifted a table*, the notion of event applies minimally to *l*. But it could also pertain to the level at which π applies. Let us take (16d): it underinforms us with respect to what really happened. In its totalising interpretation, three girls as a group lifted one table. In its distributive interpretation, we distinguish among three events, and now the notion of event seems to shift to each individual Path. So far so good: one might say that π provides for eventhood. But shifting to (16c) one should observe that it could be the result of a check on a list in which it is found out that in the past year, in different months, each of the girls lifted four tables, so that, say, the twelve liftings are distributed over twelve months. Does that count as one event? Maybe, maybe not.

It seems to me that we are concerned here with the same phenomenon observed in Verkuyl (1972) about the frequency adverbials in (33):

(33)   a. Piet warned him three times.
       b. What Piet did three times was warn him.
       c. What Piet did was to warn him three times.

Sentence (33a) can be paraphrased as (33b), and in that case it seems as if we talk about three different events, whereas the paraphrase in (33c) presents (33a) as pertaining to one event that consists of three warnings. Is it proper to say that (33a) is ambiguous and that we have to look for the minimal event in each of the two readings? Or should we simply say that the notion of event is not so appropriate for the analysis of (33a)? I do not have a precise analysis to offer for these sentences because (33a) is a case of outer aspectuality, but in the present framework a solution would be to let *three times* modify π in (33b) and *l* in (33c). In both cases we do not gain any insight if we use the term *event*. It is a handy descriptive term that we employ as language users, but as linguists it makes less sense than we are inclined to think. The real work in the building of temporal structure is done by the function *s*, which creates the counting points for the structuring of the internal argument domain into Path structure.

    The localistic notion of Path in the formalisation given above is really essential for an understanding of the notion of event. There is an event as soon as there is an l_x with a proper value of the variable *x*. Thus, it turns out to be the case that the VP is a very central element in the analysis of eventhood. Syntactically, the internal argument has closer ties with the verb than the external argument, and so a unit is formed. Semantically, it provides the second factor of a multiplication of the form exhibited in (34), which was demonstrated in (22):

(34)   ⟦NP⟧ × ⟦VP⟧.

It should be possible to refer to this VP by linguistic means—for example, by the *it* in (14). Moreover, it should be possible to make the VP central in the theory of aspectuality in the sense that some systematic form of aspectuality can be expressed by it because in sentences with a plural external argument it is necessary to copy this form. Finally, it should be possible to treat the VP as a factor in a well-organised pattern made visible in figure 7—that is, as dependent on the external argument for the calculation of the values involved. These three requirements rephrase the main problems raised in section 1. In the next section, I discuss what event semanticists have to say about these questions.

3. Event Semantics on Aspectuality

I show in section 3.1 that Davidson's problem of anaphoric reference to events is dissolved as soon as one allows for reference to functions, in section 3.2 that Vendler's proposal can be recast to fit into the localistic scheme of figure 1, and in section 3.3 that Parsons's attempts to use the aspectual predicates in (11) have nothing to do with aspectuality. In section 3.4, I discuss Krifka's event semantic approach to aspectuality.

3.1. Davidson's Anaphoric Reference

Recall that the original problem in Davidson (1967) was the use of the pronoun *it* in (35b):

(35) a. Jones buttered the toast slowly, deliberately, with a knife, in the bathroom, at midnight.
b. He did it slowly, deliberately, in the bathroom.

Davidson argued that it is not sufficient to have something such as *There is some action x such that Jones did x slowly, etc.* because *butter the toast* is not an appropriate singular term. What he did (after throwing out *slowly* and *deliberately*) was to assign (35a) the logical form in (36a):[29]

(36) a. $\exists e$(Buttering(jones, the-toast, e) $\wedge$ With(a-knife, e) $\wedge$ In(the-bathroom, e) $\wedge$ At(midnight, e)).
b. $\exists e$(Buttering(e) $\wedge$ Agent(jones, e) $\wedge$ Patient(the-toast, e) $\wedge$ With(a-knife, e) $\wedge$ In(the-bathroom, e)).

The *it* in (35b) can now be said to pertain to the *e*. In (36b), the neo-Davidsonian format of (36a) is given: the thematic roles of agent and patient are taken as two-place predicates relating the agent and patient to the event in which they have that role.

How would the anaphoric reference behave in sentences in which no action is involved, such as (37a)?

(37) a. Jones died in the bathroom at midnight.
b. It happened in the bathroom at midnight.

It is clear that one cannot continue (37a) with *He did it in . . .* but that one has to appeal to something like (37b). What is this *it* and should one expect, as Davidson does, a singular term for it (and not find any)? No, of course not. One should expect sloppy identity, as becomes clear by sentences like (38) and (39):

(38) a. Three girls buttered their toast in the bathroom.
b. They did it at midnight.

(39) a. Judith and Jessica buttered their toast in the bathroom.
b. They did it at midnight.

In (38) the anaphoric reference of *it* is sloppy. Of course, one could declare (38a) ambiguous, but as pointed out, there are at least as many arguments for assuming that (38) underdetermines what really happened: the girls may or may not have been in the bathroom together and they may or may not have shared the toast.[30] What we need in the case of (38) is that *it* may pertain to three or to two events or to just one. It must indeed be sloppy. The same applies to sentences like (39): here it is clear that for a situation in which the two girls each buttered their toast, the *it* is the sloppy identity *it* well known from the literature on *do so* constructions, for which an analysis in terms of lambda abstraction turns out to be the proper sort of solution.

I proposed such a solution (Verkuyl 1972: 142ff.) for sentences such as *Arie ate a herring and Piet did so too* to account for their terminativity. In terms of the PLUG framework of section 2, this amounts to saying that the *l*-function is the interpretation of the *it* in sentences like (35), (37), (38), and (39). In this way we may explain why it is that sentences like (40a) pertain to six sandwiches and why (40b) pertains to twelve tables.

(40)   a.   Judith ate three sandwiches at twelve o'clock and Jessica did it half an hour later.
       b.   Three girls lifted four tables and each of them did it in twenty seconds.

It is not difficult to think of *l* in terms of lambda abstraction: l_x contains a variable *x*, which needs to receive its value before the function can be applied. This is built in (D.2) and is part of the definition of the VP in the PLUG grammar (cf. Verkuyl 1993: 350). So, it turns out to be quite natural to refer to the l_x by the sloppy anaphoric *it* that is able to vary over the different values of *x*. Therefore, it seems to me that if we let *it* in (35) pertain to *l(Jones)* in the compositional framework of section 2, Davidson's problem would have been solved in principle—that is, if he had allowed quantification over functions in the way proposed by Reichenbach (1947).

Recall that Reichenbach has analysed (41a) as in (41b), which was paraphrased by Davidson as (41c):

(41)   a.   Amundsen flew to the North Pole.
       b. $\exists e(f(a, n))^*(e)$.
       c. $\exists e(e$ consists in the fact that Amundsen flew to the North Pole).
       d. $\exists e(a$ flying *e* by Amundsen to the North Pole took place).

Apart from the question of whether or not (41c) is the appropriate paraphrase—rather than, say, (41d)—it seems to me that (41b) raises the problem of why Davidson ignored the fact that the $(f(a, n))^*$ part of the formula is clearly treated as a mathematical function that can be referred to and quantified over, as in, for example, Reichenbach (1947: 307). So, the question does not seem to be whether the particular format of (41c) meets certain logical difficulties but whether Reichenbach's main point—namely, that events are entities (p. 272)—carries over to functions. In my view, the Reichenbachian position is that mathematical functions are entities as well: you may assert their existence, and so you may quantify over them. This is exactly what happens in the PLUG framework without having the (extensional substitution) problem that Davidson assigned to (41c). In short, the real issue involved in Davidson's treatment, and rejection, of (41c) is whether or not we can treat reference to events in terms of reference to functions.

My conclusion is that Davidson's problem in finding no singular term for the anaphoric *it* in (35b) is an artefact of his wish to restrict his formalism to a first-order language. I also conclude that Reichenbach's original idea can be given a better expression in a higher order language and that its strength can be made concrete by assuming that his *fact function* by and large corresponds to the VP taken as a Path, that is, as a lambda function which, once applied to an argument, yields an eventuality.[31]

3.2. Vendler's Verbs and Times

In Verkuyl (1989) I raised a series of objections against Vendler (1957) when taken as a linguistic analysis, and I also showed that Vendlerians never use the four verb classes he distinguished for making generalisations about aspectuality.

It may be helpful to put in some history at this point to explain why there is so much confusion about Vendler classes. The main source of trouble seems to me to be Dowty (1979). Dowty interpreted Vendler's notion of verb linguistically—that is, as a lexical notion. This move was very influential, and we see it back in what can be called the Vendler/Dowty tradition. Part of this tradition is in the Edinburgh approach, in which again some lip service is paid to the compositional approach, for example, in Moens (1987) and Moens and Steedman (1987). Moens and Steedman try to maintain the Vendler classes but postulate some operators to get compositionality. Consider, for example, (42):

(42) a. Mary walked.
      b. Mary walked 30 miles.
      c. Mary walked miles.

The leading idea is that *walk* in (42a) is an activity verb and that this verb is coerced into an accomplishment verb in (42b), which is coerced back again into the activity verb in (42c) and (42a). The only reason for not saying that *walk* in all three sentences of (42) has a constant meaning, and that the effect of combining *30 miles* with this *walk* is different from the effect of combining *miles* with *walk*, is the assumption that the Vendler quadripartition is lexical. This sort of coercion is in fact a rather forced notational variant of regular Fregean interpretation with the help of the features [±ADD-TO] and [±SQA] on the basis of figure 1.

Suppose that we interpret Vendler's notion of verb at the VP level, much in the way Montague used the notion of intransitive verb. Vendler can then be taken as treating *walk* and *walk a mile* as VPs. Historically, this interpretation would explain the discussion about homogeneity in the 1970s, in which Bennett and Partee (1978) played an important role. Bennett and Partee also followed Montague in treating *walk* and *walk home* as intransitive verbs; but rather than acting as linguists trying to break down a VP into its constituent parts, they simply took *walk home* as an unanalysed predicate of a certain Vendlerian type: *walk* as an activity and *walk home* as an accomplishment. So, a couple of things were mixed up: the logical Montagovian way of treating *walk* and *walk home* as being of type IV was accepted. Then a shift was made to acting as a linguist by taking *walk* as a lexical aspectual class; and then again the logician returned by declaring that *walk home* should be treated as an unanalysed verb after which it could be put in a different lexical aspectual class than *walk*; after which the coercion operators appeared, and so on.

Indeed, if Vendler's notion of aspectual classes is not lexical but rather phrasal, it would mean that the coercion operators in (42) may be abolished. There is no need for them. But it would also mean that Vendlerian verbs, whether complex (as in (42b) and (42c)) or not (as in (42a)), should be analysed along the lines of figure 1. This is another way of saying that, at best, Vendler's proposal is an unanalysed compositional approach, not paying attention to the information contributed by NPs in- and outside the VP. I rather consider it a throwback with respect to proposals in the early decennia of this century in the mainly German literature on aspectuality, where his criteria, such as the *for an hour*-test were well-established. For the present purpose, it is enough to observe that in a reinterpretation of Vendler's proposal as a proposal about verb phrases and times, the localistic approach in section 2 would be not only compatible with its rearticulation but also more appropriate because it accounts for the contribution of the arguments of the verb. And this would mean that there would not be four VP classes.

As a final remark, it should be noted that if Vendler can be reanalysed along these lines, his notion of event comes closer to that developed in the framework of section 2 than to the Davidsonian notion. It is no coincidence that event semanticists cannot express any of the Vendler classes in their representations: they use his terms only pretheoretically.

3.3. *Parsons's* Hold *and* Cul *Predicates*

In this section, I focus on Parsons's predicates *Hold* and *Cul* to see how, and how much, they contribute to a better understanding of the differences between durative and terminative sentences. The relevant rules of his grammar are given in (43).

Both *Hold* and *Cul* in R3 are treated as two-place predicates between events and times. The rule R3 is split up into two different options. Parsons adopts the first option before 1984 and opts for the second afterwards. There is an intriguing replication of the transition between these two variants of R3 in Parson's work. The transition from the first variant to the second took place around 1984, and so one expects the second to be established from that time on. But in Parsons (1990) the first variant of R3 reappears at the beginning of the book, and it is only at the close of the book that they are all rejected and the second is reintroduced. This makes it necessary to have a look at the two options:

(43) R1. If $\alpha \in V_{intr}$, then $\alpha \in VP$.

R2. If $\alpha \in V_{trans}$ and $\beta \in$ Name, then $\alpha\beta \in VP$.

R3. If $\alpha \in$ Name and $\beta \in VP$, then $\beta\alpha \in S$ and either

$\lambda e \lambda t (\alpha'(e) \wedge \text{Agent}(\beta', e) \wedge \text{Hold}(e, t))$ if α is a state or a process VP

$\lambda e \lambda t(\alpha'(e) \wedge \text{Agent}(\beta', e) \wedge \text{Cul}(e, t))$ if α is an event VP

or

$\lambda e \lambda t(\alpha'(e) \wedge \text{Agent}(\beta', e) \wedge \text{Hold}(e, t))$ if α is a state VP

$\lambda e \lambda t(\alpha'(e) \wedge \text{Agent}(\beta', e) \wedge \text{Cul}(e, t))$ if α is a process or event VP.

R10. If $\alpha \in$ Adv and $\beta \in$ VP, then $\beta\alpha = \lambda e(\beta'(e) \wedge \alpha'(e))$.

3.3.1. Hold_a and Cul_a

Consider the definition of the two predicates.

(D.6) *Hold_a* "means that an eventuality e holds at time t, which means that e is either a state and e's object is in state e or e is an event which is in development at t". *Cul_a* means "that e is an event that culminates at time t". (Parsons 1989: 220; but see also Parsons 1990: 25)[32]

Applied to the sentences in (44), this yields the primed representations:

(44) a. Mary dislikes Fred.

a'. $\exists e(\text{Disliking}(e) \wedge \text{Subj}(e, m) \wedge \text{Obj}(e, f) \wedge \text{Hold}(e, t))$.

b. Mary was crossing the street.

b'. $\exists e(\text{Crossing}(e) \wedge \text{Subj}(e, m) \wedge \text{Obj}(e, \text{the-street}) \wedge \text{Hold}(e, t))$.

c. Mary crossed the street.

c'. $\exists e(\text{Crossing}(e) \wedge \text{Subj}(e, m) \wedge \text{Obj}(e, \text{the-street}) \wedge \text{Cul}(e, t))$.

Hold and *Cul* can be seen only as being added to the stock of Davidsonian predicates to distinguish between durative and terminative aspectuality. Parsons absorbed Moens's idea of attributing to an event a development part and a culmination part. Thus, *Hold_a* in (44b') covers the development part of the crossing and expresses that the event did not (necessarily) culminate. *Cul_a* expresses the sense of culmination that Parsons attributes to (44c).[33]

In the absence of any treatment of quantification in Parsons's work, we must assume that the difference between (3a) and (4a) would be accounted for as in

(45) a. $\exists e(\text{Eating}(e) \wedge \text{Subj}(e, j) \wedge \text{Obj}(e, \text{three-sandwiches}) \wedge \text{Cul}(e, t))$.

b. $\exists e(\text{Eating}(e) \wedge \text{Subj}(e, j) \wedge \text{Obj}(e, \text{sandwiches}) \wedge \text{Hold}(e, t))$.

The following question then arises: does Parsons present here a theory about aspectuality? If so, the theory does not explain anything: *Hold_a* and *Cul_a* are at best descriptive predicates. That is, some sort of metarules may be formulated:

if $[_\alpha \ldots \text{Hold}_a(e)]$, then α is durative.

if $[_\alpha \ldots \text{Cul}_a(e)]$, then α is terminative.

However, this does not work properly. First, Lascarides (1988) devastatingly points out that there is no logical relationship between (45a) and (45b). That is, there is no *Hold_a* part in *Cul_a*. The two predicates are totally unrelated, so there is no way to provide for the one-way inference relation between sentences with a $Hold_a$ predicate and a Cul_a predicate—and, therefore, between (45b) and (45a). Second, from the purely aspectual point of view, it should be obvious that the aspectual difference between (45a) and (45b) must be found in the difference between *three sandwiches* and *sandwiches*, and it is very hard to see what $Hold_a$ and Cul_a could possibly contribute toward explaining that difference, the more so because in (44) it seems to account both for the difference between the progressive form and the simple past and for the difference between stative and certain nonstative predications. At best, the addition of the $Hold_a$ and Cul_a predicate is a way of saying that the two sentences in (45) differ, but this is what we already knew by looking at them. For Parsons there is no way of expressing that $Hold_a$ sometimes has to look at the subject NP (*nobody* in (5a)), sometimes at the object NP (*three sandwiches* and *sandwiches*), and sometimes at the verb (*dislike* in (6a)) to establish durativity. In short, $Hold_a$ and Cul_a do not do anything to connect themselves to the spots where the relevant aspectual information is. Not the slightest hint about which direction should be taken has been given in any of Parsons's articles nor in Parsons (1990).

3.3.2. $Hold_b$ and Cul_b

The definitions of $Hold_a$ and Cul_a (D.6) reappear in Parsons (1990: Part 1). So, one should expect a reaction to Lascarides (1988). In spite of the change in position from $Hold_a/Cul_a$ to $Hold_b/Cul_b$ in Parsons (1985), Parsons (1990: 23–25) simply gives the $Hold_a/Cul_a$ definitions and carries them with him far beyond p. 142. Parsons (1990: Ch. 9) is a slightly revised version of Parsons (1989). So, at the very last pages, the quite drastic change from $Hold_a/Cul_a$ to $Hold_b/Cul_b$ takes place (pp. 184–185). The differences between $Hold_a/Cul_a$ and $Hold_b/Cul_b$ are minimised: "The effect of this proposal is to broaden the scope of the earlier analysis without affecting its formulation. We just treat process verbs as a special kind of event verb and apply the theory as before" (p. 184). From this point on we have

(46)   a.   Mary ran.
      a'. $\exists e(\text{Running}(e) \wedge \text{Subj}(e, m) \wedge \text{Cul}(e, t))$.

      b.   Mary ran to the store.
      b'. $\exists e(\text{Running}(e) \wedge \text{Subj}(e, m) \wedge \text{To}(e, \text{the-store}) \wedge \text{Cul}(e, t))$.

      c.   Mary was running to the store.
      c'. $\exists e(\text{Running}(e) \wedge \text{Subj}(e, m) \wedge \text{To}(e, \text{the-store}) \wedge \text{Hold}(e, t))$.

And we may add

(47)   a.   Mary dislikes Fred.
      a'. $\exists s(\text{Disliking}(s) \wedge \text{Subj}(s, m) \wedge \text{Obj}(s, f) \wedge \text{Hold}(s, t))$.

      b.   Mary was crossing the street.
      b'. $\exists e(\text{Crossing}(e) \wedge \text{Subj}(e, m) \wedge \text{Obj}(e, \text{the-street}) \wedge \text{Hold}(e, t))$.

      c.   Mary crossed the street.

c'. $\exists e$(Crossing(e) $\wedge$ Subj(e, m) $\wedge$ Obj(e, the-street) $\wedge$ Cul(e, t)).

It is clear that some additional notions are required. It is also clear that the distinction between *Hold* and *Cul* now is just the lexical distinction between stative and nonstative verbs, or rather the way in which the events corresponding with them actualise in time. This raises a problem with (46c'): *Hold* cannot hold for events any longer. This is solved by

(48)   a.   Mary be running to the store.
       a'. $\exists e$(Running(e) $\wedge$ Subj(e, m) $\wedge$ To(e, the-store) $\wedge$ Hold(In-prog(e), t)).

The operator In-prog takes an event e and makes a state s out of it: Parsons (1990: 234) describes this operator as follows: "whenever an event e is in progress, there is a corresponding state of affairs, 'that e is in progress'. This is a state that holds while e is in progress (and at no other time). Call this the 'in-progress state' of the event e, or 'e's IP state'".

In my view the change of position can only mean that for Parsons *Hold$_b$* and *Cul$_b$* are no longer part of an aspectual theory: they are now part of the Tense system in the sense that they can be considered as accounting for the connection between states and events and real time. They have nothing (structurally) to do in making a sentence (in-)compatible with *for an hour* and *in an hour*. Parsons distinguishes between states and events and for each of the two ontological categories he needs a term to express two types of actualisation in real time: *Cul* for nonstative predications and *Hold* for stative ones. Then an aspectual notion comes in: IP state. The reasoning must be the following: *Cul* brings us in the domain of nonstative semantic objects—events—and these have a development part, a culmination part, and a consequent state part; in Parsons (1990: 235) this was called the *resultant state*. In-prog always takes the development part and yields a state.[34]

3.3.3. Conclusion

From the aspectual point of view there is a lot more to say against Parsons's analyses, but I do not pursue my discussion of his *Hold/Cul* analysis here any further because most of what I have to say follows from the framework presented in section 2. However, there is one general point that I would like to raise against the neo-Davidsonian event semantic format, which grew out of (7).

(49) $p_1 \wedge p_2 \wedge \ldots \wedge p_n$.

The format in (49) allows for inferences based on the scheme in (50):

(50)   a. $p \wedge q \to p$.
       b. $p \wedge q \to q$.

Parsons (1990: 13–15) made some restrictions on this scheme for it to work properly, but these restrictions do not bear on the point I want to make here. The point is that p and q in (50) should be independent: q may not pertain to information that is necessary for p to be asserted. This condition is not fulfilled in representations like (46), (47), (48), and so on. This can be made visible by returning to problems already raised by Davidson himself when he pointed out that from sentences such as *He sank the Bismarck*, you may not infer to *He sank*. In Dowty (1989) this problem returned in such examples as *John devoured his lunch*, from which one cannot infer *John devoured*. Likewise, one may not derive *He watered* from *He watered the plants*. Some event semanticists seem very happy in taking p_1 in (49) as 'there is some sinking' or 'there is some devouring' and 'there is some watering', and they are inclined to solve this problem in terms of ambiguity or polysemy. However, polysemy makes it impossible to cut the dependency ties between p_1 and the other members of the conjunction. And if ambiguity is the deus ex machina for dealing with polysemy, then the simple answer to that move is to point out that one thus needs a special grammar for the exclusion of unwanted inferences.

3.4. Aspectual Postulates

Krifka looks like an event semanticist, but if he is, he is quite different from neo-Davidsonians like Parsons and Higginbotham. I argue that Krifka in fact uses two different notions of event. His first notion concurs with my notion of index and is visible in his event first-order semantic representation based on mereology. His second notion is a composite one and is expressed by higher order postulates. I have criticised Krifka in some detail elsewhere (Verkuyl 1993) and do not repeat most of the points raised there. A new set of problems for Krifka is discussed in much detail in Naumann (1996).[35] I first focus on what separates Krifka's framework from the PLUG⁺ framework and then discuss some of the problems that arise in the present context.

3.4.1. Lattices

Following Link (1983), Krifka (1989a, 1989b) attributes the domain of discourse D the structure $\langle D, \sqcup \rangle$ of a join semilattice—that is, a lattice with only the join operator $\sqcup$. D is partitioned into a set O of objects and a set E of events so that there are two join operations in these subdomains: $\langle O, E, \sqcup_O, \sqcup_E \rangle$. He also assumes the (mereological) *part-of* relation P. Thus, the resulting model structure is $\langle O, E, \sqcup_O, \sqcup_E, P_O, P_E \rangle$. This move has clear ontological consequences: it helps to retain the type logic inherent to the standard format of (7) in cases like (51):

(51) a. Mary died.
      b. John and Mary died.

Standardly one has $\text{Die}_{\langle e, t \rangle}(m_e)$ for (51a), which is true iff $I(m_e) \in I(\text{Die}_{\langle e, t \rangle})$. This analysis leads to problems for (51b) because if *John and Mary* are treated as denoting a set, a type clash results. There are two ways out to save the generalisation over the two sentences in (51): either (a) we treat Mary as a singleton and take NPs as being of type $\langle \langle e, t \rangle, t \rangle$, which is the set-theoretical solution, or (b) we take John and Mary as an individual of type e. The latter possibility is obtained by extending standard predicate logic by means of a binary operator $\oplus$, interpreted as the join $\sqcup$ of two individuals. Given that the join of two individuals is still an individual, in a lattice-theoretical approach (51b) can be represented as *Die(John⊕Mary)*, where $[\![John \oplus Mary]\!]$ is considered an entity of type e.[36]

$$[\![\mathrm{Die}(\mathrm{John} \oplus \mathrm{Mary})]\!] = 1 \text{ iff } (\mathrm{I(j)} \sqcup \mathrm{I(m)}) \in \mathrm{I(Die)}.$$

Lattice theory can be used to account for the relation between mass and count nouns, although it should be observed that there are other ways to relate them, one of them being the extension of set theory to ensemble theory, proposed in Bunt (1985).

In Krifka's lattice-theoretical approach, heavy emphasis is put on the parallel structure one may attribute to the verbal (event) domain and the nominal (objects) domain. In both cases the distinction between mass and count shows up; therefore Krifka partitions the model structure into an eventive and an objectual subdomain, suitably restricting the relevant operations to them—namely, to D_O and D_E. Krifka capitalises on the parallelism between the two domains, and thus he gives his aspectual theory a rich ontological flavour. Or to put it differently, his system underscores the naive physics of the domain of discourse. We have to get interested in how Mary's dying is built up and how the three sandwiches are eaten when considering a sentences like (15a). Something of the structure on the event side must be found in the structure on the nominal side.

3.4.2. A Derivation and Some Postulates

Let us now consider the derivation of (15a), *Judith ate three sandwiches*, with enough details for a comparison. As given in (52), the derivation shows that Krifka chooses the neo-Davidsonian format by isolating in (52a) the verb *eat* from its thematic roles: there is an eating and there should be an agent x and a patient y. The NP *three sandwiches* is formed to take the verb *eat* as its argument, and the numeral expresses a relation R between the set of sandwiches and a number. The final stage of the derivation says that there is an agent Judith and that there is an complex individual y consisting of three sandwiches.[37]

(52) a. eat $\lambda e(\mathrm{Eat}(e) \wedge \mathrm{Agent}(e, x) \wedge \mathrm{Patient}(e, y))$

 b. three $\lambda R \lambda P \lambda e \exists y (P(e) \wedge \mathrm{Patient}(e, y) \wedge R(y, 3))$

 c. sandwich $\lambda n \lambda x (\mathrm{Sandwich}(x, n))$

 d. three sandwiches $\lambda P \lambda e \exists y (P(e) \wedge \mathrm{Patient}(e, y) \wedge \mathrm{Sandwich}(y, 3))$

 e. eat three sandwiches $\lambda e \exists y (\mathrm{Eat}(y) \wedge \mathrm{Agent}(e, x) \wedge \mathrm{Patient}(e, y) \wedge \mathrm{Sandwich}(y, 3))$

 f. Judith $\lambda P \lambda e \exists x (P(e) \wedge \mathrm{Agent}(e, x) \wedge x = \mathrm{j})$

 g. (15a) $\lambda e \exists x \exists y (\mathrm{Eat}(e) \wedge \mathrm{Patient}(e, y) \wedge \mathrm{Sandwich}(y, 3) \wedge \mathrm{Agent}(e, x) \wedge x = \mathrm{j})$

In one important respect, (52) deviates from Parsons's derivations: the lack of a *Cul* predicate. The question is: what makes (3a) and (15a) terminative for Krifka? And what makes (4a) durative for him? Krifka's last line for (4a), *Judith ate sandwiches*, is (53),

(53) $\lambda e \exists x \exists y (\text{Eat}(e) \wedge \text{Patient}(e, y) \wedge \exists n (\text{Sandwich}(y, n) \wedge \text{Agent}(e, x) \wedge x = j))$,

in which there is no *Hold* predicate. So, where does the aspectual information come from? The answer to this question is that Krifka does not put this information in his representations but in "meta-representations". That is, he makes use of a set of postulates by which one can determine whether a certain logical form satisfies the proper conditions for terminativity or that for durativity. The postulates are cast in a higher order language, and in this way the formulas in (52) may retain their first-order nature.[38] Sentences like (3a) and (4a) receive the correct aspectual labels by matching their logical forms with the scheme in (54), where φ is a VP:

(54) $\varphi \mapsto \lambda e \exists y (\alpha(e) \wedge \Theta(e, y) \wedge \delta(y))$.

Immediately one must take one step back: Krifka does not account for the aspectual composition above the level of φ—that is, above the level of the VP. So, no account is given of what is covered by the π function in the PLUG framework. With this reservation in mind, we continue to observe that α stands for the verb, that Θ is the patient role, and that δ stands for the internal argument NP. Given (54), Krifka says that sentences like (4a) are durative just in case α and δ are cumulative and Θ is summative. Sentence (3a) is terminative because α is cumulative, δ has quantised reference, and Θ satisfies both the constraints he terms *uniqueness of object* and *mapping to object*.

Before discussing the merits of this approach, let us have a more detailed look at the postulates:

(D.8) Cumulativity (CUM):
$$\forall R(\mathbf{CUM}(R) \leftrightarrow \forall x \forall y(R(x) \wedge R(y) \wedge R(x \sqcup y)))$$

(D.9) Summativity (SUM):
$$\forall R(\mathbf{SUM}(R) \leftrightarrow \forall e \forall e' \forall z \forall z'(R(e, z) \wedge R(e', z') \rightarrow R(e \sqcup_E e', z \sqcup_O z')))$$

(D.10) Quantised reference (QUA):
$$\forall R(\mathbf{QUA}_O(R) \leftrightarrow \forall z \forall z'(R(z) \wedge R(z') \rightarrow \neg z' P_O z))$$
$$\forall R(\mathbf{QUA}_E(R) \leftrightarrow \forall z \forall z'(R(z) \wedge R(z') \rightarrow \neg z' P_E z))$$

(D.11) Uniqueness of Objects (UoO):
$$\forall R(\mathbf{UNI}(R) \leftrightarrow \forall e \forall z \forall z'(R(e, z) \wedge R(e, z') \rightarrow z = z'))$$

(D.12) Mapping to Objects (MtO):
$$\forall R(\mathbf{MAP}_O(R) \leftrightarrow \forall e \forall e' \forall z(R(e, z) \wedge e' P_E e \rightarrow \exists z'(z' P_O z \wedge R(e', z'))))$$

(D.13) Mapping to Events (MtE):
$$\forall R(\mathbf{MAP}_E(R) \leftrightarrow \forall e \forall e' \forall z(R(e, z) \wedge x' P_O x \rightarrow \exists e'(e' P_E e \wedge R(e', z'))))$$

Cumulativity says for α that if one has $[\![Eating]\!](e)$ and $[\![Eating]\!](e')$, one may join them into $[\![Eating]\!](e \sqcup e')$; for δ it says that if you have $[\![Nice]\!](j)$ and $[\![Nice]\!](m)$, you also have $[\![Nice]\!](j \sqcup m)$. Summativity accounts for the Θ-part.

As far as (4a) is concerned, a couple of problems show up. First, Naumann observed that the cumulativity requirement on α is empty. There is no verb that is not cumulative. This means that any hope for making a distinction between stative and nonstative verbs in terms of the notion of cumulativity must be given up. It also means that all information about the role of the verb is relegated to the $\Theta(e, y)$ part. I would like to add that this holds also for the information expressed by $\delta(y)$ because in derivations like (52) and (53) there is no δ at all: the information about the patient is expressed only by $Patient(e, y)$. $R(y, 3)$ or $R(y, n)$ do not have the form $\delta(y)$. If $\delta(y)$ is in fact an abbreviatory device for the "sandwich part" of $R(y, 3)$—that is, its $R(y, \ldots)$ part—then a new problem arises: the $\delta(y)$ is the same in $R(y, 3)$ and in $R(y, n)$, so if $\delta(y)$ is cumulative in the latter it should also be in the former. And this means that the distinction between (4a) and (3a) cannot be made on the basis of $\delta(y)$.

Note that the "sandwich part" of $R(y, 3)$ and $R(y, n)$ is already expressed by the SUM postulate in (D.8), which applies to $Patient(e, y)$: its cumulativity is accounted for by $y \sqcup y'$. So, all things in (54) really boil down to $Patient(e, y)$, and here I return to Naumann, who raises the same objection to $\Theta(e, y)$ as to $\alpha(y)$: all thematic relations are cumulative. This means that the only place to look for the difference between the durative (4a) and the terminative (3a) is the second argument of $R(y, 3)$ and $R(y, n)$. But here we meet an objection I have raised (Verkuyl 1993): $\exists n(Sandwich(y, n))$ assumes that there is a specific unidentified number. But the difference between an unknown number and the number 1 cannot be the basis for a difference between unbounded and bounded. If we say, *John killed some men*, we know that there is a finite number of men killed by John, but we cannot identify the number n of men. The sentence itself is terminative. Basically Krifka treats bare plurals in the same way as quantised NPs: in both cases there is a specific number n. Recall that in PLUG$^+$ the solution was to assume that in bare plurals no cardinality information is given, so that it cannot be determined. This seems to me a more correct approach.

The second problem is that Krifka says that (3a) is terminative just in case δ has quantised reference and $Patient(e, y)$ meets the conditions UoO and MtO.[39] Note that (D.10) and (D.11) do not follow from any linguistic material inside the sentence: they just stipulate that the conditions hold for terminative cases. In my view, this keeps Krifka's theory from explaining the nature of terminativity. Naumann shows that the conditions hold good for sentences such as (3a), containing verbs like *eat*, but that, for example, UoO does not work properly in sentences like (55):

(55)   John read two books.

It is required by UoO that if someone reads a book, the event e has this book as the only object to which it relates by means of the patient role. But one may read two books simultaneously, and if humans cannot do that, computers can. One may also describe (55) as saying that there are two events in each of which a book was read. But the same situation can also be described in terms of two events meeting summativity. According to Naumann, this makes clear that whether or not the *e* relates to one or to two (complex) individuals depends on underlying individuation criteria for events, and these determine whether or not UoO holds. But this amounts to saying that UoO looses its explanatory value because as soon as one tries to solve this problem by pointing out that UoO may vary according to the verbs involved, one is doing away with the constancy in the Θ-relation.[40]

As for MtE and MtO, Naumann also raises the problem of sentences such as

(56)   a.   John drove his car from Boston to Chicago.
        b.   John peeled the apple.

In (56a), halfway the Path is not halfway the car, and in (56b) it is clear that only a part of the apple is affected. The same applies to sentences such as *Mary built a house*: the building of a house involves a lot of planning, erecting scaffolds, and so on, and these are not part of the mapping between the house and the event.

More generally, it seems to me that MtO and MtE are not appropriate for dealing with sentences like (15) and (16). For their proper analysis it is essential that we capture the underdeterminacy about which one of the possible combinatorial configurations is actualised. Note that for each of the actualisations, the interplay between *s* and *l* warrants that the structure of *l* and the internal argument denotation are in a mapping relation. This relation, however, is not a naive physical one but can be formulated at the set-theoretical level at which quantification is dealt with.

3.5. Conclusion

These objections against Krifka's lattice-theoretical approach in an event semantic framework strengthen my wish (bias, some will say) to retain the position in which the cardinality information and, for mass NPs, information about some appropriate measure along the lines of Bunt (1985) are taken as primordial for the aspectuality of a sentence. As said before, this is due to the fact that in the PLUG framework, quantificational information is considered an essential ingredient. Focusing on cardinality means that one abstracts from (naive) physics. I must admit that this results in some unnaturalness in the treatment of (3a) because the partitioning of the NP denotation $[\![a\ sandwich]\!]$ yields just a singleton, and so there is little room left for what seems at first sight so nice and natural in Krifka's treatment of this sentence in terms of MtO and MtE. In my treatment the eating is a one-swoop event, so to speak, and one may wish that there should be more to it. Actually, I am not yet sure whether PLUG$^+$ should be *mereologised* in this direction because from the point of view of aspectual composition the [+SQA] information interpreted model-theoretically as the presence of cardinality information (or some measure-function information)—as discussed, for example, in section 2—could be judged sufficient. But in my view, Krifka's lattice-theoretical approach has to solve a lot of problems before it can explain the facts explained by the $PLUG^+$ framework. In this sense, I prefer the strategy of a step-by-step extension of set theory to ensemble theory as a basis for capturing the relation between Mass and Count.

This raises the question of how Krifka's e's relate to the indices in the $PLUG^+$ framework. If he followed Naumann's advice to simply recast MtO and MtE in terms of the monotonicity property, then it would follow that the conditions would come closer to what is inherent to the interpretation of nonstative verbs in terms of the s-function. It would be another way of saying that Krifka's e's may in fact be taken as indices. Evidently, that would make Krifka's grammar part of the $PLUG^+$ framework, as far as the verbal information is concerned.

This brings us finally to the point raised earlier—namely, that Krifka actually uses two notions of event. From the fact that $\alpha(e)$ in (54) does not differentiate aspectually between verbs, if follows more or less straightforwardly that the aspectual differences are to be located at the level of φ itself, that is, at the level of VP. It is at this level that Krifka may distinguish between a terminative event and a durative event. But this means that Krifka looks at φ-events as dividuals. This is actually not what he says, but it seems the only plausible way to interpret him. It should be added that φ does not capture the role of the subject and that (54) does not say anything about the aspectual relation between VP and S.

4. Summary

In this chapter I have argued that the $PLUG^+$ framework accounts elegantly for the anaphoric reference problem, which formed the beginning of Davidson's (1967) famous article. In fact, the solution in terms of the Path function rehabilitates Reichenbach's approach, which was rejected by Davidson. Reichenbach's analysis of events is closely related to Davidson, but it offers many more attractive things, for instance, the idea of things splitting and event splitting— that is, the idea that one *may* look at a sentence "from the event side" without being forced to assume this to be an exclusive look, as grew out of Davidson's proposal. From the linguistic point of view, this mentalistic interpretation of Reichenbach (1947) is quite attractive. The Montagovian framework has provided natural tools for dealing with reference to functions, and this fits very well with the generative outlook on how to conceive of the Path notion in the localistic tradition.

Figure 7 gives a composite picture of virtual events, and it contributes to a better understanding not only of the aspectual properties of sentences but also of the quantificational structure, in particular for distributivity and collectivity. In this sense, I would like to hold that virtual events be seen as dividuals—that is, as composed of functions relating numbers to cardinality information of the verbal arguments, thus forming the structure of what is actualised in real time as the event that we talk about in the sentences under analysis. It should be added that in my view numbers are "in our head" in the sense that we order the domains of discourse by our use of number systems (e.g., our sense of progress is very closely related to counting). It seems a good way to build the notion of event on the basis of numbers rather than on some mysterious unanalysed quasi-temporal notion of event that does not appear as such in real time. In the approach illustrated here, the structure of the event we talk about is built up from the information presented in the sentences themselves. This means that depending on the linguistic material used in a sentence, we present or interpret the event structure. It seems to me that as linguists we need to speak about the relation between sentences and the domain they apply to. So we should not be amazed when there is some structural correspondence.[41]

Notes

1. In Verkuyl (1993), more structure than shown in figure 1 is involved in the construal of inner aspectuality; however, since such extra structure does not play any role in the arguments of this chapter, I do not discuss it here.

2. Whenever I refer to (7) this will also pertain to the quantified version of (7) $Qx_1 \ldots Q_m P^n(a_1, \ldots, a_n)$, with $1 \leq m \leq n$. In this way, generative logical forms obtained by Quantifier Raising, as developed by May (1977, 1985), also fall under its heading.

3. Certainly, Davidson's T-convention seems to place him on the model-theoretic side, but in his analysis of events he never employs the available model-theoretic machinery and rather operates on the syntax side.

4. The Edinburgh coercion tradition can be seen as resulting from this position.

5. Distributivity is often treated as synonymous with atomicity, and collectivity is often contaminated with the notion of, for example, spatiotemporal contiguity or joint agency. The relevant publications are Verkuyl and van der Does (1996), van der Does (1992), Verkuyl (1993), and joint work on multiple quantification by van der Does and Verkuyl (1995), among others. The discussion involves Scha (1981), Gillon (1987), Link (1987), Lønning (1987), Landman (1989), and Lasersohn (1989, 1995), among others.

6. This conclusion does not hold for Hinrichs (1986a, 1986b) which focuses on the role of aspectuality in construing discourse structure. In general, event semantic tools are very handy in the study of macrostructures. But for the study of which elements in a sentence determine aspectuality, the conclusion seems fair enough.

7. The reason for shifting from sandwiches to tables has to do with the introduction of indices.

8. This holds not only of numerals but also of all generalised quantifiers (Verkuyl 1993). It is simpler to demonstrate the system in this way.

9. The reason for distinguishing I from $\mathbb{N}$ is that I might be taken as a set isomorphic to $\mathbb{N}$ except for the property of equidistance, as argued by Verkuyl (1987).

10. The full representation of *lift* is (a) $\lambda I \lambda X \lambda i \lambda Y . [\![lift]\!](I)(i)(Y)(X)$. The verb expresses a relation between two atemporal sets Y and X, indices i and the set of indices I construed from the indices i. The treatment of tense requires a set I collecting the indices i, as discussed in section 2.4. In the PLUG+ grammar the $\lambda I \lambda X$ part of (a) is treated syncategorematically to keep derivations simple (see Verkuyl 1993: 292–297). The important point demonstrated in (17) is that the dependency structure in the VP is mirrored in the lexical

information. One might say that the i in (17) corresponds with Davidson's e, but it should be observed that indices are considered to be just part of an event rather than being events themselves.

11. To conclude with another metaphor: a clarinet player playing a score observes discrete representations (notes) and performs some structure in the reals. The s function of a [+ADD-TO] verb offers a score getting its actualisation in the reals by applying tense. Don't worry about metaphors: they are replaced by a formal machinery below.

12. In Verkuyl (1972), [+SQA] is purported to generalise over such NPs as *a sandwich, the concerto, that John was ill* in *John heard that John was ill, a piece of/from X, three concertos, some of Boccherini's cello concertos, the whisky, a draught of/from X, a Norwegian sweater, a house, many things*, and so on. That is, it covers the same ground as the theory of generalised quantification which did not exist at the time, one of the reasons that it took so long before I could give a formal treatment of this intuitively clear notion.

13. I avoid the term 'infinite' on purpose; *nonfinite* may mean 'indeterminable', as in (4a).

14. That l is defined in terms of positions is formally not so crucial as we shall see below: it is rather a tribute to the body of ideas called localism as we find it in, for example, Gruber (1976) and Jackendoff (1976, 1983, 1990), among many others, and going back to Latin grammar. An attractive linguistic feature of the localistic perspective on change and statehood is that by the use of the term 'position' a rather natural generalisation is expressed over different semantic fields, such as positional change (*Mary lifted four tables*), change of possession (*She bought four tables*), identificational change (*She melted four tables*), and other forms of change.

15. The formal machinery contains a union operator to reduce the collection p_3 to the set T.

16. In my own work, this idea was of course present in Verkuyl (1972), but it did not get a formal semantic treatment until the Groningen Conference on Tense and Aspect in 1983 and the Amsterdam Colloquium in 1984, at which I presented Verkuyl (1987). Though worked out in different ways this idea has also been adopted by Krifka (1989a) and by Tenny (1994), where it is called *measuring out*.

17. The expression 'ps' means that W is partitioned by $\mathbf{Q}$; $\mathbf{P}$ is to be restricted to lifted tables, so it should be written as $\mathbf{P}|_{\|table\|}$, but I will not bring this into the formula here; cf. Verkuyl (1993: 143–167) for details.

18. As argued in Verkuyl (1995), this explains why *Mary began to walk* is terminative: *begin* puts a restriction on l, yielding a truncated l: $\{\langle 1, \varnothing \rangle\}$, which is of the same type as l. The range of the function is bounded. The argument shows that in the case of *walk*, the l-function is present, indicating that *walk* at the lexical level is different from *walk* at the VP level.

19. The general idea is that a bare plural introduces a collection of sets and that the cardinality information is at the collection level (≥ 1) and not at the set level. For an extensive analysis of bareness of NPs, see Verkuyl (1993: 129–140).

20. In Verkuyl and van der Does (1996) and van der Does and Verkuyl (1995), the elements of $dom(\pi)$ are singletons, but nothing hinges on that; (D.3) can be adapted to take individuals of type e.

21. Contrary to (22), the law of distributivity in (23) works in only one way—that is, asymmetrically—because the combinatorial algebra underlying figure 1 is not associative. See Verkuyl (1993, 1996) for a more detailed analysis.

22. This makes it possible to formulate the first part of a "law": in all the configurations based on the injective (21a), the total number of tables is always $k \times m$, where k is

the cardinality of the external argument NP, and m is the cardinality expressed by the internal argument; in each of the configurations (24) through (26) the total number of token-dependent tables is 12. From the previous note, it follows that the total number of girls remains 3.

23. Definition (D.4) holds trivially for (3a): the function π is applied to a single argument and yields just one l, and so (D.4) applies. This is because the grammar is based on the treatment of plurality.

24. A related approach to the notion of collectivity can be found in Lasersohn (1995), but it is worked out quite differently.

25. For a more detailed discussion see Verkuyl (1994); see also Landman (1989).

26. Recall from note 10 that at the level of S the sentential structure of (16a) is (roughly) $\lambda l.[\![lift]\!](l)(i)([\![four\ tables]\!])([\![Mary]\!])$, where l, the collection of i's associated with the verb, is of type $\langle i, t\rangle$. This makes tense take an S of type $\langle\langle i, t\rangle, t\rangle$ to form an $\overline{S}$ of type t. For details, see Verkuyl (1993: 318–327).

27. Ent$^+$ is defined as a rounding-off function from the real into the natural numbers. $I = \text{Ent}^+(I_V)$ says that I is the set of representatives from the intervals in I_V. This means that the actualisation of the abstract I-structure into a real-time event takes place by Tense.

28. This means that it is of type $\langle\langle\langle i, t\rangle, t\rangle, \langle\langle i, t\rangle, t\rangle\rangle$, the modifying type.

29. Neo-Davidsonians tend to throw out the temporal adverbial as well. This sounds reasonable in view of the fact observed in Verkuyl (1993: 245–251) that Davidson can handle the inferences properly only if the agent NP in sentences like (35a) denotes a monotone-increasing quantifier. Thus, if one replaces *Jones* by *At most three students*, one cannot infer to *At most three students buttered the toast* α, where $\alpha = at\ midnight$. The problem is more general: inferences are no longer valid under monotone-decreasing quantification in cases in which $\alpha = with\ a\ knife, in\ the\ bathroom, deliberately$, or *slowly*. Event semanticists remain quite silent about this disturbing fact. Not many of them like to face the problems of quantification, so it is *Jones* and *Sebastian* rather than *three girls* and *few boys*.

30. In particular, the fact that we could speak about three bathrooms is telling in this respect. For event semanticists there is no way of getting more than one bathroom out of the information provided by *the bathroom*.

31. Not an actualised eventuality in the sense of section 2.4—that is, we are talking about the formation of S before tense applies.

32. Pred$_a$ is Pred from the first variant in (43), and Pred$_b$ from the second, and so on. Parsons sometimes writes simply *Hold(e)* or *Cul(e)*, but this is only for convenience.

33. Moens's distinction between *development part* and *culmination part* looses the advantage of the distinction on which it was partly based—namely, the distinction between [+ADD-TO] and [+SQA]. The [+ADD-TO] is indeed a development part but the [+SQA] information should not be taken as culmination, even though, of course, a sense of culmination follows from the presence of [+SQA]. In the PLUG framework, the [+SQA] information is systematically related to the development part throughout the application of the function s as part of the function l. All sorts of misunderstandings, most recently in Pustejovksy (1995), arise if one follows Moens's track, such as the need to characterise the culmination point by a proposition that expresses a state. One of the problems with this is that the *culmination proposition* is not at all determined by information given by the sentence itself. In fact, the split between *Hold* and *Cul* brings back von Wright's (1965) problem of a truth value gap between two states involved in a transition.

34. This is a problem for Parsons (1990): there turns out to be no way to distinguish processes, as they can be presented only as states. One odd consequence: the resultant state $R(e)$ and progress state are treated alike: the first argument of *Hold* in *Hold(Inprog(e), t)* is a state and the same applies to *Hold(R(e), t)*. However, the R-state is not aspectual at all; it is used to define the present perfect (pp. 234ff.). A lot remains unclear in the $Hold_b/Cul_b$ part of Parsons because it is presented very informally.

35. This impressive work gives very detailed and thorough analyses of three aspectual theories (Dowty, Krifka, and Verkuyl) and results in a dynamic theory of aspectuality combining ingredients of the three theories. In this section I sometimes draw on him.

36. This strategy is followed also in, for example, Jackendoff (1990) and formal work based on it, for example, White (1994). More generally, one can see the flattening of ontology in computational circles. An interesting mathematical example of this strategy is Touretzky (1986).

37. As I pointed out (Verkuyl 1993), the derivation does not work: there is a doubling of the *Agent(e, x)*, visible in applying (52f) to (52e) in which the free variable x of (52a) must be bound by the x in (52g), which is, of course, not allowed. This problem cannot be solved by putting lambdas in front of (52a) because there is no way to get rid of them. Krifka acknowledged this problem, but his solution (personal communication) does not convince me (cf. Verkuyl 1993: 261).

38. In general, it seems to me that an important disadvantage of Krifka's approach is that the equilibrium between what is expressed by the representations and what is determined by the postulates is out of balance—and unnecessarily so. There are many more postulates than given here. So, Krifka seems to operate on the side of the ontologists: describing the world rather than the language. The question is again: why are people so afraid of using higher order representations, especially when it can be shown that they work well empirically?

39. Roughly, QUA defines our [+SQA], but it should be observed that part of the difficulties in Krifka's system arise from the fact that his definitions focus on the N rather than on the NP. So, the role of the determiner in the determination of whether an NP is [+SQA] or [−SQA] is ignored. This point has also been made by Naumann.

40. Note in passing that the individuation problem for Krifka, as raised by Naumann, is also present in sentences like (33).

41. I would like to thank Mana Kobuchi-Philip, Ralf Naumann, Bill Philip, Yoad Winter, Martijn Spaan, and Joost Zwarts for their helpful comments on earlier versions.

References

Barwise, J., and R. Cooper, 1981. Generalised Quantifiers and Natural Language. In *Linguistics and Philosophy* 4: 159–219.

Bennett, M. R., and B. Partee, 1978. *Toward the Logic of Tense and Aspect in English*. Indiana University Linguistics Club. Bloomington.

Bunt, H. C., 1985. *Mass Terms and Model-theoretic Semantics*. Cambridge University Press, Cambridge.

Davidson, D., 1967. The Logical Form of Action Sentences. In N. Rescher (ed.), *The Logic of Decision and Action*, 81–95. University of Pittsburgh Press, Pittsburgh. Reprinted in Davidson, *Essays on Actions and Events*, 105–123.

Dowty, D. R., 1979. *Word Meaning and Montague Grammar. The Semantics of Verbs and Times in Generative Semantics and Montague's PTQ*. Reidel, Dordrecht.

Dowty, D. R., 1989. On the Semantic Content of the Notion of "Thematic Role". In G. Chierchia, B. H. Parteé, and R. Turner (eds.), *Properties, Types and Meaning, Volume II: Semantic Issues*, 69–129. Kluwer Academic Publishers, Dordrecht.

Gillon, B. S., 1987. The Readings of Plural Noun Phrases in English. In *Linguistics and Philosophy* 10: 199–219.

Gruber, J. S., 1976. *Lexical Structures in Syntax and Semantics*. North-Holland Amsterdam. *Part I. Studies in Lexical Relations* (1964); *Part II. Functions of the Lexicon in Formal Descriptive Grammars* (1967).

Halvorsen, P.-K., and W. A. Ladusaw, 1979. Montague's 'Universal Grammar'. An Introduction for the Linguist. In *Linguistics and Philosophy* 3: 185–224.

Hinrichs, E., 1981. Temporale Anaphora im Englischen. Master's thesis, University of Tübingen, Tübingen.

Hinrichs, E., 1986a. *A Compositional Semantics for Aktionsarten and NP Reference in English*. Ph.D. dissertation, Ohio State University, Columbus.

Hinrichs, E., 1986b. Temporal Anaphora in Discourses of English. In *Linguistics and Philosophy* 9: 63–82.

Jackendoff, R. S., 1976. Toward an Explanatory Semantic Interpretation in Generative Grammar. In *Linguistic Inquiry* 7: 89–150.

Jackendoff, R. S., 1983. *Semantics and Cognition*. MIT. Press, Cambridge (Mass.).

Jackendoff, R. S., 1990. *Semantic Structures*. MIT. Press, Cambridge (Mass.).

Krifka, M., 1989a. Nominal Reference, Temporal Constitution and Quantification in Event Semantics. In J. van Benthem, R. Bartsch, and P. van Embde Boas (eds.), *Semantics and Contextual Expressions*, 75–115. Foris, Dordrecht.

Krifka, M., 1989b. *Nominalreferenz und Zeitkonstitution*. Wilhelm Fink Verlag, Munich.

Landman, F., 1989. Groups I and II. In *Linguistics and Philosophy* 12: 559–605, 723–744.

Lascarides, A., 1988. *A Formal Semantics of the Progressive*. Ph.D. dissertation, University of Edinburgh, Edinburgh.

Lasersohn, P. S., 1989. On the Readings of Plural Noun Phrases in English. *Linguistic Inquiry* 20: 130–134.

Lasersohn, P. S., 1995. *Plurality, Conjunction and Events*. Kluwer Academic Publisher, Dordrecht.

Link, G., 1983. The Logical Analysis of Plurals and Mass Terms: A Lattice-theoretic Approach. In R. Bäuerle, C. Schwarze, and A. von Stechow (eds.), *Meaning, Use and Interpretation of Language*, 303–323. De Gruyter, Berlin.

Link, G., 1987. Generalised Quantifiers and Plurals. In P. Gärdenfors (ed.), *Generalised Quantifiers: Linguistic and Logical Approaches*, 151–180. Reidel, Dordrecht.

Link, G., 1991. Plural. In D. Wunderlich and A. von Stechow (eds.), *Semantics. An International Handbook of Contemporary Research*, 418–440. De Gruyter, Berlin.

Lønning, J. T., 1987. Collective Readings of Definite and Indefinite Noun Phrases. In P. Gärdenfors (ed.), *Generalised Quantifiers: Linguistic and Logical Approaches*, 203–235. Reidel, Dordrecht.

May, R., 1977. *The Grammar of Quantification*. Ph.D. dissertation, MIT, Cambridge (Mass.).

May, R., 1985, *Logical Form. Its Structure and Derivation*. MIT Press, Cambridge (Mass.).

Moens, M., 1987. *Tense, Aspect and Temporal Reference*. Ph.D. dissertation, University of Edinburgh, Edinburgh.

Moens, M., and M. Steedman, 1987. Temporal Ontology in Natural Language. In *Proceedings of the Twenty-fifth Annual Meeting of the Association for Computational Linguistics*, 1–7. Stanford University, Stanford (Calif.).

Montague, R., 1970. English as a Formal Language. In B. Visentini et al. (eds.), *Linguaggi nella società e nella tecnica*, 189–224. Edizioni di Comunità, Milano. Reprinted in Montague, R., 1974. *Formal Philosophy*, R. H. Thomason (ed.), 188–221. Yale University Press, New Haven (Conn.).

Montague, R., 1973. The Proper Treatment of Quantification in Ordinary English. In J. Hintikka et al. (eds.), *Approaches to Natural Language*, 221–242. Reidel, Dordrecht. Reprinted in Montague, *Formal Philosophy*, 247–270.

Naumann, R., 1996. *Aspectual Composition and Dynamic Logic*. Ph.D. dissertation, Heinrich Heine Universität, Düsseldorf.

Parsons, T., 1985. Underlying Events in the Logical Analysis of English. In E. LePore and B. McLaughlin (eds.), *Actions and Events: Perspectives on the Philosophy of Donald Davidson*, 235–267. Blackwell, Oxford.

Parsons, T., 1989. The Progressive in English: Events, States and Processes. In *Linguistics and Philosophy* 12: 213–241.

Parsons, T., 1990. *Events in the Semantics of English. A Study in Subatomic Semantics*. MIT Press, Cambridge (Mass.).

Partee, B. H., A. ter Meulen, and R. E. Wall, 1990. *Mathematical Methods in Linguistics*. Kluwer Academic Publishers, Dordrecht.

Pustejovsky, J., 1995. *The Generative Lexicon*. MIT. Press, Cambridge, (Mass.).

Reichenbach, H., 1947. *Elements of Symbolic Logic*. Macmillan, New York.

Scha, R., 1981. Distributive, Collective and Cumulative Quantification. In J. A. G. Groenendijk, T. M. V. Janssen, and M. J. B. Stokhof (eds.), *Formal Methods in the Study of Language*, 483–512. Mathematical Centre Tracts, Amsterdam.

Tenny, C. L., 1994. *Aspectual Roles and the Syntax-Semantics Interface*. Reidel, Dordrecht.

Touretzky, D., 1986. *The Mathematics of Inheritance Systems*. Morgan Kaufmann, Palo Alto (Calif.).

van der Does, J. M., 1992. *Applied Quantifier Logic. Collectives, Naked Infinitives*. Ph.D. dissertation, University of Amsterdam, Amsterdam.

van der Does, J. M., and H. J. Verkuyl, 1995. Quantification and Predication. In K. van Deemter and S. Peters (eds.), *Ambiguity*, 27–54. CSLI Publications, Stanford (Calif.).

Vendler, Z., 1957. Verbs and Times. In *The Philosophical Review* 66:143–160.

Verkuyl, H. J., 1972. *On the Compositional Nature of the Aspect*. Reidel, Dordrecht.

Verkuyl, H. J., 1987. Nondurative Closure of Events. In J. Groenendijk, D. de Jongh, and M. Stokhof (eds.), *Studies in Discourse Representation Theory and the Theory of Generalised Quantifiers*, 87–114. Foris, Dordrecht.

Verkuyl, H. J., 1988. Aspectual Asymmetry and Quantification. In V. Ehrich and H. Vater (eds.), *Temporalsemantik. Beitrage zur Linguistik der Zeitreferenz*, 220–259. Niemeyer Verlag, Tübingen.

Verkuyl, H. J., 1989. Aspectual Classes and Aspectual Composition. In *Linguistics and Philosophy* 12: 39–94.

Verkuyl, H. J., 1993. *A Theory of Aspectuality. The Interaction between Temporal and Atemporal Structure*. Cambridge University Press, Cambridge.

Verkuyl, H. J., 1994. Distributivity and Collectivity: A Couple at Odds. In M. Kanazawa and C. Piñon (eds.), *Dynamics, Polarity, and Quantification*, 49–80. CSLI Publications, Stanford (Calif.).

Verkuyl, H. J., 1995. Aspectualizers and Event Structure. In P. Amsili, M. Borillo, and L. Vieu (eds.), *Time, Space and Movement: Meaning and Knowledge in the Sensible World. Proceedings of the Fifth International Workshop*, 31–48. COREP, Toulouse.

Verkuyl, H. J., 1996. Syntactic and Semantic Aspects of Aspectuality. In M. Dimi-trova-Vulchanova and L. Hellan (eds.), *Proceedings from the First Conference on Formal Approaches to South Slavic Languages Plovdiv October 1995.* Trondheim Working Papers in Linguistics, Vol. 28, 329–344.

Verkuyl, H. J., and J. M. van der Does, 1996. The Semantics of Plural Noun Phrases. In J. M. van der Does and J. van Eijck (eds.), *Quantifiers, Logic and Language,* 337–374. CSLI Publications, Stanford (Calif.).

White, M., 1994. *A Computational Approach to Aspectual Composition.* Ph.D. disserta-tion, University of Pennsylvania, Philadelphia.

von Wright, G. H., 1965. And Next. In *Acta Philosophica Fennica* 18, 293–304.

9

Word Order and
Quantification over Times

Denis Delfitto and Pier Marco Bertinetto

1. Introduction

In this chapter, we consider some consequences of the assumption that verbs are endowed with an event and a time argument and that adverbs are crucially related, in ways that have to be carefully studied, with the realisation of these two arguments. The view developed here represents an extension of the hypothesis that verbal predicates are associated with an event argument and that this event argument plays a crucial role in establishing the semantics of theta-roles and adverbials (Davidson 1967; Parsons 1990; Schein 1993). The hypothesis that we put forward is that temporal adverbs of various sorts represent the realisation of a VP internal temporal argument, which is theta-marked by the verb, on full parallelism with the other arguments of the verb.[1]

Empirically, we aim at a precise definition of the modalities of interaction between locating adverbs and frequency adverbs, on the one side, and the aspectual values related to the opposition perfective/imperfective (as it surfaces in Slavic and Romance), on the other side. The central task is an elucidation of the semantic and morphosyntactic dimension of certain instances of aspectual morphology and of the ways in which the latter relates to the syntax and semantics of temporal adverbs. Theoretically, we use these results to get to grips with one of the most intriguing issues formulated by recent research in formal semantics, that of understanding the nature of the quantificational structures involved by the use of frequency adverbs (from now on, Q-adverbs) such as *often*, *always*, *rarely*, and so on. A successful line of inquiry interprets Q-adverbs as expressing relations between two classes of events/times (de Swart 1991; Rooth 1995). Semantically, there is an obvious parallelism to be drawn with the analysis of natural language determiners as developed within the tradition of the theory of generalised quantifiers (GQ), starting with the seminal work of Mostowski (1957) and its application to the linguistic domain in Barwise and Cooper (1981). The hypothesis is that both D(eterminer)-quantifiers (such as *every*) and A(dverbial)-quantifiers (such as *always*) combine with two one-place predicates to produce a sentence (the two predicates are often referred to as the *restriction* and *the nuclear scope* of the tripartite structures associated with D- and A-quantifiers). The two predicates are explicitly represented in surface syntactic structure in the case of D-quantifiers (in *Every student failed* the two predicates are constituted by N and VP, respectively). However, it is generally believed (Kamp and Reyle 1993) that surface syntax does not help to individuate the two arguments of the Q-quantifier in sentences such as

(1)   In 1975, John always had kippers for breakfast.

The common assumption is that the two arguments of A-quantifiers have to be built up by means of relatively complex semantic procedures (such as the *association with focus* algorithm proposed in Rooth 1985) and that there is no direct mapping between syntactic representations and interpretation.[2] In this respect, our main contention is that there is no reason to abandon the hope for a more compositional mapping between syntax and semantics. Once certain aspectual features (those correlating to the opposition perfective/imperfective) are properly understood as involving different modes of quantification over the temporal variable associated with locating adverbs of various sorts, a serious possibility arises that the two arguments of A-quantifiers must be in fact represented in overt syntax, even though decoding surface structure may be made difficult by the application of operations of deletion in the PF component.

We interpret the abstract level of representation at which the two arguments of an A-quantifier are syntactically encoded as the linguistic level of representation that corresponds to surface structure.[3] We also contend that the mapping into these explicit quantificational representations is directly triggered by the variety of aspectual morphology that we are investigating, that is, imperfective morphology. We claim that certain aspectual features represent the (overt) realisation on the verbal predicate of semantic information concerning the quantificational interpretation of one of the verb's arguments, that is, the temporal argument. An interesting analogy arises with the morphosyntactic expression of quantification in sign language (Petronio 1995) and in some native languages of Australia, whose verbal morphology expresses quantificational information about one of the verb's arguments by means of the mechanisms of *thematic affinity* discussed in Evans (1995).[4] If A-quantification is analysed as "regulated" by aspectual morphology, it might actually correspond to a quantificational format that is somehow intermediate between true unselective quantification (whereby a certain quantificational morpheme indifferently applies to any free variable contained in the structure) and the strongly compositional forms of quantification instantiated by the familiar cases of D-quantification. Moreover, by investigating the role of aspect as the trigger for the compositional format of A-quantification, we intend to argue in favour of the idea that (certain categories of) adverbs are not to be understood as optional modifiers but rather as a fundamental part of the clausal architecture. The suggested parallelism between nominal arguments (DPs) and temporal arguments (locating adverbs) paves the way for the hypothesis that adverbs might be involved in syntactic operations triggered by morphological requirements (such as the checking operations argued for in Chomsky 1995). In fact, we argue that not only locating adverbs but also syntactic constituents such as VPs obligatorily undergo "aspectually triggered" movement under certain conditions, as a consequence of the fact that they can properly match the quantificational features encoded in a designated aspectual projection (VPs can be interpreted as predicates of times by applying lambda abstraction to the variable that realises the temporal argument).[5]

Taken together, the proposals presented in this chapter are intended to provide an argument in favour of the relevance of surface syntactic representations for interpretation (under the crucial hypothesis that there is more syntactic movement than is detected at first glance) and for a more compositional mapping between syntax and semantics in the analysis of A-quantification. This hypothesis is feasible only if the analysis of quantification over time is enriched with the morphosyntactic dimension introduced by aspectual morphology and locating adverbials.

2. Temporal Adverbs and Aspect

2.1. Temporal Adverbs

Adopting and extending the Davidsonian insight, we would like to propose that verbs are generally associated with both an event argument and a time argument. The time argument expresses the time of the event (ET).[6] In line with standard assumptions in event semantics (Kearns 1991; Schein 1993), we assume that the variable corresponding to the event argument is not realised as a syntactic argument of the verb. We also assume that this variable is either (unselectively) bound by a quantifier on times/events or undergoes a default operation of existential closure. The question we are interested in concerns the syntactic realisation of the time argument. We propose that the time argument is syntactically realised by circumstantial temporal phrases and locating adverbs, which are thematically licensed as arguments of the lexical verb (V) and constitute the most deeply embedded arguments within VP (Larson 1988; Giorgi and Pianesi 1997).

The hypothesis that locating adverbs are arguments is apparently supported by a significant degree of syntactic evidence. In languages such as Italian, temporal phrases that fix ET tend to behave as arguments do when extracted from syntactic islands. Extraction from strong islands (2) is ungrammatical, whereas extraction from weak islands (3) yields results that are close to full grammaticality and certainly better than those produced by extraction of adverbial modifiers such as the manner adverb in (4) (Giorgi and Pianesi 1997: 106). Significantly, extraction of the same temporal phrases from weak islands is worse (comparable to (4)) when these phrases refer to the "reference time" (cf. Reichenbach 1947) instead of ET (cf. (5)):

(2)   A che ora sei partito senza chiudere il negozio?
        At which time did you leave without closing the shop?

(3)   ?A che ora ti dispiace che Mario sia partito?
        At which time do you regret that Mario left?

(4)   *Come ti dispiace che Mario sia partito?
        How do you regret that Mario has left?

(5)   *A che ora ti dispiaceva che Mario fosse già partito (da due ore)?
        At which time did you regret that Mario had already left (since two hours)?

A second argument for the VP internal status of ET-denoting temporal phrases derives from the observation that they can appear in coordination structures together with other arguments of the verbs (Pesetsky 1995), as shown by cases such as (6) or even (7). Under standard assumptions about the syntax of coordination, this shows that temporal adverbs can form a constituent with other arguments of the verbs. This cannot be the case if temporal phrases are treated as modifiers adjoined to VP (or some higher projection) but is directly compatible with the hypothesis that they are generated in the most embedded argument position within some sort of VP shell structure:

(6)   John gave presents [to Mary on Thursday] and [to Clara on Friday].
(7)   John gave presents to [Mary on Thursday] and [Clara on Friday].

Finally, anaphors contained in temporal adverbs can be bound by antecedents contained in other arguments of the verb, as shown in (8). Since syntactic binding involves c-command, the temporal phrases must be realised in a position that is c-commanded by the other arguments of the verb (arguably, the most embedded argument position in a VP shell structure):

(8)   I gave presents [to John and Mary] [on each other's birthday].

We interpret these facts, together with other somewhat more theory-internal arguments (cf. Giorgi and Pianesi 1997: 101–105), as syntactic evidence for the hypothesis that circumstantial temporal phrases and locating adverbs of various sorts have argument status and are in a thematic relation with the verb. Since these phrases are clearly interpreted as referring to the location time ET, we reach the conclusion that the time argument, contrary to the event argument, undergoes (overt) syntactic realisation.

Let us devote now some attention to the semantics of circumstantial temporal phrases. Here, the most striking result consists in the observation that the different semantic types of nominal arguments (DPs) are arguably paralleled by analogous semantic types expressed by temporal phases (which are distributed over different syntactic categories). This clearly provides a crucial confirmation of the thematic status of locating adverbials. The formulation of the relevant interpretive generalisations clearly depends on the semantic framework that one chooses. For the sake of the exposition, we will adopt the theoretical vocabulary of Discourse Representation Theory (DRT), the choice being mainly motivated by the in-depth analysis of the different classes of temporal phrases that has been attempted within this theoretical framework (Kamp and Reyle 1993). We believe that nothing crucial hinges on this particular choice, and the reader is obviously free to try to rebuild the considerations that follow in the theoretical vocabulary of his or her preference.

As is well known, argument DPs come out in at least three semantic types: they can correspond to referential expressions (proper names such as *John* or *Mary*), predicative expressions (definite and indefinite descriptions, that is, expressions introducing a variable and a restriction for the variable in the discourse representation, such as *the post office* or *a student*), and quantifiers (quantified DPs headed by determiners that express a relation between the two sets of objects referred to by N and VP, respectively). Let us briefly consider how these semantic types are matched by those expressed by different categories of locating adverbials.

Calendar expressions like *on April 5, 1992*, are intuitively an obvious candidate for the status of proper name since they seem to rigidly designate one particular date/time. Whether this rigid designation property of calendar names is compositionally derived from their internal syntax (on the model of the syntax of proper names developed in Longobardi 1994) constitutes a separate question, which we will not address in this contribution. It is enough to say that in a DRT perspective the rigid designator can be identified with the NP *April 5, 1992*, with the preposition *on* interpreted as a dyadic predicate establishing identity between this time and the location time ET (Kamp and Reyle 1993: 614).

Quite different is the semantic contribution of "context-dependent" calendar expressions like *in April* or *on Sunday* and of punctual adverbials like *at eight o'clock*. If we abstract away from the information provided by the context (i.e., if we consider the DRT condition *Sunday(t)* in isolation), these expressions cannot be interpreted as referring to a particular time: rather, they have to be interpreted predicatively—that is, as referring to a nonfinite set of times (under the metaphysical assumption that the world will never have an end). In other words, there are (potentially) infinitely many times of which the property *at eight o'clock* or the property *on Sunday* holds. The actual interpretation of this class of adverbials is the result of the interaction of a number of grammatical and contextual factors (technically captured by means of the insertion of additional (presuppositional) DRT conditions to *Sunday(t)*), among which tense plays a prominent role. Consider for instance the following sentence (Kamp and Reyle 1993: 614):

(9)   Mary wrote the letter on Sunday.

Semantically, one can simply assume that the locating adverbial "on Sunday" is a predicate of times (logical type $\langle e, t \rangle$), which refers to the different sets of times that have the property of belonging to some Sunday or other. In DRT, the contribution of context and tense to interpretation is captured by enriching the condition *Sunday(t)* with a quantified condition which informally states that no time t' that is entirely after t but not later than the time ST at which the sentence is uttered is part of another Sunday. In plain terms, the locating adverbial in (9) ends up referring to the set of times belonging to the Sunday that is closest to the utterance time ST in the direction of the past. Putting these complications aside, we propose that the semantic contribution of context-sensitive calendar expressions, as captured by the DRT condition *Sunday(t)*, consists in introducing a time variable and a predicative restriction in the discourse representation.[7] We conclude that the semantic role of this class of temporal adverbials exactly parallels the role of (definite and indefinite) descriptions in the nominal domain. This also entails that the logical type ($\langle e, t \rangle$) of the adverbials instantiated in (9) is different from the logical type that has to be assigned to calendar names ($\langle e \rangle$ under a non-Montagovian treatment of names).

The last step in our argument consists of the identification of the temporal equivalents of quantifiers. As already emphasised, a conspicuous tradition in formal semantics takes frequency adverbs (e.g., *mostly*, *always*, and *often*) as expressing a relation between two classes of events/times (de Swart 1991; Rooth 1995). A sentence such as (1), restated here as (10), is most naturally interpreted as stating that all events e such that John had breakfast in e are events in which John ate kippers (i.e., the set of eventualities of having breakfast in which John participated as agent is included in the set of eventualities in which John ate kippers). Intuitively, the role of the preposed locating adverb (a *frame adverbial* in the terminology adopted by Bonomi 1995) in (10) consists in providing temporal boundaries to the set of eventualities that represents the range of the quantified variable e and must be accurately kept apart from the role played by the locating adverbials discussed above, which just consists, as we emphasised, in providing a range for the time variable.

(10)   In 1975, John always had kippers for breakfast.

In a nutshell, sentences containing Q-adverbs can be understood as tripartite structures in which a determiner-like expression (the frequency adverb) takes two open formulas as arguments:

(10') $\forall e[\text{breakfast}(e) \wedge \text{Agent}(\text{John}, e)]$ [$\text{eating}(e) \wedge \text{Theme}(\text{kippers}, e)$
         $\wedge \text{Agent}(\text{John}, e)$].

Under the relational GQ treatment of determiners as second-order two-place predicates, (10') can be rewritten as

(10") $\forall[\lambda e.(\text{breakfast}(e) \wedge \text{Agent}(\text{John}, e))]$ [$\lambda e.(\text{eating}(e) \wedge \text{Theme}(\text{kippers}, e)$
         $\wedge \text{Agent}(\text{John}, e))$]

However, (10') presents an important problem with respect to the usual forms of D-quantification. Although the operator present in (10') is explicitly represented in (10) as the frequency adverb, the division of (10) into a restriction and a nuclear scope (the material contained within squared brackets in (10') and (10")) is not syntactically explicit in the sense that it does not seem to be made manifest by the surface phrase structure of (10). In the familiar cases of D-quantification, restrictor and scope are explicitly individuated by the lexical material contained under the nodes N and VP. This is the problem that mainly concerns us in this chapter, that is, the so-called *separation problem*. On the grounds of the preceding discussion, we choose to formulate it in the form of the following question: *to which extent does syntax contribute to the mapping from sentences like (10) to abstract, nonlinguistic representations like (10') and (10")?* The seriousness of the separation problem is immediately confirmed, at the empirical level, by the observation that (10) admits alternative ways of distributing the lexical material between restriction and scope. In the appropriate context and with the appropriate intonational pattern (the main stress must fall on *breakfast*), (10) can be interpreted as stating that whenever John has kippers, it is with his breakfast. This interpretation corresponds to the separation between restriction and scope indicated in (10''').

(10''') $\forall e$[eating(e) $\wedge$ Theme(kippers, e) $\wedge$ Agent(John, e)] [breakfast(e)
          $\wedge$ Agent(John, e)].

The different forms of mapping to tripartite structures permitted by (10) strongly contrast with the strongly deterministic form of mapping induced by lexical determiners in the familiar cases of D-quantification. As far as the quantifier over events/times can be realised as a determiner that selects NP as its complement, the deterministic form of separation is the only option left. This is clearly shown by cases such as (11), which is unambiguously interpreted according to the tripartition indicated in (11'): the set of time intervals that correspond to morning periods in the year 1975 is included in the set of time intervals at which John had kippers for breakfast .

(11)   In 1975, John had kippers for breakfast every morning.
(11') $\forall t$[morning(t) $\wedge$ $t \subseteq$ 1975] [$\exists e$(eating(e) $\wedge$ Theme(kippers, e)
        $\wedge$ Agent(John, e) $\wedge$ at(e, t))].

The logically conceivable interpretation according to which every time interval at which John had kippers for breakfast was a morning period does not seem to be available. This reading entails that if there had been days in 1975 in which John had kippers in the morning and in the afternoon, (11) is false. However, speakers have a clear intuition that (11) is true in the context just described. Since this reading corresponds to the projection of the complement NP *morning* into the nuclear scope, we conclude that when the quantifier over times is realised as a determiner there is a unique form of separation to the effect that the NP complement of the determiner is obligatorily projected into the restriction. The indeterminacy of mapping is thus a feature of sentences containing frequency adverbs. In these structures, there is no obvious syntactic candidate for the projection into the restrictive clause (as the NP complement of D in the standard cases of D-quantification). This state of affairs has led some scholars to propose that the process of partitioning a clause that contains a Q-adverb depends on the application of a syntactic operation of abstract adjunction that is basically unconstrained, modulo issues of semantic coherence and pragmatic plausibility

(Chierchia 1995a, 1995b). According to this proposal, Q-adverbs can be freely adjoined to any propositional constituent (VP, IP, or CP) and virtually any other syntactic constituent can undergo an abstract operation of adjunction to the Q-adverb. At the syntactic level of representation produced by this form of unconstrained scrambling, the restrictive clause of the Q-adverb is identified with the lexical material which is not c-commanded by the Q-adverb.

Let us briefly consider how this procedure would work in the case of (10), which has been shown to be ambiguous between the partitioning in (10') and the partitioning in (10'''). The abstract syntactic representation underlying (10') would have both the subject *John* and the PP *for breakfast* in positions external to the Q-adverb *always* (this probably entails abstract scrambling of the PP over the Q-adverb). In the case of (10''') it is the direct object *kippers* that is scrambled over the Q-adverb, whereas the PP *for breakfast* remains in a position that is in the c-command domain of the adverb. Syntax can indifferently produce both abstract representations. The choice of one format over the other depends on issues of semantic and pragmatic plausibility (which truth conditions are more appropriate to the intentions of the speaker in a given context).

It is worth emphasising that Chierchia's position is tantamount to assuming that the syntactic constraints on separation are not represented in surface phrase structure since they are the effect of covert operations of adjunction that apply after the mapping to PF (as an instance of the unconstrained operation Move-α). In section 3, we argue against this position, showing that there are serious empirical reasons to believe that the separation is already encoded at the level of surface structure. In section 4, we also contend that Chierchia's "mapping hypothesis" is empirically inadequate since it leads to wrong predictions for languages with overt scrambling. Moreover, the position endorsed by Chierchia is hardly compatible with models of syntax that do not rely on an unconstrained operation Move-α and in which adjunction turns out to be a quite constrained, if not marked, option (Chomsky 1995). In fact, the position that we endorse is more akin to the clause-splitting algorithm proposed by Rooth (1995), according to which focus is the crucial factor for the projection of some lexical material contained in the sentence into the restrictor of the Q-adverb (cf. also de Swart 1991; Krifka 1992).

What is relevant for the mapping into tripartite structures is surface structure information.[8] As a matter of fact, informational focus is commonly held to correlate with main phrasal stress, and according to some recent proposal (Reinhart 1995) this PF characterisation exhaustively defines focus phenomena. In Rooth's approach, sentences are conceived of as *event abstracts*—that is, predicates of events/times—and constitute the nuclear scope of Q-adverbs. The restrictive clause is provided by a semantic procedure that replaces the focused constituent with an existentially quantified variable. In the case of (10), this procedure will take the reading corresponding to (10') as consisting of a relation between the set of events in which John eats *something* for breakfast and the set of events in which John eats kippers for breakfast (focus = *kippers*). As for the reading corresponding to (10'''), it is formulated as a relation between a set of eventualities in which John eats kippers *at some meal or other* and the set of eventualities in which John eats kippers at breakfast (focus = *for breakfast*). Although we believe that the focus algorithm endorsed by Rooth plays an important role for an adequate solution to the separation problem, we propose to reinterpret the proposed semantic mechanism (substitution of the focused constituent with an existentially quantified variable) as a proper subpart of an essentially syntactic operation. Moreover, we argue that it is the application of this more general syntactic procedure that permits us to avoid some apparent empirical shortcomings of the "association-with-focus" procedure. Before turning to these issues, let us briefly try to establish some crucial properties of aspectual morphology.

2.2. Aspect

In Slavic and Romance, the interpretive contrast between episodic and habitual sentences is aspectually encoded by means of the opposition between perfective and imperfective morphology (Bertinetto 1986; Schoorlemmer 1995; Delfitto and Bertinetto 1995). This interpretive contrast is most evident in structures where there is no overt Q-adverb, as shown by the Italian minimal pair in (12):

(12)   a. Nel 1975, Gianni fumava.   (habitual)
           In 1975, Gianni smoke-PAST-IMP.

        b. Nel 1975, Gianni ha fumato.   (episodic)
           In 1975, Gianni smoke-PAST-PERF.

The interpretation of (12a) is essentially relational: in the relevant period of time, Gianni always smoked on occasions that naturally favoured smoking. This entails that (12a) is necessarily understood as involving an implicit Q-adverb, which triggers the mapping into a tripartite structure. For the sake of concreteness, we may think of the restrictive clause as expressed by an implicit *when* clause (something like "whenever Gianni found himself in situations when a smoker tends to exhibit his typical behaviour") and of the Q-adverb as an implicit operator with intensional force (i.e., the implicit *Gen*, which is usually assumed to be present in characterising sentences such as (12a)).[9] The generalisation we want to capture is that the presence of imperfective morphology on the verbal predicate clearly triggers the presence of an (implicit) Q-adverb. This is not the case with episodic sentences such as (12b), where the verbal predicate is perfectively marked. The interpretation of (12b) simply involves existential closure of the event/time variable: in the relevant period of time, Gianni has been involved in one or more events of smoking. This interpretation is not relational and there is no mapping into a tripartite structure. The relational reading of perfective sentences requires the presence of an overtly realised Q-adverb, as confirmed by the observation that the variant of (12b) exemplified in (13) also expresses a relation between events/times, on a par with (12a).

(13)   Nel 1975, Gianni spesso ha fumato.
      In 1975, Gianni often smoke-PAST-PERF.

The difference between (12a) and the variant of (12b) with a lexically realised Q-adverb concerns the presence of a characterising (i.e., generic) reading.
Intuitively, (12a) involves quantification into a set of *possible* events that naturally favour smoking, whereas (13) simply involves quantification into the set of
events favouring smoking that occurred in 1975. This strongly suggests that imperfectively marked habitual sentences have an essentially modal dimension that
is absent from the semantics of perfectively marked habitual sentences such as
(13). On the grounds of these considerations, one might expect that (12a) is exclusively compatible with intensional Q-adverbs such as *usually, generally,* and
so on, which essentially constitute the overt counterpart of the implicit *Gen.*
However, the prediction is not borne out since a sentence like (14), containing
the extensional Q-adverb *often,* is perfectly acceptable with the intensional
reading associated with (12a)—the claim is that for any possible set of events
favouring smoking, Gianni would actually smoke in a large part of them. This
observation might be assumed to cast some doubts on the hypothesis that the
intensional reading of (12a) depends on the interpretation of the imperfective
morpheme realised on the verb as a polarity item that has to be licensed by an
intensional Q-adverb such as *Gen.*[10] In fact, (14) shows that the intensional
reading of (12a) is not sensitive to the extensional/intensional nature of the
Q-adverb.

(14)   Nel 1975, Gianni spesso fumava.
        In 1975, Gianni often smoke-PAST-IMP

The conclusion we want to draw from these considerations is that one of the
aspectual values encoded by the imperfective morphology, as instantiated in
Slavic and Romance, triggers the presence of an (implicit) Q-adverb. This explains why the interpretation of imperfectively marked habitual sentences is inherently relational, essentially encoding a form of mapping into tripartite structures, quite independently of the presence of a phonologically realised Q-adverb.
This sharply contrasts with the situation found with perfectively marked predicates, where the relational reading has been shown to be dependent on the presence of a lexically realised Q-adverb. As for the characterising/nomic interpretation of imperfective habituals, an author of this chapter, Delfitto, does not
want to commit himself to the view that this interpretation follows from the
presence of an implicit Q-adverb (i.e., the view that habitual morphology is necessarily licensed by *Gen,* as in Chierchia 1995a, 1995b) since the compatibility
of the characterising reading with extensional Q-adverbs seems rather to require
a *predicational* analysis, according to which habituality roughly corresponds to
the ascription of a property to an individual.[11] In fact, as explicitly emphasised
by Bertinetto (1997: 209), the truth conditions associated with sentences such as
(12a) seem to be independent of the frequency with which the relevant event
occurs (a single occurrence of the event of *smoking by Gianni* seems sufficient
to make the sentence true).

Nevertheless, for the purposes of this chapter, we largely disregard the issue
of intensionality. The basic fact that we want to account for is the observation

that habitual morphology encodes some form of mapping into tripartite structures. The question that we want to address is in which way morphosyntactic factors affect the nature of this mapping.

2.3. The Interaction of Temporal Adverbs and Aspect

The basic question that we want to discuss concerns the relevance of the surface position of locating adverbials for the truth conditions of imperfectively marked habitual sentences. If the temporal adverb is VP internal (superficially occurring in sentence-final position), it is projected into the nuclear scope, whereas it gets projected into the restrictive clause whenever it occurs in a dislocated position.[12] This is shown by the contrast manifested by (15') and (16').

(15)   Nel 1975, Gianni andava (sempre) a nuotare alle otto di mattina.
        In 1975, Gianni (always) go-PAST-IMP swimming at 8 A.M.

(15') $\forall t[\exists e(\text{go-swimming}(e) \wedge \text{Agent}(\text{Gianni}, e) \wedge \text{at}(e, t))]$ [8am(t)].

(16)   Nel 1975, alle otto di mattina Gianni andava (sempre) a nuotare.
        In 1975, at eight o'clock Gianni always go-PAST-IMP swimming.

(16') $\forall t[8\text{am}(t)]$ [$\exists e$ (go-swimming$(e) \wedge$ Agent(Gianni, $e) \wedge$ at$(e, t))$].

The different mapping represented in (15') and (16') is intended to capture the insight that there are situations that falsify (15) but do not falsify (16). For instance, if Gianni went swimming at 8 A.M. and 5 P.M. in the relevant period, there is a clear intuition that this suffices to make (15) false but does not suffice to make (16) false. This difference is directly captured by the tripartite structure associated with (16) and represented in (16'), which simply states that for every time t contained in 1975 such that the property *8am* holds of t, there has been an event of going to swim by Gianni at t. Such truth conditions obviously leave the possibility open that Gianni went swimming at times different from 8 A.M. This is why (16) remains true in the context mentioned above—that is, a situation in which Gianni went swimming twice in a day. The same considerations hold for all structures in which the punctual adverbial is replaced by an arbitrary locating temporal adverb. The presence of separation algorithms of the kind instantiated in (15) and (16) can be taken to suggest that overt syntax might play a crucial role for a precise formulation of the clause-splitting algorithm in cases of A-quantification, thus paralleling the crucial role that it is often assumed in the canonical cases of D-quantification (cf. Heim 1982 and especially Diesing 1992).

As a matter of fact, this is the thesis defended in the next section. However, we should first consider the alternative analysis, the hypothesis that the projection rules apply in the way exemplified in (15') and (16') as a consequence of some straightforward, purely semantic procedure. A good candidate is the "association-with-focus" procedure first proposed in Rooth (1985) and subsequently extended to more complex cases, involving indefinites and predicates as focused elements (Rooth 1995). According to this procedure, the lexical material

projected into the nuclear scope overlaps with the lexical material contained in
the sentence, to the exclusion of the Q-adverb, whereas the restrictive clause is
obtained by replacing the focused constituent contained in the sentence with an
existentially quantified variable. As for the determination of the focused constituent, let us assume that focus is related to the assignment of the main phrasal
stress in the way stated in (17) (Reinhart 1995: 62; see section 4 for further discussion).

(17)   *The focus rule*: The focus of IP is a(ny) constituent containing the main
        stress of IP, as determined by the stress rule. The stress rule assigns the
        most prominent stress to the most embedded element on the recursive
        side of the syntactic tree.

The application of (17) to (15) yields the result that the punctual adverbial *8am*
is one of the members of the focus set associated with (15)—that is, a member
of the set of constituents that may be assigned focus according to (17). The application of the association-with-focus procedure projects (15) into the tripartite
structure represented in (18).

(18) $\forall \langle t, e\rangle [\text{go-swimming}(e) \wedge \text{Agent}(\text{Gianni}, e) \wedge \exists P(P(t)) \wedge \text{at}(e, t)]$
        $[\text{go-swimming}(e) \wedge \text{Agent}(\text{Gianni}, e) \wedge \text{at}(e, t) \wedge 8\text{am}(t)].$

In (18), the restrictive clause has been built up by replacing the focused constituent—that is, the punctual adverbial *8am*—with an existentially quantified
variable. More particularly, we have followed Rooth (1995) in proposing that
when the focused constituent is a predicate, it has to be replaced by a second-
order variable ranging over properties. In other words, $\exists P(P(t))$ is read as "there
exists a property P such that P holds of t". Since this is trivially true, (18) can be
rewritten as (18'), roughly stating that "every pair $\langle e, t\rangle$ of events and times
whereby e is an event of swimming by Gianni taking place at t is such that e
took place at 8 A.M.", intuitively the correct result. Although (18') is slightly
different from (15'), it seems to provide an adequate characterisation of the truth
conditions of (15).

(18') $\forall \langle t, e\rangle [\text{go-swimming}(e) \wedge \text{Agent}(\text{Gianni}, e) \wedge \text{at}(e, t)] [\text{go-swimming}(e)$
        $\wedge \text{Agent}(\text{Gianni}, e) \wedge \text{at}(e, t) \wedge 8\text{am}(t)]$

Let us consider now what happens if we apply the association-with-focus
procedure to sentences involving adverb preposing, such as (16). If we make use
of the ancillary hypothesis that subjects (i.e., specifiers) and adjuncts are invisible for the stress assignment procedure described in (17)—as extensively argued
in Zubizarreta (1994) on the grounds of convincing evidence from Germanic
and Romance—it is reasonable to assume that the preposed adverbial in (16)
cannot be a member of the focus set associated with (16) since it fills either an
adjoined position or the specifier position of a designated functional projection
in the left periphery of the clause. However, the IP to the right of the preposed
constituent *is* a member of the focus set of (16). This gives rise to the tripartite
structure shown in (19), where the whole IP has been interpreted in focus and

has therefore been replaced by a variable ranging over times, in full accordance with Rooth's interpretation of sentences as temporal abstracts.

(19) $\forall t[8\text{am}(t) \land \exists P(P(t))]$ [8am(t) $\land \exists e$(go-swimming(e) $\land$ Agent(Gianni,e) $\land$ at(e, t))].

Since $\exists P(P(t))$ is a trivial condition on the variable t, (19) reduces to (19'), roughly stating that every time t such that the property *8am* holds of t is a time t satisfying both the property *8am* and the property that an event of going to swim by Gianni takes place at t, arguably the correct result.

(19') $\forall t[8\text{am}(t)]$ [8am(t) $\land \exists e$(go-swimming(e)$\land$ Agent(Gianni, e) $\land$ at(e, t))].

Despite this partial success, there is evidence that the application of the association-with-focus procedure, even though it plays a role in the application of the separation algorithm, cannot be the whole story—that is, it cannot be identified with the separation algorithm tout court. This evidence has to do with the cases in which the preposed adverbial is not a temporal adverbial and can be assumed to correspond, semantically, to a predicate of events instead of a predicate of times. As exemplification, let us consider the following examples, which involve a manner/instrumental adverbial, a locative adverbial, and an iterative adverbial, respectively.

(20)   a.   Con questo coltello, Gianni minacciava sempre Maria.
            With this knife, John always threaten-PAST-IMP Mary.

        b.   A Parigi, Gianni incontrava sempre il suo vecchio professore.
            In Paris, Gianni always meet-PAST-IMP his old professor.

        c.   Due volte, Gianni bussava sempre alla porta di Maria.
            Twice, John always knock-PAST-IMP at Mary's door.

Since the association-with-focus procedure applies to (20) in exactly the same way as it applies to (16), the output will be a tripartite structure in which the whole constituent corresponding to the IP has been replaced by an existentially quantified variable in the restrictive clause. For (20a), this tripartite structure can be represented as follows:

(21) $\forall \langle t, e \rangle$[WITH(this-knife, e)$\land \exists P(P(t)) \land$ at(e, t)] [threatening(e) $\land$ Agent(John, e) $\land$ Theme(Mary, e) $\land$ WITH (this-knife, e) $\land$ at(e, t)].

This is not the correct result since what (21) roughly expresses is that "every $\langle t, e \rangle$ pair whereby e is an event involving the use of a knife which occurs at t is such that e consists in John threatening Mary with a knife". Similar wrong results are produced with all the sentences in (20), as the reader can easily verify—for instance, (20b) is not intended to mean that "every time t at which some event occurred in Paris is a time at which John met his old professor". It is evident that (21) does not represent the correct interpretation of (20a), even in contexts in which the focused constituent is best identified with the IP to the right of the preposed adverbial, for instance, when (20a) is used as an answer to the

question *What has been done with this knife?* Even in such a context, the paraphrase that we want is something like "every pair ⟨*t, e*⟩ whereby *e* is event occurring at *t* in which John threatened someone with a knife is such that *e* is an
event in which John threatened Mary with a knife"—that is, a paraphrase corresponding to a tripartite structure where some extra material, in addition to the
preposed adverbial, has been projected into the restrictive clause. It might be
objected that we can derive (one of) the correct paraphrase(s) by applying the
association-with-focus procedure since focus assignment under (17) will also
have *Mary* (or a larger constituent containing *Mary*) as one of the members of
the focus set. This is certainly true. However, the point is that at least one of the
possible outputs of the focus algorithm is generally not acceptable as a paraphrase of sentences in which a nontemporal adverbial has been preposed, such
as those in (20). The wrong paraphrase corresponds to the separation algorithm
that maps only the preposed adverbial phrase into the restrictive clause. We have
just seen that even in contexts in which the focus assignment clearly favours this
sort of mapping, these readings tend to be nonaccessible. Conversely, this sort of
mapping provides a quite natural set of readings in structures where the preposed adverbial is a locating temporal adverb, as we have seen in the case of
(16).[13] In the next section, we argue that this striking asymmetry between temporal adverbs and nontemporal adverbs is not due to pragmatic constraints on the
syntax/semantics mapping. We rather argue that the asymmetry has its roots in
the nature of the mapping itself—that is, in the way the separation algorithm
operates on syntactic representations.

The relevance of formal factors of a morphosyntactic nature is immediately
confirmed by the observation that the surface position of locating temporal adverbs does not seem to affect the truth conditions of the perfective counterparts
of (15) and (16). This claim is illustrated by the fact that both (22) and (23) are
assigned the very same reading (the one represented in (24)) in structures where
the verbal predicate is perfectively marked, quite independently of the choice
between the compound Past (morphologically, but not always functionally,
equivalent to the English Present Perfect) and the simple Past (roughly equivalent to the English Simple Past).

(22)   Gianni è andato a nuotare alle otto di mattina.
        Gianni has-gone-PERF swimming at 8 A.M.

(23)   Alle otto di mattina Gianni è andato a nuotare.
        At 8 A.M. Gianni has-gone-PERF swimming.

(24) $\exists t \exists e$(swimming(e) $\wedge$ Agent(Gianni, e) $\wedge$ at(e, t) $\wedge$ 8am(t)).

The surface position of the locating adverbial *at 8 A.M.* only affects the informational package associated with (22) and (23), in the sense that the latter, contrary to the former, has the preposed adverbial as part of the presupposition. As
already emphasised, however, there is no effect on the truth conditions assigned
to these sentences since both are interpreted as shown in (24), roughly stating
that in 1975 "there has been one or more events of swimming by John, which

has taken place at 8 A.M.". The conclusion that we want to draw from these observations is that the role of locating temporal adverbs in the mapping from syntactic representations to quantificational structures is crucially affected by the choice of aspectual morphology. Explaining the interaction between imperfective morphology and locating adverbials in the case of habitual sentences should be a part of a more general enterprise also attempting to explain the interaction between perfective morphology and locating adverbials exemplified in (22) and (23).

At the same time, we have to take into consideration that the imperfective morphology is not able to overcome a rigidly deterministic form of mapping in structures where the quantifier over times is syntactically realised as a determiner and the locating expression as the NP complement of this determiner. As already pointed out in secttion 2.1, in the course of our discussion of structures such as (11), sentences like (25) are rigidly mapped into the tripartite structure represented in (26), quite independently of the presence of contexts that would favour, on pragmatic grounds, readings in which the NP complement is projected into the nuclear scope.[14]

(25)   Nel 1975, Gianni andava a nuotare ogni mattina.
        In 1975, John go-PAST-IMP swimming every morning.

(26) $\forall t[\text{morning}(t) \land t \subseteq 1975] [\exists e(\text{swimming}(e) \land \text{Agent}(\text{John}, e) \land \text{at}(e, t))]$.

Given the puzzling state of affairs described above, it is time to lay out the essential ingredients of our theoretical proposal.

3. Aspect as a "Regulator" of A-quantification

The proposal for a syntax of aspect to be presented in this section (as an attempt to provide a principled analysis of the interaction between aspectual marking on the verb and temporal adverbials; cf. section 2.3) is based on the syntax of tense developed in Zagona (1995) and Stowell (1996). According to Stowell, tense is a dyadic operator expressing a temporal ordering relation between the speech time, ST, and the event time, ET, both syntactically represented as time-denoting Z(eit)P(hrase) arguments, the first of which is realised in the specifier of the T(ense) projection, and the second of which corresponds with the complement of T.

(27)

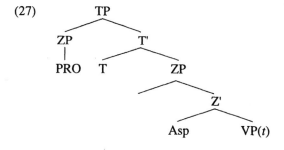

The external ZP argument is realised as an empty anaphoric element, PRO, which is interpreted as referentially dependent from the ET of a superordinate clause when (27) corresponds to an embedded structure (potentially accounting for sequence of tense effects) and as coinciding with ST when (27) corresponds to an independent clause. The part of Stowell's proposal that is relevant for our present concerns is the hypothesis that the ZP argument of T(ense) in (27) is interpreted as a quantified argument, in the sense that it is assigned the same semantics as a quantified DP. More exactly, Stowell assumes that either Z itself or an empty operator in Spec-ZP saturates the VP by binding a null temporal variable in a VP internal argument position, which is theta-marked by the verb. In this way, under the straightforward interpretation of the past morpheme in T as the dyadic predicate *after*, an English sentence such as *John hit the ball* is read as "The speech time, ST, is after some time ZP at which John hit the ball" (Stowell 1996: 281). The most obvious analogy with the analysis proposed above concerns the fact that there is a syntactic level of representation that encodes quantification over times. To put it more concretely, the event time, ET, is syntactically realised as a temporal argument that is thematically marked by the verb and can give rise to quantificational structures.

At the same time, the observations of sections 2.1 and 2.2 immediately suggest some integrations and modifications of Stowell's proposal. First, we have seen that context-depending locating adverbials such as *on Sunday* and *at 8 A.M.* are best interpreted as time predicates (type $\langle e, t \rangle$). As explicitly suggested in section 2.1, we can simply assume that these adverbials constitute the syntactic realisation of the temporal argument expressing ET, their semantic role essentially consisting of the introduction of a free variable with a predicative restriction, in full analogy with the semantics assigned to indefinite DPs in the DRT framework. Moreover, there is no need to assume that the ZP level necessarily involves the presence of an empty variable-taking operator, which binds the free temporal variable within the VP. In fact, since we have proposed to view quantification over times as the essential dimension of A(dverb) quantification, the null hypothesis is that the free temporal variable typically introduced by locating adverbials is bound by Q-adverbs like *often* and *always*, which are interpreted as second-order dyadic predicates in full analogy with the G(eneralised)Q(uantifier) analysis of nominal determiners (cf. de Swart 1991). In structures that do not contain any frequency adverb, a process of default existential closure will apply, in full analogy with the standards assumptions on nominal indefinites. If the ZP projection is no longer intended to host a binder for the temporal variable, we should, of course, wonder whether its presence is legitimate at all. We contend that the most straightforward and principled answer to this question consists in the hypothesis that Stowell's ZP complement of T(ense) has in fact to be understood as a functional category that encodes some of the features realised on the temporal phrase—that is, the locating adverbial—in strict analogy with the functional projections that instantiate some of the (quantificational) features realised on nominal arguments, under standard syntactic assumptions. In this view, if DP arguments are characterised as sets of features entering *checking* relations in syntax (Chomsky 1995), there is no principled reason to believe that the same does not apply to temporal phrases. The ZP-complement of T is therefore best identified with the aspectual projection which encodes the morphological opposition perfective/imperfective, crucially involving the realisation of some quantificational features of the temporal argument.

According to this proposal, aspect, at least as far as the opposition perfective/imperfective is concerned, is thus the syntactic level at which a particular set of *interpretable* features of temporal phrases are realised and checked (as we shall see). As a conclusion, the syntactic representation in (27) can be made more perspicuous in terms of (28).

(28)

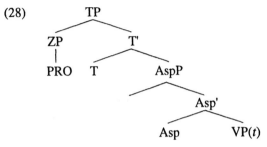

At this point, the obvious question concerns the nature of the features that are realised in the aspectual head. As emphasised in section 2.2, the crucial property of imperfectively marked habitual sentences is constituted by the obligatoriness of a relational interpretation, even in absence of a phonologically realised frequency adverb. In other words, it seems that the presence of imperfective marking on the verb suffices for the interpretation of habitual sentences as expressing relations among two sets of times. The hypothesis that we would like to put forward is that the interpretable feature realised on the aspectual head (let us label it [+*quant*]) encodes the semantic instruction that the temporal argument is part of a G(eneralised)Q(uantifier) structure. As for the specific technical implementation of this insight, at least two possibilities come to mind. In the hypothesis that syntactic structures are projected into discourse representation structures, [+*quant*] might be literally interpreted as encoding the instruction that the variable introduced by the temporal argument is necessarily interpreted within a *duplex condition* of the kind proposed in DRT (i.e., the temporal variable has to appear in two open formulas that are interpreted as the arguments of a variable-taking operator). Alternatively, we may assume, slightly modifying the proposal put forward in Chierchia (1995a), that [+*quant*] is essentially realised as a sort of polarity feature, which requires being in the scope of a frequency adverb in order to be formally licensed. Since the presence of this polarity feature obligatorily induces the presence of a GQ interpretation, and duplex conditions are intended as the representational equivalents of GQ interpretations, the two approaches are empirically indistinguishable, the choice between them depending on general theoretical options regarding the mapping between syntax and semantics. As for perfectively marked verbal predicates, we assume that the aspectual head is underspecified for the feature *quant*, roughly encoding the semantic instruction that the variable introduced by the temporal argument does not need to be interpreted within a duplex condition. Notice that this does not exclude the possibility that perfective sentences be assigned a GQ interpretation, provided a frequency adverb is syntactically realised in the relevant structure, arguably the correct result, in view of the discussion in section 2.2. If there is no frequency adverb, the free time variable introduced by the locating adverbial will end up existentially quantified, giving rise to the episodic readings that are normally associated with perfective sentences.

Let us try to give these basic insights a more precise technical implementation. The hypothesis that we want to put forward consists of two parts. The first part is that certain aspectual features realised on the aspectual head that selects the VP and superficially detectable on the verb (at least in Slavic and Romance) have to be interpreted as imposing semantic constraints on the quantificational interpretation of the time argument—most likely in the form of constraints on the interpretation of the time variable introduced by the locating temporal adverb. The second part is that the aspectual feature realised on the aspectual head has in fact to be checked (in the technical sense proposed by Chomsky 1995, involving a formal relation of Spec-head agreement and deletion of one of the features entering the checking procedure) by an identical feature realised on some lexical head—the verb and/or the temporal argument. We contend that there is convincing empirical evidence for both claims. In particular, the second part of the hypothesis seems able to provide a principled solution for the separation problem, whose analysis has led to the empirical issues formulated and discussed in section 2.3. The basic insight here is that the aspectual projection behaves as a sort of "regulator" of the algorithm that maps syntactic representations into tripartite structures.

Let us start with the first claim. At first glance, the hypothesis that verb-related morphology encodes semantic instructions on the quantificational interpretation of one of the verb's arguments appears to correspond to some highly stipulative and vaguely defined mechanism.[15] However, the point is that recent cross-linguistic investigation into the quantificational structures attested in human languages has revealed the presence of general mechanisms of *lexical quantification* (cf. Partee 1995 for the use of this term), which are quite similar, in the spirit if not in the letter, to the mechanism that we are proposing in the present contribution. Lexical quantification concerns cases in which "an operator with some quantificational force (and perhaps further content as well) is applied directly to a verb or other predicate at a lexical level, with (potentially) morphological, syntactic and semantic effects on the argument structure of the predicate" (Partee 1995: 559). Two cases in point are constituted by American Sign Language (ASL) (Petronio 1995) and indigenous languages of Australia such as Warlpiri and Gun-djeymi (Evans 1995). There is a complex agreement system in ASL according to which certain verbs are specified for which of their arguments they agree with: quantificational information concerning the agreeing argument(s) is encoded in the form of morphological modification of the verbal sign, most typically by changes in the space-time trajectory of the verbal sign (Klima and Bellugi 1979). Some of these quantificational instructions concern the singular or dual interpretation of the agreeing argument (29a), but they can also express information about the reciprocal or distributive reading of the agreeing argument (29b), as shown by the English paraphrases below (drawn from Partee 1995).

(29)   a.   [Woman]$_{TOP}$ book I-give-singular.
            I gave a/the woman a/the book.

       b.   [Woman]$_{TOP}$ book I-give-exhaustive.
            I gave each woman a book.

A distinct, although conceptually related, case concerns the presence of an incorporated classifier in motion verbs; the classifier clearly encodes quantificational information about the singular/plural or collective interpretation of the argument of the motion verb, along the lines suggested by the English paraphrase in (30), where CL indicates the classifier and @ a spatial locus.

(30)   [Student]$_{TOP}$ @CL:44(plural) went west.
       The/some students went west.

Even more striking, from the perspective of the present study, is the quantificational meaning expressed by a specific class of verbal affixes in Warlpiri and Gun-djeymi, which has been investigated by Evans (and Hale 1989, quoted in Evans 1995). Hale reports that Warlpiri has an open class of affixlike elements that obligatorily form a constituent with the verb and express quantificational features such as *universal, reciprocal, distributive*, and so on. According to Evans, these features do not apply randomly to any argument of the verb, showing instead a strong tendency to select a specific argument of the verb and leading to at least four distinct patterns of *thematic affinity*: actor/subject scope, absolutive scope, VP scope, and time/place/manner/theme/action scope. An exemplification of the cases of subject-scope, concerning the verbal prefix *–djarrk*, is given in (31) for Gun-djeymi (drawn, again, from Partee 1995). Naturally a detailed investigation of the cases of time scope might be of great interest for the claims made in the present study.

(31)   Garri-djarrk-dulubom duruk.
       We.pl-together-shootPST-PF dog.
       We all shot the/a dog/dogs.   (crucially not distributive)

We believe that even a superficial consideration of these cases of lexical quantification suffices to shed an entirely different light on the view that we have taken on the interpretation of aspectual morphology. The hypothesis that the perfective/imperfective opposition corresponds to two different instructions on the quantificational interpretation of the temporal argument is best analysed, in view of the data presented above, as a case of lexical quantification that involves a mechanism of *thematic affinity* (i.e., aspectual morphology selects the temporal argument of the verb, exactly as a certain verbal affix selects the actor argument or any other argument of the verb in Gun-djeymi). Lexical quantification is no stranger to (at least) Slavic and Romance when it comes to quantification over times. In this perspective, it is quite tempting to conclude that the separation problem deserves a quite radical reformulation. The reason that A-quantification has been generally felt to be problematic was the lack of an explicit algorithm for the mapping of syntactic representations into the tripartite structures that express the GQ analysis of quantification. Although the operator is syntactically realised in the form of a frequency adverb, there is no obvious syntactic correlate for scope and restriction, in sharp contrast with the standard cases of D-quantification. Moreover, since at least the seminal study of Lewis (1975), Q-adverbs are normally conceived of as unselective binders, with no exclusive connection with quantification over time variables. This may well be correct.

However, the point is that there is much more, in the structures involving A-quantification, than the mere presence of an unselective binder. Once locating temporal adverbials are understood as indefinite temporal arguments of the verbal predicate, introducing, as any other indefinite argument, a restricted variable into the domain of discourse (section 2.1), the aspectual morphology realised on the verb can be interpreted as effectively constraining the quantificational interpretation of this variable. In the case of habitual morphology, the aspectually encoded instruction is that the temporal argument has to be interpreted as one of the two arguments of a generalised quantifier. This immediately accounts for the inherently relational reading of imperfectively marked habitual sentences (section 2.2): the quantificational instruction encoded by aspectual morphology triggers the projection into a tripartite structure; hence the presence of a Q-adverb, which does not need to be lexically realised, but may simply be recovered from context. In other words, given the role of aspect, there are serious morphosyntactic reasons to believe that Q-adverbs select syntactically represented time predicates as their natural semantic arguments, rather than simply behaving as unselective binders. On these grounds, we think that the next step to be taken is exploiting the link between verbal morphology and the functional structure of language, which has been the core of recent research in formal syntax. If aspectual features can be assumed to give rise to a specific aspectual projection, it is this projection that constitutes the most obvious candidate as the regulator of time quantification—that is, the essential ingredient for the definition of an explicit mapping algorithm. This directly leads us to a careful examination of the second part of the hypothesis formulated above.

As stated at the onset, we propose that Stowell's ZP complement of T(ense) is to be understood as an aspectual projection (AspP), which contains features that are related to the quantificational interpretation of the temporal argument of the verb. Suppose we now ask this question: where are these aspectual features actually interpreted in the semantic component? Since we have argued that these features express selective information on one of the verb's arguments—namely, the temporal argument—there are only two natural syntactic candidates. One is the verb itself, under the natural hypothesis that lexical quantification encodes some change of information about the argument structure of the predicate (in our case, some specific constraint on the interpretation of the time argument), as proposed by Partee. The other obvious candidate is the temporal argument of the verb. If the aspectual feature [+ *quant*] is realised on the time argument, it simply encodes the instruction that the latter is to be interpreted as one of the two arguments of a generalised quantifier over times. If [+*quant*] is realised on the verb, it encodes the instruction that it is the whole verbal projection that has to be interpreted as one of the two arguments of a generalised quantifier over times. This can be regarded as the null hypothesis. The question is whether this makes any sense semantically. We think it does. Under the VP internal subject hypothesis, all arguments of the verb are realised VP-internally. Since the temporal argument is interpreted as a free restricted variable, the possibility arises of interpreting the whole VP as a *predicate of times* (a *temporal abstract* in Rooth's sense), informally referring to the set of times at which the event referred to by the verb takes place. This interpretation can be formally represented in terms of lambda abstraction on the time variable:

(32) $\lambda t.\ \exists e(P(e) \wedge \theta_1(c_1, e) \ldots \wedge \theta_n(c_n, e) \wedge Q(t))$,

where $c_1, \ldots, c_n$ are individual constants, P is a predicate of events, and Q is a predicate of times. As for the second option, in which [+*quant*] is directly realised on the temporal argument, we have already seen that locating temporal adverbials are normally interpreted as predicates of times, as formally represented in (33).

(33) $\lambda t.\ [Q(t)]$,

where Q is a predicate of times

Let us thus assume that the aspectual features we are investigating are interpreted either on the verb or on the locating temporal adverbial. In syntactic terms, this entails that the aspectual features that are phonetically realised on the verb can be syntactically realised either on the verb or on its temporal argument.[16] The [+*quant*] feature that constitutes the lexical content of the aspectual head (Asp in the structure (29)) is therefore noninterpretable in that position and must be deleted by means of a formal procedure of checking (i.e., by moving a constituent that bears an identical feature to the Spec,AspP position). Suppose that this is actually what takes place whenever we have an imperfectively marked habitual sentence. Remember that in the case of (16), we want to account for the fact that the preposed adverbial is necessarily interpreted as the restrictive clause. We can do that by simply assuming that the temporal adverbial, in its way to the left-dislocated position, where it is interpreted as a topic, has moved through the Spec,AspP position, checking and erasing the noninterpretable aspectual feature realised in that position. Intermediate movement to Spec,AspP is necessary since noninterpretable features have to be deleted. At the same time, the phonologically unrealised copy of the temporal adverbial in Spec,AspP is interpreted as a predicate of times, as we have seen above. *We can thus formulate the hypothesis that it is the constituent in Spec,AspP that provides the restriction of the Q-adverb.* In other words, the explicit definition of the mapping algorithm for A-quantification that we are proposing has the constituent in Spec,AspP as the restrictive clause and the material contained in the VP as the scope.[17]

Let us consider now how this solution to the separation problem applies to sentences like (15), where the locating temporal adverb surfaces in sentence-final position. We interpret the syntactic position of the locating adverbial in (15) as direct evidence that it has not undergone syntactic displacement to the Spec,AspP position. If this is the case, the issue is how it is possible, for the syntactic derivation corresponding to (15), to achieve erasure of the noninterpretable aspectual feature realised on the aspectual head. Our answer to this problem is that it is the whole VP that has undergone overt syntactic displacement to the Spec,AspP position in (15), the effects of this movement operation having been partially obliterated by the application of other movement operations in the course of the syntactic derivation. As emphasised above, the VP can also be interpreted as a predicate of times, receiving the abstract representation in (32). At the same time, we may assume that the derivation, which has the whole VP displaced to Spec,AspP, involves the realisation of the interpretable [*+quant*] feature on the verb, one of the two syntactic options contemplated above. It is this feature (under percolation to the top of the verb's projection) that formally checks the noninterpretable aspectual feature realised on the aspectual head, producing its elimination as required. The result of the sort of hidden movement that we are proposing is that both the restrictive clause and the scope are syntactically represented, the latter as the phonologically unrealised copy of the VP in its base position and the former as the VP copy in Spec,AspP. Empirically, this is not yet the correct result since we do not want the restriction to be identical to the scope. However, all we have to do to make the algorithm work properly is to apply Rooth's association-with-focus procedure to the VP in Spec,AspP. The reason to make this move is that we want our "mapping algorithm" to capture the fundamentally correct insight that focus and topic act as a sort of filter on the material projected into the restrictive clause. The hypothesis that focused material cannot be part of the restriction constitutes the basic insight behind Rooth's proposal, whereas the observation that topicalised constituents are necessarily interpreted as part of the restriction is based on a considerable amount of empirical evidence (cf. especially the discussion in Partee 1995). We propose thus the following interface filter:

(34)   Constituents interpreted as topics must be part of the restrictive clause, constituents interpreted as foci cannot be part of the restrictive clause

After (34) has applied to (15), interpreting the temporal adverb as the focused constituent and replacing it with an existentially quantified variable in the higher VP, (15) gives rise to the tripartite representation in (18), arguably the correct result. It is important to emphasise that (34) should not be identified with the mapping algorithm. What our mapping algorithm does is identify the restriction with the constituent present in Spec,AspP in overt syntax. The fact that there always is a syntactic constituent in Spec,AspP depends on the purely syntactic requirement that the noninterpretable aspectual feature realised in Asp be erased. The fact that this syntactic requirement successfully fits the semantics depends on the possibility of interpreting both syntactic candidates for displacement to Spec,AspP as predicates of times, as required by the interpretation of A-quantification as quantification over times. This entails that (34) should rather be understood as an interface filter on the output of the mapping algorithm. This captures the basic insight formulated above that the association-with-focus procedure plays a role in the mapping to tripartite structures but cannot be the whole story.

The crucial evidence in favour of the proposed approach concerns the treatment of the cases of adverb preposing exemplified in (20), which involve adverbial phrases that cannot be interpreted as predicates of times and have been shown to be problematic for an unconstrained application of the association-with-focus algorithm. As the reader will remember, the problem is that there is no accessible reading that has only the adverbial phrase in the restriction. This is not expected since the clausal constituent to the right of the preposed adverbial is certainly one of the members of the focus set obtained from the application of the focus rule in (17). On the contrary, this fact follows straightforwardly from the approach that we are proposing. Since the restriction of the tripartite structure is identified with the constituent contained in Spec,AspP, the syntactic derivation that most directly corresponds to the reading under scrutiny involves intermediate movement of the preposed adverb to Spec,AspP. However, this movement does not lead to acceptable results, neither syntactically nor semantically.

Syntactically, we have seen that the [+*quant*] feature is a prerogative of the temporal argument and cannot be freely generated on other adverbial phrases as a consequence of the interpretation of aspectual morphology in terms of a mechanism of thematic affinity that involves exclusive selection of the temporal argument. Since the displaced adverbial in (20) is not endowed with the interpretable feature [+*quant*], movement to Spec,AspP does not ensure checking and erasure of the noninterpretable feature on Asp. Semantically, manner/iterative/locative adverbials are not interpreted as predicates of times. This entails that the constituent in Spec,AspP is not suitable as the restriction of a Q-adverb. We conclude that the reading we want to exclude on empirical grounds cannot be produced under adverb displacement, a positive result. The only converging syntactic derivation has the whole VP displaced to Spec,AspP, followed by further movement of the preposed adverb to the left-peripheral position. This is legitimate since the VP is interpretable as a predicate of times and can activate the checking procedure, as emphasised above.

Interpretively, we know that VP movement necessarily triggers the application of the association-with-focus procedure to differentiate the higher VP copy, which is projected into the restriction, from the lower VP copy, which is projected into the scope. As repeatedly emphasised, this is done by replacing a proper subpart of the higher VP copy with an existentially quantified variable (ranging on objects or properties, depending on the semantics of the replaced constituent, as in Rooth 1995). In other words, we propose that the application of Rooth's algorithm is strictly tied to the syntactic operation of VP displacement to Spec,AspP, in the form of the general constraint on the syntax/semantics mapping formulated in (35).

(35)   The syntactic operation of VP displacement to Spec,AspP triggers the semantic procedure of association-with-focus.

Moreover, there are reasons to believe that constituents that are interpreted as topics are not computed in the application of the focus procedure. This additional condition is imposed by the necessity of avoiding the condition that constituents that are marked as topics be interpreted as focused. This would lead to the contradictory requirement that the very same constituent be projected into the restriction (as is the case with topics) and substituted within the restriction (as is the case with focused constituents). It follows that (35) is relevant to the part of the VP copy in Spec,AspP that is obtained by abstracting away from the constituents that are interpreted as topics (in the case of (20), the preposed adverbials). It is thus a proper subpart of this "reduced" VP that must be interpreted as focused and be replaced by an existentially quantified variable, as required by (35). In this way, we derive the fact that the tripartite structures associated with the sentences in (20) (involving adverb preposing of nontemporal phrases) will normally have some extra material, besides the preposed constituent, in the restrictive clause.[18]

Let us try to conclude. Our main source of concern in the analysis of imperfectively marked habitual sentences is the asymmetry between temporal and nontemporal phrases: *why are preposed temporal adverbials exhaustively identifiable with the restrictive clause, whereas this is impossible (or at least rather more difficult) with preposed nontemporal phrases?* We have proposed that this interpretive asymmetry has its roots in the way the mapping algorithm applies to syntactic representations. The restrictive clause is uniformly identified with the constituent that fills the Spec,AspP position (modulo further computations involving topic and focus). Structures with preposed temporal phrases are cases of adverb displacement to Asp, whereas structures that involve other sorts of preposed adverbials are cases of VP displacement to Spec,AspP. On these grounds, the detected asymmetry is explained in terms of the interaction between a relatively well-defined set of syntactic and semantic conditions, without having to resort to arbitrary forms of mapping that are exclusively constrained by pragmatic conditions.

Before closing this section, let us briefly consider the positive consequences of our proposal for a satisfactory analysis of adverb preposing with perfectively marked sentences. As the reader will remember, the basic fact to be accounted for is that in sentences such as (22) and (23) the truth conditions are not modified according to whether the locating temporal adverb is realised in sentence-final position (as in (22)) or in left-dislocated position (as in (23)). In other words, both (22) and (23) receive the reading expressed in (24). However, the interpretation of (22) and (23) exactly parallels that of (15) and (16) as soon as (22) and (23) contain a frequency adverb such as *sempre* ('always'). These two facts can be shown to follow from our analysis. Remember that part of our hypothesis is that the aspectual marking found on verbs in the appropriate contexts encodes the morphological instruction that the aspectual head—that is, Asp in (29)—is underspecified for the feature *quant*. In (22) and (23) no Q-adverb has been added to the structure; therefore, there is no way for the underspecified aspectual feature to get a positive specification—that is, [+*quant*]—in the course of the syntactic derivation. The usual default procedure will therefore apply, with the insertion of an abstract existential operator that binds the free temporal variable introduced by the temporal argument. Semantically, it is a standard assumption that the existential operator just applies to an open formula to close some free variable contained in it (Heim 1982; Diesing 1992). As a consequence, it does not give rise to tripartite structures—that is, a duplex condition in the sense of Kamp and Reyle (1993).

We can reasonably assume that the abstract existential operator is endowed with the specification [−*quant*], encoding the semantic instruction that it is not part of a duplex condition, in full compliance with the general interpretation of *quant* that has been proposed above. For the sake of concreteness, we may think of the abstract existential quantifier as generated in Spec,AspP, a position from which it provides a negative specification to the underspecified aspectual slot in Asp, at the same time erasing it under checking. This is arguably why adverb preposing does not change truth conditions in (23). Syntactically, intermediate movement of the preposed temporal adverb to Spec,AspP is likely to be impossible, Spec,AspP being filled by the existential operator. Even if it were possible (with the existential operator in a higher position), the application of the mapping algorithm would be blocked by the fact that the temporal phrase present in Spec,AspP, being in the scope of the existential operator, must be specified as [−*quant*], encoding the semantic instruction that there is no mapping of some syntactic constituent into a restrictive clause.

Suppose now that a frequency adverb is added to the structure (let us assume that it is generated as adjoined to the aspectual phrase or some higher (functional) projection). Being in scope of a Q-adverb (i.e., of an element bearing the feature [+*quant*]), the originally underspecified aspectual head can get a positive specification for *quant* in the course of the syntactic derivation.[19] In turn, this entails that the noninterpretable aspectual feature in Asp has to be deleted through movement of some lexical constituent endowed with exactly the same feature (we crucially assume that Q-adverbs are generated in positions higher than Spec,AspP). If the constituent displaced to Spec,AspP is the temporal argument, we get (23), with the locating temporal phrase projected into the restrictive clause. Otherwise, we get (22), involving hidden VP displacement to Spec,AspP and subsequent application of the focus algorithm, which essentially gets rid of the temporal phrase in the restriction, as desired. We conclude that the facts concerning the interaction of temporal adverbs and perfective aspect follow from our analysis of aspectual morphology under a small set of plausible syntactic and semantic assumptions.

Given the perspective suggested above, the fact that structures such as (25) (where the quantifier over times is realised as a determiner and the locating temporal expression as the NP complement of the determiner) exhibit a form of rigid mapping, completely insensitive to the surface position of the temporal phrases, does not seem to require any special explanation. In fact, it is no longer the case that certain cases of quantification over times (those involving DP structures) are explicitly encoded in syntax, whereas other cases (those involving (implicit) frequency adverbs) are not. In both cases, the constituent to be projected into the restrictive clause is identified with a designated syntactic position (the NP complement of D and the specifier of AspP, respectively). The second case is obviously more complex: it involves aspectual features phonologically realised on the verb and crucially represented in functional structure, the basic insight being that the aspectual projection is a regulator of the mapping into a tripartite quantificational format. However, the formal analogy between the two cases should be quite evident at this point of the discussion.[20] Once aspectual morphology is understood in terms of mechanisms of lexical quantification and thematic affinity, the possibility that the mapping into the tripartite quantificational format be syntactically represented becomes much less remote than it appeared at first glance.

4. Adjunction, Focus, and the "Separation Problem"

The main theoretical issue addressed in this chapter concerns the role of syntactic representations for the interpretation of the structures involving adverbial quantification. In section 3, we have advocated a form of mapping that is essentially compositional since it is based on the hypothesis that both arguments of the frequency adverb are explicitly represented in overt syntax. Compositionality has been achieved by assigning a central role to aspectual features and aspectual functional structure. It is important, in this perspective, to compare not only conceptually but also empirically the present analysis with different solutions to the separation problem that have been proposed in the literature. In this final section, we try to assess the empirical merits of the proposed form of the clause-splitting algorithm by considering the empirical predictions made by the competing analysis developed in Chierchia (1995b) with respect to object-scrambling phenomena in Germanic SOV languages such as Dutch.

In the cases in which the frequency adverb expresses a sentence-internal relation, we have assumed that the nuclear scope coincides with the VP copy in the original position, whereas the restriction is provided by the VP copy (or the locating temporal adverb) that has been moved to the specifier of the aspectual phrase.[21] For a sentence such as (36) (drawn from Chierchia 1995b), the application of the proposed splitting algorithm produces the logical representation in (37), expressing the interpretation of the Q-adverb in terms of a relation between two classes of times:

(36)   Computers always route modern planes

(37) $\forall \langle t, e \rangle [\exists x((\text{route}(e) \wedge \text{Agent}(x, e) \wedge \text{Theme}(\text{modern-planes}, e) \wedge \text{at}(e, t))]$
       $[\text{route}(e) \wedge \text{Agent}(\text{computers}, e) \wedge \text{Theme}(\text{modern-planes}, e) \wedge \text{at}(e, t)].$

Clearly, the possibility that syntactic representations involving VP movement to Spec,AspP give rise to logical forms of the kind in (37) crucially depends on the possibility that the displaced VP (or the displaced temporal phrase) be interpreted as a predicate of times. This predicate of times constitutes one of the two arguments of the second-order dyadic predicate expressed by the frequency adverb. An important corollary of the position we have taken is that there is no requirement that in the syntactic representation that constitutes the input for (37) the lexical material that is projected into the restriction be realised outside the c-command domain of the Q-adverb. The mapping we have proposed relies on the insight that the material realised in Spec,AspP is uniformly projected into the restrictive clause at the interpretive interface, as a consequence of the general formulation of the mapping algorithm.

Chierchia (1995b) deals with the cases exemplified in (36) in a different way. He assumes that Q-adverbs may be freely adjoined to propositional constituents, essentially CP, IP, and VP, and that the nuclear scope coincides with their c-command domain (roughly, all the lexical material that is c-commanded by the adjunction site of the adverb must be mapped into the scope of the frequency adverb). As a logical consequence of this strictly configurational approach, the restrictive clause is assumed to coincide with the part of the m-command domain of the adverb that is not also c-commanded (roughly, the material in the same local environment as the adverb, which is not included in its the scope/c-command domain). This splitting algorithm provides us, in the case of (36), with the logical representation in (38), where the Q-adverb is represented as an unselective operator, expressing a relation between two classes of "objects". The syntactic input for (38) at the LF interface arguably corresponds to the representation in (39):

(38) $\forall x(\text{plane } (x)) (\exists y(\text{computer}(y) \wedge y \text{ route } x)).$

(39)

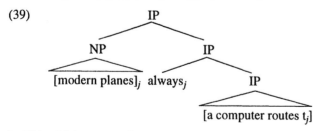

In Chierchia's approach, structures such as (39) are an instantiation of the possibility that the correct input for interpretation is created by movement operations that involve adjunction to maximal projections. Adjunction structures are rather unconstrained since it is assumed that frequency adverbs can be generated as adjoined to any propositional maximal projection. In fact, Chierchia assumes that the process of partitioning the clause is basically free, being exclusively subject to standard conditions on movement and issues of pragmatic plausibility.

At the syntactic level, Chierchia's proposal clearly represents a variant of Diesing's mapping hypothesis, the main difference having to do with the fact that the syntactic domain that is assumed to correspond to the nuclear scope is not rigidly identified with the VP but with any propositional constituent to which the Q-adverb is adjoined. The conceptual similarity between the two proposals is clearly shown by the fact that Chierchia adopts Diesing's view that sentence partitioning applies overtly in some languages (for instance, German and Dutch), that is, prior to Spell-Out. A mechanical extension of this proposal to the structures involving quantificational adverbs "would mean that the movement that may extract elements out of the intended scope of a quantificational adverb, making them part of the restriction, takes place before the operation that maps syntactic representations into phonetic ones—i.e., before Spell-Out" (Chierchia 1995b: 121).

This approach leads to some important empirical expectations. For instance, the view that sentence partitioning is *overtly* represented in Dutch naturally leads to the expectation that object scrambling, which gives rise to structures in which an internal argument of V occurs to the left of a frequency adverb, is exclusively compatible with the interpretation in which the scrambled argument is mapped into the restrictive clause. In other words, the expectation arises that scrambling of the object to the left of the Q-adverb takes place exactly in the cases in which the object must be mapped into the restrictive clause (whether this interpretive requirement has to be intended as the trigger of scrambling is a separate question).[22]

The version of the clause-splitting algorithm that has been advocated in this chapter makes quite different predictions. According to our proposal, the adequate syntactic input for the process of restrictive clause formation is provided by the displacement of a constituent interpreted as a predicate of times to the specifier of the aspectual phrase. As emphasised above, this syntactic operation is independently motivated by the checking requirement on noninterpretable features (in this case, the [+*quant*] feature encoded in Asp). Since the lexical material found in Spec,AspP at the LF interface is systematically mapped into the restrictive clause, there is no need to move internal arguments of V outside of the c-command domain of the Q-adverb, and hence no need to interpret object scrambling as triggered by the requirement that the object be projected into the restriction. In fact, the version of the splitting algorithm argued for here turns out to be immediately compatible with the hypothesis that at least certain instances of scrambling correspond to focus-driven operations, a view recently advocated in Reinhart (1995). According to this proposal, scrambling of the object to the left of an adverbial depends on the application of the unmarked focus assignment procedure as formulated in (17). Putting aside irrelevant details, scrambling can be conceived of as representing a *defocusing* effect. As is well known (and as widely discussed in Reinhart 1995), there is an important class of scrambling facts that seems to strongly support the view that scrambling corresponds to a defocusing operation. As originally pointed out in de Hoop (1992), the contrast exemplified in (40) and (41)—scrambling of the *generic* object is illegitimate in (40) and perfectly acceptable in (41)—seems to correspond to the descriptive generalisation according to which, in Dutch, scrambling of the object yields the same semantic effect as the contrastive predicates obtained by stressing the verb in English (de Hoop 1992: 165). The English equivalents of (40) and (41) are given in (42) and (43), respectively:

(40)   *. . . omdat ik een kat altijd heb.
       . . . because I cat always have.

(41)   . . . omdat ik een kat altijd liefheb.
       . . . because I a cat always love.

(42)   ?? . . . because I always HAVE a cat.

(43)   . . . because I always LOVE a cat.

Accounting for the long-standing issue raised by (40) and (41) becomes a relatively easy matter under the view that scrambling may correspond to a defocusing operation. Consider, first, the (relevant part of the) algorithm for unmarked stress assignment in Dutch (cf. Gussenhoven 1984):

(44)   Adv - O - V   (stress on O)

(45)   O - Adv - V   (stress on V)

Essentially, this means that the unmarked stress is assigned to the object in the contexts in which the latter immediately precedes the verb and is assigned to the verb in the contexts in which the latter is immediately preceded by an adverbial. Second, let us restate, as (46), the algorithm formulated in (17), which relates focus to unmarked stress assignment.

(46)   *The focus rule.* The focus of IP is a(ny) constituent containing the main stress of IP, as determined by the stress rule. The stress rule assigns the most prominent stress to the most embedded element on the recursive side of the syntactic tree.

Application of (46) constitutes the unmarked strategy for focus assignment. However, it is also possible to assign focus to a given constituent by means of marked prosodic procedures, essentially consisting in deaccenting the lexical material to the right of the focused constituent (see especially Zubizarreta 1994). The contrast between (40) and (41) should now naturally follow. According to the approach briefly sketched above, scrambling of the object in (40) and (41) is assumed to take place to derive the structure (45) from the structure (44). The only legitimate motivation for such an operation is the requirement that the verb be assigned focus in accordance with the unmarked strategy described in (46): the verb is permitted to receive the main stress (hence focus, according to (46)) only in configurations where it is *not* immediately preceded by the object.

Scrambling ensures that the appropriate syntactic output is created for the application of (46) to create the required result. As emphasised in Reinhart (1995), we do not expect scrambling to be possible when it is unlikely that the verb is interpreted as the focused constituent. This is arguably the case in (40) since *have* clearly constitutes a "light" verb which can be focused only under very special circumstances. In other words, there is no trigger for scrambling in (40) under the view that scrambling is defocusing, which is why the output of scrambling is of dubious grammaticality in (40). Conversely, scrambling is expected to yield an acceptable result if it applies to creating the appropriate syntactic configuration for the verb *love* to receive main stress (hence focus, in accordance with (46)). The perfect status of (41) confirms that the prediction is indeed borne out.

We think that there is compelling empirical evidence that object scrambling (at least as far as "generic" indefinites are concerned, as in (40) and (41)) is actually *not* triggered by the requirement that the object vacate the c-command domain of the adverbial to be interpreted in the restrictive clause. As explicitly acknowledged by Chierchia, the reading of (36) according to which the object is mapped into the restrictive clause, roughly corresponding to the logical paraphrase in (38), is favoured by putting focal stress on the subject *computers*, which receives in this way an existential interpretation:

(36') COMPUTERS always route modern planes.

If the subject is not assigned stress, it tends to receive a quasi-universal interpretation, according to which (36) roughly expresses the meaning "it is a general property of computers that they route some modern planes". Essentially the same procedure can be adopted in Dutch, producing the two variants exemplified in (47) and (48), depending on whether object scrambling applies:

(47) (Ik denk dat vliegen veilig is) omdat COMPUTERS altijd moderne vliegtuigen besturen.
      (I think that flying safe is) because COMPUTERS always modern planes route.

(48) ??(Ik denk dat vliegen veilig is) omdat COMPUTERS moderne vliegtuigen altijd besturen.
      (I think that flying safe is) because COMPUTERS modern planes always route.

If object scrambling corresponds to a defocusing operation (as we want to claim), the prediction is that it should not apply in structures such as (36'). The reason is that assignment of focal stress to the subject *computers* involves the adoption of a marked "prosodic" strategy, essentially involving deaccenting of the lexical material following *computers*. In other words, according to Reinhart's analysis, the only possible trigger for scrambling in (48) is the requirement that the object be displaced for the verb to be assigned main stress and focus: however, main stress/focus is independently assigned to the subject (via a marked prosodic procedure), to the effect that there is in fact no trigger for scrambling. In this way, we can easily explain why (48), involving scrambling, is rather more degraded than (47), where scrambling has not taken place.

Chierchia's theory makes entirely different predictions. If object scrambling is triggered by the requirement that the object vacate the c-command domain of the frequency adverb every time the object must be mapped into the restrictive clause, the object is expected to scramble in contexts such as (36') under the interpretation roughly expressed in (38), quite independently of the distribution of focus. The expectation is clearly not fulfilled, given the better status of (47) with respect to (48). Of course, one might propose some weaker version of Chierchia's splitting algorithm, by assuming that adjunction may apply covertly also in Dutch. However, this would yield a considerable empirical loss since the fact that the splitting applies overtly in certain languages has generally been viewed as the main piece of empirical evidence in favour of Chierchia's (and Diesing's) version of the clause-splitting algorithm. More important, weakening the algorithm would still not allow us to capture the important correlation that seems to exist between the application of object scrambling and the distribution of focus. What we have proposed is that scrambling is only *indirectly* relevant for the application of the splitting algorithm, in the sense that it represents a focus-driven operation and focus *is* relevant for the correct application of the splitting algorithm. Summarising, we have claimed that the approach to clause splitting developed here makes more accurate predictions than competing proposals with respect to a well-defined class of object-scrambling phenomena. On the other hand, our analysis supports the view of scrambling of generic objects as a defocusing operation independently advocated in Reinhart (1995).

5. Conclusions

In this chapter we have examined some issues concerning the interaction between aspect and temporal adverbials, trying to show how the position of locating temporal adverbs affects interpretation. The picture that emerges appears to confirm the validity of a research program according to which the operations performed in overt syntax have an essentially morphological trigger—that is, checking of features realised in designated syntactic positions and possibly encoding specific semantic instructions used for the mapping to logical representations at the interface with the system of interpretation (cf. Chomsky 1995). On the other hand, adverbial quantification is arguably amenable to a more compositional mapping between syntactic and semantic representations than it is usually assumed. In fact, we have argued that *both* arguments of a frequency adverb are represented in overt syntax, under the hypothesis that the restrictive clause is uniformly provided by the (copy of the) constituent that has been displaced to the aspectual projection before the syntactic representation is projected into a phonetic one. The clause-splitting algorithm we have argued for differs significantly from some of the solutions to the *separation problem* that are found in the literature since it is crucially based on the interpretation of aspectual morphology as involving some form of lexical quantification, in the sense of Partee (1995). The Davidsonian insights about the pervasiveness of the quantification over events in natural language have been adopted and extended to quantification over times. Surprising and deep analogies between the nominal and the temporal domain have emerged, strongly suggesting that the extension of the domain of quantification to events and times does not simply reflect an arbitrary interpretive choice but also has deep roots in the form of the syntactic component and in the nature of the feature system encoded in syntax. By taking aspect and quantification over times into account, it becomes possible to reduce the role of adjunction within the syntax of adverbial modification and to look at the traditional dichotomy between argument and adjuncts from an entirely new perspective.

Notes

1. Cf. especially Larson (1988), Stowell (1996), and Giorgi and Pianesi (1997).

2. Following Rooth (1995), we assume that the *association-with-focus* procedure works in the following way. A Q-adverb denotes a relation between sets of times. The second argument of the Q-adverb (nuclear scope) is provided by the whole sentence the Q-adverb combines with (this sentence is interpreted as a *temporal abstract*—that is, a set of times). The first argument of a Q-adverb coincides with the *presupposition set* associated with the sentence that combines with the Q-adverb. Informally, the presupposition set associated with a proposition A consists of the times referred to by the proposition A' such that $A = A'$ except for the fact that the focused constituent in A has been replaced by an existentially quantified variable in A'. Given a sentence such as (a), the focus procedure derives the following two arguments for the relation expressed by the Q-adverb *always*:

(a)   [$_F$ Mary] always takes John to the movies.
      Second argument: λt(Mary takes John to the movies (t))
      First argument: $\lambda t(\exists x$ (x takes John to the movies (t)))

3. Surface structure does not need to be a formal level of syntactic representation. We assume that a syntactic derivation $\mathcal{D}$ involves a series of derivational steps $d_1 \ldots d_n$ and that there is a k, $1 \leq k \leq n$, such that d_k gets projected into a phonetic representation, PF (cf. Chomsky 1995). We contend that the syntactic information that is relevant for the projection of a syntactic representation into the tripartite quantificational structure that expresses the GQ interpretation of the Q-adverb is already available at the derivational step d_k. Of course, the syntactic representation at d_k may be considerably richer than is made visible by the phonetic realisation of part of the syntactic material present at d_k. For example, certain instances of movement may be difficult to detect because one of the two copies created by movement is uniformly deleted at PF and/or other instances of movement have applied to the material contained in one of the copies. The syntactic input to the mapping into tripartite structures is abstract in the sense that this input is more complex than it appears at the surface structure but not in the sense that it involves abstract operations that do not feed PF—that is, covert movement is irrelevant.

4. Cf. Partee (1995) and the discussion below (section 3).

5. Cf. also note 2.

6. Notice that it would not be correct to assume that the lexical information expressed by the temporal argument simply *locates* the event on the time axis. In fact, fixing the location of the event on the time axis is often the result of the convergence of lexical and contextual information and can even be forbidden in the case of perfect tenses (the English present perfect, for instance, is hardly compatible with localising adverbials such as *yesterday* or *at four o'clock*, an issue that is often referred to, in the literature, as the *present perfect puzzle*).

7. As brought to our attention by F. Pianesi, the actual interpretation of context-dependent calendar expressions is clearly sensitive to the internal syntax of these expressions. In Italian, for instance, a temporal adverbial such as *on Sunday* can be realised as the bare form *Sunday* in perfective contexts such as (a)—where it refers to a particular contextually relevant Sunday—but requires a determiner/preposition in habitual contexts such as (b)—where it refers to a whole set of times for which the property *Sunday* holds:

(a)   Giorgio è partito domenica.
      Giorgio left-PAST-PERF Sunday.

(b)   Giorgio partiva (sempre) *(di/la) domenica.
      Giorgio left-PAST-IMP (of/the) Sunday.

8. More exactly, we think that a compositional semantic input for the mapping into tripartite structures can be obtained without resorting to covert movement. This entails that all the relevant information is already contained in the abstract syntactic representation that corresponds to surface structure; cf. also note 3.

9. For a general discussion of the properties of the implicit *Gen* operator, cf. especially the introduction to genericity in Carlson and Pelletier (1995).

10. Cf. Chierchia (1995a, 1995b).

11. See Delfitto (1997, 1998) for a detailed criticism of the quantificational approach to genericity.

12. For an overview of the syntactic issues around adverb preposing, cf. Cinque (1990: 86-94).

13. The general observation to be made is that neither Rooth's focus algorithm nor the hypothesis that the restriction is provided by the syntactic constituent interpreted as topic leads to adequate empirical predictions for the cases of adverb preposing. The dislocated adverb uniformly counts as topic in (16) and (20). However, it corresponds to the restriction of the tripartite structure only in (16), whereas (20) requires additional material to be mapped into the restrictive clause. We conclude that the separation algorithm cannot be exclusively based on the notions of *focus* and *topic* since other factors—for example, the semantic category of the preposed adverbial—apparently play a crucial role.

14. The deterministic nature of the mapping associated with (25) emerges more clearly when we consider minimal pairs, such as the one instantiated below:

(a)   Nel 1975, Giorgio faceva colazione ogni domenica.
      In 1975, Giorgio had breakfast every Sunday.

(b)   Nel 1975, Giorgio faceva sempre colazione di domenica.
      In 1975, Giorgio always had breakfast on Sunday.

Of the two logically conceivable interpretations of (a) and (b)—that is, "All days in which Giorgio had breakfast were Sundays (= Giorgio had breakfast only on Sundays)" and "Giorgio had breakfast on all Sundays"—only the former can be expressed by (b), whereas (a) can express only the latter.

15. However, there are various proposals in the literature that passive morphology should be analysed exactly along these lines; cf. Partee (1995).

16. Technically, we can assume that the possibility that features of the temporal argument are phonetically realised on the verb is part of the abstract mechanism of thematic affinity, which creates a formal dependency between the verb and its temporal argument.

17. The mapping algorithm applies *modulo* reconstruction—that is, the activation of phonologically unrealised copies to neutralise the effects of syntactic displacement.

18. It is possible that the prohibition on readings that have only the preposed nontemporal adverb in the restriction is less absolute than we have suggested, in view of examples such as (a):

(a)   Con questo pugnale, il sacerdote Azteco eseguiva (sempre) i sacrifici.
      With this dagger, the Aztec priest (always) performed sacrifices.

It seems that (a) refers to an exclusive use of the dagger—that is, it can be interpreted as roughly stating that "every event *e* such that this dagger was used in *e*, was a sacrificial event in which the Aztec priest was involved as agent". This reading seems to correspond to a tripartite structure in which the restriction is exclusively constituted by the preposed adverb. If this is correct, it would entail that the hypothesis according to which constituents marked as topics are not computed by the focus procedure might be too strong. We should rather assume that the focus procedure applies to the whole VP in Spec,AspP, including the constituent interpreted as topic. Conflicting interpretive requirements would still be avoided since topics are generally realised in adjoined or specifier positions, which are invisible for the unmarked stress assignment procedure (Zubizarreta 1994) and cannot therefore be interpreted as members of the focus set associated with the VP in Spec,AspP. This modification would not essentially alter our basic proposal. The point would still be that preposed temporal adverbs are generally identified with the restrictive clause, a situation that is rather exceptional for other preposed adverbials. This asymmetry is not accounted for under versions of the mapping algorithm in which the restriction is simply identified with the dislocated constituent, whereas it naturally follows from the hypothesis that the association-with-focus procedure applies only in cases of VP displacement to Spec,AspP—that is, in cases that involve preposing of a nontemporal adverbial.

19. We are assuming that linguistic elements that are underspecified for a quantificational feature are able to inherit the relevant specification if they are realised in the c-command domain of a scope-taking element that is either positively or negatively specified for the quantificational feature.

20. An important question that arises (and that we will not address here) concerns the role of the imperfective morphology in structures such as (25). Since the mapping into tripartite structures is not regulated by aspectual morphology in structures in which the restriction is provided by an NP complement of D, one might expect imperfective marking to be ruled out in these cases, contrary to the facts. We believe that the answer to this question consists in the hypothesis that imperfectively marked predicates may involve the realisation of more than one interpretable feature. The presence of imperfective marking in (25) can thus be assumed to correspond to the realisation of some interpretable feature distinct from *quant*. See Delfitto (1997) for some hypotheses concerning the status of this feature, to be linked to the *predicational* status of habituals as involving the ascription of a property to an individual.

21. It is worth noticing that the solution to the "separation problem" proposed in this chapter might be understood as suggesting that the "separation" into tripartite structures is *always* syntactically represented. The cases in which the Q-adverb does not express a

sentence-internal relation (i.e., the material contained in the restriction is mainly provided by contextual information) might correspond to structures in which there is a phonetically unrealised *when* clause. The fact that the lexical content of the *when* clause has to be recovered from context does not exclude compositionality—that is, movement of the empty *when* clause through the Asp projection. We leave a more detailed discussion of this point to a future occasion.

22. It should be emphasised that Chierchia empirically motivates his proposal concerning the splitting algorithm with data on the distribution of German bare plurals with respect to the VP adverb *ja doch*, without extending his hypothesis to the interpretation of object scrambling. These data (originally discussed in Diesing 1992) are purported to show that subject bare plurals are obligatorily projected into the restriction when they occur to the left of the VP adverb, as in (a):

(a)   Weil Haifische ja doch sichtbar sind.
      . . . Since (in general) sharks are (indeed) visible.

(b)   Weil ja doch Haifische sichtbar sind.
      . . . Since there are (indeed) sharks visible.

Our discussion of object scrambling intends to show that the data on the interpretation of subject bare plurals cannot be used to argue for the strong hypothesis that sentence partitioning in Dutch is generally determined by the relative position of indefinite arguments and frequency adverbs in overt syntax.

References

Barwise, J., and R. Cooper, 1981. Generalised Quantifiers and Natural language. In *Linguistics and Philosophy* 4: 159–219.

Bertinetto, P. M., 1986. *Tempo, Aspetto e Azione nel verbo italiano. Il sistema dell'indicativo.* Accademia della Crusca, Firenze.

Bertinetto, P. M., 1997. *Il dominio tempo-aspettuale. Demarcazioni, intersezioni, contrasti.* Rosenberg & Sellier, Torino

Bonomi, A., 1995. Aspect and Quantification. In P. M. Bertinetto, V. Bianchi, J. Higginbotham, and M. Squartini (eds.), *Temporal Reference, Aspect and Actionality. Volume 1: Semantic and Syntactic Perspectives*, 93–110. Rosenberg & Sellier, Torino.

Carlson, G. N. and F. J. Pelletier, 1995. *The Generic Book.* University of Chicago Press, Chicago.

Chierchia, G., 1995a. Individual-level Predicates as Inherent Generic. In G. N. Carlson and F. J. Pelletier (eds.), *The Generic Book*, 176–223. University of Chicago Press, Chicago.

Chierchia, G., 1995b. A Note on the Contrast between Individual Level vs. Stage Level Predicates in German. In P. M. Bertinetto, V. Bianchi, J. Higginbotham, and M. Squartini (eds.), *Temporal Reference, Aspect and Actionality. Volume 1: Semantic and Syntactic Perspectives*, 111–123. Rosenberg & Sellier, Torino

Chomsky, N., 1995. *The Minimalist Program.* MIT Press, Cambridge (Mass.).

Cinque, G., 1990. *Types of A'-dependencies.* MIT Press, Cambridge (Mass.).

Davidson, D., 1967. The Logical Form of Action Sentences. In N. Rescher (ed.), *The Logic of Decision and Action*, 81–95. University of Pittsburgh Press, Pittsburgh. Reprinted in Davidson, D., 1980. *Essays on Actions and Events*, 105–123. Clarendon Press, Oxford

Delfitto, D., 1997. Aspect, Genericity and Bare Plurals. *OTS Working Papers*. Utrecht University, Utrecht.

Delfitto, D., 1998. On the Morphosyntactic Roots of Genericity. In *The Proceedings of the KNAW Colloquium on "Interface Strategies"*, Amsterdam, September 24–26, 1997.

Delfitto, D., and P. M. Bertinetto, 1995. A Case Study in the Interaction of Aspect and Actionality: The Imperfect in Italian. In P. M. Bertinetto, V. Bianchi, J. Higginbotham, and M. Squartini (eds.), *Temporal Reference, Aspect and Actionality. Volume 1: Semantic and Syntactic Perspectives*, 125–142. Rosenberg & Sellier, Torino.

de Hoop, H., 1992. *Case Configuration and NP Interpretation*. Ph.D. dissertation, Rijksuniversiteit Groningen.

de Swart, H., 1991. *Adverbs of Quantification: A Generalised Quantifier Approach*. Ph.D. dissertation, Rijksuniversiteit Groningen.

Diesing, M., 1992. *Indefinites*. MIT Press, Cambridge (Mass.).

Evans, N., 1995. A-quantifiers and Scope in Mayali. In E. Bach, E. Jelinek, A. Kratzer, and B. H. Partee (eds.), *Quantification in Natural Language*, 207–270. Kluwer Academic Publishers, Dordrecht.

Giorgi, A., and F. Pianesi, 1997. *Tense and Aspect*. Oxford University Press, New York and Oxford.

Gussenhoven, C., 1984. *On the Grammar and Semantics of Sentence Accents in Dutch*. Foris, Dordrecht.

Hale, K., 1989. Warlpiri Categories. Talk in Quantification Lecture Series. Linguistic Institute, Tucson.

Heim, I., 1982. *The Semantics of Definite and Indefinite Noun Phrases*. Ph.D. dissertation, University of Massachusetts, Amherst.

Kamp, H., and U. Reyle, 1993. *From Discourse to Logic*. Kluwer, Dordrecht.

Kearns, K. S., 1991. *The Semantics of the English Progressive*. Ph.D. dissertation, MIT, Cambridge (Mass.).

Klima, E. S., and U. Bellugi, 1979. *The Signs of Language*. Harvard University Press, Cambridge (Mass.).

Krifka, M., 1992. A Framework for Focus-sensitive Quantification. In C. Barker and D. Dowty (eds.), *Proceedings of the Second Conference on Semantics and Linguistic Analysis*, 215–236. Ohio State University, Columbus (Ohio).

Larson, R., 1988. On the Double Object Construction. In *Linguistic Inquiry* 19: 335–391.

Lewis, D., 1975. Adverbs of Quantification. In E. L. Keenan (ed.), *Formal Semantics of Natural Language*, 3–15. Cambridge University Press, Cambridge.

Longobardi, G., 1994. Reference and Proper Names. In *Linguistic Inquiry* 25: 609–666.

Mostowski, A., 1957. On a Generalisation of Quantifiers. In *Fundamenta Mathematicae* 44: 12–36.

Parsons, T., 1990. *Events in the Semantics of English: A Study in Subatomic Semantics*. MIT Press, Cambridge (Mass.).

Partee, B. H., 1995. Quantificational Structures and Compositionality. In E. Bach, E. Jelinek, A. Kratzer, and B. H. Partee (eds.), *Quantification in Natural Language*, 541–601. Kluwer Academic Publishers, Dordrecht.

Pesestky, D., 1995. *Zero Syntax*. MIT Press, Cambridge (Mass.).

Petronio, K., 1995. Bare Noun Phrases, Verbs and Quantification in ASL. In E. Bach, E. Jelinek, A. Kratzer, and B. H. Partee (eds.), *Quantification in Natural Language*, 603–618. Kluwer Academic Publishers, Dordrecht.

Reichenbach, H., 1947. *Elements of Symbolic Logic*. Macmillan, New York.

Reinhart, T., 1995. Interface Strategies. *OTS Working Papers*. Utrecht University, Utrecht.

Rooth, M., 1985. *Association with Focus*. Ph.D. dissertation, University of Massachusetts, Amherst.

Rooth, M., 1995. Indefinites, Adverbs of Quantification, and Focus Semantics. In G. N. Carlson and F. J. Pelletier, *The Generic Book*, 265–299. University of Chicago Press, Chicago.

Schein, B., 1993. *Plurals and Events*. MIT Press, Cambridge (Mass.).

Schoorlemmer, M., 1995. *Participial Passive and Aspect in Russian*. Ph.D. dissertation, Utrecht Institute of Linguistics OTS, Utrecht.

Stowell, T., 1996. The Phrase Structure of Tense. In J. Roorick and L. Zaring (eds.), *Phrase Structure and the Lexicon*, 277–291. Kluwer Academic Publishers, Dordrecht.

Zagona, K., 1995. Temporal Argument Structure: Configurational Elements of Construal. In P. M. Bertinetto, V. Bianchi, J. Higginbotham, and M. Squartini (eds.), *Temporal Reference, Aspect and Actionality. Volume 1: Semantic and Syntactic Perspectives*, 397–410. Rosenberg & Sellier, Torino

Zubizarreta, M. L., 1994. Word Order Prosody and Focus. Unpublished ms., University of Southern California, Los Angeles.

10

Aspect, Adverbs, and Events
Habituality vs. Perfectivity

Alessandro Lenci and Pier Marco Bertinetto

1. Introduction

Adverbial quantification is a widely debated topic in model-theoretic semantics. Its relevance depends not only on the fact that it deals with an important class of lexical items but also on its being part of the broader field that Partee (1995) refers to as *A-quantification*, where 'A' is a mnemonic for adverbs, auxiliaries, affixes, and argument-structure adjusters. This label intends to subsume a (possibly) nonhomogeneous set of phenomena, which share the relevant feature of introducing the quantificational structure of sentences in a more "constructional" way than determiners do. On the other hand, aspect is a fundamental linguistic category that covers the different modalities in which the development of events can be represented. The basic opposition between perfective and imperfective aspect finds a precise morphological realisation in many languages, and notwithstanding the difficulty of eliminating much of the vagueness still present in their use, these categories correspond to really different semantic values.

Aspect and quantification are clearly related and interacting phenomena; since it is possible to give a quantificational interpretation of aspectual values, we can look at aspect as one of the ways in which the quantificational force of sentences is established. Thus, it seems straightforward to include aspect in the class of A-quantification. But then an interesting question arises concerning the way morphologically realised aspectual features are related to other types of constructional quantification, like the adverbial one. This is our main concern in this chapter, and we tackle it by discussing two facets of the general problem. More precisely we (a) investigate the way in which explicit quantificational adverbs interact with aspectual values and (b) examine whether one of these two features could (or should) be reduced to the other.

In the next section we mainly deal with point (a). However, a survey of the data also brings evidence supporting a negative answer to the question concerning point (b). Section 3 is devoted to an outline of a formal analysis of aspectual oppositions, which should be able to explain the distribution of data that we illustrate. Our leading hypothesis is that the habitual imperfective aspect introduces a modal generic quantifier, which eventually co-occurs with overt quantificational adverbs. This allows us to capture the difference between perfective and imperfective sentences even when they contain the same explicit adverbials. In section 4, we try to give a principled explanation of a largely debated phenomenon—namely, the tendential incompatibility of imperfective habitual aspect with iterative adverbs.

2. Quantificational Adverbs and Aspect

In de Swart (1993), quantificational adverbs like *spesso* ('often'), *sempre* ('always'), *due volte al giorno* ('twice a day'), and so on, are called *frequency adverbs*, as opposed to *due volte* ('twice'), *molte volte* ('many times'), and *poche volte* ('few times'), which are referred to as *iterative adverbs*.[1] According to de Swart, iterative adverbs "count events as individual entities and specify the absolute cardinality of a set of situations" (p. 316). In contrast, frequency adverbs never express absolute quantities of situations but rather relative ones. De Swart also distinguishes two further readings of frequency adverbs, a *relational reading* and a *pure frequency reading*, which can be illustrated by (1):

(1)   Gianni va spesso al mare con Anna.
         John often goes to the beach with Ann.

In the relational reading, the quantificational adverb simply establishes a proportion between two sets of events or situations, which are identified either by means of the material inside the sentence or with the help of external material. For instance, in (1) we have a set A of events of going to the beach by John and a set B of events of going to the beach by John with Ann. The relational reading simply compares the extension of the intersection of A and B with the cardinality of A itself, and the quantifier specifies the ratio of this comparison that makes the sentence true. Thus (1) is roughly equivalent to saying that most of the situations in which John goes to the beach are situations in which he goes there with Ann. On the contrary, the pure frequency reading of (1) does not establish any proportion between sets of situations, and consequently there is no partition of the material inside the sentence: the quantifier simply refers to the totality of events of going to the beach by John with Mary and specifies that they have happened with a high frequency. The notion of frequency is then characterised as the expression of the number of occurrences of an event per time unit.

De Swart also claims that frequency adverbs can be distinguished according to whether they allow for just one interpretation or both. For instance, *sempre* ('always') and *il più delle volte* ('most of the times') have only a relational reading. Thus de Swart calls them *strong frequency adverbs* since they resemble strong nominal quantifiers like *ogni* ('every') which are intrinsically relational.

On the other hand, *spesso* ('often') and *raramente* ('rarely') are completely ambiguous between a relational reading and a pure frequency one; these quantifiers are referred to as *weak frequency adverbs*.

To sum up, de Swart distinguishes three notional features that define different classes of adverbs: iteration, frequency, and relationality. Concerning frequency, she claims that it is expressed both by weak frequency adverbs, when they are interpreted nonrelationally, and by adverbs like *due volte al giorno* ('twice a day') and *settimanalmente* ('weekly'), the only difference being that the latter type explicitly specifies the time unit that is necessary to compute the frequency of an event.[2]

2.1. Iteratives

Many scholars have noticed that habitual imperfective sentences are incompatible with iterative adverbs:

(2)   a.   *Gianni andava al mare con Maria due volte.
            John went-IMP to the beach with Mary twice.

       b.   *Gianni vedeva *Blade Runner* molte volte.
            John watched-IMP *Blade Runner* many times.

On the contrary, perfective tenses can occur freely with iterative adverbs:

(3)   a.   Gianni è andato al mare con Maria due volte.
            John has gone to the beach with Mary twice.

       b.   Gianni ha visto *Blade Runner* molte volte.
            John has watched *Blade Runner* many times.

Many hypotheses have been suggested to explain these data: Hoepelman and Rohrer (1980) claim that the ungrammaticality of (2) is to be connected with the unbounded, *masslike* nature of the imperfective aspect, in opposition to the bounded, *countlike* nature of perfective one. As mass nouns cannot occur with cardinal determiners (unless with a shift in their meaning), similarly habitual imperfective sentences cannot contain iterative adverbs, whose function is to express a bounded quantity of events (cf. Kleiber 1987). Bertinetto (1986) connects this restriction with the inherent indeterminacy that characterises the imperfective aspect; in other words, habitual sentences would represent the number of iterations of an event as tendentially indeterminate.[3]

De Swart (1993) proposes a formal implementation of Hoepelman and Rohrer's hypothesis. She gives a procedural interpretation of quantificational adverbs in terms of semantic automata, extending the analysis of nominal quantifiers given in van Benthem (1987). Specifically, de Swart interprets iterative adverbs as finite state automata and explains the ungrammaticality of (2) by stating that finite state automata have to reach a definite evaluation point, which is incompatible with the imperfective aspect, that refers to "an open, potentially growing domain" (p. 328).

This line of analysis is grounded on the idea that there is a total incompatibility between the notional categories of unboundedness, expressed by the imperfective aspect, and cardinality, expressed by iterative adverbs. However, this assumption runs up against some problems. First, notwithstanding the data in (2), the sentences in (4) and (5) are perfectly acceptable:

(4)   Il mio postino suona due volte.
         My postman rings twice.

(5)   a. Un film interessante, Gianni lo vedeva due volte.
          An interesting movie, John watched-IMP it twice.

       b. Un uomo intelligente non commette lo stesso errore più volte.
          An intelligent man does not commit the same error several times.

Both these sentences are generic or habitual and contain a (present or past) imperfective tense. If there were an absolute incompatibility between imperfectivity and iteratives, these data could not be explained. Second, iterative adverbs are acceptable in imperfective sentences with a temporal adverb or clause:

(6)   a. In quel periodo, la domenica, Gianni mi telefonava tre volte.
          In that period, on Sundays, John called-IMP me three times.

       b. In quel periodo, quando veniva in città, Gianni mi telefonava tre volte.
          In that period, when he came-IMP downtown, John called-IMP me three times.

The sentences in (5) and (6) show that there might be some precise structural restrictions governing the compatibility of iterative adverbs with imperfective sentences. We return to these problems in section 4.

2.2. Relational Adverbs

The precise semantic analysis of habitual sentences remains an open problem in contemporary linguistic research. All the different formal approaches to genericity and habituality share the idea that explaining these phenomena requires assuming the existence of a special *generic* operator. However, whereas in the first proposals (cf. Carlson 1977) this operator was interpreted as a monadic sort-shifting function over predicates, it is now widely accepted that habituality is rather a quantificational phenomenon and that the generic operator is actually a particular kind of adverbial quantifier (Krifka 1988; Schubert and Pelletier 1989; Krifka et al. 1995). According to this idea, nomic sentences always contain a quantificational adverb, either overtly or covertly.[4] In the latter case, the logical representation of the sentence is equipped with a so-called generic quantifier *Gn*, whose meaning is stated as being roughly equivalent to *typically, in general*, and so forth. Thus, nomic sentences are given the following general logical structure:

(7) $Q[x_1,\ldots,x_i; y_1,\ldots,y_j]$ [Restrictor $(x_1,\ldots,x_i)$; Matrix $(x_1,\ldots,x_i, y_1,\ldots,y_j)$].

This structure involves a segmentation of the lexical material of the sentence, which must partly be assigned to the restrictive clause and partly to the matrix one.

In this section, we discuss the relationship between habituality and overt quantificational expressions. Adverbs like *generally* or *typically* (conventionally, we call them *generic* adverbs) are the best candidates to make explicit the notion of habituality; thus, it is reasonable to regard them as the spelling out of the generic operator. This move seems to be supported by data from English, which lacks a tense like the imperfect, which is intrinsically able to express habits in the past:

(8)   John walked to school.

As Krifka et al. (1995) claim, this sentence is ambiguous between a habitual interpretation and a semelfactive-existential one. The former reading can be singled out by adding a suitable quantificational adverb like *generally*:

(9)   John generally walked to school.

These data suggest the following picture: (8) is structurally ambiguous between a reading containing the generic operator and a reading with an existential quantifier. Such an ambiguity is part of the semantic potential of the simple past. Moreover, the presence of an explicit operator, as in (9), helps to select the proper interpretation—that is, the one structurally similar to (7).

However, in Italian (and more generally in Romance) the question is somewhat different. In fact, compare the following sentences:

(10)   a.   In quel periodo, Gianni generalmente/di solito si svegliava alle 6.
             In that period, John generally/usually woke-IMP up at 6 o'clock.

        b.   ?? In quel periodo, Gianni generalmente/di solito si è svegliato alle 6.
             In that period, John generally/usually woke up at 6 o'clock.

The first sentence contains the *imperfect* and has a habitual interpretation, which in this case is also made explicit by the adverbs; if we leave out the quantificational adverbs, the sentence has only a habitual interpretation. In contrast, the second sentence contains a perfective tense like the simple past, and it is somehow anomalous with a generic adverb. If we drop the quantifier, the sentence is correct, but only in a semelfactive reading. These data reveal two facts that distinguish Italian from English. First, the imperfect univocally expresses habituality (in the appropriate contexts), and this feature opposes it to the simple past. Second, the role of explicit generic adverbs must be stated more carefully.

As far as the second point is concerned, consistently with the idea that expressions like *generally* contain some sort of modality, we could take them as modal operators similar to items like *possibly* or *necessarily*.[5] Compositionally, this would imply assuming that *generally* takes as input a semelfactive sentence and turns it into a habitual one, similarly to the case of standard modal operators, that apply to nonmodal sentences and modalise them. But then the prediction would be that applying such adverbs to a perfective sentence would produce a habitual reading. The problem is that this prediction is not borne out because, as (10b) reveals, such a move results in an anomalous sentence.

A plausible conclusion seems to be that in a language like Italian, which has a specialised aspectual device to express habituality as part of the domain of imperfectivity, the aspectual dimension cannot be overruled by overt adverbial expressions. In other words, the intrinsic nature of perfective tenses cannot be turned into habituality by quantificational adverbs, even by those like *generally* that seem more suitable to perform this operation. Rather, to express habituality a different aspectual value must be chosen—namely, the imperfective one. This also suggests a particular relationship between habituality and overt generic adverbs, at least for Italian. If a sentence is habitual, its meaning can be made more explicit by means of these adverbs, but if a sentence does not aspectually express habituality, such a reading cannot be produced by the mere use of the given adverbs. Therefore, we can take generic adverbs as being able to make explicit the semantics of habitual sentences, but habituality cannot be obtained by simply juxtaposing these adverbs to any sentence.

Another related problem concerns the common assumption that the operator *Gn* in the logical form of habitual sentences is a *default* quantifier, in the sense that it appears in the representation of a sentence unless other explicit quantificational adverbs are present. Compare, then, the following examples:

(11)   a.   Gianni usciva con Maria.
            John went-IMP out with Mary.

       b.   Gianni usciva raramente con Maria.
            John rarely went-IMP out with Mary.

       c.   Gianni è uscito raramente con Maria.
            John has rarely gone out with Mary.

Although both (11a–b) are imperfective and express habits, nevertheless they are not equivalent.[6] If *Gn* is simply a default type of quantificational adverb, which appears in the logical form unless an overt adverb is specified, (11a) and (11b) come to have exactly the same logical structure, the only difference being that in the case of (11b) *rarely* replaces *Gn*. The interesting fact is that (11c) also contains an explicit quantifier (the same as in the former sentence), which gives rise to a tripartite structure. Therefore, (11b) and (11c) would also end up having the same logical form and, unless we want to say that *rarely* is actually homophonous between two different operators, the same truth conditions, too. The problem is that these two sentences are not equivalent; although they both express a relation between sets of events, it is clear that the imperfective sentence is a real nomic statement, whereas the perfective one simply expresses a factual, accidental statement.

Moreover, the alleged identification between (11b) and (11c) shows a conflict between some reasonable assumptions about the aspectual system that are considered to be uncontroversial. First, typological studies usually describe habituality as a subtype of imperfectivity, (cf. Comrie 1976; Bertinetto 1986); and there are good reasons to state this fact as a kind of semantic universal. Second, adverbial quantification is an essential ingredient for habituality, not only because habitual sentences often contain overt quantificational structures, but also because the truth conditions of these sentences seem to require the recovering of such a structure, even when there is not an overt one. Third, quantificational adverbs often occur in perfective sentences, too. Given these facts, if the semantic contribution of habitual imperfective sentences simply consisted of an adverbial-like quantification over events, since the sentence in (11c) also contains the same kind of quantifier as (11b), then it might be straightforward to include the perfective sentence in the domain of habituality. However, the consequence of this solution is that we would lose the correlation between habituality and imperfectivity. In fact, if sentences like (11c), which contain a perfective tense, were described as habituals, this would mean that habituality could be expressed either with an imperfective tense or with a perfective one. Consequently, habituality could no longer be univocally associated with imperfectivity. This seems to suggest that the hypothesis of characterising the semantic contribution of the habitual imperfective aspect as simply consisting of the introduction of an adverbial tripartite structure, plus a default value for the operator, is too weak. In fact, this hypothesis is not able to capture a really specific feature of habituality, to distinguish it from other related, yet different, types of event quantification, such as the one that can be expressed by perfective sentences also.

Notice that in certain circumstances perfective sentences without overt quantificational adverbs may express the iteration of an event, but they still differ from imperfective habitual ones. Take, for instance, the following minimal pair:

(12) a. Lo scorso anno, Gianni incontrava Maria all'Università.
          Last year, John met-IMP Mary at the University.

      b. Lo scorso anno, Gianni ha incontrato Maria all'Università.
          Last year, John met Mary at the University.

The latter sentence does not exclude the fact that John met Mary several times during the time period specified by the temporal adverb, and the iterative interpretation may be the favoured one in certain contexts. However, this is a kind of factual statement, and the event does not have any normative character but rather one as a matter of fact. On the other hand, in (12a) the imperfective tense represents the meeting of Mary by John as a truly regular event. This means that multiple occurrences of an event do not automatically turn it into a habit; only imperfective sentences are actually able to express habituality.

The different behaviour of imperfective and perfective sentences with quantificational adverbs is also shown by the constraints on the distribution of arbitrary null objects in Italian. Since Rizzi (1986), it is well known that null objects in Italian receive an arbitrary (generic) interpretation, which is responsible for the fact that they can occur only in habitual sentences, as the contrast between the following examples reveals:

(13)   a. In passato, la musica rendeva *proarb* felici.
           In past times, music made-IMP (people) happy.

       b. *In passato, la musica ha reso *proarb* felici.
           In past times, music made (people) happy.

If we adopt Rizzi's proposal to represent the null object as an empty pronominal—namely, *pro* with an arbitrary interpretation—it is clear that the perfective sentence is not able to license it for some reason. Moreover, the same contrast remains if we add an explicit quantificational adverb:

(14)   a. In passato, la musica rendeva spesso/generalmente/sempre *proarb* felici.
           In past times, music often/generally/always made-IMP (people) happy.

       b. *In passato, la musica ha reso spesso/generalmente/sempre *proarb* felici.
           In times past, music often/generally/always made (people) happy.

However, if the object is overt, the perfective sentence is correct:

(15)   In passato, la musica ci ha resi (spesso) felici.
           In times past, music (often) made us happy.

The plausible conclusion to be drawn is the following: whatever licensing factor is responsible for the arbitrary null object pronominal in Italian, it cannot be identified with any quantificational adverb but rather with the habitual imperfective morphology of the verb. Moreover, the semantics of habituality cannot reduce to a default quantifier that can be freely substituted with an overt one since overt quantifiers alone in perfective sentences are not able to license the object *proarb*.

Finally, temporal adverbs indicating a time frame or background for the main sentence have a different function in perfective and imperfective sentences:

(16)   a. Nel 1998, Gianni è andato spesso al cinema con Maria.
           In 1998, John often went to the cinema with Mary.

       b. Nel 1998, Gianni andava spesso al cinema con Maria.
           In 1998, John often went-IMP to the cinema with Mary.

In the perfective sentence, the temporal frame adjunct actually restricts the domain of the quantificational adverb to the events of going to the cinema that occurred in 1998, so that in most of the cases John was with Mary. In the imperfective habitual sentence, the role of the background expression is different: it says that in 1998 the generalisation that most of the events of John's going to the cinema were with Mary was true, without entailing that the quantification is restricted to the occurrences contained within the limits of 1998. The possibility is completely open that the same habit was already true in the years before and is possibly still true (the use of the past comes with an implicature that the generalisation does not hold anymore, but it is easy to verify that this is just a pragmatic, defeasible inference). This fact is also proven by the insertion of an adverb like *già* ('already'), which implies that the series of events went on beyond the right boundary of the interval specified by the background clause:

(17) a. *Nel 1998, Gianni è già andato spesso al cinema con Maria.
          In 1998, John already-often went to the cinema with Mary.

      b. Nel 1998, Gianni andava già spesso al cinema con Maria.
          In 1998, John already-often went-IMP to the cinema with Mary.

All these facts imply that the nomic nature of a sentence does not depend on the presence of a relational quantificational adverb but rather on its being imperfective. We can then state the following tentative generalisation: in a language like Italian, overt adverbs are neither a necessary nor a sufficient condition for habituality. They are not necessary because the imperfect can be interpreted habitually even without any overt quantificational device; but they are also not sufficient because the presence of a quantificational adverb in a perfective, semelfactive sentence does not turn it into a nomic one. Moreover, there is a certain variation among the adverbs: those such as the generic ones that are semantically close to the interpretation of *Gn* are anomalous in perfective sentences (10), whereas strong frequency adverbs are acceptable, although they simply express a quantificational statement over a bounded set of events, rather than a truly nomic proposition (11).

3. A Model for Aspect

The domain of imperfectivity is usually assumed to be further distinguishable in the two subclasses of habitual and progressive aspects.[7] In Italian, the present and the imperfect are potentially ambiguous between these two interpretations, whereas in English the habitual aspect is typically realised with the simple present and with some defective past periphrases like *used to* and *would*; moreover, in both languages the progressive periphrasis is a specialised device to express progressivity. The semantic opposition between imperfectivity and perfectivity is normally characterised in terms of bounded vs. unbounded representations of events, as we have already reported in section 2.1. Notwithstanding the intuitive appeal of this solution, there are several problems with it. First, it is extremely difficult to detail the content of these features and to clearly state their semantics; second, the same notions of boundedness vs. unboundedness are often used for event classification, especially to capture the distinction between telic and atelic predicates. Thus, it might not be appropriate to use the same features to describe two related but nevertheless distinguished phenomena, like Aktionsart and aspect.

In model-theoretic semantics, semelfactive perfective sentences like (18a) and habitual imperfective sentences like (18b) are distinguished in terms of the type of quantification over events:

(18)   a.   Gianni è andato al mare con Maria.
            John has gone to the beach with Mary.

       b.   Gianni andava al mare con Maria.
            John went-IMP to the beach with Mary.

Starting from Davidson (1967), the idea that predicates carry an extra argument (usually called the E-argument), ranging over occasions or events, has become widely accepted. Another standard assumption is that the E-argument is existentially closed by default at some point during the derivation of the logical form. This closure is usually operated by a functional projection (tense or mood) dominating the VP.[8] In his discussion of the interaction between aspect and the interpretation of *when* clauses, Bonomi (1995) related the existential closure of the E-argument with a specific aspectual value—namely, the perfective one. The result is the semelfactive reading of sentences like (18a), which is assigned the following logical form:

(19) $\exists e(\text{go-to}(e) \wedge \text{theme}(\text{John}, e) \wedge \text{to}(\text{beach}, e) \wedge \text{with}(\text{Mary}, e))$.

By contrast, imperfective habitual sentences would contain a sort of quasi-universal quantification over events. Apart from the formal details, the core idea of Bonomi's proposal is that "aspect plays a systematic role in the determination of the relevant quantificational structures." (p. 99). Similarly, Delfitto and Bertinetto (1995) suggest that the essential feature of an imperfective tense like the Italian imperfect is to introduce a strong quantifier over times.

   In the following section, we extend and provide detail for the hypothesis that aspect is connected with particular types of quantification over events, and we try to suggest a general framework that will allow us to deal with the problems concerning the interaction of aspect and overt quantificational adverbs that we discussed in section 2.

3.1. Aspectual Operators

The proposal we want to outline here is that distinguishing perfective and habitual imperfective sentences only in terms of the default quantificational force assigned to the E-argument is not enough. The reason that this solution is inadequate comes from the data discussed in the previous section. In fact, such a hypothesis predicts that when the default value of the event quantifier is replaced by other quantificational adverbs, the difference between imperfective (habitual) and perfective sentences should disappear. The facts show that this prediction is not borne out, suggesting that aspectual values differ in at least another respect besides the type of quantification over the E-argument. Our amendment to the current view amounts to stating that the perfective and habitual imperfective aspects also differ because the former is typically intensional whereas the latter is typically extensional.

   Intensionality covers different phenomena. But there is a sense in which this term can be useful in describing the habitual imperfective aspect. The most salient feature of nomic sentences is that they express lawlike generalisations, which cannot be reduced to quantifications over specific and limited sets of objects and which show a sort of intensional behaviour.[9] This point was already convincingly defended in Dahl (1975:100), who argued that "in an accidental generalisation, we talk only about a set of actual cases, whereas nomic statements concern also possible, non-actual cases." In the rest of this section we argue that this opposition exactly corresponds to the one between perfective and imperfective sentences containing quantificational adverbs—that is, since they contain quantifiers, they both express generalisations, the difference being that perfective sentences express accidental ones and habitual imperfective sentences nomic ones. Finally, following Dahl and other scholars, we reserve the term *habitual* only for nomic generalisations about events.[10]

This aspectual difference also interacts with the semantics of nominal phrases. Dahl (1975) argues that whereas in (20a) the definite DP refers to the actual members of the club, in (20b) the bare plural does not refer only to the actual members of the golf club but also to the possible ones, and this would reveal the intensional character of generic sentences:

(20)   a.   The members of this club vote for the Democrats.
       b.   Members of this club vote for the Democrats.

In fact, the latter case allows us to make a prediction concerning the behaviour of future members of the same association. In Italian, it is well known that bare plurals cannot have a generic, universal interpretation. However, the aspectual shape of the sentence helps us to determine when a definite plural DP can also have a generic interpretation:

(21)   a.   Nel 1998, i membri di questo club raramente indossavano la cravatta.
            In 1998, the members of this club rarely wore-IMP a tie.

       b.   Nel 1998, i membri di questo club raramente hanno indossato la cravatta.
            In 1998, the members of this club rarely wore a tie.

In the perfective sentence, the subject DP can refer only to a specific group of individuals, either to those individuals that happened to be members of the club in 1998 (if the nominal is interpreted within the scope of the temporal adverb) or to the specific individuals that are the current members (if the nominal is interpreted externally to the adverb). Conversely, in the habitual sentence (21a), the subject DP also has an interpretation similar to an authentic generic bare plural in English, an interpretation that is instead excluded in the perfective case. The interesting fact is that in this interpretation, the generalisation is quite independent of which set was actually denoted by the DP in 1998, and more generally of any specific set of individuals. Rather, the sentence specifies that a general tendency, typical for whoever could possibly be a member of the club, was in force in 1998. Thus, given the minimal pair in (21), it seems that it is the imperfective aspect that makes available the intensional, classlike reading of the plural DP.

The same hypothesis can be used to explain the difference in acceptability between the following sentences:

(22)   a. ?*Nel 1998, gli abitanti di Pisa sono andati al mare una volta ogni dieci anni.
       In 1998, the inhabitants of Pisa went to the beach once every ten years.

       b. Nel 1998, gli abitanti di Pisa andavano al mare una volta ogni dieci anni.
       In 1998, the inhabitants of Pisa went to the beach once every ten years.

The first sentence is anomalous because there is a clash between the frequency adverb *una volta ogni dieci anni* ('once every ten years') and the perfective tense, which locates the event strictly within the time boundary of 1998. Conversely, the habitual sentence (22b) is perfectly acceptable under the reading that a certain nomic generalisation was true of the inhabitants of Pisa in 1998—that is, that they had the habit of going to the beach once every ten years. The generalisation represented by the habitual is thus not restricted to the time period indicated by the temporal adverb.

The intensional nature of habituality can be represented by interpreting the generic operator as a modal quantifier, along the lines of Kratzer (1981). This analysis of genericity dates back to Heim (1982) and, more recently, has been adopted by Condoravdi (1994) and Krifka et al. (1995). Modal operators, such as *must* and *can*, are defined within possible-world semantics along three parameters. First, these operators are distinguished according to the *modal relation* they express (e.g., necessity or possibility), which is represented in terms of different quantifications (e.g., universal or existential) over possible worlds. Second, there is a *modal base* (or *conversational background*) that is contextually determined and specifies the set of possible worlds quantified over by the modal operator. The modal base represents the set of presuppositions that constitutes the necessary background for the interpretation of the modal operator.[11] Kratzer defines different classes of interpretations for such expressions, depending on the assumptions contained inside the modal base. Following Stalnaker (1978), we represent each proposition as a set of possible worlds and the conversational background as the set of possible worlds compatible with the presuppositions assumed to be relevant for a certain modal interpretation. Third, there is an *ordering source* (also contextually determined) that gives us an ordering among possible worlds; this relation restricts the evaluation of modal sentences to worlds that are maximally normal—that is, that are most similar to the real world. Therefore, given two worlds w_i and w_j, $w_i \leq_w w_j$ is true iff w_i is at least as normal as w_j with respect to the actual world w. According to this definition of modality, the truth conditions of a nomic sentence like (23) can be stated informally as follows: the sentence is true in the actual world iff everything that is a man in the worlds of the modal base B_w is such that, in every world that is most normal according to the ordering source, it has two legs.

(23)   A man has two legs.

Since we restrict ourselves to most normal worlds, we exclude exceptional cases (e.g., the ones in which a man has lost his leg in a war). Similarly, this definition does not presuppose the existence of men because the actual world might not be included in B_w. Moreover, we quantify over *all* the most normal worlds, and thereby the operator has a necessity-like modal force. As for the choice of the modal base, since the sentence expresses a descriptive generalisation, we can assume that B_w contains the worlds in which the biological facts about men are identical to the ones of the actual world; similarly, the context will force the ordering source to express a kind of ideal situation, where no external intervention or casual modification has occurred.[12]

We have argued that habitual imperfective sentences express nomic generalisations, whose salient features can be suitably captured within an intensional analysis. We could then raise the question of whether it is possible to conceive of the whole realm of imperfectivity as altogether intensional. Of course, habituality is just a subtype of the imperfective aspect; but turning to the other possible uses of this aspect, we can see that if an intensional analysis is not the only possible solution, nevertheless it is surely apt to highlight some common features of imperfectivity in general. What about the progressive, for instance? Actually, the debate about its nature and semantics is still open, but some data seem to suggest that this aspectual value shows a behaviour that can also be described as intensional. Landman (1992) brings interesting evidence to support this view. Obviously, extensional models of progressivity, as well as of habituality, have been proposed and opposed to the intensional approach. However, other uses of the imperfective aspect, which do not fall within the major classes of progressive and habituality, seem to confirm the *modal* nature of this aspect, and some scholars have also claimed that imperfectivity is the realm of irreality.[13] Therefore, even though we commit ourselves to the weaker claim concerning the intensional nature of habituality, we believe that a stronger version of the statement is also plausible, suggesting that imperfectivity might be analysed as an intrinsically intensional phenomenon.[14]

In order to give a formal representation to the contribution of aspect to the semantics of sentences, we adopt a version of intentional logic (IL) as a representation language, and we assume models defined in the following way (see Chierchia 1995d):

(D.1) A model for IL is a tuple $M = \langle \langle D, \leq, \oplus \rangle, W, \leq_w, F \rangle$, where

    a. D is a multisorted domain of individuals, containing objects, events, and times; D_o, D_e, D_t are the proper subsets of D associated to the respective sorts; the extension of each of these sets is an algebra with the structure of a *join semilattice*, where $\leq$ is a partial order (*part of*) over $D_k \times D_k$ with $k \in \{o, e, t\}$, and $\oplus$ is a two-place operation on $D_k \times D_k$ (the join operation);

    b. W is a set of possible worlds;

    c. $\leq_w$ is an *ordering source* over the possible worlds;

    d. F is an interpretation function.

This kind of model allows us to refer to plural entities and groups of events as individuals, according to the classical analysis of Link (1983). Moreover, we assume the following definition of an *assignment* to variables:

(D.2)   An *assignment* is a function g from IL's variables into values of the appropriate type or sort, such that for any v_a, $g(v_a) \in D_a$, where a is a given type or sort.

To define the temporal extension of an event we borrow the notion of temporal trace τ from Krifka (1992): τ is a function from D_e to D_t, that maps an event to its *run time*. Formally, it is a homomorphism relative to the join operation:

(D.3) $\forall e, e_1 (\tau(e) \oplus \tau(e_1) = \tau(e \oplus e_1))$.

Again following Krifka, we assume that D_t contains a proper set of atomic times T_a, or instants (variables $t_1, \ldots, t_n, \ldots$ will range over instants); moreover we adopt a relation of precedence between instants $\leq_t$, which is a linear order for time points. Finally, we define the set of convex times or intervals in the standard way:

(D.4) $\forall t (\text{CONV}(t) \leftrightarrow \forall t_1, t_2, t_3 (t_1 \leq t \land t_2 \leq t \land t_1 \leq_t t_3 \leq_t t_2 \rightarrow t_3 \leq t))$.

We also adopt the convention that interval variables $i_1, \ldots, i_n \ldots$ will range onto elements of D_t, satisfying (D.4), and we augment IL with a special relation $\subseteq$ between events and intervals, which is interpreted in the following way:[15]

(24) $[\![e \subseteq i]\!]_{w,g} = 1$ iff $\tau(g(e)) \leq g(i)$.[16]

Chierchia (1992) develops a version of dynamic semantics in which sentences denote context change potentials.[17] This means that the semantic contribution of a sentence is not only to present a certain content—that is, to express a proposition—but also to change the context of information that is assumed by the participants at the conversation. Chierchia defines the system of Dynamic Type Theory (DTT), which is like Montague's IL, except that assignments to variables take the place of worlds. Therefore, given a sentence φ, the proposition expressed by that sentence, $\hat{}\varphi$ of type $\langle s, t \rangle$, is the set of assignments with respect to which the sentence is true. However, the crucial notion in DTT is the *context change potentials* (henceforth *ccp*) expressed by a sentence. Informally, the ccp of a sentence is the set of propositions that are compatible with the truth of that sentence. Given a formula φ, the corresponding ccp, $\uparrow\varphi$, is as follows:

(25) $\uparrow\varphi = \lambda p(\varphi \land \check{}p)$.

The ccp of a sentence determines the set of possible alternatives that remain open after the sentence has been uttered. The propositional variable p stands for possible continuations of the sentence. Conversely, given a ccp A, $\downarrow A$ is the truth-functional component of A.

The core part of Chierchia's proposal consists in refusing DRT's claim that indefinites are free variables and, therefore, type–theoretically different from strong quantifiers. To this purpose, indefinites are actually existentially quantified terms, as in the classical Montagovian analysis. Chierchia also assumes that adverbs of quantification are able to turn indefinites into free variables, by means of a rule of *existential disclosure* (Dekker 1993). Quantificational adverbs are interpreted as polyadic generalised quantifiers. They form tripartite structures and select (via indexation) one or more indefinite DPs, which appear in the restrictive clause, as that which is actually quantified over. The existential disclosure is a type-shifting mechanism that applies to these selected items. It first *opens* the variable of an existential quantifier and then λ-abstracts over it to form a predicate, which represents the restrictor of the adverbial quantifier (see Chierchia 1992 for details). The existential disclosure is then the operation by which quantificational adverbs determine what they quantify over. To sum up, the relevant assumptions in DTT concerning quantification are the following:

(26)   a.   Indefinites are existentially quantified.
       b.   Adverbs of quantification *disclose* the indefinites they are coindexed
            with and λ-abstract over them.

This approach has some clear advantages over other model-theoretic semantic systems, such as, for instance, the DRT. In fact, it has an intrinsic dynamic character, while at the same time guaranteeing strict compositionality and dispensing with the mechanism of existential closure. For instance, as Chierchia (1995a) points out, whereas existential closure has to apply to a seemingly arbitrary class of environments, existential disclosure applies to only one environment. This is surely an appealing and simplifying feature, which makes it an ideal mechanism to build a compositional semantics of aspect and quantificational adverbs.

Consistently with the model we have assumed, we adopt an intensional version of DTT. Accordingly, propositions are not simply sets of assignments verifying a sentence but sets of world-assignment pairs:

(27) $[\![^\wedge\varphi]\!] = \{ \langle w, g \rangle : [\![\varphi]\!]_{w,g} = 1 \}$.

To realise a correct mapping between syntactic structures and logical representations that incorporates the process of aspectual interpretation of sentences, we adopt a principles and parameters approach to syntactic analysis. Similarly to Chierchia (1995b), we assume that VP is dominated by an aspectual projection AspP, headed by aspectual morphemes. The latter have agreement features that require a suitable operator in their checking domain. Thus, we introduce the morphological features *pf* and *hab*—for perfective sentences and for habitual ones, respectively—which will be projected under Asp^0. Moreover, we introduce the two *aspectual operators Perf* and *Gn*, which are adjoined to AspP and check *pf* and *hab*, respectively. Consequently, we also augment the language of DTT with the corresponding operators. If other explicit relational quantificational adverbs occur, they will be further adjoined to AspP, according to the following configuration:

(28)

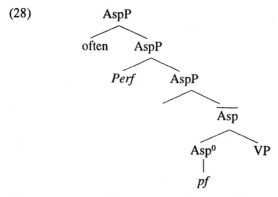

The aspectual operators are not default. Rather, they are always projected, given a certain aspectual value, and they co-occur with overt quantificational adverbs instead of being replaced by them. Moreover, we assume that verbs are basically translated as the properties of (or relations between) the participants of an event that takes place at a certain time (interval) i:

(29)   walk $\Rightarrow \lambda x \lambda i \exists e(\text{walk}(e) \wedge \text{theme}(x, e) \wedge e \in i)$.

The E-argument in (29) is existentially closed, forming a sort of indefinite description of an event. Its status as an indefinite makes it available for existential disclosure. Thus, like with standard indefinite DPs, the existentially quantified event variable can be disclosed in order to be bound by other quantificational devices. The higher tense phrase TP will expand this formula by adding information concerning the reference time with respect to which the interval is located. In section 3.4 we outline an analysis of the interaction between aspect and tense.

As far as the perfective operator is concerned, we define it as an existential-like operator binding a time variable, whose structure is

(30) $Perf[i](C(i) \wedge \varphi(i))$.

The formula $\varphi(i)$ contains some quantification over events, and the interval i restricts the quantification to those events that happened in that interval: the first conjunct states some (contextual) condition about the size of the interval. The semantics of $Perf$ can be defined as follows:

(D.5) $[\ \wedge \varphi(i))]\!]_{w,g} = 1$ iff for some assignment h such that $h = g[i'/i]$, $[\![C(i) \wedge \varphi(i)]\!]_{w,h} = 1$.

Thus, the whole representation in (30) captures the idea that perfective sentences refer to bounded events or series of events. Moreover, $Perf$ is an extensional operator in the sense that the interpretation of its component clause is in the current world (the actual one, by default).

The relevant mapping to IL for a perfective sentence is as follows:

(31)   a. Gianni fumò.
            John smoked.

b. *Perf* [i] ($C(i) \land \exists e$ (smoke(e)$\land$ agent(John, e) $\land$ $e \subseteq i$)).

We can say that (31a) is true iff there is an interval i (of a certain contextually specified size) such that there is at least an event of smoking by John that happened in it (tense information is added in section 3.4). In other words, the perfective aspect selects a temporal interval and makes a predication on it concerning the occurrence of an event.

As for habitual sentences, we assume that the generic operator that is triggered by the feature *hab* is translated into an intensional operator, composed of a restrictor and a matrix that correspond to open formulas of the following kind:

(32)   *Gn* [$\varphi(d_1, \ldots, d_n)$] [$\psi(d_1, \ldots, d_n)$].

Gn is interpreted as a modal operator, which is also able to bind the variables that occur free in its restrictor. The truth conditions for *Gn* are stated as follows (where d_i is a variable of type e of a certain sort):

(D.6) $[\![Gn$ [$\varphi(d_1, \ldots, d_n)$] [$\psi(d_1, \ldots, d_n)$]$]\!]_{w,g} = 1$ iff given a (contextually determined) modal base B_w, for every assignment h such that $h = g[d_1', \ldots, d_n'/d_1, \ldots, d_n]$ and every $w_1 \in B_w$ such that $[\![\varphi(d_1, \ldots, d_n)]\!]_{w_1, h} = 1$ there is a world $w_2 \in B_w$ such that $w_2 \leq_w w_1$, and for every world $w_3 \leq_w w_2$ it holds that $[\![\psi(d_1, \ldots, d_n)]\!]_{w_3, h} = 1$.

This definition is a slight variation of that in Condoravdi (1994) and Krifka et al. (1995), and it characterises the truth conditions of generic sentences as similar to those of conditional statements. The usual restriction against vacuous quantification applies; as Krifka et al. (1995: 32) say, nomic sentences "must have at least one variable to generalise over." That is, there must be at least one variable that is not explicitly tied to some particular object. Moreover, whereas *Perf* is existential in nature, *Gn* is an operator that resembles strong quantifiers (for the strong character of the generic operator, see Diesing 1992).

It is today an accepted fact that the content of the restrictor depends on the presuppositions of the sentence. More specifically, Schubert and Pelletier (1989) claim that habituals are always interpreted according to the background of certain situations or cases that can be determined on the basis of the presuppositions of the sentence. For instance, the truth conditions of (33) depend on the cases in which John goes to school:

(33)   John walks to school.

Therefore this sentence is felt to be roughly equivalent to

(34)   Whenever John goes to school, he walks.

The presuppositional basis that fills in the restrictor can be explicitly stated by means of a *when* or an *if* clause (as in (34)); otherwise it must be contextually recovered. For instance, the presence of a question to which the habitual is an answer can be decisive in determining the presupposition set and therefore the structure of the restrictor:

(35)   a.   (i) Where does John smoke?
            (ii) John smokes in the garden.

       b.   If John smokes, he smokes in the garden.

The question in (35a) determines the cases in which John smokes as the presuppositions for the habitual, whose truth conditions are roughly equivalent to (35b). Establishing a precise algorithm to determine the semantic presuppositions of a sentence is beyond the limits of this chapter. Therefore, we limit ourselves to assuming that the relevant presuppositions for the interpretation of habitual sentences are accommodated into the restrictor of Gn. Moreover we assume that existentially quantified variables expressed by the linguistic material in the sentence, and which must occur in the restrictor of the operator, are turned into free variables.

To implement this procedure, we assume that certain elements in the sentence are marked with a feature *top* (topic).[18] In some languages this marking is realised by specialised linguistic devices—for example, the topic particle *wa* of Japanese. Alternatively, we can imagine that at LF the topic elements are moved to a projection c-commanding the generic operator, and we can adopt the *splitting algorithm* proposed in Chierchia (1995b, 1995d) to determine the partition of the sentence material in the restriction and the scope of quantificational adverbs. According to this proposal, quantificational adverbs are free to choose their scope via LF adjunction, and the DPs that c-command the adverb at LF will fill its restriction. Similarly, the aspectual operators, too, will be able to adjoin to some higher projection, after they have checked the relevant feature in Asp^0. Finally, we define the following mapping rule from LF to logical representations (for the sake of simplicity, we just mark the topic elements in their positions at spell-out):

(D.7) $[_{AgrS-P} XP_1^{top} \ldots XP_j^{top} [_{AspP} Gn \ldots XP_n^{top}, YP] \ldots] \Rightarrow Gn\, [C(i) \wedge \ldots$
        $!_{di}XP_i \wedge \ldots] [\phi]$ for every i, $1 \leq i \leq n$,

where $!_{di}XP_i = \lambda P.P(\lambda d_i(d_i = d_i'))$ if P is an existential quantifier, else undefined.[19]

The generic operator discloses (and accommodates into its restrictor) every existentially quantified variable that is contained in the expression corresponding to the translation of a topic-marked constituent. Therefore, the rule is sensitive to two factors: (a) the indefinite character of a constituent—that is, the fact that it contains an existential quantifier binding any sort of variable, eventive or objectual—and (b) the topic status of the constituent. This idea is consistent with the assumption that presuppositions are accommodated into the restrictor; in fact, it is a standard assumption in model-theoretic semantics that sentential topic elements determine the restrictor of operators and quantifiers (cf. Partee 1995). The definition (D.7) also states that Gn will bind an interval variable whose size is (contextually) restricted by a condition C; this amounts to saying that habitual sentences always contain a quasi-universal quantification over the intervals where events occur.

As an example, let us take (18b):

(36) [Gianni andava al mare]^{top} con Maria.
      John went-IMP to the beach with Mary.

Let us assume that we have selected the bracketed section of (36) as the part to be accommodated into the restrictor since it provides the background set of cases for the interpretation of the whole habitual. The relevant logical form will be as follows:

(37) $Gn \ [C(i) \land go(e) \land theme(John, e) \land to(beach, e) \land e \subseteq i] \ [C(i) \land go(e) \land theme(John, e) \land to(beach, e) \land e \subseteq i \land with(Mary, e)]$.

In this specific case, the part of the sentence that has been selected by the topic-marking algorithm to fill the restrictor of Gn contains only the existentially quantified event argument, which is disclosed and bound by Gn according to the rule of translation in (D.7). The sentence (36) is true iff, in any world of the modal base, every interval of a certain size and every event of John's going to the beach occurring in this interval are such that, in every world that is most normal according to the ordering source, the events of John's going to the beach that happened in these intervals took place in the company of Mary. This representation seems suitable to capture the normative character of habituality.

3.2. Adding a Relational Quantificational Adverb

We now turn to cases like (11b–c) to analyse the interplay between the aspectual operators, which in our model are not default, and explicit quantificational adverbs:

(11) b. Gianni usciva raramente con Maria.
          John rarely went-IMP out with Mary.

      c. Gianni è uscito raramente con Maria.
          John has rarely gone out with Mary.

Let us assume that in (38) both *Perf* and the quantificational adverb are free to move at LF and to select their scope. Thus, different resulting configurations are possible. A first possibility is that *Perf* has scope over *spesso*, maybe as a consequence of its adjunction to AgrS-P:

(38) a. Gianni lesse spesso romanzi di spionaggio.
          John often read spy stories.

      b. [$_{AgrS-P}$ *Perf*$_i$ [$_{AgrS-P}$ Gianni$_j$ lesse$_k$ [$_{AspP}$ spesso[$_{AspP}$ t_i[$_{VP}$ t_j t_k romanzi di spionaggio]]]]].

The restriction and the nuclear scope for the relational adverb can be built out of the following expressions:

(39) a. $\exists e(read(e) \land agent(John, e) \land e \subseteq i)$.
      b. $\lambda e \exists x(spy\text{-}stories(x) \land theme(x, e))$.

This partition corresponds to the reading in which the quantificational adverb establishes a relation between the set of events of reading and the set of the events of reading spy stories. Obviously, other partitions are possible according to contextual and linguistic factors (for details, see de Swart 1993).

Since the quantificational adverb must bind the E-argument, existential disclosure applies to (39a) to turn the quantifier over events into a free variable, which is then λ-abstracted:

(40) $\lambda e(\text{read}(e) \land \text{agent}(\text{John}, e) \land e \subseteq i)$.

This property defines the set of events that represents the restriction of the quantificational adverb—that is, what the quantifier is about. Furthermore the free variable i is bound by the aspectual operator *Perf*, which will have scope over the adverb. The logical form we get is the following:

(41) *Perf* $[i]$ $(C(i) \land \text{Most} [\lambda e(\text{read}(e) \land \text{agent}(\text{John}, e) \land e \subseteq i)] [\lambda e \exists x(\text{spy-stories}(x) \land \text{theme}(x, e))])$.

Applying the truth conditions for the perfective operator, we find that the sentence in (38) is true iff most of the events of reading something by John, *which occurred within the boundary of a certain interval*, were events of reading spy stories. This formalisation accounts for the data concerning perfective sentences containing relational adverbs that we have discussed in section 2.2. That is, although they contain a quantificational adverb, nevertheless these sentences do not express normative generalisations. The quantifier merely establishes a relation between bounded sets of events because it is restricted to events that happened in a certain interval.

Another possibility is that the quantificational adverb c-commands at LF the aspectual operator. In this case, *Perf* will appear inside the nuclear scope of the relational adverb. Thus the following logical form could also be generated:

(42) Most $[\lambda e(\text{read}(e) \land \text{agent}(\text{John}, e) \land e \subseteq i)] [\lambda e(\text{Perf} [i] (C(i) \land \exists x(\text{spy-stories}(x) \land \text{theme}(x, e))))]$.

However, this representation is not well formed because the interval variable in the restrictor clause of the quantificational adverb remains unbound, and accordingly the whole formula cannot be properly interpreted. Therefore, although the scope configuration that generates (42) is syntactically well formed, the logical form is ruled out at the interpretative level, and this is consistent with the fact that (38a) is not ambiguous and its only reading is the one represented in (41).[20]

If the relational quantificational adverb is contained in a habitual sentence (as in (43)), the relevant representation at LF, in which the aspectual operator has scope over the adverb, will be as follows:

(43) a. Gianni leggeva spesso romanzi di spionaggio.
         John often read-IMP spy stories.

      b. [$_{\text{AgrS-P}}$ Gn_i [$_{\text{AgrS-P}}$ Gianni$_j$ leggeva$_k$ [$_{\text{AspP}}$ spesso [$_{\text{AspP}}$ t_i [$_{\text{VP}}$ t_j t_k romanzi di spionaggio]]]]].

The mapping algorithm will proceed similarly to the perfective case in (38). The output is the following logical representation:[21]

(44) $Gn\ [C(i)]$ [Most [λe(read(e) $\land$ agent(John, e) $\land e \subseteq i$)] [$\lambda e \exists x$(spy-stories(x) $\land$ theme(x, e))]].

This proposition is true iff for every possible interval of a certain contextually fixed size, in the worlds that are most normal, most of the events of John's reading that occurred in this interval were events of John's reading spy stories. Notice that the restrictor of Gn is not filled with material from the sentence but simply contains a contextual condition about the interval within which the events have occurred.[22]

Moreover, it is interesting to compare the logical forms in (41) and (44), corresponding to a perfective and an imperfective sentence, respectively, both containing a relational adverb. In both cases, the adverb establishes a proportion between two sets of events. However, in the perfective sentence, the members of these sets are events that happened in the actual world and within the boundaries of a time interval that is existentially closed; by contrast, in the imperfective case, the events quantified over are from different possible worlds and the adverb establishes a proportion between sets of events that happened in every possible interval of a certain implicit size. In this way, although the quantificational adverb is the same in both sentences, only the habitual corresponds to an intensional generalisation, stating that the proportion expressed by the quantifier is not just an episodic fact but also a normative one. Therefore, this solution accounts for the data concerning the semantic differences of imperfective and perfective sentences containing relational adverbs, as discussed in section 2.2.

The idea that the generic operator is not a default one, but rather co-occurs with quantificational adverbs, allows us to explain the ambiguity of (45):

(45)   In passato, un marito raramente usciva insieme alla moglie.
          In past times, a husband rarely went-IMP out together with his wife.

In one reading, this sentence means that few husbands used to go out with their wives; in the second reading, it means that it was a characteristic of any husband that few of his events of going out occurred in the company of his wife. This ambiguity can be captured in terms of the possible scope configurations between the aspectual operator and the quantificational adverb. The logical representation of the two readings is given in (46):

(46)   a. Few [λx(husband(x))] [$\lambda x\ Gn[C(i)$ $\land$ go-out(e) $\land$ theme(x, e)$\land$ $e \subseteq i$] [with(wife, e)]].

        b. $Gn\ [C(i)$ $\land$ husband(x)] [Few [λe(go-out(e) $\land$ theme(x, e) $\land$ $e \subseteq i$)] [λe(with(wife, e))]].

Thus, (46a) is true iff few husbands had the habit of going out with their wives. In contrast, (46b) is true if it was typical of any husband that in the most normal worlds few of his events of going out were events of going out with his wife. The perfective sentence corresponding to (45) shows a pair of readings, too:

(47)   In passato, un marito è uscito raramente con sua moglie.
        In past times, a husband rarely went out with his wife.

In one case, (47) means that for few husbands there was an interval in which an event of going out with his wife occurred; in the second reading, the sentence means that there was a husband and there was an interval in which few of his events of going out that occurred within that interval took place with his wife. These two readings correspond to the following representations because of different scope configurations of the operator and the adverb:

(48)   a.   Few $[\lambda x(husband(x))]$ $[\lambda x\, Perf\,[i]\,(C(i) \wedge \exists e(go\text{-}out(e) \wedge theme(x, e) \wedge$
            $with(wife, e) \wedge e \subseteq i))]$.

        b. $Perf\,[i]\,(C(i) \wedge \exists x(husband(x) \wedge$ Few $[\lambda e(go\text{-}out(e) \wedge theme(x, e) \wedge$
            $e \subseteq i)]\,[\lambda e(with(wife, e) \wedge e \subseteq i)]))$.

The difference between perfective and imperfective cases is predicted by the representation we gave to the aspectual values; in fact, *Perf* does not perform any variable disclosure, and therefore an indefinite DP that appears outside the quantificational adverb is forced to keep its existential force.

3.3. Habituality and Existence

In section 3.1 we have seen that the truth of a generic sentence like (23) does not presuppose the existence of men. The lack of existential presuppositions in generic noun phrases is a well-known phenomenon, and the intensional analysis of the generic operator allows us to derive it easily. Now, the point is that habituals behave quite differently with respect to the presupposition of events. In particular, sentences containing overt quantificational adverbs, such as (43a), always seem to presuppose the existence of some events of the specified type:

(49)   Gianni leggeva spesso romanzi di spionaggio.
        John often read-IMP spy stories.

The intuitions concerning this point are quite clear, and it is almost impossible to find a context in which the truth of this sentence does not also license the inference that some events of reading spy stories by John actually occurred. The problem is that the interpretation of the generic operator we have given in (D.6) does not seem to be able to account for this fact. In fact, in the semantics of *Gn* there is nothing that forces the actual occurrence of events.[23]

The question of the interaction between habituality and the actual occurrence of events is a wide and complicated one, and we cannot hope to explore it completely in this chapter. However, we do try at least to outline a possible solution within the model for habituals we have proposed. The basic question can be restated in the following way: how many events must actually occur for a habitual sentence to be true? The problem is that it does not seem possible to give a precise and universal answer to this question—that is, there is a wide variability between different cases of habituals, and this variability is connected with linguistic and extralinguistic factors. For instance, compare the following sentences:[24]

(50) a. Gianni fumava.
          John smoked-IMP.

      b. Questa macchina tritava noccioline.
          This machine crushed-IMP peanuts.

      c. Gianni fumava raramente in giardino.
          John rarely smoked-IMP in the garden.

The truth of the first sentence licenses the inference that at least two events of smoking have occurred, but even in this case the variance is high; for some speakers and in certain circumstances, two events do not suffice to classify a person as a smoker, but at the same time we can also imagine circumstances in which even one occurrence is enough (e.g., in a very strict society in which the fact of having smoked once immediately labels you as a smoker). What is sure is that if someone is a smoker, he or she must have smoked some times. In contrast, the truth of (50b) does not license the same inference. The sentence can be true, even though the machine actually never crushed a single peanut. Simply, it was designed to do that, but in fact it was never started. At the opposite pole stands (50c), whose truth seems to imply not only the actual existence of some events of smoking but also that they occurred in a considerable number. The semantics itself of the adverb *raramente* imposes the connotation that the events of smoking are at least more than two.

Given that habituals express nomic generalisations over events, it seems that the inference concerning the actual occurrence of some of these events depends on the source of the generalisation. In fact, generic statements can be either inductively or deductively derived. In the former case, they are the result of a generalisation on the grounds of some specific occurrence of a certain type of event or behaviour; in the latter, their truth can be deduced by a number of other facts. This is actually what happens with (50b): its truth is independent of the actual occurrence of peanut-crushing events, only because it can be deduced by the facts concerning the internal design of the machine and its structural organisation. In other words, the truth of this generalisation can be derived from the purpose this machine has been designed for. In contrast, no such a deduction is possible for the other two sentences, (50a) and (50c), whose truth can only have an inductive grounding. There is nothing in the constitution of John that makes him a smoker, or a smoker with a certain given frequency: the truth of this generalisation can therefore be justified only on the basis of some past behaviour of John, and in particular of the existence of actual occurrences of that event.

As Krifka et al. (1995) also suggest, it is possible to represent these differences within the formal definition of genericity by exploiting the notion of the modal base and ordering sources, on which the generic operator depends. We have seen that the generic operator, being intrinsically modal, quantifies over a suitably restricted set of worlds, and the definition of this set depends on the choice of the modal base and the ordering source. Moreover, the choice of these two entities is heavily context-dependent. The difference between deductively based sentences like (50b) and inductively based habituals like (50a) and (50c) can therefore be stated in terms of the difference in the nature of the modal base. Specifically, a generic sentence is inductively based iff the modal base on which it is evaluated contains the real world (i.e., it is a *realistic* modal base) and the proposition that there have been some events of the specified type is true in it (and in all the other words of the modal base).

The choice of the modal base, and the consequent distinction between habituals with and without existential presuppositions, is contextually determined but surely also largely linguistically influenced. As Laca (1990) claims, for instance, the fact that the subject is an artefact facilitates the possibility of a reading without existential presuppositions of the events. In the light of this, we can try to explain why sentences containing overt quantificational adverbs, like (43a) or (50c), always license the inferences concerning the occurrence of the events. Along the line of the present proposal, this amounts to saying that these quantificational adverbs always select inductive modal bases. This fact is reasonable both from a commonsense point of view and from a technical one. Since these adverbs express a relation between sets of events, when they are part of habitual sentences, they necessarily determine inductive statements, whose truth presupposes the actual occurrence of an adequate set of events. Moreover, quantificational adverbs like *spesso* and *sempre* are relational adverbs; if we extend to the event domain the same characteristic of nominal quantifiers, relational readings are also presuppositional, in the sense that they presuppose the fact that the domain of quantification is not empty. Therefore, we could say that quantificational adverbs, being intrinsically presuppositional, always select inductive modal bases, where their existential presuppositions are accommodated.

An alternative way to implement these facts is to assign a default value to the choice of the modal base for habituals. Since habituals are generalisations concerning the more or less regular occurrence of events, we could assume that this default value is set to select an inductive, presuppositional modal base. This would represent the idea that standardly habituals are generalisations grounded on the past experience of the repetition of events in certain conditions. However, the default value could be cancelled under special circumstances, such as those represented by sentences containing artefact DPs (50b) or sentences like (51), whose truth can be deduced by John's job contract, rather than by his actual success in selling cars:

(51)   Gianni vendeva macchine usate.
        John sold-IMP used cars.

When these special circumstances occur, we would be authorised to choose a different, non-presuppositional modal base. An argument supporting this hypothesis can be given by the fact that the habitual sentences that license non-presuppositional readings always license presuppositional ones, too, whereas the reverse is not true. It is then plausible to claim that presuppositional readings are the standard and normal case, whereas the non-presuppositional readings are instead interpretations that can arise only when certain special circumstances license the choice of a noninductive modal base for the evaluation of the sentence. Therefore, given this line of analysis, the case to be explained is not the fact that sentences containing quantificational adverbs have only presuppositional readings, which is indeed the standard situation, but rather how and when it is possible to have a non-presuppositional interpretation, too.[25]

To sum up the results of this discussion, we can say that habituals differ according to whether they presuppose or not the actual occurrence of a certain number of events. This presupposition is part of the way the generalisation expressed by a habitual is grounded. Both linguistic and extralinguistic factors participate in determining the appropriate reading in a certain context. What is essential is that the modal base for the evaluation of the generic operator and its context-dependent nature allow us to capture this variability inside a formal representation of habitual and generic sentences.

3.4. Aspect and Tense

In this section we want to debate the question of the relationship between aspect and tense since aspectual features are carried by inflectional morphemes that also anchor sentences to time. Our goal is to discuss the following three points: (a) what information tense features bring into the derivation of the logical form of sentences; (b) whether and how aspect and tense interact; (c) the role of certain temporal adverbs that are used to set the temporal background of the events. As to the representation of tense, we adopt the Reichenbachian proposal that tenses can be defined according to the respective relationships among three salient times—the *utterance time*, t_u; the *event time*; and the *reference time*, t_r. However, whereas Reichenbach (1947) claims that every tense has to be defined in terms of all three salient times, we instead follow Bertinetto (1986) and others in using the reference time only for the representation of tenses that express the notion of perfect.[26]

In Italian, the imperfective aspect is typically represented by two tenses, the *simple present*, and the *imperfect*, which is a past tense. By contrast, the perfective aspect is represented by a whole range of tenses: the simple past, compound past, pluperfect, simple future, and future perfect. Moreover, the very notion of perfectivity needs to be further specified in two aspectual subtypes, which we refer to as *perfect aspect* and *aoristic aspect*, adopting the terminology in Comrie (1976) and Bertinetto (1986). In both cases, the event is represented as a completed and bounded entity. However, the two subtypes of perfectivity differ in the way the event is connected with time. In the case of the perfect value, perfective tenses express the fact that the result of an event lasts up to the reference time. By contrast, the aoristic perfective value simply represents the event as totally anterior or posterior to the utterance time, so that no part of the event or its effects are connected to the utterance time or to a contextually relevant reference time. The interesting fact of this distinction within the perfective domain is that it allows us to group the different perfective tenses according to the particular value they may carry. Specifically, the perfect aspect is expressed only by the compound tenses; in turn, these differ according to the location of the reference time, which coincides with the utterance time, a time in the past and a time in the future, respectively, for the compound past (in its perfect reading), the pluperfect, and the future perfect. By contrast, the aoristic aspect is typically expressed by the simple past and the simple future (besides the compound past in its aoristic meaning).

To implement this picture in the analysis of aspect we have proposed, it is necessary to keep in mind the following points: (a) there is a common feature that all perfective aspectual values share; (b) the subtypes of perfectivity are (normally) associated with different tenses and depend on the way the *bounded* event is related to different salient times (the reference time for the perfect tenses and the utterance time for the aoristic tenses). These considerations suggest a natural distribution of the semantic information associated with the perfective aspect between different functional heads in the following way. First, the common part of perfectivity is given by the content of AspP, which in every case will head the feature *pf* and will contain the operator *Perf* in an adjoined position. Second, there are two different possibilities, depending on whether the tense is compound or simple. In the former case (leaving aside the aoristic reading of the compound past), we adopt the representation proposed by Belletti (1990), according to which the auxiliary is generated under the head of a functional projection AuxP that is located under TP (in our analysis, AuxP will also dominate AspP):

(52)   AgrS-P

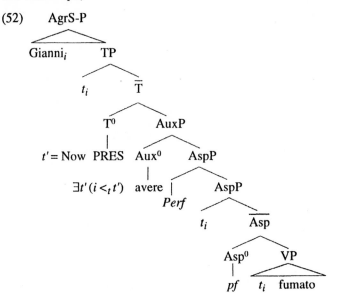

The semantic contribution of the relevant nodes to the logical representation of the sentence is shown on the left of the tree. The basic idea is that the Aux⁰ *introduces* the reference time, by means of an existential quantifier over instants, and sets the interval, which includes the event time as anterior to the reference time. The tense phrase (to which the auxiliary will move to check the relevant morphological features) *specifies* the reference time; in the case of the compound past the reference time is indexically identified with the utterance time (here indicated with the constant *Now*), whereas with the pluperfect and the future perfect the reference time is some (familiar) time, respectively, anterior or posterior to the utterance time. This corresponds to the classical Reichenbachian analysis for compound tenses.[27] The result is the following representation:

(53)   [Il portacenere è pieno]
        [The ashtray is full]

    a. Gianni ha fumato.
        John has smoked.

    b. *Perf* [i] $(C(i) \land \exists t_1 (i <_t t_1 \land t_1 = Now \land \exists e(smoke(e) \land agent(John, e) \land e \subseteq i)))$.

The case of the simple past is similar but differs because AuxP is not projected. Since the reference time is associated with Aux⁰, this implies that the logical form of a sentence with the simple past will not contain the reference time, and the event will be simply represented as being anterior to the utterance time. Therefore, we can associate to (31a), now (54a), the following structure and logical representation:

(54)   a. Gianni fumò.
            John smoked.

        b.
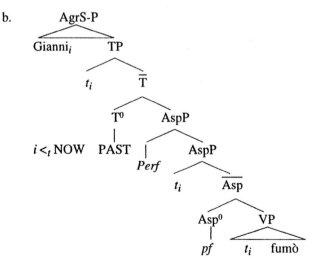

(55)   *Perf* [i] $(C(i) \land i <_t NOW \land \exists e(smoke(e) \land agent(John, e) \land e \subseteq i))$.

Since there is no reference time and the event is represented as being strictly anterior to the utterance time, the logical form in (55) seems to be a suitable formalisation of the semantics of the aoristic perfective aspect.

Thus we have not only given a representation of the interplay of tense and aspectual information but also we have formalised the different facets of the perfective aspect—that is, the perfect and the aoristic values. The core of our proposal amounts to a precise division of labour among the different functional heads that make up the description and location of the reported event. The common feature is the aspectual operator *Perf*, which is shared by every perfective sentence, and the distinguishing element is the presence or absence of the reference time, which is carried only by the auxiliary of compound tenses, which typically expresses the perfect value of perfectivity.

The issue of the relationship of habituals and tense is not an easy one. A possible answer to this problem is that since habituals express normative generalisations, they are intrinsically atemporal. The flaw in this solution (which has been adopted by many scholars) is that it runs against linguistic and common-sense evidence. Starting from the latter, habits (like smoking) begin at some time, last for a certain period, and then finish, notwithstanding their tendentially stable character. Apart from metaphysical and mathematical laws, most generic sentences express general statements that may be true now but that may have been false some time ago. On the linguistic side, the obvious evidence is that habits can be expressed both in the present and in the past, as well as in the future (although with certain pragmatic restrictions). If tense connects language with time, then the fact that habituals occur with all the three tense values means that general statements are well situated in time.

A related question concerns the role that background clauses have in perfective and imperfective sentences:

(56) a. Nel 1998, Gianni è andato al cinema con Maria.
          In 1998, John went to the cinema with Mary.

      b. Nel 1998, Gianni andava al cinema con Maria.
          In 1998, John went-IMP to the cinema with Mary.

According to our discussion in section 2.2 (see examples (16) and (17)), the temporal adverb that occurs with the habitual in (56b) does not fix the boundaries of the habit, which may still hold in 1999. By contrast, in the perfective case we refer to events that occurred within the boundaries of the interval denoted by the temporal adverb. It is thus necessary to explain the apparent paradox of imperfective habituals—that is, their possibility of co-occurring with expressions that introduce a finite interval as a background for the habit while still maintaining the character of unboundedness typical of imperfectivity.

To accommodate these facts, we suggest that the generic operator should be translated into IL in a more complex way than we have assumed in the former sections. Following and adapting some insights in Chierchia (1995b), we assume the following representation of the generic operator, which therefore substitutes for the one in (32):

(57) $\exists i(C(i) \wedge Gn [\text{overlap}(i, i') \wedge D(i') \wedge \varphi(d_1, \ldots, d_n)] [\psi(d_1, \ldots, d_n)])$.

We refer to the existentially quantified interval i as the *external interval*, which is assumed to be anchored to time. This interval is contextually restricted, and the value of C can be overtly specified by temporal adverbs. Thus, the condition $C(i)$ corresponds to the background clause in (56b). We call the second interval i' the *internal interval*, which is bound by the generic operator (these intervals will be of a contextually specified size D). The core of this proposal concerns the relation between the external and the internal interval, which must overlap (i.e., have at least one common subpart). Therefore, the logical translation of (56b) is as follows:

(58) $\exists i(i = 1998 \wedge i <_t \text{Now} \wedge Gn [\text{overlap}(i, i') \wedge D(i') \wedge \text{go}(e) \wedge \text{theme(John,}$
       $e) \wedge \text{to(cinema, } e) \wedge e \subseteq i'] [\text{with(Mary, } e)])$.

Notice that the background adverb and the relevant tense information restrict the external interval.[28] The sentence in (56b) is true iff there is a past interval coinciding with 1998 such that, in any world of the modal base, every interval (of a contextually relevant size) overlapping with the external one and every event of John's going to the cinema that occurred in this interval are such that, in every world that is most normal according to the ordering source, the events of John's going to the cinema that happened in these intervals took place in the company of Mary. The relation of overlapping between the external and internal intervals allows us to capture the interplay between the boundedness of the background interval, and the intrinsic unboundedness of habituality. In fact, although the external background interval is a finite one, yet *Gn* quantifies over all possible intervals that simply overlap with the external one. Therefore, the habit holds even for periods of time that extend beyond the boundaries of the background clause. In other words, we can say that in habitual sentences, background adverbs and tense information locate the habit in a certain time period, but at the same time they do not restrict the habit only within the boundaries of this period. As it is easy to verify, the treatment of habituality in the previous section naturally extends to this new version of the generic operator.[29]

4. Iterative Adverbs

Languages differ in the way multiple events are represented. Various morphemes can be used to express the distribution of events among multiple agents, the repetition of events in time, the scattering of events in space, and so forth. Lasersohn (1995) refers to all these devices as *pluractional markers*, to stress the parallelism with the plural morphemes that occur with nominal elements. The interesting fact is that plurality in the event domain is a much more composite phenomenon than its counterpart in the objectual domain because of the multidimensional nature of events. In fact, events can be plural with respect to time, space, or one of their arguments, or with respect to more than one of these variables at the same time.

Iterative adverbs like *twice* can surely be described as plurality expressions because they specify the multiple occurrence of an event. However, the question of the dimension of plurality they express is less obvious, as the following example reveals:

(59)   Yesterday, the gun shot twice.

This sentence is ambiguous: it can mean that there was a single occasion yesterday in which the gun fired two shots or that there were two different times in which the gun fired an undefined number of shots.[30] However, the same ambiguity does not arise in (60):

(60)   Yesterday, John called me twice

which simply means that there were two moments of the day in which John called me. As Lasersohn says, the ambiguity of (59) is shared by sentences containing verbs like *knock*, *ring*, *nibble*, *wink*, and so on. The characteristic of these verbs is that, for instance, an event of knocking at the door is normally (although not necessarily) composed of repeated knockings and nibbling usually consists of repeated small bites. We take from Lasersohn the distinction between *repetitive* and *repeated* actions, corresponding, respectively, to the case of firing many shots on the same occasion and to the case of many different occasions of firing.

The main goal of this section is to give an explanation of the tendential incompatibility of iterative adverbs with the habitual imperfective aspect. In particular, we derive it from our quantificational analysis of habituals. The model we propose will also be suitable for predicting the cases in which iterative adverbs *can* occur in habitual sentences. First, remember that we have represented verbs as containing indefinite descriptions of events:

(61)   run $\Rightarrow \lambda x \lambda i \exists e(\text{run}(e) \wedge \text{theme}(x, e) \wedge e \subseteq i)$.

Thus, we can say that verbs like *run* resemble singular indefinite nominal predicates like *a man* or *a house*. On the other hand, we suggest that some verbs, those denoting repetitive events, should be represented as being intrinsically collective, in the same way as collective nominal predicates like *flock* or *cattle*. Furthermore, we assume that so-called iterative adverbs are actually ambiguous between a *repeated* and a *repetitive* interpretation. In the former case they count the number of occurrences of events in the sense of bounded units temporally separated one from another. In the latter case, iterative adverbs count the elements that compose a single occurrence of a repetitive event. The existence of such an ambiguity is supported by data from languages that have lexically distinct adverbs to express the repeated and the repetitive interpretation (Hengeveld 1992).

As Lasersohn suggests, the difference between repeated and repetitive readings of iterative adverbs lies in the level of granularity of the entities we count with these expressions. Let us consider:

(62)   John knocked twice.

We can assume that the denotation of the predicate corresponds to a *sum* of events of type P, where P is some contextually relevant predicate that can also be similar to the original predicate.[31] The events of type P will be called the *atoms* of knocking. For instance, an occurrence of knocking can actually be composed of multiple atomic knockings, and an occurrence of shooting can be composed of the firing of multiple shots, each corresponding to an atom of shooting. In this way, *knock* or *shoot* is similar to collective predicates: for instance, the word *committee* denotes an object that is actually the sum of atomic individuals. Using Link's notation, we can represent repetitive predicates as indefinitedescriptions of an event that is the *material fusion* of atomic events of a given type P:

(63)   knock $\Rightarrow \lambda x \lambda i \exists e(\text{knock}(e) \wedge \text{agent}(x, e) \wedge e\text{»}\sigma e_1 P(x, e_1) \wedge e \subseteq i)$

where » stands for *constitutes* and $\sigma e_1 P(x, e_1)$ denotes the sum of atomic events of type P (see Link 1983 for details); we call each e_1 that constitutes e a *phase* of e.

However, atoms can also be defined in a different way. Lasersohn suggests that events are cut or packaged in bounded units, with respect to different parameters—that is, time, space, and participants. He also shows that languages provide different devices to refer to multiply bounded units of events along one of these three dimensions. It seems plausible to state that repeated adverbs really count temporally packaged events, which now constitute sorts of atoms. Notice also that the compatibility of iterative quantifiers with event predicates depends on the possibility of carrying out this sort of packaging:

(64)   a. Yesterday, John called twice.
         b. Yesterday, John ran twice.
         c. ?? Last night, John slept twice.

Whereas *call* in (64a) has a clear partition in temporally bounded units, each corresponding to a single call, (64b) is correct only if we are able to distinguish two runs by John. By contrast, in normal conditions the packaging operation is more difficult to carry out with sleeping. Following Lasersohn, we refer to each temporally packaged event as an *event unit*. Thus, each event predicate P will denote a set of event units (somehow determined with different criteria, depending on the event type), whereas for some predicates Q each event unit of type Q is further equivalent to a sum of phases of a certain type.

Given a sentence like (64a), let us assume that the VP is translated in the following way:[32]

(65)   [VP t_i call] $\Rightarrow \exists e(\text{call}(e) \wedge \text{agent}(x, e))$.

In the previous section we have adopted the idea that quantificational adverbs perform an operation of variable disclosure and abstraction, turning an existentially quantified formula into a first-order property. We now define iterative adverbs in the repeated interpretation as generalised quantifiers of type $\langle\langle e, t \rangle, t \rangle$. Consistent with this characterisation, they perform an operation of disclosure and abstraction over the E-argument. Since syntactically iterative adverbs are VP-internal, these operations apply at the level of VP. What we get is the following property over events:

(66) $\lambda e(\text{call}(e) \wedge \text{agent}(x, e))$.

We can thus define the repeated reading of *due volte* ('twice') as follows:[33]

(67) $\lambda P \exists e(e = \sigma e_1 \check{} P(e_1) \wedge \text{two}(\sigma e_1 \check{} P(e_1)))$.   (repeated interpretation)

The adverb will then apply to the event property, producing a description of a sum of events, whose cardinality is two:

(68) $\exists e(e = \sigma e_1(\text{call}(e_1) \wedge \text{agent}(x, e_1)) \wedge \text{two}(\sigma e_1(\text{call}(e_1) \wedge \text{agent}(x, e_1))))$.

The other iterative adverbs can be defined in a similar way; the essential part of the definition is that these adverbs are now considered as sorts of pluralising operators, which turn indefinite descriptions over events into descriptions of sum of events, specifying their cardinality.

We noted that iterative adverbs in languages like Italian or English also have a repetitive interpretation. We suggest that in this reading, adverbs like *due volte* actually behave like a normal first-order predicate, with a selection restriction concerning their argument—that is, that it must be a sum (the restriction states that the values of e must not be single atoms):

(69) $\lambda e(\text{two}(e))$ such that $\neg \exists g, w \ [\![\lambda e(\text{two}(e))]\!]_{w,g} \subseteq \text{ATOM}$.   (repetitive int.)

This restriction allows us to derive the observed fact that only a set of verbs give rise to a repetitive interpretation—namely, collective verbs that denote events corresponding to sums of phases of a certain predicate P. Therefore, at the VP level, the repeated and repetitive readings of (62) are represented as follows:

(70) a. $\exists e(e = \sigma e_1(\text{knock}(e_1) \wedge \text{agent}(x, e_1)) \wedge \text{two}(\sigma e_1(\text{knock}(e_1) \wedge \text{agent}(x, e_1))))$
      b. $\exists e(\text{knock}(e) \wedge \text{agent}(x, e) \wedge e \gg \sigma e_1 P(e_1) \wedge \text{two}(\sigma e_1 P(e_1)))$.

In the repeated case (70a), there is a group of event units of knocking, whose cardinality is equal to two; in the repetitive case (70b), there is a single event of knocking, which consists of a group of phases of type P and whose cardinality is equal to two. The crucial difference is that the existentially bound variable in (70a) is a group one; that is, it is not an atomic event unit. In contrast, in (70b), the existentially closed variable is an atomic one, which nevertheless corresponds, at a finer level of description, to the sum of different parts. For comparison, this is reminiscent of the difference between *platoon*, which denotes a group of soldiers, and *John*, which denotes a single individual constituted by the sum of other entities (e.g., its body parts).

Given this analysis of iterative adverbs, it is possible to derive the anomaly of sentences like (2), repeated here:

(2) a. *Gianni andava al mare con Maria due volte.
      John went-IMP to the beach with Mary twice.

b. *Gianni vedeva *Blade Runner* molte volte.
John watched-IMP *Blade Runner* many times.

Remember that we have analysed habitual sentences as containing a generic operator that binds the event variable in the proper cases, producing a generalisation over events of a certain type. The same operator is responsible for the generic interpretation of indefinite singular DPs, and in general of so-called *I-generics*, following the terminology of Gerstner-Link and Krifka (1993). Notice now that singular indefinite generic DPs are incompatible with collective predicates:

(71)   *A lion gathers near water holes.

This restriction can be explained on the grounds that the truth conditions of the generic operator that is contained in nomic sentences have the form of a conditional statement:

(72)   If x is a lion, then x gathers near water holes.

Given the singular indefinite predicate *a lion* in the restrictor of the conditional, x can only be an atomic individual, but surely not a plural sum. Therefore, there is a clash between the atomic nature of x in the restrictor and the fact that the collective predicate in the matrix clause requires x to range over plural individuals—that is, over sums and not atoms. Hence the anomaly of (71).

A similar argument can be given for the sentences in (2). Notice that if the former example were correct, then its truth conditions should be roughly equivalent to the following conditional statement:

(73)   If John went-IMP to the beach with Mary, John went-IMP to the beach with Mary twice

or equivalently

(74)   Everything that was an event of John's going to the beach with Mary, was an event of going to the beach with Mary twice.

Besides their self-evident oddness, these restatements show that the restrictor of *Gn* contains an indefinite singular description of an atomic event, which is disclosed and bound by *Gn*. Thus, the sentence is actually about a singular, atomic event, while at the same time the matrix clause attributes a property to a group of events. The anomaly of (2a) would therefore amount to the resulting incompatibility between the restrictor and the matrix clause of the habitual operator. The logical representation corresponding to (2a) would then be something like this (for simplicity we henceforth omit tense information in the representation of the aspectual operators):

(75)   *Gn* $[C(i) \wedge$ went$(e) \wedge$ theme(John, e) $\wedge$ to(beach, e) $\wedge$ with(Mary,e) $\wedge e \subseteq i]$
$[\exists e_1(e_1 = \sigma e_2($went$(e_2) \wedge$ theme(John, e_2) $\wedge$ to(beach, e_2) $\wedge$ with(Mary, e_2))
$\wedge$ two$(\sigma e_2($went$(e_2) \wedge$ theme(John, e_2) $\wedge$ to(beach, e) $\wedge$ with(Mary, e_2))))].

The logical form in (75) is ill formed because, although the generic quantifier ranges over an atomic event, the matrix clause does not predicate anything but rather introduces a sum of events that are completely unrelated to the one in the restrictor. Thus, the oddness of the paraphrases in (73) and (74) also corresponds to the anomaly of the logical form in (75). To sum up, the anomaly of the sentences in (2) is similar to the impossibility of singular indefinite DPs to be generically interpreted in sentences with collective predicates. The reason for such a similarity is that the event description appearing in the restrictor of *Gn* in habitual sentences is a singular predicate over event units, whereas iterative adverbs in the matrix clause behave like collective predicates—that is, they range over sums of events.

How is it, then, that (4) (repeated here) is correct despite its habitual aspect?

(4)   Il mio postino suona due volte.
       My postman rings twice.

Notice that *ring* belongs to the class of repetitive verbs, such as *knock* or *shoot.* They are intrinsically collective—that is, each event of ringing is constituted by a sum of phases. The repetitive reading of (4) can then be paraphrased as in (76a) and formalised as in (76b):

(76)   a. If my postman rings (at my door), he rings twice.
       b. $Gn \, [C(i) \wedge \text{ring}(e) \wedge \text{agent}(\text{postman}, e) \wedge e_2 \text{»} \sigma e_1 P(e_1) \wedge e \subseteq i]$
           $[\text{two}(\sigma e_1 P(e_1))].$

The E-argument bound by *Gn* ranges over event units since we are dealing with a singular description of an event atom. The point is that, as a repetitive verb, each atom is also formed by other subparts of a certain type. It is the cardinality of this sum that is expressed by the cardinal adjective in (76). This analysis predicts that with verbs like *ring* iterative adverbs in sentences like (4) can only have the repetitive interpretation. This prediction is actually borne out, as is shown by the comparison of (4) with the corresponding perfective sentence:

(77)   a. Il mio postino suona due volte.
           My postman rings twice.

       b. Oggi, il mio postino ha suonato due volte.
           Today, my postman has rung twice.

The former sentence is not ambiguous, and it can only mean that every time my postman rings at the door, he generally makes two rings. In contrast, the latter sentence can mean either that there have been two occasions during the present day in which my postman has rung at the door (repeated interpretation) or that there has just been one event composed of two rings (repetitive interpretation).

We now analyse other cases of imperfective habituals containing iterative adverbs—that is, sentences like (6a), here reproduced as (78):

(78)   In quel periodo, la domenica, Gianni mi telefonava tre volte.
       In that period, on Sundays, John called-IMP me three times.

We can plausibly assume that the adverb *la domenica* ('on Sundays') denotes a kind whose atoms are intervals and that the generic operator binds instances of this kind.[34] The habitual sentence in (78) roughly states that for every contextually fixed interval i of size C, every Sunday in i was such that, in most normal cases, John called me three times. Formally, we get something like this:

(79) $Gn\ [C(i_1) \wedge i \leq \text{Sunday} \wedge i \subseteq^* i_1]\ [\exists e(e= \sigma e_1(\text{call}(e_1) \wedge \text{agent}(\text{John}, e_1)) \wedge$
$\text{three}(\sigma e_1(\text{call}(e_1) \wedge \text{agent}(\text{John}, e_1))) \wedge e \subseteq i)]$.

The generic operator binds here the interval variable, and the event predication is wholly contained in the matrix. Therefore, in contrast to the case of (75), the logical form in (79) is structurally correct. Moreover, notice that in this case the iterative adverb has a repeated interpretation, although the sentence is habitual.[35]

Similarly, we can explain the fact that both the perfective and the imperfective sentences in (80) are correct:

(80) a. Ogni domenica, Gianni mi veniva a trovare tre volte.
          Every Sunday, John came-IMP and visited me three times.

      b. Ogni domenica, Gianni mi è venuto a trovare tre volte.
          Every Sunday, John has come and visited me three times.

These sentences will get the following logical representations:

(81) a. *Gn* $[C(i)]$ [Every $[\lambda i_1(\text{Sunday}(i_1) \wedge i_1 \subseteq^* i)]$ $[\lambda i_1 \exists e(e= \sigma e_1(\text{visit}(e_1) \wedge$
          $\text{agent}(\text{John}, e_1) \wedge \text{theme}(\text{me}, e_1)) \wedge \text{three}(\sigma e_1(\text{visit}(e_1) \wedge \text{agent}(\text{John}, e_1)$
          $\wedge \text{theme}(\text{me}, e_1))) \wedge e \subseteq i_1)]]$.

      b. *Perf* $[i]$ $[C(i) \wedge \text{Every} [\lambda i_1(\text{Sunday}(i_1) \wedge i_1 \subseteq^* i)]$ $[\lambda i_1 \exists e(e= \sigma e_1(\text{visit}(e_1)$
          $\wedge \text{agent}(\text{John}, e_1) \wedge \text{theme}(\text{me}, e_1)) \wedge \text{three}(\sigma e_1(\text{visit}(e_1) \wedge \text{agent}(\text{John},$
          $e_1) \wedge \text{theme}(\text{me}, e_1))) \wedge e \subseteq i_1)]]$.

In either case, the quantifier *ogni* (every) is the same, the difference lying in the presence of *Perf* or of *Gn*. In the perfective one, the sentence is true iff there has been a time interval of a certain size such that every Sunday occurring within its boundaries John called me three times. Therefore, if on one Sunday John actually called me just twice, the sentence turns out to be false. However, (81a) is true iff for every possible interval i of a given size, in most normal cases, every Sunday in i John called me three times. Thus, if it has happened that John actually called me twice on one Sunday, this fact does not make the sentence false because the actual world may not belong to the most normal ones. Therefore, the representation we have given to those sentences explains the normal intuition that although both sentences contain the same universal quantifier, the imperfective but not the perfective one allows for exceptions.

A similar case is represented by (5a) (now (82)):

(82) Un film interessante, Gianni lo vedeva due volte.
      An interesting movie, John watched-IMP it twice

In this case, the restriction of the generic operator is filled by the left-dislocated DP, which is topic-marked. Therefore the event and the iterative adverb both appear in the nuclear scope of the *Gn*, as in (79) and (81a).

Finally, it is possible to explain why imperfective habitual sentences are always compatible with frequency adverbs expressing cyclic iteration, as shown by the following sentences:

(83)   a. Gianni mi telefonava tre volte alla settimana.
            John called-IMP me three times a week.

        b. Gianni andava al cinema due volte al mese.
            John went-IMP to the cinema twice a month.

We can assume that the cyclic interpretation depends on the fact that these adverbs contain a universal quantification over time intervals of the specified type. Therefore their semantic representation resembles that of (80a)—that is, (81a)—and the grammaticality of (83) is due to the same reasons. However, sentences containing frequency adverbs like (83) differ in an important respect from sentences with a universal quantifier over time intervals overtly adjoined at AgrS-P:

(84)   a. Uno studente ha telefonato tre volte alla settimana.
            A student has called three times a week

        b. Ogni settimana, uno studente ha telefonato.
            Every week, a student has called

The difference concerns the scope domain of the quantifier over time intervals: in fact, whereas (84b) can mean that each week a different student called me, according to our intuitions, this reading is impossible with (84a), which can mean only that the same student has called me three times a week. In other words, the universal quantifier that is contained in the frequency adverb cannot have scope over the subject DP. Therefore, (84a) will have only the following representation:

(85)   *Perf* [*i*] $(C(i) \wedge \exists x(\text{student}(x) \wedge \text{Every } [\lambda i_1(\text{week}(i_1) \wedge i_1 \subseteq *i)] [\lambda i_1 \exists e(e= \sigma e_1(\text{call}(e_1) \wedge \text{agent}(x, e_1)) \wedge \text{three}(\sigma e_1(\text{call}(e_1) \wedge \text{agent}(x, e_1))) \wedge e \subseteq i_1))])$.

A possible explanation of this scope restriction can be given in terms of the impossibility of extracting the PP *alla settimana* out of the whole adverbial phrase: such an hypothesis is plausible because of the well-known limitations operating on extractions out of DPs. If this is the case, QR will adjoin the PP at most at the DP. Thus, given the definition of scope in May (1985), the quantifier will have wide scope over the VP but not over the subject DP.

5. Conclusions

We have claimed that language represents a series of events in two different modes: as *nomic* habits or as *episodic* pluralities of occurrences. The first option is expressed by habitual sentences: it requires a very specific aspectual value available, for example, in Romance languages, where it is conveyed by the imperfective tenses. The second option, by contrast, is conveyed when the aspectual parameter is set to perfectivity. In both these options, quantificational adverbs can specify some properties of the series of events—namely, their frequency or the proportion between alternative sets of events. But it is important to realise that quantificational adverbs and aspectual values operate on two independent, although interacting, levels; furthermore, the effect produced by this interaction varies dramatically along the divide nomic/episodic (see section 2). It is therefore necessary to disentangle the mere expression of quantification over events, mainly realised by specific lexical items, from the expression of truly normative and intensional generalisations, which is manifested by the (imperfective) habitual aspect (see section 3).

We have also provided a fine-grained analysis of the relationships between iterative and habitual aspect. This has been explained partly in terms of the type of event denoted by the predicate (depending on whether or not it is a repetitive event) and partly in terms of the distribution of sentence material in the restrictor and nuclear scope of the generic quantifier associated with the habitual aspect (see section 4).

Broadly speaking, our analysis represents a strong plea in favour of a quantificational representation of aspectual features, differently expressed according to the specific value implemented in the sentence, and of an intensional analysis of habituality.[37]

Notes

1. Actually, de Swart's original analysis is on French; however, her classification is easily adaptable to the Italian case.

2. This assimilation might turn out to be too coarse-grained. An interesting difference between adverbs like *due volte alla settimana* ('twice a week') and *raramente* ('rarely') is represented by their interaction with aspectual values. As the following examples reveal, *raramente* has a real frequency interpretation only when it occurs with the habitual imperfective aspect, whereas in perfective sentences it has a sort of cardinal interpretation, roughly equivalent to *few times*:

(a) i.   Da piccolo, mio padre mi picchiava raramente.
          When I was a child, my father beat-IMP me rarely.

      ii.   Da piccolo, mio padre mi ha picchiato raramente.
          When I was a child, my father beat me rarely.

The same contrast does not appear with the other kind of adverbs, which maintain their frequency interpretation even in perfective sentences:

(b) i.   Da piccolo, mio padre mi picchiava due volte alla settimana.
          When I was a child, my father beat-IMP me twice a week.

      ii.   Da piccolo, mio padre mi ha picchiato due volte alla settimana.
          When I was a child, my father beat me twice a week.

Therefore, it might be the case that the pure frequency reading of weak adverbs actually arises as the byproduct of the interaction with the semantic features of the habitual aspect. However, for lack of space, we do not discuss this problem any further.

3. It is important to keep distinct this notion of indeterminacy or unboundedness typical of the imperfective aspect fromthe intrinsic vagueness of certain iterative adverbs like *molte volte* ('many times'), which are also incompatible with this aspectual value.

4. In this field, the terminology can be rather confusing, especially for the notion of habitual sentences. In fact, in formal semantics, generic and habitual sentences are usually considered to be disjointed classes, which differ for the type of their subject; the subject of generics is interpreted in a classlike way, whereas the subject of habituals is an individual object. However, habituality is also an aspectual category, which encompasses both types of sentences. Since this chapter mainly deals with aspectual problems, we always use the term *habituality* in this latter sense. Moreover, we employ the term *nomic sentences* to globally qualify the class of sentences that do not have an episodic, factual interpretation, and we reserve the term *generic* to refer exclusively to those habituals that assign a classlike interpretation to the subject DP.

5. See below and Krifka et al. (1995).

6. For some issues concerning habituals without explicit quantificational adverbs, see Lenci (1995).

7. Actually, Bertinetto (1986) also distinguishes a third subtype of imperfectivity, the *continuous aspect*. For simplicity, we do not discuss it here.

8. See Higginbotham (1985), Kratzer (1994), and many others.

9. See also Carlson (1989), who stresses the widespread role of intensionality inside nomic sentences.

10. Carlson (1977: 211) also argues that generic sentences create intensional contexts. He claims that in the sentence *Procedure P picks out the coldest state*, you cannot substitute *salva veritate* for the object DP, either *Alaska* or *the least populous state*. Actually this kind of argumentation can also be extended to the opposition between perfective and imperfective sentences containing explicit quantificational adverbs:

(a)   Nel 1998, Maria usciva spesso con il direttore del dipartimento.
       In 1998, Mary often went-IMP out with the head of the department.

(b)   Nel 1998, il direttore del dipartimento = il capo dei Boy Scouts.
       In 1998, the head of the department = the head of Boy Scouts

(c)   Nel 1998, Maria usciva spesso con il capo dei Boy Scouts.
       In 1998, Mary often went-IMP out with the head of Boy Scouts.

The truth of (c) does not follow from the truth of (a) and (b). In fact, suppose that Mary was very ambitious and aimed at getting a promotion: in this situation, it might be the case that in 1998 Mary had the habit of going out with the head of her department with a certain frequency (because in this way she hoped to get the promotion), but she did not have the habit of going out with the head of Boy Scouts, even though the two descriptions actually happened to denote the same individual in that period. In fact, (a) could have been true even if the head of the department had not been the head of Boy Scouts. Things are different with perfective sentences:

(d)   Nel 1998, Maria è uscita spesso con il direttore del dipartimento.
       In 1998, Mary often went out with the head of the department.

(e)   Nel 1998, il direttore del dipartimento = il capo dei Boy Scouts.
       In 1998, the head of the department = the head of Boy Scouts.

(f) Nel 1998, Maria è uscita spesso con il capo dei Boy Scouts.
     In 1998, Mary often went out with the head of Boy Scouts.

In this case, the substitution of the DP preserves the truth of the sentence. As these examples show, the contrast is independent from the presence of the quantificational adverb, and it is sensible rather to the imperfective vs. perfective aspect of the verb. This fact seems again to support the difference between habituals and perfective sentences in terms of intensional vs. extensional generalisations.

11. Alternatively, the modal base can be seen as a function that maps the actual world onto a set of possible worlds, which roughly corresponds to the relation of accessibility for possible worlds in modal logic.

12. As Dahl (1975) suggests, nomic generalisations come at least in two forms—*descriptive* generalisations and *normative* generalisations. Whereas the former, for example, express biological and physical laws, the latter express social norms, regulations, and so on. This difference can be captured in terms of the modal base that is adopted to evaluate the sentence; whereas descriptive generic sentences are evaluated in the *physically possible* worlds, normative ones are evaluated in the *morally perfect* worlds, to use Dahl's words. Similarly, the ordering source will also be different. The ordering source of descriptive generics will try to capture the notion of the *ideal* or *stereotypical* case, whereas the ordering source in normative generalisations will usually have a *deontic* character, where the ideal is adherence to that which laws prescribe. For some problematic cases, see Condoravdi (1994), who also proposes some solutions to overcome the apparent difficulties that the modal version of the generic operator can encounter.

13. For a discussion about the modal uses of the imperfect, see Bertinetto (1986). An interesting example is the following:

(a) Se Gianni studiava di più, passava l'esame senza problemi.
     If John studied-IMP more, he passed-IMP the exam without any problem.

The imperfect here has a clear counterfactual interpretation, roughly equivalent to *If John had studied more, he would have passed the exam without any problem*. Moreover, notice that this reading is impossible with a perfective tense, which makes the sentence odd, too:

(b) ?? Se Gianni ha studiato di più, ha passato l'esame senza problemi.
     If John has studied more, he has passed the exam without any problem.

Finally, this contrast also proves that conditional clauses do not perform any aspectual neutralisation between the imperfective and perfective aspect, as is often claimed.

14. This also means a shift from the standard description of the opposition between imperfectivity and perfectivity in terms of boundedness vs. unboundedness. However, the intuition behind this classical approach can be captured in the intensional analysis, too. For instance, Carlson (1989) adopts the features *bounded* and *unbounded* for the description of the domain of quantifiers and interprets them as being equivalent to extensional vs. intensional. Similarly, we can interpret the intensionality of the imperfective aspect as a realisation of its intrinsic unboundedness.

15. We also define the relation of strict precedence of an interval to an instant:

$$\forall i, t_1 \, (i <_t t_1 \leftrightarrow \forall t_2 (t_2 \leq i \rightarrow (t_2 \leq_t t_1 \wedge t_2 \neq t_1))).$$

16. The representation language will also contain the relation $\subseteq *$ between intervals, interpreted in the following way: $[\![i \subseteq * i']\!]_{w,g} = 1$ iff $g(i) \leq g(i')$.

17. This is a short exposition of the parts of the theory that are relevant for the present discussion. For the complete details of the system, see Chierchia (1992, 1995d).

18. This solution is adopted in Chierchia (1992).

19. This definition adopts the implementation of the existential disclosure proposed in Chierchia (1995b), which has the form of a type-shifting operation !yXP defined on existential quantifiers.

20. The only ambiguities being those due to different ways in which the clauses of the quantificational adverb can be filled.

21. Differently from the habitual case analysed in the former section, the variable disclosure is now operated by the quantificational adverb itself, as in perfective sentences. This is due to the fact that *Gn* opens only the indefinites that are to be inserted into its restrictor, but in the current case, the clauses in (44) are part of the structure of the quantificational adverb *spesso*, which instead forms the nuclear scope of *Gn*.

22. Again, the configuration in which *Gn* has narrow scope with respect to the quantificational adverb is ruled out at the interpretative level because in that case the interval variable would remain unbound.

23. Thanks to Andrea Bonomi and Gennaro Chierchia for long discussions about this problem.

24. Cf. Laca (1990: 28) and Krifka et al. (1995).

25. If we want to extend this line of analysis to generic DPs also, we can say that they set the default value for the choice of the modal base of the generic operator to the non-presuppositional one. This difference can be motivated by the fact that generalising over individuals and generalising over events are two well-distinguished operations, even though sometimes they come to be linguistically expressed by similar devices—that is, the imperfective aspect. Standard generalisations over events are made on the grounds of past experiences of those events. In contrast, we can make generalisations about men, dogs, or atoms, even though there are no instances of these concepts, simply on the basis of the internal features of the concepts themselves. For instance, when we say that *A man has two legs* is true independently of the existence of men, this is due to the fact that the truth of this sentence can be evaluated simply on the grounds of the biological-genetic history of mankind, which would still hold true even if men were completely extinct.

26. See Bertinetto (1986) for the evidence in favour of such an analysis.

27. We can assume that at LF, after having checked the aspectual features in Asp^0, *Perf* scopes out and adjoins first to TP (to whose head the auxiliary has simultaneously adjoined) and then to AgrS-P; in this way, it is possible to capture the natural connection between aspectual and tense information. The semantic reflex of the chain formed by the movement of the operator would be the restriction of the interval variable quantified over by *Perf* with the formulas associated to Aux^0 and T^0. At the same time, the verb moves to Asp^0 to check the aspectual information.

28. As in the perfective case, we assume that the syntactic operator *Gn* first adjoins to TP, picking up the tense information, and then moves up to AgrP.

29. This account of the relation between habituality and tense is similar to the idea in Dahl (1975) that generic sentences state that a law of some sort holds at a certain time. The time is now represented by the external interval.

30. Cf. Bertinetto (1986) and Hengeveld (1992).

31. A *sum* can be defined as a relation between an object of the domain D and a subset of D in the following way:

$$(x \text{ Sum } \alpha) \leftrightarrow \forall y (y \in \alpha \rightarrow y \leq x).$$

Each sum is atomistic, in the sense that it has atoms or minimal elements.

32. We have adopted some version of the internal subject hypothesis, and we interpret the trace left by the subject as a variable of type $\langle e \rangle$. Thus, (65) represents the output of applying the translation of V to this variable. The same variable will be λ-abstracted at some higher projection and then applied to the subject DP.

33. We assume the analysis of cardinal adjectives in Ojeda (1993) and in Moltman (1997), according to which they count the atoms of a sum.

34. As in Chierchia (1995b), the disclosure type-shifting operation $!_yXP$ can easily be extended to kind-denoting DPs also.

35. If a temporal adverbial is adjoined to (4), this sentence may also get a repeated interpretation:

(i)   La domenica, il mio postino suona due volte.

       On Sundays, my postman rings twice

36. For useful comments, we would like to thank Andrea Bonomi, Gennaro Chierchia, Denis Delfitto, and Jim Higginbotham. Of course, all the errors are ours. This chapter was jointly developed by the two authors. For academic purposes, Pier Marco Bertinetto bears responsibility for sections 1 and 2 and Alessandro Lenci for sections 3 through 5.

References

Belletti, A., 1990. *Generalised Verb Movement. Aspects of Verb Syntax.* Rosenberg & Sellier, Torino.

van Benthem, J., 1987. Semantic Automata. In J. Groenendijk, D. de Jongh, and M. Stokhof (eds.), *Studies in Discourse Representation Theory and the Theory of Generalised Quantifiers*, 1–25. Foris, Dordrecht.

Bertinetto, P. M., 1986. *Tempo, Aspetto e Azione nel verbo italiano. Il sistema dell'indicativo.* Accademia della Crusca, Firenze.

Bonomi, A., 1995. Aspect and Quantification. In P. M. Bertinetto, V. Bianchi, J. Higginbotham, and M. Squartini (eds.), *Temporal Reference, Aspect and Actionality. Volume 1: Semantic and Syntactic Perspectives*, 93–110. Rosenberg & Sellier, Torino.

Carlson, G., 1977. *Reference to Kinds in English.* Ph.D. dissertation, University of Massachusetts, Amherst.

Carlson, G., 1989. On the Semantic Composition of English Generic Sentences. In G. Chierchia, B. H. Partee, and R. Turner (eds.), *Properties, Types and Meaning. Vol. II: Semantic Issues*, 167–192. Kluwer, Dordrecht.

Chierchia, G., 1992. Anaphora and Dynamic Binding. In *Linguistics and Philosophy* 15: 111–183.

Chierchia, G., 1995a. *Dynamics of Meaning. Anaphora, Presupposition and the Theory of Grammar.* University of Chicago Press, Chicago.

Chierchia, G., 1995b. Individual-level Predicates as Inherent Generics. In G. Carlson and F. J. Pelletier (eds.), *The Generic Book*, 176–223. University of Chicago Press, Chicago.

Chierchia, G., 1995d. The Variability of Impersonal Subjects. In E. Bach, E. Jelinek, A. Kratzer, and B. H. Partee (eds.), *Quantification in Natural Language*, 107–143. Dordrecht, Kluwer.

Comrie, B., 1976. *Aspect.* Cambridge University Press, Cambridge.

Condoravdi, C., 1994. *Descriptions in Context.* Ph.D. dissertation, Yale University, New Haven (Conn.).

Dahl, Ö., 1975. On Generics. In E. L. Keenan (ed.), *Formal Semantics of Natural Language*, 99–111. Cambridge University Press, Cambridge.

Davidson, D., 1967. The Logical Form of Action Sentences. In N. Rescher (ed.), *The Logic of Decision and Action*, 81–95. University of Pittsburgh Press, Pittsburgh. Reprinted in Davidson, D., 1980. *Essays on Actions and Events*, 105–123. Clarendon Press, Oxford

Dekker, P., 1993. Existential Disclosure. In *Linguistics and Philosophy* 16: 561–587.

Delfitto, D., and P. M. Bertinetto, 1995. A Case Study in the Interaction of Aspect and Actionality: The Imperfect in Italian. In P. M. Bertinetto, V. Bianchi, J. Higginbotham, and M. Squartini (eds.), *Temporal Reference, Aspect and Actionality. Volume 1: Semantic and Syntactic Perspectives*, 125–142. Rosenberg & Sellier, Torino.

de Swart, H., 1993. *Adverbs of Quantification: A Generalised Quantifier Approach.* Garland, New York.

Diesing, M., 1992. *Indefinites*. MIT Press, Cambridge (Mass.).

Gerstner-Link, C., and M. Krifka, 1993. Genericity. In J. Jacobs, A. Von Stechow, and W. Sternefeld (eds.), *Syntax. An International Handbook of Contemporary Research*, 966–978. De Gruyter, Berlin.

Heim, I., 1982. *The Semantics of Definite and Indefinite Noun Phrases*. Ph.D. dissertation, University of Massachusetts, Amherst.

Hengeveld, K., 1992. Adverbial quantification in British Romani, Dutch and Turkish. In *Eurotyp Working Papers* 4: 19–29.

Higginbotham, J., 1985. On Semantics. In *Linguistic Inquiry* 16: 547–593.

Hoepelman, J., and C. Rohrer, 1980. On the Mass-count Distinction and the French Imperfait and Passé Simple. In C. Rohrer (ed.), *Time, Tense and Quantifiers. Proceedings of the Stuttgart Conference on the Logic of Tense and Quantification*, 85–112. Niemeyer, Tübingen.

Kleiber, G., 1987. *Du côté de la référence verbale. Les phrases habituelles*. Lang, Berne.

Kratzer, A., 1981. The Notional Category of Modality. In H.-J. Heikmeyer and H. Rieser (eds.), *Words, Worlds and Contexts. New Approaches in Word Semantics*, 38–74. De Gruyter, Berlin.

Kratzer, A., 1994. On External Arguments. In E. Benedicto and J. Runner (eds.), *Functional Projections. University of Massachusetts Occasional Papers* 17, 103–130. University of Massachusetts, Amherst.

Krifka, M., 1988. The relational theory of genericity. In M. Krifka (ed.), *Genericity in Natural Language. Proceedings of the 1988 Tübingen Conference* (Seminars für natürlichsprachliche Systeme), 88–42. Tübingen.

Krifka, M., 1992. Thematic Relations as Links Between Nominal Reference and Temporal Constitution. In I. Sag and A. Szabolcsi (eds.), *Lexical Matters*, 29–54. CSLI Publications, Stanford (Calif.).

Krifka, M., F. J. Pellettier, G. N. Carlson, A. ter Meulen, G. Chierchia, and G. Link, 1995. Genericity: An Introduction. In G. N. Carlson and F. J. Pellettier (eds.), *The Generic Book*, 1–124. University of Chicago Press, Chicago.

Laca, B., 1990. Generic Objects. Some More Pieces of the Puzzle. In *Lingua* 81: 25–46.

Landman, F., 1992. The Progressive. In *Natural Language Semantics* 1: 1–32.

Lasersohn, P., 1995. *Plurality, Conjunction and Events*. Kluwer, Dordrecht.

Lenci, A., 1995. The Semantic Representation of Non-quantificational Habituals. In P. M. Bertinetto, V. Bianchi, J. Higginbotham, and M. Squartini (eds.), *Temporal Reference, Aspect and Actionality. Volume 1: Semantic and Syntactic Perspectives*, 143–158. Rosenberg & Sellier, Torino.

Link, G., 1983. The Logical Analysis of Plurals and Mass Terms: A Lattice-theoretic Approach. In R. Bäuerle, C. Schwarze, and A. von Stechow (eds.), *Meaning, Use and Interpretation of Language*, 303–323. De Gruyter, Berlin.

May, R., 1985. *Logical Form: Its Use and Derivation*. MIT Press, Cambridge (Mass.).

Moltmann, F., 1997. *Parts and Wholes in Semantics*. Oxford University Press, Oxford.

Ojeda, A., 1993. *Linguistic Individuals*. CSLI Publications, Stanford (Calif.).

Partee, B. H., 1995. Quantificational Structures and Compositionality. In E. Bach, E. Jelinek, A. Kratzer, and B. H. Partee (eds.), *Quantification in Natural Language*, 541–601. Kluwer, Dordrecht.

Reichenbach, H., 1947. *Elements of Symbolic Logic*. Macmillan, London.

Rizzi, L., 1986. Null Objects in Italian and the Theory of Pro. In *Linguistic Inquiry* 17: 501–557.

Schubert, L. K., and F. J. Pelletier, 1989. Generically Speaking, or, Using Discourse Representation Theory to Interpret Generics. In G. Chierchia, B. H. Partee, and R. Turner (eds.), *Properties, Types and Meaning. Vol. II: Semantic Issues*, 193–268. Kluwer, Dordrecht.

Stalnaker, R. C., 1978. Assertion. In P. Cole (ed.), *Syntax and Semantics. Vol. IX: Pragmatics*, 315–332. Academic Press, New York.

Author Index

Subject Index

ADD-TO, 176
Adjunction, 62, 213–214, 232–233,
    237–238, 261–262
Adverb dropping, 19, 21–23
Adverbial modification, 19, 22–27, 39,
    57–60, 63, 82–83, 95–96, 124, 238
— manner interpretation of, 58
— thematic interpretation of, 57–63
— with stative predicates, 84–95
Adverbial quantification, 28, 37, 207–
    208, 212–214, 232, 237, 243–253
— and iterative adverbs, 247–248,
    273–280
— and relational adverbs, 248–253,
    263–266
Algebra of events, 30–31, 130, 193–
    194
Anaphoric reference, 23, 55–56, 126–
    127, 174, 186–188
Arbitrary *Pro*, 252
ASP, 41, 39, 223–224, 226, 259
Aspect, 4, 34, 40–41, 128, 130, 151–
    154, 164, 173, 180, 200, 208–209,
    215–226, 231, 237, 243–246, 249–
    259, 268–270, 273, 277, 280–283
Aspectual class, 152–153, 188–189
Aspectual composition, 169–170, 195,
    197
Aspectual operator, 253, 258, 261–264,
    270, 276
Aspectual postulate, 193
Aspectuality, 34, 41, 169–176, 184–
    190, 197–199, 215–232, 245, 254–
    256
Atelicity, 28–35, 64– 71, 77, 152, 170,
    252

Boundedness, 252, 272, 282

Causal dependence, 110
Causal statement, 17, 38–40, 112–119
Causation, 11, 21–22, 38–40, 72, 105–
    120
Checking, 222–224
Chronoscope, 155–167
Closure principle, 129–132
Consequent state, 71–72, 192
Context change potential, 159, 258
Control, 56–59
Continuous aspect, 34
Cul, 29–30, 81, 173–174, 189–195,
    201–202
Cumulativity, 30–32, 176, 196

Discourse relation, 137–149
Discourse Representation Theory
    (DRT), 40, 123, 130, 135–153, 159,
    165–167, 182, 211–223, 257
Distributivity, 175, 119
Dividual, 169
Dynamic Aspect Tree (DAT), 151,
    154–167
— vs. Discourse Representation The-
    ory (DRT), 155–156
Dynamic inference, 161, 165
Dynamic involvement, 159–160
Dynamic semantics, 137, 152, 257

Event, *passim*
— as concrete universal, 101–103
— as dividual, 169–199
— as particular, 4–5, 8–12, 21–23, 50–
    51, 95–101

Printed in the United States
3968